ON THE DIVIDE

Willa Cather on railroad handcar. Courtesy of the Willa Cather Pioneer Museum, Red Cloud, Nebraska.

On the Divide

The Many Lives of Willa Cather

DAVID PORTER

University of Nebraska Press
Lincoln and London

Acknowledgments for previously published materials
appear on p. xvii, an extension of the copyright page.

♾

LIBRARY OF CONGRESS
CATALOGING-IN-PUBLICATION DATA

Porter, David H., 1935–
On the divide : the many lives of Willa Cather /
David Porter.
p. cm.
Includes bibliographical references and index.
ISBN 978-0-8032-3755-1 (alk. paper)
1. Cather, Willa, 1873–1947. 2. Novelists, American—
20th century—Biography. I. Title.
PS3505.A87Z77 2008   813'.52—dc22
[B]   2008008845

Set in Adobe Caslon.
Designed by Ashley Muehlbauer.

In memory of Laudie,
*   without whom I would never have written this book,*

and for Helen,
*   without whom I could never have completed it.*

Contents

Illustrations

Frontispiece. Willa Cather on railroad handcar

Preface

How does it happen that someone whose background is in classics and music, and who had never read a book by Willa Cather until his late forties, now has the audacity to write a book about her?

It all began when my late wife, Laudie, who had read and loved Cather since her high school years, finally got around to reading *The Song of the Lark* in 1982, when we were living in Minnesota and both teaching at Carleton College. One summer day, when she was about halfway through, she said to me, "I've decided two things about this book. First, it's about a musician, and I love it so much that I'm not going to finish it yet—I want to save that for the future. I've also learned that Cather cut a good bit out of her original text when she published the version I'm reading. I don't want to finish the book until I have the first edition and can read everything she wrote." As a fellow musician—she was a flutist, I a pianist—I was touched by her first comment, and the second came suddenly to mind when I was in New York several months later and realized that Christmas was coming soon, and that I didn't have a present for Laudie. I visited several New York bookshops and was lucky enough to find a first edition of *The Song of the Lark*—a bit stained and battered, and without a dust jacket, but the real thing. While I was at it, I picked up a couple of other Cather firsts as well.

The gifts were a great hit with Laudie—about the best I'd ever done at this uncertain business of finding presents for one's spouse—and they fired both her enthusiasm and mine for finding other first editions of Cather. It's an addictive pastime, as other bibliomanes know well, and before long we were moving beyond Cather to Edith Wharton and to Virginia and Leonard Woolf's Hogarth Press. By 1985 we had completed a nice run of Cather firsts—one of my most poignant memories is of

Laudie's delight in the book that completed our set, a lovely copy of *The Troll Garden*, which I'd found as a gift for Christmas 1985, just weeks after we learned of the lung cancer that would take Laudie's life less than a year later.

As we assembled the collection, I of course began to read the books, and as any Cather enthusiast knows, once one starts reading this remarkable author, one book leads to another: it seems impossible to get enough. After Laudie's death I continued to add to our collection, partly because doing so reminded me of her, partly because I'd become hooked myself. Somewhere in the mid-1990s I realized that both the Hogarth Press and the Cather collections contained some items that were rare and little known, and when in 1999 I returned to teaching after a spell as a college president, I began to study these materials in depth, to write a few short articles on them, to organize shows of these two collections at Skidmore College and Williams College, and even to offer a seminar on Cather at Williams.

That my interest in Cather began in collecting her books relates not only to the genesis of this book but also to its focus. Among the items I happened to find in the 1990s were two rare advertising pieces, one written to promote Cather's first book, *April Twilights*, in 1903, the other to promote *The Song of the Lark* in 1915. Though published anonymously, the earlier piece is clearly by Cather herself, and there is documentary evidence of Cather's extensive role in writing the later one. During the same period I also acquired a Cather draft that showed that as late as the time of her last novel, *Sapphira and the Slave Girl*, published in 1940, Cather was personally involved not only in reviewing dust-jacket copy for her books but even in writing it herself. The clear evidence in these pieces that Cather throughout her career was actively involved in promoting and advertising her books led me both to a close examination of her other promotional activities and to the suspicion, and later the certainty, that her interest and skill in this area owed a good bit to the time she had spent in 1906–8 working on a series of articles about Mary Baker Eddy, the founder of Christian Science—and a genius at self-promotion. It is thus that the first two chapters of this book focus on the promotional copy Cather helped produce and publish, always anonymously—a body of writing that has not been readily available to Cather readers and scholars. Similarly, a second focus throughout the book is on the many ways in which Cather's writing reveals the impact of the time she spent working on Mary Baker Eddy, a relationship that Cather herself repeatedly downplayed, but that in fact keeps bubbling to the surface throughout her career.

My journey from total ignorance about Cather to something approaching understanding has been possible only through the help of many people and institutions. Given its origin in book collecting, I must begin with a number of booksellers who have not only helped build our collection but have also educated me in the process. Among the many whose names I might include are Robert Dagg, John DeMarco, Barbara Farnsworth, Glenn Horowitz, Peter Howard, and the late Howard Mott. I am particularly grateful to Thomas Goldwasser, who put me onto what may be the one extant copy of the 1903 "Literary Note" Cather wrote to accompany her first book, and to Jeffrey Marks, through whom I acquired not only many of the rarest books in the collection but also the drafts of the *Sapphira* dust-jacket blurb.

As anyone who has been associated with it knows, the community of Cather scholars is wise, articulate, and generous, and a number of these colleagues have taken this neophyte in hand, ignoring his blunders, helping in all manner of circumstances, and lending encouragement even when it was not deserved. Again the list is too long to name everyone who falls into this category, but I would voice special thanks to Bruce Baker, Richard Harris, Mark Madigan, John Murphy, Guy Reynolds, Steve Shively, Janis Stout, Steve Trout, and Joe Urgo. I had the great good fortune to come to know Sue Rosowski before she died, and I shall not forget her gracious encouragement. Robert Thacker has generously shared his knowledge of the Cather-Greenslet archive at Harvard University. Merrill Skaggs and Ann Romines edited the first pieces I published on Cather and have been exemplars and inspirations ever since. John Swift read two drafts of this book and made invaluable suggestions on both.

Betty Kort and her colleagues at the Willa Cather Foundation in Red Cloud have helped me at point after point in my Cather journey.

Skidmore College granted me two welcome leaves during my presidency, both of which contributed materially to my evolving interest in Willa Cather. Williams College has granted generous financial support for a wide range of research materials and activities. The six students in my 2005 Willa Cather seminar at Williams provided questions and insights that made me see Cather in new ways, as did the lively participants in Cather seminars and colloquia at Bread Loaf, Red Cloud, Lincoln, and Drew University. A number of libraries have offered invaluable assistance, among them the Enoch Pratt Free Library in Baltimore; the Houghton Library at Harvard University; the Pierpont Morgan Library in New York City; the Rare Books division of the New York Public Library; the Willa Cather Pioneer Memorial archives in Red Cloud; the Lucy Scribner Library at Skidmore College; the Bailey-Howe Library at the University of Vermont; the Alderman Library at the University of Virginia; and the Sawyer and Chapin libraries at Williams College. I am particularly indebted to the Caspersen Collection in the University Library at Drew University in Madison, New Jersey, where Andrew Scrimgeour and Lucy Marks have both given invaluable advice and support for several years. I am grateful to David Seiler of Skidmore College, Masato Okinaka of Drew University, and Eric Reed of the Cather Foundation in Red Cloud for their ready and skillful assistance with the illustrations. Special thanks are due to a number of people at the University of Nebraska Press. From my earliest communications with the press until the publication of this book, Ladette Randolph as editor has been a warm, candid, wise, and ever-helpful colleague. Acquisitions assistant Kristen Rowley has led me through a labyrinth of complex and essential issues with skill, persistence, and grace; without her guidance this book would still be in its preliminary stages, and I would be insane. Lona Dearmont has brought critical acumen, a sharp ear for the English language, a welcome attention to detail, and an equally welcome sense of humor to her work as copyeditor, and the book is materially better thanks to her efforts. To those several other press staff members whom I cannot list by name but who have made substantial contributions toward making this book a reality, my warm thanks.

My deepest debts are to my family. My four children, Hugh, Everett, Helen, and David, were very much part of the early stages of our Cather collecting. Not only did they endure the lengthy bookstore outings that Laudie and I visited upon them in the early days of our mania, but all four of them have become astute and enthusiastic Cather readers themselves, and they have actively encouraged their father's excursion into these new territories. My stepdaughter, Cathrin Lawton, has in recent years become an enthusiastic supporter as well as a delightfully sardonic kibitzer. As I have said, Laudie Porter's keen interest in Cather was the start of this whole journey. In the same way, Helen Porter has given constant support and encouragement to my burgeoning Cather efforts in the years since our marriage in 1987—and has graciously put up with the attendant invasions on our time and budget. My work on Cather has for me involved an opening of new vistas of the same sort as Cather's fiction so often offers her readers. This ongoing adventure is unthinkable without the inspiration, love, and wisdom of these two women to whom this book is dedicated.

Acknowledgments

Portions of chapters 1, 2, and 4 contain material revised from four articles that appeared in the *Willa Cather Newsletter and Review*: "'She had only to touch an idea to make it live': Willa Cather and Mary Baker Eddy," vol. 44 (2000): 38–44; "Cather on Cather: Two Early Self-Sketches," vol. 45 (2002): 55–60; "Cather on Cather II: Two Recent Acquisitions at Drew University," vol. 46 (2003): 49–58; and "Cather on Cather III: Dust-Jacket Copy on Willa Cather's Books," vol. 48 (2005): 51–60. They are used by permission of the Cather Foundation.

A portion of chapter 4 contains material revised from the chapter entitled "From Violence to Art: Willa Cather Caught in the Eddy," in *Violence, the Arts, and Willa Cather*, ed. Joseph R. Urgo and Merrill Maguire Skaggs (Madison: Fairleigh Dickinson University Press, 2007), 295–309. This material is used by permission of the Fairleigh Dickinson University Press.

Several chapters cite materials from the Houghton Mifflin archive at Harvard University: four letters from Ferris Greenslet to Willa Cather and two letters from Cather to Greenslet, all with the call number *bMS Am 1925 (341)*, as well as house memos on *Alexander's Bridge*, *O Pioneers!*, and *My Ántonia*, with the call number *MS Stor 245*. These materials are used by permission of the Houghton Library, Harvard University.

Photograph 106, "Willa Cather Drives a Handcar—Cheyenne, Wyoming," is used by permission of the Cather Foundation.

Several chapters make use of two 1926 Cather typescripts now in the Caspersen Collection at Drew University, "A Biographical Sketch" and "[Interview at Grand Central]." These two typescripts, and the illustrations of them (figures 5 and 6), are used by permission of the Drew University Library.

The following materials from books by Willa Cather are used by permission of Alfred A. Knopf, a division of Random House, Inc.: jacket blurbs and photograph of entire jacket of *Youth and the Bright Medusa*; blurb on front cover and photograph of front cover of *One of Ours*; blurb on rear cover of *A Lost Lady*; blurb on rear cover of *The Professor's House*; blurb on rear cover of *My Mortal Enemy*; blurbs on front and rear covers, and photographs of front cover of first-edition dust jacket and front cover and spine of first-edition, fifth-issue dust jacket of *Shadows on the Rock*; blurb on inner front flap of *Obscure Destinies*; blurb on inner front flap of *Lucy Gayheart*; blurb on front cover of *Not Under Forty*; blurb on inner front flap of *Sapphira and the Slave Girl*; and "A Biographical Sketch" from *Willa Cather: A Biographical Sketch, an English Opinion, and an Abridged Bibliography*.

Introduction

With Willa Cather, the imagination was a way of being. What came to her of experience, in any form, became a part of her. And in turn she became an actress creating and recreating for herself and in her writing new landscapes, voices, rooms. There were hidden selves, as she said often in her novels, and created selves, and masks to transform the literal. The person, who is also the artist, becomes the instrument by which experience is absorbed and translated.
—BERNICE SLOTE

Willa Cather associated her Nebraska childhood with "the Divide," the height of rolling prairie that rises between the Republican River to the south of Red Cloud and the Little Blue River to the north, and these two evocative words sound again and again in *O Pioneers!*, the first novel in which, drawing on childhood memories, Cather found her own voice: "The houses on the Divide were small and were usually tucked away in low places; you did not see them until you came directly upon them" (*OP* 19); "Then came the hard times that brought every one on the Divide to the brink of despair; three years of drouth and failure, the last struggle of a wild soil against the encroaching plowshare" (47); "The Divide is now thickly populated. The rich soil yields heavy harvests; the dry, bracing climate and the smoothness of the land make labor easy for men and beasts" (76); "It was three months now since the news of the terrible thing that had happened in Frank Shabata's orchard had first run like a fire over the Divide" (275–76).

Both the name itself and the mixed resonances it carries in these and other passages are appropriate to Willa Cather, for in a very real sense, she lived not just her childhood but her whole life "on the Divide." Bartley Alexander, the title character of her first novel, *Alexander's Bridge*, protests that he is "not a man who can live two lives" (*AB* 104), but Cather herself from the beginning of her career to the end of her life constantly lived a divided life. The fact that as a lesbian she often felt alienated from society, "queer," both added to this sense of division and encouraged her to explore it in her writing.[1] This book explores the rifts in her own life, the many lives she lived, and the manifold ways in which she wrote these "divides" in her life into her fiction and her characters.

Part 1 focuses on two sets of promotional materials that Cather either wrote or helped write, autobiographical vignettes published between 1903 and 1926, and dust-jacket blurbs dating from her first novel in 1912 to her last in 1940. These materials exemplify Cather's penchant for playing different roles, for tolerating and even fostering a life simultaneously lived on different planes, and with different objectives in mind. On the one side, these biographical sketches and jacket blurbs evoke an iconic Willa Cather who is "our greatest living woman novelist" and the author of "novel[s] to rank with the finest of this or any age" (to quote one of her jackets). This is a Cather we easily recognize, as she wanted us to do, an author whose first goal throughout her career was to reach the heights of what she had during her university years called the "kingdom of art." On the other side is a less familiar Willa Cather, again an author, but one who throughout her career repeatedly devoted her writing skills to penning advertising copy and to otherwise promoting herself. This other Cather is a tireless and savvy go-getter out to foster her career, win public recognition, and reap the attendant financial rewards. In imagining these two Willa Cathers it is useful to recall different graphic images of her. For the one Cather there are the familiar paintings that portray her as rather formal and distant, and immensely impressive—for example, the familiar portraits of her by Leon Bakst and Nicolai Fechin. Other images, however, suggest a different Cather, among them the photograph used for the frontispiece of this book, which shows her tooling along in her self-driven railroad handcar, hell-bent to go as fast and as far as she can. Both Cathers are real, and both find voice in the materials discussed in part 1: for though its focus is on Cather as writer of promotional copy, the purpose of the materials this Cather creates is to promote the career, and shape the image, of the other.

These contrasting roles serve both as our starting points and as continuing points of reference throughout the book. Succeeding sections focus on ways these roles transmute into others, on the different directions in which Cather's many roles take her, and especially on the diverse and changing after-images they leave in her books and the characters who people these books. Part 2 shows her identifying and exploring these divergent roles during two early periods of her career. During the sixteen years she is in Lincoln and then Pittsburgh (1890–1906), working much of the time as a reporter and reviewer, she writes a vast number of essays and reviews, most of them focused on artists and their art. A recurrent theme of these writings is a central "divide," the choice the artist must make between following art's highest calling or selling oneself and one's "wares," and as Cather writes about different authors, actors, and singers during this period, she constantly comments on and assesses the choices they make at such intersections.

In the next six years Cather finds herself tested at similar crossroads. When in 1906 she moves to New York to work for S. S. McClure, her first major assignment takes her to Boston to write a series of essays on Mary Baker Eddy, the founder of Christian Science. In her second year there Cather meets Sarah Orne Jewett, and for the rest of her life she identifies this meeting as a turning point in her career. In the event, however, and despite Cather's efforts to distance herself from Eddy, *both* women emerge as alter egos, with Jewett embodying dedication to one's art, Eddy exemplifying what one can achieve through self-promotion. We shall see how these models pull against each other in the fiction Cather writes in 1906–12, and how her first novel, *Alexander's Bridge*, reflects the choices she faced in 1911–12 as she stood at the crossroads between continuing a brilliant career at *McClure's* and hazarding the uncertain life of a full-time writer—a divide similar to those at which she had placed so many artists in her early essays and reviews.

In part 3 the tug of war continues into the great novels that Cather writes in the teens. For although these works differ radically in scope and feel from what Cather had written during her years at *McClure's*, they continue to reflect the divisions and dividedness of her own life. The sharp differences between the two heroines of *O Pioneers!*, Alexandra and Marie, each with clear affinities to Cather, play variations on the rift at the heart of *Alexander's Bridge*; Thea Kronborg, the heroine of *The Song of the Lark*, ends up living the double life of the operatic diva—iconic on the one hand, pressured and lonely on the other—a life analogous to that of Willa Cather, on whom Thea is closely modeled; and while the heroine of *My Ántonia* by the end of the novel breathes integration and harmony, the novel itself exists on the divide between its heroine, Ántonia, and its narrator, Jim Burden, a New York professional whose life and experience closely recall Cather's own.

Part 4 shows Cather in 1916–22 moving closer to this model of the New York professional. Although she garners increasing recognition during this period, she also finds she must devote ever more time and energy to promoting her books and making a living, and again these conditions leave their mark on her writing. At the same time as she is working on *My Ántonia* in 1916–17, she is also writing a series of stories about women consumed by mercenary concerns, three of them singers—and self-promoters—who achieve considerable success but have little of Thea Kronborg's transcendent artistic ambition. In 1919 Cather writes another story of the same ilk, and when in 1920 she publishes her first book with Alfred A. Knopf, these four stories constitute the first half and are matched against four earlier stories that in their different ways project a loftier vision of what art can be. Cather explains that the book's title, *Youth and the Bright Medusa*, evokes "youth's adventure with the many-colored Medusa of art," a theme that mirrors her own ongoing struggle with the opposing pulls of the artist's life. The theme of youth wrestling with difficult choices is focal also in the novel Cather writes during these same years, *One of Ours*, whose hero abhors the commercialism that surrounds him in his small Nebraska town and chooses to escape it by joining what he sees as the noble cause of fighting the Great War in France, where he dies.

The quest to live a life that rises above the mundane remains central to the three novels considered in part 5. Marian Forrester, the heroine of *A Lost Lady*, manages still to retain something of her unique aura even as her life falls to pieces and the world around her succumbs to greed and crassness. The focal characters in *The Professor's House*, Godfrey St. Peter and Tom Outland, define their lives by consuming passions that separate them from the more material concerns of the people who surround them—the professor's mammoth history of Spanish adventurers in North America, Tom's discovery of an ancient city on the Blue Mesa. Myra Henshawe, the heroine of *My Mortal Enemy*, displays a similar inclination to rise above the ordinary in the two defining acts of her life, her early choice to abandon her inheritance by eloping with Oswald Henshawe, and her efforts at the end to die in a manner consonant with her dreams. As she herself acknowledges, however, she is also a woman for whom the daily comforts of life, and having the wherewithal to possess and enjoy them, remain crucial.

The tension in all three of these novels, as in *One of Ours*, between two modes of life, one focused on material success, the other on more visionary goals, plays variations on the tension Cather had felt in her own life, and had explored in earlier works, between two contrasting visions of the artist, one devoted to "success," the other to transcendent achievement. It is a tension that finds expression also in the collection of Sarah Orne Jewett stories that Cather edits in 1924–25, with Cather's preface voicing reverence for Jewett's consummate artistry but her actual editing of the stories betraying her own keen and even intrusive promotional side. In addition, just as in *One of Ours* Cather ultimately exposes the folly of the "noble cause" to which its hero devotes his life, so in her three succeeding novels she raises questions as to the validity of the aspirations by which her heroes and heroines define their lives. As this happens, Cather's focus in the teens on the artist's different roles transmutes in the 1920s into an ongoing meditation on the opposing poles of our lives, mortal limitations on the one hand, immortal aspirations on the other. Once again, her theme reflects the facts of her own life: she is now closer to the artistic goals she had set for herself, but she also feels more keenly the looming fact of her own mortality. Cather continues to live a double life, but the central divide has shifted. Where formerly it had been between the lofty goals of the artist and the irksome realities of promoting one's career, it is now between the immortal dreams that artists—and humans—can entertain and the grim fact that artists—like all humans—are but mortal. As this shift occurs, the contrasting roles of her life begin to feel like unsatisfying versions of those she had earlier played with zest. In the teens, the energetic pursuit of success had been wearying, but it was certainly better than her life in the twenties, when the daily round mainly provided reminders of her mortal limitations. In the teens, the quest to scale the artistic heights had felt as daunting as it was exhilarating, but that too was better than feeling, as she often did now, that she had gained those heights only to wonder whether that was where she wanted to be, and whether the ascent justified all the efforts entailed.

Part 6 takes a retrospective look at ground covered to this point, with a focus on the ongoing and evolving "conversation" between Cather's anonymously composed promotional materials and the books she was writing. The placement of this chapter at this point in the book honors the fact that this conversation peaks in 1926, when Cather not only publishes *My Mortal Enemy*, with its terse but powerful jacket blurb, but also writes her two last anonymous biographical "puff pieces," a "Biographical Sketch" for an Alfred A. Knopf booklet and a brief but revealing "Interview" at Grand Central.

Nineteen twenty-six is a key turning point also in that Cather is already working on *Death Comes for the Archbishop*, a novel that differs dramatically from those that precede it—and for which Cather chooses to have no promotional blurb whatsoever. Along the same lines, after 1926 she never composes another anonymous biographical sketch. She does, however, gradually move back into preparing dust-jacket copy, and part 7 explores the continuing fascination of the interplay between that copy and her books. Of particular interest is that the two later books in which she herself is most intimately involved, *Obscure Destinies*, where she appears as Vickie in "Old Mrs. Harris," and *Sapphira and the Slave Girl*, where she herself appears as a five-year-old in the epilogue, also have the most intriguing jacket copy. In addition, the reappearance of substantial and penetrating blurbs on these two books accompanies the reappearance in the books themselves of strong personal ambition, a motive largely absent from *Death Comes for the Archbishop* and *Shadows on the Rock* and one that begins to drive the heroine of *Lucy Gayheart* only in the final chapters of that novel. Along the same lines, Cather gives herself a prominent role as both narrator and participant in her 1936 collection of essays, *Not Under Forty*, a natural lead-in to *Sapphira*, where she will be the narrator throughout and will make a cameo appearance as a child in the novel's epilogue.

Recent years have brought new recognition of the emotional depths that lie beneath the limpid surface of Willa Cather's writing. Critical to this enhanced appreciation has been a growing awareness of the complexities that similarly lie beneath the dignified, even impassive, exterior that Cather herself, especially in her later years, presented to the public. Understanding more fully how vigorously Cather could hate, how fierce a temper she had, how keenly she strove for recognition and success, how complex was her quest to define and confront her sexuality, how difficult she could be to live with, has not only thrown new light on her life but has also led to new recognition of the human and moral profundity of her fiction. If, as I suggest, Cather in many ways resembled both Mary Baker Eddy, whom Cather portrays as repugnant, and Sapphira, who strikes many readers the same way, these similarities are but further evidence of how well Cather understood the depths to which humans can plunge as well as the heights to which they can climb. My hope for this book is that its exploration of the tensions by which Cather was torn, the variant roles she played, the Divides upon which she lived, will further enhance our appreciation for her achievement as both artist and human being.

Abbreviations

Part I

Cather on Cather

Willa Cather has been called "the most autobiographical of writers," but she earns this designation because she draws so heavily on her own life in writing her fiction.[1] As for autobiography itself, Cather wrote little of it, and nothing remotely resembling the book-length autobiographies written by two close contemporaries, Edith Wharton's *A Backward Glance*, published in 1934, three years before her death, and Ellen Glasgow's two "backward glances," *A Certain Measure* in 1943 and *The Woman Within* in 1944, both also published shortly before her death. In Cather's case we also have nothing comparable to what another contemporary left us, the extensive diary and the thousands of letters that provide such insight into the life and work of Virginia Woolf. There is no evidence that Cather kept a diary, and if she did, we may be sure that she took care to destroy it.[2] As for letters, close friends such as Isabelle Hambourg and Edith Lewis burned the great majority of letters they had from Cather, and in her will Cather ruled out direct quotation of all surviving letters (hence the paraphrases in this book). It is against this backdrop that the materials presented in the two chapters of this first part take on such interest and importance, for they are filled with information about Cather's life, with "backward glances" at her evolving career, and with commentary on individual books both as they appear and in retrospect. Chapter 1 deals with four autobiographical vignettes written at different stages of Cather's career, chapter 2 with the jacket blurbs that Cather either wrote or vetted to herald and promote her books' initial appearances.

By its nature, autobiography skews the truth, as even so candid an autobiographer as Leonard Woolf admits: "I have tried in the following pages to tell the truth, the whole truth, and nothing but the truth, but of course I have not succeeded. I do not think that I have anywhere deliberately manipulated or distorted the truth into untruth, but I am sure that one sometimes does this unconsciously."[3] Cather's autobiographical statements also take liberty with what they include and omit, even with the facts themselves, and the portraits they create differ sharply one from another. That they date from different periods of her life explains these differences in part, but other factors come into play as well.

Two features in particular distinguish these materials from the autobiographical writings mentioned above and shape the choices Cather makes in writing them: all are unsigned, with the expectation that a reader will assume someone else has written them, and all are written as promotional pieces. From one point of view, both of these conditions encourage Cather to play free with the truth: no one will know that it is she who has done so, and hyperbole and license are the givens of "puff pieces" such as these, the purpose of which is less to "tell the whole truth" than to sell the author and her books. From a different point of view, however, both features encourage their own honesty and candor. Most autobiographers, aware as they are that readers will know who has written the book, are reluctant either to play too free with the facts or to overstep the bounds of modesty. Cather feels no such constraints. Inasmuch as she is writing what are by nature puff pieces, and without mention of her authorship, she can attribute to herself whatever qualities she believes she possesses, whatever vision she has of the position she occupies, or would like to occupy, as a writer. The genre, and its anonymity, encourage a kind of honesty that is unlikely in a signed autobiography. Thus even at a time when she knows her reputation is in decline, she can claim on the jacket of *Shadows on the Rock* what she may well have believed—that she is an author "whose title to foremost of living, if not of all, American novelists few would challenge." The statement on the jacket of *Sapphira and the Slave Girl* that "Sapphira's African slaves . . . are, and doubtless were meant to be, the most interesting figures in the book," is even more telling: it is the sort of candid comment Cather rarely makes about her fiction, but here, protected by the anonymity of a blurb, she types it on her own typewriter.

CHAPTER ONE

Three Autobiographies
and an (Auto)interview

The four biographical sketches discussed in this chapter date from three different decades and three important junctures in Willa Cather's career. The first accompanied the publication of her first book in 1903, the second the publication of her longest and most autobiographical novel in 1915, and the third was the opening essay in a promotional pamphlet published in 1926, three years after she won the Pulitzer Prize and shortly before the appearance of what many consider her greatest novel, *Death Comes for the Archbishop*. The fourth, an interview with Cather in Grand Central station, also dates from 1926.

Although all four of these pieces were published without indication that Cather was their author, and all four were created as puff pieces, it seems clear that in writing them Cather wished to convey, as only she could do, important insights into herself and her books. Their primary purpose, however, was to attract readers and sell books, and their very existence exemplifies the conflict Cather faced for so many years between presenting herself candidly on the one hand and shaping her image to entice the public on the other. It is a conflict that finds frequent reflection in Cather's fictional characters, a number of whom are similarly split between public and private concerns, integrity and ambition, what they know of themselves and how they want the world to perceive them. Indeed, a 1938 jacket blurb for *The Song of the Lark* describes its heroine, who rises to stardom as an opera diva, in words that fit Cather herself: "Thea Kronborg is sublimely egotistic and every influence, natural and human, she turns into account to help her in her career. There is always the struggle between the human and the artistic in the woman herself. . . ."

A principal purpose of this first chapter is simply to make these four autobiographical pieces readily available. Two circumstances have prevented this from occurring before: the 1903 and 1915 sketches are very rare—excellent examples of what bibliophiles call "ephemera"—and only recently have we learned that the 1926 "Interview" is in fact a fiction composed entirely by Cather herself. Although the 1926 "Biographical Sketch" is relatively accessible, it is included here so that it can be read in concert with these other pieces.

Literary Note (1903)

Cather published her first book, a collection of poems entitled *April Twilights*, with a vanity press in Boston, sharing a portion of the costs herself. Her publisher, Richard Badger, not only produced a handsome, albeit slight, volume but also made considerable efforts to market it. A few months before its release he included one of its poems, "Paris," in an attractive little booklet, *The Garden of the Heart*, specifically created to promote Cather and other poets whose books he was publishing (fig. 1). He also circulated an advance flyer containing an advertisement for the book and a mail-in order form (fig. 2). The "Literary Note," which is written on a single sheet about seven inches long and three and one-half inches wide, was probably designed to accompany this flyer (fig. 3).[1]

LITERARY NOTE

Miss Willa Sibert Cather, whose first book, a delightful volume of poems entitled *April Twilights*, will be published at once, was born near Winchester, Va., in 1876. When she was ten years old, the family moved to a ranch in Southwestern Nebraska, and for two years the child ran wild, living mostly on horseback, scouring the sparsely-settled country, visiting the Danes and Norwegians, tasting the wild-plum wine made by the old women, and playing with the little herd girls, who wore men's hats, and were not in the least afraid of rattlesnakes, which they killed with clods of earth. Even when the family moved later to Red Cloud, she still kept up her friendship for the Norwegian farmer folk, whose business brought them often to her father's office. During the ranch period and for some time after going to Red Cloud, Miss Cather did not go to school at all, and her only reading was an old copy of Ben Jonson's plays, a Shakespeare, a Byron, and *The Pilgrim's Progress*, which latter she said she read through eight times in one winter.[2] The first two years of her course at the University of Nebraska, where she graduated in 1895, were spent in the hardest kind of study, but then she discovered herself and began to write a little, mostly for her own pleasure and to satisfy the new craving for expression. She edited a creditable college magazine, and did remarkably discriminating dramatic criticism for the *Nebraska State Journal*. With all this she read voraciously, both in French and in English, and laid the foundation of her wide acquaintance with both literatures. Every vacation she went back to the sunflowers and the Norwegians, where she says she found her real life and her real education. After graduation she wrote for the *Lincoln* (Neb.) *Courier*, and in 1896 she came to Pittsburg,[3] where she was for several years on the staff of the *Leader*, doing clever dramatic and literary criticism in addition to her regular work.

This "Literary Note" is unsigned, but in style and substance it closely resembles the biographical portions of the 1915 "Development of an American Novelist" and the 1926 "Biographical Sketch," both of which we know Cather wrote. One doubts also that anyone else could have penned the vivid picture of the "little herd girls" who "wore men's hats, and were not in the least afraid of rattlesnakes, which they killed with clods of earth"; the description of Cather "living mostly on horseback, scouring the sparsely-settled country . . . tasting the wild-plum wine made by the old women"; or the comment on her university years: "Every vacation she went back to the sunflowers and the Norwegians, where she says she found her real life and her real education." The most telling evidence for Cather's authorship, however, is that Edith Lewis uses this "Literary

Note" in the same way that she uses the 1926 "Biographical Sketch" in describing Cather's childhood in her 1953 book, *Willa Cather Living*. We know, and Lewis must have known, that Cather herself wrote the 1926 statement; that Lewis—without attribution—cites whole passages virtually verbatim from both statements suggests strongly that she viewed both as Cather's own.[4]

Written when Cather was teaching in Pittsburgh, with her move to New York and *McClure's* three years in the future, this brief note predates Cather's decision to become a full-time professional writer. That *April Twilights* was being published by a vanity press, in part at Cather's own expense, was no doubt the source of some insecurity, and in this note she trumpets her prior achievements in ways that feel amateurish and overdone: the "hardest kind of study" of her early university years, the "creditable college magazine" she edited, her "remarkably discriminating dramatic criticism for the *Nebraska State Journal*" and her "clever dramatic and literary criticism" for the *Pittsburgh Leader*.[5] It is the sort of language that Cather would later castigate as belonging to "the purple flurry of my early writing . . . my florid, exaggerated, foamy-at-the-mouth, adjective-spree period."[6]

The same insecurity must also have led Cather in this note to alter her date of birth from 1873 to 1876, thus moving the publication of her first book from her thirtieth year to her twenty-seventh. Until the reappearance of this note, scholars had credited this revision of her age to a suggestion from S. S. McClure, who published Cather's *The Troll Garden* in 1905, but it is clearly her own.[7] This alteration of the truth persists through the remainder of Cather's career, and even onto her gravestone in Jaffrey, New Hampshire.[8]

This note was in circulation early enough in 1903, probably as part of a publicity packet, for it to serve as primary source for an article on Cather published in the winter 1903 issue of the journal *Poet-Lore*.[9] While the second half of this article briefly reviews Cather's new book of poems, its first half is lifted directly (and without attribution) from the "Literary Note," including Cather's distinctive spelling of "Pittsburg," her reference to Ben Jonson (transmuted into Ben Johnson), and her mention of the "little herd girls."

"The Development of an American Novelist" (1915)

The brochure produced to market *The Song of the Lark* immediately reveals the impact of the twelve years that have passed since the publication of *April Twilights*. Cather's publisher is now the venerable Houghton Mifflin, not a vanity press. The brochure may be small (about six inches by three and one-half inches), but it is skillfully designed, with a cover that reproduces the jacket of the novel and its silhouette of Jules Bréton's "The Song of the Lark" (fig. 4). Cather already has two novels to her credit, *Alexander's Bridge* and *O Pioneers!*, and the brochure cites reviews and notices of both. A detachable picture postcard, with instructions for ordering all three novels, is folded into the back cover.[10] The brochure includes a portrait of Cather, and it devotes eleven pages to the novelist and her work, space for more than five times as many words as in the 1903 "Literary Note."

WILLA SIBERT CATHER

THE DEVELOPMENT OF AN AMERICAN NOVELIST

I. A Prairie Childhood

Willa Sibert Cather was born near Winchester, Virginia, the daughter of Charles Fectigue Cather and Virginia Sibert Boak. Though the Siberts were originally Alsatians, and the Cathers came from county Tyrone, Ireland, both families had lived in Virginia for several generations.[11] When Miss Cather was nine years old her father left Virginia and settled on a ranch in Nebraska, in a thinly populated part of the state where the acreage of cultivated land was negligible beside the tremendous stretch of raw prairie. There were very few American families in that district; all the near neighbors were Scandinavians, and ten or twelve miles away there was an entire township settled by Bohemians.

For a child, accustomed to the quiet and the established order behind the Blue Ridge, this change was very stimulating. There was no school near at hand, and Miss Cather lived out of doors, winter and summer. She had a pony and rode about the Norwegian and Bohemian settlements, talking to the settlers and trying to understand them. The first two years on the ranch were probably more important to her as a writer than any that came afterward. The change from mountain-sheltered valleys to unprotected plains, the experiences of pioneering, and the contact with people of strange languages and customs impressed her deeply and inspired in her the broad, human understanding so essential to a writer of fiction. Foreign speaking people often talk more freely to a child than to grown persons, and even though they spoke very little English the settlers were social with the lonely little girl and somehow managed to tell her a great many stories about the old country. Miss Cather says:—

"I have never found any intellectual excitement more intense than I used to feel when I spent a morning with one of these pioneer women at her baking or butter-making. I used to ride home in the most unreasonable state of excitement; I always felt as if they told me so much more than they said—as if I had actually got inside another person's skin. If one begins that early, it is the story of the man-eating tiger over again—no other adventure ever carries one quite so far."[12]

II. Journalism and Editing

After some preparation in the high school at Red Cloud, Nebraska, Miss Cather entered the State University of Nebraska, graduated at nineteen, and immediately went to Pittsburgh and got a position on the *Pittsburgh Leader*. She was telegraph editor and dramatic critic on this paper for several years and then gave it up to take the place of the Head of the English Department in the Allegheny High School. While she was teaching she published her first book of verse, "April Twilights," and her first book of short stories, "The Troll Garden."

"The Troll Garden" attracted a good deal of attention, and six months after it was published, in the winter of 1906, Miss Cather went to New York to accept a position on the staff of McClure's Magazine. Two years later she became Managing Editor of McClure's. The duties of this position, the demands of life in New York, and the claims of her new social and business connections occupied her entire attention and for four years she did no writing at all. Then in 1912 she gave up office work and took a house in Cherry Valley, New York.

III. Her First Novel

"Alexander's Bridge," a short novel, was published in 1912. Avoiding alike the Western backgrounds and the newspaper and magazine world, with which she felt she was still too closely connected to "see them from the outside," Miss Cather laid the scene of her story in Boston and London.

Bartley Alexander was a builder of bridges. A man of elemental, restless force, he realized that the success which had made him famous had forced upon him exactly the kind of life he had determined to escape. Confronted by the possibility of a calm, secure middle age, he felt as if he were being buried alive. At this critical period he met again a girl whom he had known in his struggling student days at the Beaux Arts. She was like his youth calling to him. Yet he could respond only through deception and he was not the sort of man who could live two lives.

The situation is treated with subtlety, in a manner both restrained and penetrating. Struggle and tragedy are always near the surface, but there is no hint of sordidness, and Miss Cather has told the story with great artistic skill, brilliant and sympathetic in its reflections of character and life.

IV. "O Pioneers!"

When Miss Cather first began writing, she tried to put the Swedish and Bohemian settlers, who had so profoundly influenced her childhood, into short stories. The results never satisfied her. In explaining her feeling Miss Cather says:—

"It is always hard to write about the things that are near your heart, from a kind of instinct of self-protection you distort them and disguise them. Those stories were so poor that they discouraged me. I decided that I wouldn't write any more about the country and people for which I had personal feeling.

"Then I had the good fortune to meet Sarah Orne Jewett, who had read all of my early stories and had very clear and definite opinions about them and about where my work fell short. She said, 'Write it as it is, don't try to make it like this or that. You can't do it in anybody's else [*sic*] way—you will have to make a way of your own. If the way happens to be new, don't let that frighten you. Don't try to write the kind of short story that this or that magazine wants—write the truth and let them take it or leave it.'

"It is that kind of honesty, that earnest endeavor to tell truly the thing that haunts the mind, that I love in Miss Jewett's own work. I dedicated 'O Pioneers' to her because I had talked over some of the characters with her and in this book I tried to tell the story of the people as truthfully and simply as if I were telling it to her by word of mouth."

Perhaps it is the simplicity and truthfulness of it which makes "O Pioneers!" stand out preëminently above the sort of novel which we have come to designate as "typically Western." There is a certain sameness about most Western stories. The characters and the country seem stamped into a mechanical similarity with blurred edges and automatic effects. Miss Cather has departed from conventional lines. She took no pattern, but from her own knowledge and love of her subject she wrote with a virility and art that mark her book as a novel of moment. Alexandra, the woman of the story, is forty years old, has brought up her brothers after the death of their parents, and wrested a subsistence from the land by dint of sheer force of will. She is passionately attached to the country. "We come and go, but the land is always here. And the people who love and understand it are the people who own it—for a little while."

That is the note struck throughout and wrought with consummate art into the framework of the story. Even the exquisite and tragic episode of the love of Alexandra's brother for the little Bohemian, Marie Shabata, is handled with a ruthlessness in keeping with the country and the stark simplicity of its moral code. Although pure fiction, the vividly sketched background of Nebraska prairies and the faithful character drawing of a class of settlers who are becoming more and more a power in the political and economic life of the country give to "O Pioneers!" a definite historical value.

v. Miss Cather's Latest Novel

In whatever Miss Cather writes the reader may be sure of excellent workmanship and interesting theme. Other than that, one book in no way prepares him for what is coming next.

"The Song of the Lark" is a story of a great American singer, her childhood in the Colorado desert, her early struggles in Chicago, her romantic adventures among the Cliff Dweller ruins in Arizona, her splendid triumphs on the operatic stage.

There is a diverting picture of musical Chicago in the early years of Theodore Thomas's leadership when the young Swedish-American heroine, Thea Kronborg, not yet appreciating the possibilities of her voice, is spending all her money and almost more than all her strength for the sake of her lessons and the drudgery of choir work. There are wonderful chapters on the Cliff Dweller ruins, which first awoke in her the historic imagination so necessary to a great Wagnerian singer and where, away from drudgery for the first time in her life, she grew all at once into a powerful and willful young creature, got her courage, and began to find herself. Thea Kronborg, the Swedes and Mexicans of the little Colorado town where she spent her childhood, the Polish musicians and art-loving German and Jewish capitalists of Chicago and New York—these are to-day as typically American as any descendant of Pilgrim father or southern chevalier.[13]

The author's familiarity with the West has already been accounted for. She is equally intimate with New York, and has gained her knowledge of the ways of the operatic world through journalistic work and through personal friendship with many well-known singers.

VI. Present Life and Future Work

Miss Cather's present home is an apartment in that picturesque and interesting old part of New York known as Greenwich Village. In the summer she goes abroad or returns to the West. This summer she refused a tempting offer to write a series of articles on the war situation in Europe, preferring instead to explore the twenty-odd miles of Cliff-Dweller remains that are hidden away in the southwest corner of Colorado, near Mancos and Durango.

What may be Miss Cather's plans for future work she has not disclosed. One thing is certain—she will not repeat herself. There will never be a stereotyped Cather heroine or Cather hero. She finds the appeal of the West compelling, but "Alexander's Bridge" shows how well she knows and loves not only wild nature and the conquering spirit of the new West but also the old, fine culture and traditions of New England.

Few young authors have so broad a field to choose from, and few are so thoroughly equipped for their work. Three books establish her position in the front rank of American writers. "The Song of the Lark," especially, places her definitely in the little group of American novelists that count; the novelists that present American life with full knowledge and convincing reality.

Like the 1903 literary note, this statement is unsigned. Ferris Greenslet wrote Cather on July 21, 1915, about plans for this booklet and asked her "to provide a 200–500-word story of her life"; five days later he noted that he had received "the biography section of the booklet." He indicated that he himself would write the "literary history," and sections 3–5 at times draw on the house memos he wrote on Cather's first three novels.[14] But much of section 4 consists of direct quotations from an earlier Cather interview; section 5 draws heavily on promotional copy Cather herself had written for the *Song of the Lark* jacket (some of it not used when the book was published); and all three sections mesh with the portions of the brochure that Cather wrote herself (sections 1, 2, and 6, which far exceed the five-hundred-word maximum that Greenslet had suggested). Cather warmly thanks Greenslet for his work on the brochure when he runs it by her for a final prepublication review in September 1915, but it is clear that she herself wrote the opening and concluding biographical portions and contributed significantly to the whole project.[15]

The tone of this 1915 essay differs markedly from that of the "Literary Note." Where in 1903 Cather struggled to inflate the importance of the writing she had done as a student and the criticism she had written for papers in Lincoln and Pittsburgh, she now has four books to her credit. Her enhanced self-confidence is especially evident in the final section, "Present Life and Future Work," where she boldly places herself "in the front rank of American writers, . . . in the little group of American novelists that count; the novelists that present American life with full knowledge and convincing reality."

Given the success of *O Pioneers!* just two years earlier, it is not surprising that Cather again emphasizes her Nebraska upbringing. In addition, this time she specifically ties this childhood period to her subsequent success as a novelist. Not only does she identify "[t]he first two years on the ranch" as "probably more important to her as a writer than any that came afterward," but she also emphasizes how visiting the pioneer women made her feel "as if I had actually got inside another person's skin." Once again she stresses the importance of her early and close acquaintance with foreign languages and cultures, though here with reference not to her university studies, as in the "Literary Note," but to her childhood: "[T]he contact with people of strange languages and customs impressed her deeply and inspired in her the broad, human understanding so essential to a writer of fiction. Foreign speaking people often talk more freely to a child than to grown persons, and even though they spoke very little English the settlers were social with the lonely little girl and somehow managed to tell her a great many stories about the old country." She also has space this time to include a few details about her early years in Virginia and to comment on the move to Nebraska: "For a child, accustomed to the quiet and the established order behind the Blue Ridge, this change was very stimulating."

One means by which Cather lends authority to this 1915 statement is by frequent quotation of her own previous statements, drawing on a 1913 interview in the *Philadelphia Record*.[16] But if there is a hint of legerdemain in Cather citing interviews of herself in an essay she herself is composing, this is nothing compared to her freedom with all manner of facts about herself. Her claim that she graduated from the University of Nebraska at age nineteen is not true—she was twenty-one and a half—and presumes again her adjusted date of birth.[17] As she had done in the 1903 note, she exaggerates the length of time she lived on the prairie: "the first two years on the ranch" not only fudges the fact that her family moved to Red Cloud after only a year and a half on the Divide but also suggests that they lived there for even more than two. She also implies, as she had done in 1903, that she had no schooling prior to attending high school in Red Cloud: in fact, she spent some time in school even during the eighteen months on the Divide (cf. "there was no school near at hand"), and she attended school regularly from the time she moved at age eleven to Red Cloud.[18] It is also not true that after finishing university she "immediately went to Pittsburgh and got a position on the *Pittsburgh Leader*." To the contrary, she spent a good part of a year in Red Cloud, eagerly hoping for a job that would take her away from home, and when she did go to Pittsburgh it was to edit the *Home Monthly*, a women's magazine far less prestigious than the *Leader*.[19] When she left the *Leader*, it was not to become head of English at Allegheny High School but to take a temporary position teaching Latin, composition, and algebra at Central High School; only two years later did she become head of English at Allegheny High.[20] As for "refus[ing] a tempting offer to write a series of articles on the war situation in Europe," in fact she and S. S. McClure had planned to go to Europe in hopes of making money off stories from the war, but they abandoned the project when Judge McClung persuaded Cather and his daughter Isabelle, who also was planning to go on the trip, that the undertaking was too dangerous.[21] One other fiction is more poignant: when Cather says that she did "no writing at all" in the time when she was managing editor at *McClure's*, she again overstates the case—several fine stories date from these years (1907–11). That said, this may well be how the period felt to her as she looked back upon it.

Cather is, of course, a storyteller, someone who both in her fiction and her signed essays constantly transforms mere facts into persuasive stories, whether about herself or in the fictional worlds she creates.[22] None of the distortions we have identified is especially egregious in itself. Nonetheless, all but the last one mentioned move toward making Cather appear more impressive, more accomplished, more dashing than the facts warrant. What's more, these twistings of the truth appear in a brochure which quotes Cather herself stressing that truthfulness is at the heart of both her work and the novelist's art, a theme she roots in advice she had received from Sarah Orne Jewett (italics mine):

> She said, "*Write it as it is, don't try to make it like this or that.* You can't do it in anybody else's way—you will have to make a way of your own. If the way happens to be new, don't let that frighten you. Don't try to write the kind of short story that this or that magazine wants—*write the truth* and let them take it or leave it."
>
> *It is that kind of honesty, that earnest endeavor to tell truly the thing that haunts the mind,* that I love in Miss Jewett's own work. I dedicated "O Pioneers" to her because I had talked over some of the characters with her and *in this book I tried to tell the story of the people as truthfully and simply as if I were telling it to her by word of mouth.*

As if to seal the point, immediately after this passage the brochure comments on "the simplicity and *truthfulness*" of *O Pioneers!* The essence of Cather's comments is that the writer of fiction must above all tell the truth, but here is Cather, in this very brochure, repeatedly advancing false information about herself. My point is not to impugn her as a liar but to note a contradiction of which she herself must have been aware. Advertising copy often stretches the truth in promoting a book, but usually it is the publisher, not the author, who produces such copy. Here

Cather herself writes the prose, crafts its distortions, and does so in the course of identifying truthfulness as central to herself and her writing. Further underscoring the disjunction is an authorial comment in the climactic scene of the very book she is promoting, *The Song of the Lark*: "Artistic growth is, more than it is anything else, a refining of the sense of truthfulness. The stupid believe that to be truthful is easy; only the artist, the great artist, knows how difficult it is" (*SOL* 477).

Cather's compromise between artistic principles and advertising priorities extends to the way this brochure treats *Alexander's Bridge*. Cather within months had found flaws in this first novel, as she recalled in a 1931 article: "Soon after the book was published I went for six months to Arizona and New Mexico. The longer I stayed in a country I really did care about, and among people who were a part of the country, the more unnecessary and superficial a book like *Alexander's Bridge* seemed to me."[23] In the same essay she compares the novel unfavorably to *O Pioneers!*, and in this second novel she abandoned the model of *Alexander's Bridge* and took a markedly different novelistic tack. None of this, however, prevents her from including warm praise of her first novel, and of herself as its creator, in the 1915 brochure: "Miss Cather has told the story with great artistic skill, brilliant and sympathetic in its reflections of character and life.... 'Alexander's Bridge' shows how well she knows and loves not only wild nature and the conquering spirit of the new West but also the old, fine culture and traditions of New England." Here Cather either writes or approves promotional copy that contradicts her artistic judgment and puts selling copies of this first novel above her perception that it falls short of her best. At work here are two quite different Willa Cathers—one the artist, the other the promoter. It is a duality that finds reflection in those many figures in Cather's fiction who are also divided within themselves—among them, of course, the very hero of *Alexander's Bridge*.

"A Biographical Sketch" (1926)

In 2002 Drew University acquired a number of Cather materials that had been owned by Frederick B. Adams Jr., former head of New York's

Pierpont Morgan Library, and creator of a major Cather collection. Among them was the typescript of the "Biographical Sketch" that was published without attribution in Alfred A. Knopf's 1926 pamphlet, *Willa Cather: A Biographical Sketch, an English Opinion, and an Abridged Bibliography*. Whereas for the 1903 and 1915 statements we must piece together evidence of Cather's authorship, we can actually see her writing this 1926 statement. Cather's corrections also document the care she took even with this sort of promotional material.[24]

A BIOGRAPHICAL SKETCH[25]

Although Willa Cather is generally spoken of as a Western writer, she was born in Virginia, on a farm near Winchester, and lived there until she was eight years old. Her ancestors, on both sides, had been Virginia farmers for three or four generations; they came originally from England, Ireland, and Alsace. When Willa Cather was eight years old, her father took his family to Nebraska and bought a ranch near Red Cloud, a little town on the Burlington Railroad named for the famous Sioux warrior.

Life on a Nebraska ranch, in those days when the country was thinly settled, was full of adventure. Farming was then a secondary matter; the most important occupation was the feeding of great herds of cattle driven up from Texas, and most of the great prairie country from the Missouri River to Denver was still open grazing land. The population of the country about Red Cloud was largely foreign. Swedes, Danes, Norwegians, Bohemians, Germans, a few Russians, and to the north the prosperous French Canadian colony of St. Anne.

Willa Cather did not go to school. She had a pony[26] and spent her time riding about the country and getting acquainted with the neighbors, whose foreign speech and customs she found intensely interesting. Had she been born in that community, she doubtless would have taken these things for granted. But she came to this strange mixture of peoples and manners from an old conservative society; from the Valley of Virginia, where the original land grants made in the reigns of George II and George III had been going down from father to son ever since, where life was ordered and settled, where the people in good families were born good, and the poor mountain people were not expected to amount to much. The movement of life was slow there, but the quality of it was rich and kindly. There had been no element of struggle since the Civil War. Foreigners were looked down upon, unless they were English or persons of title.

An imaginative child, taken out of this definitely arranged background, and dropped down among struggling immigrants from all over the world, naturally found something to think about. Struggle appeals to a child more than comfort and picturesqueness, because it is dramatic. No child with a spark of generosity could have kept from throwing herself heart and soul into the fight these people were making to master the language, to master the soil, to hold their land and to get ahead in the world. Those friendships Willa Cather made as a little girl still count immensely for her; and she says she could never find time to be bored in that community where the life of every family was like that of the Swiss Family Robinson. Lightning and hail and prairie fires and drouths and blizzards were always threatening to extinguish this family or that.[27]

All the while that she was racing about over the country by day, Willa Cather was reading at night. She read a good many of the English classics aloud to her two grandmothers. She learned Latin early and read it easily.[28] Later her father moved his family into the little town of Red Cloud, and she went to the high school, but she learned her Latin from an old English gentleman, who had the enthusiasm of the true scholar and with whom she used to read even after she entered the University of Nebraska. She was graduated from that University at nineteen and spent the next few years in Pittsburgh teaching and doing newspaper work. She chose that city to work in rather than New York because she had warm personal friends there. These were the years when she was learning to write, doing all that work and experimenting that every writer and painter must do at some time or other to find and perfect his medium.

But it was only the winters that Miss Cather spent in Pittsburgh. Every summer she went back to Nebraska and Colorado and Wyoming. For although she says it was in these years that she was learning to write, Miss Cather admits that she spent very little time sitting at a desk. She was much too restless for that and too much interested in people, east and west. She believes that there is no use beginning to write until you have lived a good deal, and lived among all kinds of people. But wherever she went, whatever ties she formed, she always went back to the plains country. The first year she spent in Europe she nearly died of homesickness for it. "I hung and hung about[29] the wheat country in central France," she says, "sniffling when I observed a little French girl riding on the box between her father's feet on an American mowing machine, until it occurred to me that maybe if I went home to my own wheat country and my own father, I might be less lachrymose. It's a queer thing about the flat country—it takes hold of you, or it leaves you perfectly cold. A great many people find it dull and monotonous; they like a church steeple, an old mill, a waterfall, country all touched up and furnished, like a German Christmas card. I go everywhere, I admire all kinds of country. I tried to live in France. But when I strike the open plains, something happens. I'm home. I breathe differently. That love of great spaces, of rolling open country like the sea,—it's the grand passion of my life. I tried for years to get over it. I've stopped trying. It's incurable."

Miss Cather's first published book was a volume of verse, "April Twilights" (reissued in 1923 as "April Twilights and Later Verse"). While she was in Pittsburgh she had been working from time to time on a collection of short stories. In 1904 she sent the manuscript[30] of this volume of stories, entitled "The Troll Garden," into the publishing house of McClure-Phillips. The manuscript came under the eye of that most discerning of American editors, S. S. McClure, who had already so many discoveries to his credit. He telegraphed Miss Cather to come to New York at once for a conference. He published her book, and published several stories from it in "McClure's Magazine." Two of these, "The Sculptor's Funeral" and "Paul's Case," attracted wide attention, and for several years imitations of them kept turning up in the manuscript bags of New York editors.

Two years after he accepted her book of short stories, S. S. McClure offered Miss Cather a position on his magazine. She joined the McClure staff in the winter of 1906. Two years later she became managing editor of McClure's and held that position for four years. During that period of editorial work she wrote very little. She traveled a great deal, in Europe and in the American Southwest, Arizona and New Mexico. In 1912 she gave up editorial work and wrote her first novel, "Alexander's Bridge." This was followed by "O Pioneers!" "The Song of the Lark" and "My Antonia [sic]," "Youth and the Bright Medusa," "One of Ours," "A Lost Lady," "The Professor's House," and "My Mortal Enemy."[31] Nearly all of these books have been translated into various European languages, and Willa Cather has a rapidly growing European reputation.

This 1926 "Biographical Sketch" is two-thirds as long as the 1915 "Development of an American Novelist," about twelve hundred words compared to about eighteen hundred. Although it notes the attention accorded Cather's early stories and ends with a reference to her "growing European reputation," it is also largely free of the occasionally obtrusive puffery of the 1903 and 1915 sketches.[32] Since the next piece in the pamphlet, Porterfield's "An English Opinion," discusses and praises Cather's writings up through *The Professor's House*, Cather need do little more than list her bibliography, as she does in the final paragraphs.[33]

While Cather in this 1926 sketch retreats from the more overt self-promotion of the earlier statements, she does not hesitate to alter facts about herself, especially those relating to her childhood. She still casts herself as younger than she is, now making herself eight at the time of the move to Nebraska and maintaining the fiction that she graduated from the university at nineteen. The statement that "Willa Cather did not go to school" creates an even more erroneous impression of her pre–high school years than does the 1915 sketch, and the lengthy description of her life on the prairie similarly outstrips the 1915 statement in implying that she lived there for many years rather than just eighteen months. And when she writes, "All the while that she was racing about over the country by day, Willa Cather was reading at night," she does not mention that most of this reading was done after, not before, the family moved from the Divide, a misperception she bolsters by adding, "Later her father moved his family into the little town of Red Cloud."

Despite the distortions, Cather weaves these details into a childhood portrait so evocative and consistent that it rings true. To begin with, she devotes far more space to her early childhood than in the 1903 and 1915 sketches, in the process creating an artful counterpoint between Virginia and Nebraska: "an old conservative society" against "this strange mixture of peoples and manners"; the "slow" (albeit "rich and kindly") "movement of life" in Virginia against "adventure" and "struggle" in Nebraska; her own rather conventional family background—"England, Ireland, and Alsace"—against the polyglot mixture she found in Nebraska: "Swedes, Danes, Norwegians, Bohemians, Germans, a few Russians, and to the north the prosperous French Canadian colony of St. Anne."; predictable continuities there, constant uncertainties here, the latter evoked in a sentence whose breathless profusion of conjunctions contrasts sharply with the measured cadences of her description of Virginia: "Lightning and hail and prairie fires and drouths and blizzards were always threatening to extinguish this family or that."[34]

Not only does the first part of the 1926 sketch contain numerous details of her childhood not present in the earlier statements, but Cather also works her western background into the portions of the sketch that deal with later periods of her life, noting that when she was in Pittsburgh she returned each summer to "Nebraska and Colorado and Wyoming" and adding that "wherever she went, whatever ties she formed, she always went back to the plains country." And where in the earlier statement Cather relates the Nebraska background mainly to her work as a writer, implicit throughout the 1926 sketch is her emotional connection to the land itself. This theme builds to a powerful climax in her description of the nostalgia she felt on her first trip to Europe. Once again she adopts the ploy of quoting herself, but this time with reference not to her writing (as in 1915) but to her feelings for Nebraska: "'I hung and hung about the wheat country in central France,' she says, 'sniffling when I observed a little French girl riding on the box between her father's feet on an American mowing machine, until it occurred to me that maybe if I went home to my own wheat country and my own father, I might be less lachrymose.'"[35]

It is instructive to compare this passage with the "Barbizon" chapter of *Willa Cather in Europe*, which contains Cather's original account of that trip, in 1902, to "the wheat country in central France."[36] Here too she dwells on the details of the country and its people, associating them specifically with the Nebraska she knew as a child and noting that they "recalled not a little the country about Campbell and Bladen." "To complete the resemblance," she adds, "there stood a reaper of a well-known American make, very like the one on which I have acted as supercargo many a time. There was a comfortable little place where a child might sit happily enough between its father's feet, and perhaps if I had waited long enough I might have seen a little French girl sitting in that happy sheltered place, the delights of which I have known so well" (*WCE* 122). This passage, written twenty-four years earlier, is clearly the source of her 1926 description of the little French girl. Not only has Cather in the 1926 sketch recast this memory as a quotation that she places in her own mouth, but she also transforms the little French girl she "might have seen" into one she did see![37] It is one more example of her freedom with facts in these puff pieces, but here one senses less Cather the advertiser at work than Cather the novelist, always ready—as in her fiction—to enhance the emotional impact of her story by giving play to her imagination.[38]

The revisions Cather made on the typescript further suggest the importance she attached to this climactic section, with its focus on the lasting emotional pull of the prairies of her childhood (see fig. 5).[39] The typescript shows that this paragraph originally ended as follows: "I go everywhere, I admire all kinds of country. But when I strike the open plains, something happens. I'm home. I breathe differently. That love of great wide spaces, of rolling open country like the sea,—it's the grand passion of my life. I tried to go to France to live, I tried for years and years to get over it. I've stopped trying. It's incurable." One can then see Cather working on this passage. A deleted quotation mark suggests that at one point she thought of ending the quotation after "I breathe differently." She crosses out "wide" in "great wide spaces" and eliminates "and years" from "for years and years." She has problems with the phrase about living in France. She adds a comma ("I tried to go to France, to live"); notes in longhand, then inks through, a transposition ("I tried to go to live in France"); finally she draws a line through the whole phrase and writes it by hand, as a separate sentence, into an earlier position, where we find it in the final version: "I go everywhere, I admire all kinds of country. I tried to live in France. But when I strike the open plains, something happens. I'm home. I breathe differently. That love of great spaces, of rolling open country like the sea,—it's the grand passion of my life. I tried for years to get over it. I've stopped trying. It's incurable." A comparison of this final version with where Cather began reveals the degree to which her several changes give the final version a grace, directness, and emotional resonance it originally lacked.

The trimming of "wide" and "and years" is similar to what Cather does elsewhere in this manuscript. "Struggle is the thing which appeals to a child" becomes "Struggle appeals to a child"; "after she entered the freshman class of the State University of Nebraska" becomes "after she entered the University of Nebraska"; before the sentence that begins "Later her father moved his family . . ." Cather has crossed out "When she was old enough to . . . ." Slight in themselves, these and other such changes help give the 1926 sketch a spare eloquence that contrasts sharply not only with the "adjective-spree" language of the 1903 note but also with the relative wordiness of her 1915 brochure, a contrast comparable to that between the language of the chronologically proximate *Song of the Lark* and *Professor's House*. Albeit in microcosm, Cather's revisions of this typescript display the same quest for an "unfurnished" style that was shaping her fiction of the 1920s.[40]

In retrospect, what remains most striking about this sketch is the degree to which Cather's focus almost throughout is on her childhood. The first five of its eight paragraphs concern this topic, and as we have seen, the sixth mentions her move to Pittsburgh and her European trip only to circle back in both instances to the western plains. Porterfield's survey of her writing, which immediately follows this sketch, permits Cather to devote the bulk of her attention to her Nebraska upbringing, an emphasis interesting in light of her resistance elsewhere (including at the start of this very essay) to being typecast as a "Western writer," and suggestive of a growing comfort with acknowledging her roots and the part they play in her writing. The very prevalence of this topic, however, and especially the way it recurs at the end of the sixth paragraph, suggest also a nostalgic return to a time earlier and better than the present: "That love of great spaces, of rolling open country like the sea,—it's the grand passion of my life. I tried for years to get over it. I've stopped trying. It's incurable." Both tone and language recall *My Ántonia*, even down to Jim Burden's comparison of the prairie to the sea: "As I looked about me I felt that the grass was the country, as the water is the sea" (*MA* 16). The recollection of *My Ántonia* is apt, for that novel is filled with overtones of a distant, lost past, a theme emphasized from the start by its Virgilian epigraph, *optima dies . . . prima fugit*—"the best days are the first to flee," as Jim translates it. And despite its assurance, this 1926 sketch leaves us above all with a sense that this writer, the winner of a Pulitzer Prize three years earlier, and by now recognized here and abroad as one of America's greatest novelists, is looking back on better days. Indeed, the last two paragraphs, the one devoted to Cather's first two books, the other to her later work, seem almost afterthoughts to the lines that end Cather's section on her French trip and that fix the overall mood of the piece: "[I]t's the grand passion of my life. I tried for years to get over it. I've stopped trying. It's incurable."

That this essay's final paragraphs, with their promotional content, are less memorable than what has preceded fits the overall character of this 1926 sketch, which throughout retreats from the self-advertisement of the 1903 and 1915 pieces. As such, it leads naturally into this chapter's final example of Cather's anonymous promotional writing, a short piece written a few months later and so lacking in self-advertisement that it was apparently never used for the promotional purposes that called it forth. Like the 1926 sketch, this piece too seems to reveal more of Cather's true feelings than perhaps she herself realized. Both, of course, date from four years after 1922—which Cather would subsequently identify as the year the world broke in two.[41]

A Willa Cather "Interview" (1926)

While the typescript just discussed proves what we have long known, that Cather herself wrote this 1926 "Biographical Sketch," a second typescript from the same year, also from the Adams collection, provides evidence of a more surprising sort. It shows that a short "Interview" with Cather, originally published in the *Nebraska State Journal* and in 1986 reprinted as a bona fide interview in a standard reference book, is not an interview at all but a fiction composed by Cather herself.[42] How it got from her desk to the *Nebraska State Journal*, where it appeared on September 5, 1926, we do not know, but that it is entirely her creation is beyond doubt: the handwritten corrections to the typescript are in Cather's hand, and comparison of the typing with that of the 1926 sketch confirms that it too is hers.[43] A short note appended to the typescript, written in pencil and in a different hand (and missing from previously published versions), is also revealing, for it suggests that Cather wrote this brief piece—like the 1926 sketch—for promotional purposes.

[UNTITLED][44]

Interviewed at the Grand Central Station where she was waiting for a train one hot July day, Willa Cather said:

"Yes, I'm going out of town,—it's rather evident. No, not West this time. I have just come back from three months in New Mexico. Now I'm going up into New England."[45]

"What part of New England?"

"Oh, several places! Mr. Knopf and Mr. Reynolds will always have my address, if you should wish to reach me about something important. Seriously, I'm going away to work and don't want to be bothered."

"But this is vacation time."

"I've just had a long vacation in New Mexico. I need a rest from resting."

"Are you beginning a new novel?"

"No, I'm in the middle of one."

"When will it be published?"

"The book? About a year from now. The serial publication will begin sometime this winter. I want to finish the manuscript by the middle of February and get abroad in the early spring."

"I suppose, Miss Cather, it's no use to ask you for the title. You told me several years ago that you never announced the title of a new book until it was completed."

"Did I tell you that? Well, this time I'll make an exception. I don't like to get into a rut about anything.[46] I call this book 'Death Comes for the Archbishop'."

"And the scene?"

"Oh, that remains to be seen! My train is called."

"One general question on the way down, please. What do you consider the greatest obstacle American writers have to overcome?"

"Well, what do other writers tell you?"

"Some say commercialism, and some say Prohibition."

"I don't exactly agree with either. I should say it was the lecture-bug. In this country a writer has to hide and lie and almost steal in order to get time to work in,—and peace of mind to work with. Besides, lecturing is very dangerous for writers. If we lecture, we get a little more owlish and self-satisfied all the time. We hate it at first, if we are decently modest, but in the end we fall in love with the sound of our own voice. There is something insidious about it, destructive to ones [*sic*] finer feelings. All human beings, apparently, like to speak in public. The timid man becomes bold, the man who has never had an opinion about anything becomes chock full of them the monent [*sic*] he faces an audience. A woman, alas, becomes even fuller! Really, I've seen people's reality quite destroyed by the habit of putting on a rostrum front. It's especially destructive to writers, ever so much worse than alcohol, takes their edge off."

"But why, why?"

"Certainly, I can't tell you now. He's calling 'all aboard'. Try it out yourself; go lecture to a Sunday School or a class of helpless infants somewhere, and you'll see how puffed-up and important you begin to feel. You'll want to do it right over again. But don't! Goodbye."

[Appended note, handwritten, by someone other than Willa Cather:][47]

Miss Cather's most recent published work is "the [*sic*] Professor's House", which turned out to be a national bestseller. Mr. Knopf, her publisher, announces a short novel, "My Mortal Enemy" by Miss Cather, for October.

The addendum pinpoints the composition of this piece to the period between September 4, 1925, and October 20, 1926, the respective publication dates for *The Professor's House* and *My Mortal Enemy*. One also assumes that its composition must fall not far from the "dramatic date" implicit in the interview itself, a hot day in July 1926, "about a year" before the publication of *Death Comes for the Archbishop*, and with serial publication of that novel to begin "this winter" (serial publication of *Death* began in January 1927, and the book itself appeared on September 2, 1927).[48]

Though even less self-promoting than the "Biographical Sketch," the interview by its very form carries to new lengths Cather's habit of putting words into her own mouth in her puff pieces, and of playing free with the facts. That this piece has hitherto been taken for an actual interview is testimony to Cather's skill in catching the tone of this sort of hasty interview. And while the three sketches provide fascinating glimpses of Cather the writer of promotional copy, this interview is something more—a fictional skit replete with its own setting, plot, and vividly realized characters. Its polish is the more remarkable in that the paucity of corrections in the typescript, and the presence of two uncorrected typos, suggest that Cather dashed it off quickly—a snapshot rather than a posed self-portrait. Her keen ear is again apparent, this time in her deft evocation of her own voice—jaunty, insouciant, self-assured, brusque at times. A change she makes at the end not only underscores the urgency of the conductor's "All aboard!" a few lines earlier but also shows her working to capture her own crisp manner (see fig. 6).

Her conclusion originally ran, "You'll want to do it right over again; your mind will bubble with platitudes. Goodbye." In the typescript she has inked through the second clause and replaced it with a sharp admonition: "You'll want to do it right over again. But don't! Goodbye."[49] The only other substantive change noted in the typescript is of the same ilk. The passage about the "lecture-bug" originally read, "In this country a writer can get on at all only by being rude to womens [*sic*] clubs and colleges. He, her, she, has to hide and lie . . . ." Cather has inked out from "can get on" through "He, her, she," a change that both makes for economy of language and also again captures her own blunt manner: "In this country a writer has to hide and lie and almost steal in order to get time to work in,—and peace of mind to work with."

Cather also has fun toying with her imaginary interviewer. She tells him that if he has something really important to ask, he can always call her office, then leavens her brusqueness with the "seriously" that follows. When he notes that she is heading off to work during vacation, she answers that she needs "a rest from resting," and when he asks if she is beginning a new novel, she snippily replies, "No, I'm in the middle of one." To bring home her point about the addictive effect of speaking in public, she encourages him to "go lecture to a Sunday School or a class of helpless infants somewhere."

The game Cather is playing in writing this "Interview," and that her persona is playing with her interlocutor, is especially apparent in the way its opening mimics an actual interview Cather had given to the *Cleveland Press* when she lectured in that city in 1925:

"And are you working on a new novel now?" I asked Miss Cather.
"Yes."
"When will we have it?"

A period of ominous silence. Then, flushed with a slight peeve, Miss Cather brusquely exploded. "Say, even my publishers don't dare ask me that! I get my books out when I can, and not before."

"And its title, please?"

"I never give out titles or any information about my books until they are ready," she replied.[50]

Since in her 1926 ersatz interview Cather herself is creating both interviewee and interviewer, she for once lets down her guard and reveals the title of her next book!

The peevishness captured in the 1925 Cleveland interview, however, suggests some serious undercurrents in this fictional interview that Cather crafts the following year. The theme she sounds in it—finding "time to work in,—and peace of mind to work with"—was in fact very close to her heart in 1926. "As she became more widely known, as her books became celebrated," comments Edith Lewis, "the demands on her time and strength of course greatly increased. The luxury she prized above all others was freedom; and she now found her freedom hampered at every turn.... She was, of course, continually pressed to give interviews, to give lectures, to join societies, to work for charities—all the clutter of irrelevant activities that obstruct the life of any artist who becomes famous."[51]

Prominent among this "clutter of irrelevant activities" was the "lecture-bug." In late 1921 Cather gave several speeches in Nebraska, and in 1922 she delivered a series of lectures at the Bread Loaf School in Vermont, experiences she often enjoyed but that just as often left her exhausted and even ill.[52] In the following years, especially after she won the Pulitzer Prize in 1923, lecture invitations poured in. In early 1923 she reports that her secretary has turned down almost a hundred requests; late the same year she declines to give the William Vaughn Moody lectures in Chicago; in March 1924 she notes that she can hardly write for fending off people inviting her to speak.[53] In 1925 she relents and lectures at Bowdoin College in May, in Chicago (the Moody Lecture she'd earlier declined) and in Cleveland in November (the lecture that leads to the *Cleveland Press* interview).[54] Though her 1926 interview strikes a light-hearted note and tempers the pique that sounds in the *Cleveland Press* article, behind it one hears a serious Cather reminding herself of what she has long known, and what the 1925 lectures had brought home to her: "[L]ecturing is very dangerous for writers. . . . There is something insidious about it, destructive to one's finer feelings. . . . You'll want to do it right over again. But don't!"[55] The "talking to" she gave herself apparently worked. A few months later she tells Marion Edward Park, president of Bryn Mawr College, that she refuses to speak at colleges but will relent in this one case—on condition that Park not spread the word to other college presidents.[56] From this time on, Cather gives almost no public talks, heeding her own words about this habit: "destructive to writers, ever so much worse than alcohol, takes their edge off."[57]

As with anything Willa Cather writes, there is yet more to be said. Both the 1915 and the 1926 anonymous sketches hint at the presence of two Willa Cathers. In the 1915 piece there is the split between the high-minded author who stresses truthfulness as her touchstone and the essay's anonymous writer who skews the facts about herself at point after point. In the 1926 sketch there is the split between the assurance with which this much-fêted writer traces so much of her current success to her western roots and the unmistakable longing with which she evokes times and places now irrevocably in the past. In the 1926 interview the rift is yet closer to the surface. On the one hand there is the author, jealous of her time, painfully aware that "in this country a writer has to hide and lie and almost steal in order to get time to work in,—and peace of mind to work with," and it is this self-protective side that predominates early on: "Seriously, I'm going away to work and don't want to be bothered." Present also, though, is the author who has learned from her own experience what fun it can be to play to an audience: "[Y]ou'll see how puffed-up and important you begin to feel. You'll want to do it right over again." She goes so far as to admit that such activities can even change one's personality: "The timid man becomes bold, the man who has never had an opinion about anything becomes chock full of them the moment he faces an audience. A woman, alas, becomes even fuller! Really, I've seen people's reality quite destroyed by the habit of putting on a rostrum front." It is easy to see in "the habit of putting on a rostrum front" a refraction of

Cather's activities as publicist and promoter, playing to potential readers in the same way skilled lecturers play on the emotions of their listeners. This piece suggests that she was tired of putting on that "rostrum front," had become aware of the addictive dangers of courting public favor, and was longing for a place where she could work in peace, escape intruders like her Grand Central interviewer, and avoid assuming a different voice to speak to the public.[58]

The interview casts that place as the New England to which she is fleeing, but it could as well be the childhood Eden she recalls with such love in her 1926 "Biographical Sketch." In retrospect, these two 1926 pieces form a fascinating pair. Though both are written as promotional pieces, the sketch abandons most of the self-promotion that marked earlier pieces of this sort, while the interview is so lacking in promotional promise that it was never used for this purpose. Both pieces seek simpler, quieter places, the sketch constantly returning to the Nebraska of Cather's childhood, the interview catching Cather as she flees the hustle and bustle of New York. Both focus on powerful inclinations in Cather herself, the sketch acknowledging the irresistible passion she feels for the plains of her childhood, the interview zeroing in on the addictive dangers of the "lecture-bug," an admonition one senses Cather is voicing above all for herself.

What makes Cather's puff pieces so fascinating is that within this avowedly promotional medium she comments so thoughtfully about both her art and the life of the artist. In reading the 1903, 1915, and 1926 biographical sketches we not only meet Cather the public-relations maven but also learn a great deal about how she perceives herself at three different stages of her career. The same is true of the 1926 interview, and perhaps to an even greater degree, in that the topic that takes over the conversation suggests a host of concerns that were on her mind at this time. The very introspection that renders this interview so revealing, however, undermines its value as a puff piece, and on the only two occasions it is published—in the *Nebraska State Journal* and the *Webster County Argus*—it appears without the handwritten promotional conclusion found in the typescript. While in her three biographical pieces Cather shows a keen instinct for writing material that will both promote her books and provide insight into herself and her work, for the bulk of this interview she is riding a pet hobbyhorse. She does so wittily, but the hobbyhorse relates to private concerns far more relevant to herself than to her public: strictures on the "lecture-bug" seem unlikely to sell copies of her latest book! That someone so experienced in writing this sort of copy miscalculates so badly in this instance suggests that the motivation for her tirade against the "lecture-bug" is indeed something far deeper and more personal than just the addictive dangers of public speaking.

CHAPTER TWO

Dust-Jacket Copy

Cather involved herself at every stage in the production of her books. Among the issues she raises in letters to Houghton Mifflin during the production of *My Ántonia* are the color of the cover and the jacket, the "physical design of the novel," the type and paper to be used and the "visual effect" of the pages, the clarity of the accent on "Ántonia," the deletion of her middle initial from the title page, and the illustrations.[1] Promotional matters especially engaged her attention. In connection with *The Song of the Lark*, she not only writes the biographical statement for the advertising brochure but also suggests that her publisher capitalize on the current interest in cliff dwellings, advertise at women's colleges ("girls will like the book's aggressive careerism"), and reprint favorable reviews. When she scans her publisher's ads and finds them wanting, she herself crafts different copy, and when similar concerns arise two years later in connection with *My Ántonia*, they are the critical factors in her decision to move from Houghton Mifflin to Alfred A. Knopf.[2]

Given all this, it is not surprising that Cather also paid close attention to jacket blurbs, knowing as she did that such blurbs not only suggest what lies within a book but can also encourage a purchase. In 1915, for instance, she comments favorably on the *Song of the Lark* jacket but corrects its copy and suggests further improvements; soon after *My Ántonia* appears, she suggests new promotional possibilities for a revised jacket.[3] And when she finally decides to leave Houghton Mifflin, one reason she gives is that Knopf will allow her a free hand in the preparation of jacket copy and advertising blurbs.[4]

A draft I own of the jacket blurb for *Sapphira and the Slave Girl* offers striking evidence for Cather's active involvement in preparing such copy even at the time of her last novel. The first of its two pages appears to be a blue carbon copy *not* typed by Cather (fig. 7).[5] She has noted minor changes to the beginning and end of this draft (all adopted in the final jacket blurb), has begun revising its central portion, which describes the novel itself, and has then circled this entire section. The second page has faded badly, but it is nonetheless clear that the typing on this page, unlike that on the first, is Cather's own, a fact established both by typographic details that match other Cather typescripts and also by three pencil corrections that are clearly in her hand (and that have not faded).[6] Below this typed section Cather has written the lead-in to the next sentence of the blurb ("and it is treated etc"), and at the bottom of the sheet she has noted, again in pencil, "I suggest the above paragraph take the place of the paragraph in your copy which I have enclosed in pencil. Hastily W. S. C." (fig. 8). When the book appears, Cather's typed revision on this page becomes the central paragraph of the jacket blurb.[7]

The substance of Cather's *Sapphira* jacket revision is fascinating, and we shall return to it; for now, the important point is that in this typescript we see Cather, at the time of her last novel, not only reviewing and revising jacket copy but also completely rewriting the portion that describes the novel itself. What this document reveals squares with what we find elsewhere. Portions of Ferris Greenslet's house memos reappear in the jacket blurbs of Cather's Houghton Mifflin books, but we shall hear her voice as well in the jacket copy for all four of these novels. Similarly, though Alfred A. Knopf suggests that Edith Lewis helped draft some of Cather's jacket copy, one of Knopf's draws for Cather was his assurance that she herself could write such copy.[8] Taking everything together, it seems that though others may often have drafted initial jacket copy, Cather herself reviewed and revised it. When it came to descriptions of her books or herself, she is likely, as in the *Sapphira* typescript, to have played an even more active role.

Like the 1903 literary note and the 1915 brochure, many of Cather's dust jackets are fragile and rare—those for *The Troll Garden* (1905), *Alexander's Bridge* (1912), and *O Pioneers!* (1913) are close to, or more than, one hundred years old. One purpose of this chapter, as with the materials considered in chapter 1, is simply to make available the jacket blurbs from all the books Cather published to the time of her death. Not only is the copy on these jackets intrinsically interesting, but it too creates an intriguing counterpoint with Cather's other writings, including her anonymous puff pieces.

The following pages include all jacket copy that contains original commentary.[9] The copy transcribed is that of the first-edition jacket, both because such jackets are the hardest to access and because, as Susan Rosowski comments, "the first edition represents Cather's most intense creative engagement with her work."[10] Just as the sketches reviewed in chapter 1 provide information on Cather's life, so this chapter's survey of jacket copy provides an overview of the books Cather published during her lifetime. But just as that biographical scan is unbalanced and skewed—a great deal about Cather's childhood, relatively little about her life as a New York writer, and nothing about her life after 1926—so her jacket copy tells us a great deal about some works (e.g., *My Ántonia*, *Obscure Destinies*), disappointingly little about some others (e.g., *The Professor's House*, *Lucy Gayheart*), and nothing about still others (e.g., *The Troll Garden*, *Death Comes for the Archbishop*). Although I have postponed detailed commentary on individual jackets until later in the book, I offer here some general remarks after *My Ántonia* (Cather's last Houghton Mifflin novel) and after *My Mortal Enemy* and *Not Under Forty* (two groups of Knopf books). Comments on the *Sapphira* jacket lead into some concluding observations.

The Troll Garden (1905)

The jacket for this book contains no copy relating to Cather or to the stories in the book.

Alexander's Bridge (1912)

Some six or eight years ago, Miss Cather's collection of short stories entitled "A Troll Garden" [*sic*] was hailed by critics both in this country and in England as a collection of the first distinction, and fit companion to the stories of Mrs. Wharton; and a novel by the same hand was eagerly desired. This now comes in "Alexander's Bridge," a story that will take its place among the brilliant first novels of American writers. It is dramatic, powerful, and haunting to the memory,—marked in an uncommon degree by the qualities of distinction, of excellence of workmanship, perceptiveness, actuality and the spiritual sense of life.

O Pioneers! (1913)

A stirring romance of the Western prairies, embodying a new idea and a new country. There are two heroines,—the splendid Swedish girl, Alexandra, who dares and achieves, and the beautiful Bohemian whose love story is the very story of Youth. It is only by a happy chance that a creature so warm and palpitating with life is ever enticed into the pages of a novel.

S. S. McClure, My Autobiography (1914)

It is an inspiring story—and a typical story—this life of a North of Ireland boy. The vicissitudes through which he rose make a fascinating narrative as he tells it in a quiet style well colored with humor and anecdote.

"My Autobiography" is more than a human document however, for S. S. McClure has been in the forefront of many movements in the last decade—from the exposure of predatory corporations by the Tarbell articles on "Standard Oil" to the revolution in child education through the Montessori Method. Kipling, Stevenson and many other famous authors were introduced to an American audience by Mr. McClure, and the writers, editors and famous men of a generation have been his friends and intimates." [sic]

The Song of the Lark (1915)

The story of a great American singer,—her childhood in the Colorado desert, her early struggles in Chicago, her romantic adventures among the ruins of the Cliff Dwellers in Arizona, her splendid triumphs on the operatic stage. It is a story of aspiration and conflict, of the magnificent courage of young ambition, and of the influence of four men upon the singer's career.

The title of the book was suggested to the author by Jules Breton's famous painting, "The Song of the Lark," reproduced on the front jacket.[11]

My Ántonia (1918)

Of all the remarkable women that Miss Cather has created no other is so appealing as Ántonia, all impulsive youth and careless courage. Miss Cather has the rare quality of being able to put into her books the flame and driving force of unconquerable youth.

MY ÁNTONIA is a love story, brimming with human appeal, and a very distinguished piece of writing.

We unreservedly recommend it to all lovers of good stories and to those who appreciate the very best in fiction.

HOUGHTON MIFFLIN COMPANY [front cover]

A New York lawyer, whose worldly and successful career has been shaped by a brilliant marriage, tells the story of the one woman who has most influenced his inner life and stirred his imagination,—a Bohemian girl, Ántonia Shimerda, whom he first knew in his boyhood on the Nebraska prairies. Her family are poor homesteaders. Their tragic adventures among the unexpected hardships of the wild frontier form the first thrilling and memorable chapters of the book. Out of their grim tragedy arises the beautiful figure of Ántonia. One sees her as a child, running about the red prairies in her rabbit-skin cap, or huddling in the draw-side cave with her family, so burning with vitality that no disaster can crush her; as a girl, gallant and defenseless in her struggle with the world; as a young woman, surrounded by the sordid gossip of a little town, too simple and unreflecting to arm herself against the misfortune which overtakes her, but so valorous that she conquers in spite of it.

Of all the remarkable portraits of women that Miss Cather has done, no other is so poetic and appealing. Ántonia has the freshness and vitality of the new soil from which she springs, the vigor of the great prairies on which her vivid and enthralling personal drama unfolds. [inner front flap]

Comparison of the four Houghton Mifflin jackets with Ferris Greenslet's "house memos" in Harvard's Houghton Library reveals a situation similar to what we find in the *Sapphira* draft. Greenslet has, in differing degrees, contributed to these jackets, but Cather's hand is also very much in evidence. The bulk of the *Alexander's Bridge* jacket comes from Greenslet's memo, including the comparison of Cather to Edith Wharton (fig. 9). The jacket's assertion that the novel is "dramatic, powerful, and haunting to the memory," however, has no counterpart in that memo, and in it one suspects both Cather's own voice and an allusion to Sarah Orne Jewett's emphasis on the evocative power of memory. While Cather has left creation of jacket copy for this first Houghton Mifflin book largely to Greenslet, by the time of her third novel she herself is taking the lead.[12] The result is at once apparent: in place of the generalities of the *Alexander's Bridge* jacket (e.g., its "excellence of workmanship, perceptiveness, actuality and the spiritual sense of life," all verbatim from Greenslet's memo), the *Song of the Lark* blurb abounds in specifics—the heroine's "magnificent courage of young ambition," "her childhood in the Colorado desert, her early struggles in Chicago, her romantic adventures among the ruins of the Cliff Dwellers in Arizona, her splendid triumphs on the operatic stage." The brief *O Pioneers!* blurb seems also to be hers: not only has it no ties to Greenslet's house memo, but it too is rich in what the *Alexander's Bridge* jacket lacks—vivid description of the novel's central characters: "the splendid Swedish girl, Alexandra, who dares and achieves, and the beautiful Bohemian whose love story is the very story of Youth."[13] In particular, the language in tone and substance recalls the second half of "Prairie Spring," the poem Cather places at the beginning of *O Pioneers!*:

Against all this, Youth,
Flaming like the wild roses,
Singing like the larks over the plowed fields,
Flashing like a star out of the twilight;
Youth with its insupportable sweetness,
Its fierce necessity,
Its sharp desire . . .

Given this history, it is initially surprising to find that most of the long blurb on the *My Ántonia* jacket comes directly from Greenslet's house memo. He has clearly learned from Cather in the interim since *Alexander's Bridge*. He had admired her suggestions for the *Song of the Lark* blurb and had worked closely with her on the brochure for that same book. His letters reveal also his keen response to the lyrical language of *My Ántonia*, and—on a more negative note—he must have seen letters Cather had written castigating the wooden, generality-ridden advertising Houghton Mifflin had suggested to her.[14] The result is that his house memo for *My Ántonia*, and the resulting jacket blurb, contain vivid evocations of character such as Cather herself had written for the *Song of the Lark* jacket and brochure, and apparently for the *O Pioneers!* jacket. Indeed, his description of Ántonia "running about the red prairies" echoes Cather's description of herself as a child in the 1915 brochure—riding about the prairie, coming to know the settlers. His description of Ántonia, "gallant and defenseless in her struggle with the world," recalls that brochure's picture of Alexandra "wrest[ing] a subsistence from the land by dint of sheer force of will," and his eloquent peroration ("Ántonia has the freshness and vitality of the new soil from which she springs," etc.) is of a piece with the jacket blurb on *O Pioneers!*, with its capsule portraits of "the splendid Swedish girl, Alexandra, who dares and achieves, and the beautiful Bohemian whose love story is the very story of Youth."

The short blurb on the cover expands on a sentence in the inner jacket blurb (fig. 10): "Of all the remarkable women that Miss Cather has created no other is so appealing as Ántonia, all impulsive youth and careless courage. Miss Cather has the rare quality of being able to put into her books the flame and driving force of unconquerable youth. MY ÁNTONIA is a love story, brimming with human appeal, and a very distinguished piece of writing." The start of the first sentence is Greenslet's ("Of all the remarkable . . . appealing"), as is the last comment ("a very distinguished piece of writing"). What comes in between, though, has no counterpart in his house memo and must have been added either by Cather or with her approval. The additions again focus on youth, energy, and courage, the very qualities Cather had emphasized in her descriptions of Alexandra and Marie. And while in later years Cather would claim that *My Ántonia* contains "no struggle for success," at the book's first appearance she accepts a description of an Ántonia who "conquers" in "her struggle with the world."[15] The cover's emphasis on "the driving force of unconquerable youth" further underscores the point. In retrospect, Cather faulted the final portions of *The Song of the Lark*, the novel that preceded *My Ántonia*, for focusing on Thea's success and commented, "Success is never so interesting as struggle."[16] One suspects that Cather came to this conclusion as she worked on *My Ántonia*, and that it helped shape not only the novel but also a jacket blurb designed to attract readers to her new book: no lack of struggle here!

The jacket for *My Autobiography* sounds a theme familiar from the jackets of *O Pioneers!*, *Song of the Lark*, and *My Ántonia*: it too is the tale of someone who, like Alexandra (and, of course, Thea and Ántonia), "dares and achieves." Inasmuch as Cather wrote *My Autobiography*, she probably wrote its jacket material as well; that its themes so resemble those of these Houghton Mifflin jackets is unlikely to be mere accident.[17]

Youth and the Bright Medusa (1920)

There are not many living writers from whom a new book commands the mixture of excitement, anticipation, and curious respect with which each successive volume of Miss Cather's is now awaited.

This collection of eight stories is a new exhibition of the writer's power and remarkable artistry. The theme on which all the stories more or less loosely hang—youth's adventure with the many-colored Medusa of art—is in itself fascinating; but it is the writer's quick, bold cutting into the very tissues of human experience and emotion, the daring play of her imagination, that make each of these stories stand out as a separate new discovery about character and life.

Coming, Aphrodite! the first story in the book is perhaps the most interesting from an artistic point of view. Its savage and purely pagan theme loses nothing from being set to an accompaniment of New York asphalt streets and studio skylights. This story of a young painter, drawn by accident under the overwhelming obsession of a woman's beauty, has both the grace and the naked ruthlessness that one expects to find only in a fragment of Greek art. *The Diamond Mine*, the story of a great singer's life, is a whole novel resolved into its elements and foreshortened with an ironic simplicity.

The last four stories in the volume are republished from Miss Cather's early work. *The Sculptor's Funeral* and *Paul's Case* are the stories that first won a reputation for their author. *Paul's Case* has been studied, imitated, plagarized [*sic*] by young writers as perhaps only O. Henry's "The Unfinished Story" has been. In finish and execution Miss Cather has travelled a long way, but the same ardor and restless energy of imagination which give her work the stamp of genius, flame out amazingly in these earlier tales. [front cover, continuing onto back]

Willa Cather wrote her first short story some fifteen years ago. It was published in *McClures* [*sic*], having been accepted by correspondence with the author, who was in the West. She was also asked to come east as a member of the magazine's staff. For several years she devoted herself to editorial work in New York and abroad. It was in Italy curiously enough, that she wrote her first story about the prairie country of the West, where she spent her childhood, and which has since become so much her field. The next summer, which she spent in London on magazine business, found an echo in her first novel, "Alexandra's [*sic*] Bridge," published in 1912.

"My Antonia" [*sic*] was her last published work prior to the present one. [inner front flap]

One of Ours (1922)

More and more have we come to recognize in Willa Cather our greatest living woman novelist. ONE OF OURS, a novel to which she has devoted nearly three years (she is one of the few writers of today who refuses to be hurried) is her first long novel since MY ANTONIA [*sic*] (1918), and shows her at the very fullness of her powers. Nothing that Miss Cather has ever written has quite prepared one for this book—and yet everything that she has written has been a preparation for it. Here, you will say, is an authentic masterpiece—a novel to rank with the finest of this or any age.

All the magic of Miss Cather's subtle and flexible style, all the passion of her daring, impatient mind, are lavished upon the presentation of a single figure—a sort of young Hamlet of the prairies— and upon the haunting story of his struggle with life and fate. ONE OF OURS is the intimate story of a young man's life. Claude Wheeler's stormy youth, his enigmatic marriage, and the final adventure which releases the baffled energy of the boy's nature, are told with almost epic simplicity. But behind the personal drama there is an ever deepening sense of national drama, of national character, working itself out through individuals and their destiny.

ALFRED A. KNOPF

April Twilights and Other Poems (1923)

Miss Cather's first published work was a volume of verse, entitled APRIL TWILIGHTS.[18] The book has been off the market for some years, but has been greatly in demand by collectors, and a number of the poems have been constantly reprinted in anthologies of American verse. In this new volume, Mr. Knopf publishes Miss Cather's selections from the original volume, as well as all her later verse which has appeared from time to time in periodicals, together with a number of poems which have never before been published.

In reviewing Miss Cather's new novel ONE OF OURS for the *Atlantic*, Mr. Gamaliel Bradford said: "The sense of mystery and the sense of beauty make the charm of this latest book of Miss Cather's, as they made the charm of the lovely APRIL TWILIGHTS years ago. And I like to turn back from Claude's heroic sacrifice to the verses which have sung so long in my memory."

A Lost Lady (1923)

In an atmosphere as individual and full of color as that of the old manor-houses in Russian novels, Miss Cather unfolds this romance of the old West; not the West of the pioneer this time, but of the railroad aristocracy that grew up when the great trans-continental lines were being built across the plains[.]

A whole epoch lives again in the little group of people so wonderfully pictured in this story of an incorruptible man and the beautiful woman who was his wife, and of the house in which their moving drama took place[.]

In every page there is a melancholy beauty, a thrilling pathos; it underlies the easy brilliance of the writing, the vivacity with which Miss Cather gives us all the idiosyncrasies of that lavish, generous, careless era. Through the whole story one figure stands out with irresistible fascination—the figure of Marian Forrester, full of feminine mystery and charm, inscrutable in her weakness and her reckless courage. She is one of Miss Cather's greatest triumphs[.]

The Professor's House (1925)

To those who do not know or who doubt the American youth, to those who may be interested in the environment which their son's and daughter's [sic] find in college [sic] Miss Willa Cather addresses herself in "The Professor's House". [sic] With great economy of words and an equally great simplicity of manner she pictures America—the richness of its earliest civilization, the struggle of its pioneer life, the small railroad town of the South, work on a Western ranch and the life among professional classes. Her portraiture of America's many social groups, sympathetic but honest, shows a mastery of the story form never excelled even by her own previous work.

The publication of a novel by this winner of the Pulitzer prize is an event in American literary history. Moreover, "The Professor's House" will, undoubtedly, be more widely read and discussed than any of Miss Cather's previous works because of the interest in the people whom she treats here and because it represents her highest achievement in the art of fiction.

My Mortal Enemy (1926)

My Mortal Enemy is a work of tragic passion—an astounding and profound study of a woman's heart. While directly presenting the end of a great love story, it sketches unforgettably the entire life of a woman, and the nineteenth century surroundings that produced her greatness of character. As the story proceeds to the disclosure of the mortal enemy's identity, the reader feels the growing intensity of relations between the characters which provides the climax not of an episode, but of a life.

Alfred A. Knopf offered Cather a free hand in composing jacket copy, and in her first Knopf jackets she used this license to the full. One notices immediately the keen and personal glimpses these early Knopf jackets give a prospective reader into the very souls of their books. Claude Wheeler, the hero of One of Ours, is "a sort of young Hamlet of the prairies" whose "final adventure . . . releases the baffled energy of the boy's nature" and whose "personal drama" is set against "an ever deepening sense of national drama."[19] A Lost Lady creates "an atmosphere as individual and full of color as that of the old manor-houses in Russian novels" for its story of a woman "inscrutable in her weakness and her reckless courage." *My Mortal Enemy* is "an astounding and profound study of a woman's heart" which "sketches unforgettably the entire life of a woman, and the nineteenth century surroundings that produced her greatness of character."

The 1923 publication of *April Twilights and Other Poems* demonstrates Cather's continued determination to seize marketing opportunities as they arose. Cather had long since shown her scorn for the original *April Twilights*, and at one point she tried to destroy any extant copies.[20] But the éclat achieved by *One of Ours* may have suggested that a reissue of her first book would appeal to readers, a motivation implicit in the *One of Ours* reviews on the back of the new *April Twilights* jacket and in the excerpt on its front from a review that links the two books. Although Cather's negative assessment of the first *April Twilights* led her to exclude thirteen of its poems, her blurb for this reissue nonetheless praises "this first published work," pointing with pride to "the great demand" for it and to the frequent appearance of its poems in anthologies.[21] In its touting of a book she had long deprecated, this blurb recalls Cather's praise for *Alexander's Bridge*—which she had also previously criticized—in the *Song of the Lark* brochure, and both this blurb for *April Twilights* and the reissue itself reveal Cather's alertness to the "main chance." Her promotional instincts are apparent also in her use of the poem "Grandmither, think not I forget," from the original collection, for a 1922 circular to advertise the forthcoming reissue.[22]

The *Professor's House* jacket seems a special case. Although it makes interesting comments about the book's broad scan of American life ("the richness of its earliest civilization, the struggle of its pioneer life, the small railroad town of the South," etc.), in it, as in the jacket for *Alexander's Bridge* (which we know is primarily Greenslet's), I hear little of Cather's voice. What I miss in both blurbs is precisely what I find in the others—and what we see Cather contributing to the *Sapphira* jacket: an evocation of the vibrant tale within. To juxtapose the rich humanity of the jacket descriptions on *One of Ours*, *A Lost Lady*, and *My Mortal Enemy* with what appears in that of *The Professor's House* is to marvel that there is no mention of Godfrey St. Peter or Tom Outland, no allusion to the novel's inner drama. The blurb's first sentence confirms one's suspicions: even if we ignore the egregious punctuation, we cannot imagine Cather herself perpetrating the absurdity of casting *The Professor's House* as an introduction to college life.[23]

In contrast, Cather's voice sounds unmistakably throughout the jacket of *Youth and the Bright Medusa*, as though she were reveling in her new-found promotional freedom (fig. 11). Where the *Professor's House* jacket unaccountably bypasses the book's characters, that for *Youth* bills each of its stories "as a separate new discovery about character and life" and introduces us enticingly to the protagonists of "Coming, Aphrodite!"—"a young painter, drawn by accident under the overwhelming obsession of a woman's beauty." At the risk of scanting the rest of the collection, the jacket draws us into the "savage and purely pagan theme" of this opening story, making us curious to experience "both the grace and the naked ruthlessness that one expects to find only in a fragment of Greek art" (Cather's use of "naked" seems a wave at the role nudity plays in the story itself—perhaps a slightly naughty way of drawing the reader into an act of voyeurism like that of its hero).

By no means does more conventional hype disappear in these jackets. The *Youth and the Bright Medusa* cover blurb begins with the "excitement, anticipation, and curious respect" that await each new Cather book; the *One of Ours* jacket calls Cather "our greatest living woman novelist" and the book itself "a novel to rank with the finest of this or any age"; the *Professor's House* jacket dubs the novel "an event in American literary history." What remains memorable, though, are not phrases like these but the jackets' vivid evocations of the books themselves. And that, of course, is precisely Cather's purpose: if a jacket can capture a book's al-lure, can take potential readers inside its covers, the book will sell itself. Indeed, conventional hype disappears completely from the jacket of *My Mortal Enemy*: all there is by way of promotion is the back cover's terse but penetrating description of the book itself—a statement that, to be sure, suggests the power of Cather's writing but that says nothing about her previous triumphs, or her stature as a writer.

Death Comes for the Archbishop (1927)

The jacket quotes reviews of earlier Cather books but contains no blurb for the novel itself.

Shadows on the Rock (1931)

> Seldom has any novel been as widely bought and as dearly loved as *Death Comes for the Archbishop*. I assure Miss Cather's readers that Shadows on the Rock is of the same superb vintage[.]
>
> ALFRED A. KNOPF [front cover]

> The setting of *Shadows on the Rock* is for Miss Cather a new one— Quebec, in the last year of Frontenac's life—and she recaptures the very tone and feeling of the seventeenth century in this old French city, built on a rock on the great St. Lawrence.
>
> For me to praise this novel would smack of impertinence. It is enough to say that it is every bit as good as we have come to expect from one whose title to first and foremost of living, if not of all, American novelists few would challenge.
>
> ALFRED A. KNOPF [rear cover]

Obscure Destinies (1932)

> SHADOWS ON THE ROCK won for Willa Cather what is probably the largest and most enthusiastic audience of any American novelist today. And now, a year later, it is a pleasure to offer to those same readers a book written with all the charm and artistry which they have come to expect from one who unquestionably ranks with the greatest of living authors.
>
> In the three stories which make up this volume Willa Cather returns with fresh enthusiasm to the Western scene of her earlier novels.

In *Neighbour Rosicky* admirers of *My Ántonia* will discover a story that is almost like a pendant to that remarkable book (which is much more popular today than when it was first published fifteen years ago). Anton Rosicky is a Bohemian exile, who, after many experiences in London and New York, lives out his life on a prairie farm.

Either of the *Two Friends* might have stepped out of the pages of *A Lost Lady*, and might have belonged to the circle of Marian Forrester's chivalrous admirers. They are American business men of the Old West, the age of railroad-building, large outlook, liberal methods, romantic feeling, "when business was still a personal adventure."

Old Mrs. Harris stands alone. Miss Cather has never written anything in the least like this before. Tragic human meanings underlie its apparently careless and light-hearted mood. The scene is a Colorado town in the brilliant sand-hill country; the story is the old riddle of human relationships, the struggle of three women who live under one roof each to live her own life and follow her own destiny.

Lucy Gayheart (1935)

Willa Cather's new novel needs no introduction: I will comment only as to place and time. It is Romantic . . . Western . . . Modern . . . a story of the passionate enthusiasms of youth, which triumph even when they seem to fail.

ALFRED A. KNOPF

Not Under Forty (1936)

Studies of Literary Personalities and Certain Aspects of Literature. This short book is the first collection of essays Miss Cather has published. Its revealing chapters concern some of the authors she admires and what she admires in them, so that the result is a considerable expression of her convictions about the art of writing generally.

Knopf's use of favorable reviews to advertise an author's work, and what Cather perceived as Houghton Mifflin's recalcitrance in this same regard, ranked high among the considerations that led her to change publishers, and from *A Lost Lady* on, all the Knopf jackets adopt this practice.[24] The jackets from *Death Comes for the Archbishop* through *Not Under Forty* devote much space to squibs from such reviews, and the rear covers of *Obscure Destinies* and *Lucy Gayheart* are devoted entirely to citing reviews of *Shadows on the Rock*, with such copy largely replacing self-crafted promotional language. Only the *Shadows* jacket ("first and foremost of living, if not of all, American novelists") and the first paragraph of the *Obscure Destinies* blurb ("unquestionably ranks with the greatest of living authors") hype Cather's preeminence in the manner familiar from earlier jackets.

Noteworthy also, again in contrast to earlier jackets, is how little space these five jackets devote to the books themselves. *Death Comes for the Archbishop*—remarkably—receives no blurb at all, *Not Under Forty* only a brief description squeezed in at the bottom of the front cover. Placement, typography, and Alfred A. Knopf's signature lend weight to the blurbs describing *Shadows* and *Lucy Gayheart*, but these too are relatively brief. That said, these jackets still contain much to pique our interest: *Not Under Forty*'s statement that taken together its essays represent "a considerable expression of [Cather's] convictions about the art of writing generally"; the attention paid to setting in the *Shadows* jacket, to the exclusion of plot and character; the return on the *Lucy Gayheart* jacket to youth and its triumphs, a theme central to many early jackets but that, with this one exception, virtually disappears from jackets beginning with *A Lost Lady*.[25]

As was the case with *Youth and the Bright Medusa*, it is again a collection of shorter fiction that receives the most extended treatment. Unlike the *Youth* jacket, however, which focuses primarily on one story out of the book's eight, the *Obscure Destinies* jacket gives brief but memorable descriptions of each of its three stories. The fact that diffuse generalities in the first two paragraphs yield to telling specificity in the final three, at the very point where the blurb turns to the stories themselves, again suggests Cather's hand, especially given the cogent descriptions we find (and the parallel with the *Sapphira* jacket, where Cather makes modest adjustments to the first and last paragraphs but totally rewrites the portion that describes the novel itself). The reference to "the three women" of "Old Mrs. Harris" sounds like Cather's own, for "Three Women" was her original title for the story.[26] The association of "Neighbour Rosicky" with *My Ántonia*, of "Two Friends" with *A Lost Lady*, must come from Cather herself, and the parenthetical comment on *My Ántonia* reflects Cather's recurrent recollection that this novel had begun poorly but gained in reputation over the years.[27] That "Old Mrs. Harris" is an entirely new departure picks up another Cather theme, that she never repeats herself.[28] What follows is full of telling aperçus—for example, the contrast between the story's "tragic human meanings" and its "apparently careless and light-hearted mood," its focus on "the old riddle of human relationships," comments that are especially significant given the story's roots in Cather's own life. One notes too that the first and third descriptions end with humans living out their lives, the theme that, in contrast to *Lucy Gayheart*'s "passionate enthusiasms of youth," has been so much on Cather's mind from *A Lost Lady* on, and that sounds again in her portrayal of Mrs. Harris in the central story of *Obscure Destinies*.

Sapphira and the Slave Girl (1940)

For some time past it has been known that Miss Cather was at work on a new novel, but the setting remained, until very recently, her own well-kept secret. For *Sapphira and the Slave Girl* she has gone to Virginia—just west of Winchester, where she lived as a little girl before the family moved to Nebraska.

The chief theme of the novel is the subtle persecution of a beautiful mulatto girl by her jealous mistress. The unconventional opening chapter at the breakfast table strikes the keynote of the whole story, in which strong feelings and bitter wrongs are hidden under the warm atmosphere of good manners and domestic comfort. The period is 1856, just before the outbreak of the Civil War. The setting is the beautiful Virginia countryside, and the narrative is peopled with unusual characters: the mountain people, grim disapproving "Republicans," and Sapphira's African slaves, who are, and doubtless were meant to be, the most interesting figures in the book. These colored folk are presented in an unusual way. They are attractive to the writer as individuals, and are presented by a sympathetic artist who is neither reformer nor sentimentalist.

The theme is moving and dramatic; and it is treated with the sensitiveness and imagination of a master. Here again is the calm dignity of her beautiful style—matchless among those of writers of today—and a story that is moving and satisfying. It is indeed a proud privilege to round off my first quarter-century of publishing with so memorable a novel.

Like all the jackets from *A Lost Lady* on, that for *Sapphira and the Slave Girl* promotes Cather's earlier work, in this case listing twelve previous books on its inner rear flap. The rear cover mentions that *Sapphira* "is Miss Cather's first novel in five years. Her last previous novel was *Lucy Gayheart*"—a deft lead-in to the citation of two *Lucy Gayheart* reviews. The blurb for *Sapphira* itself, located on the inner front flap, is considerably fuller than those for most of her recent books, thanks in part to the revised and expanded description of the novel that Cather herself wrote.

Here is the description originally proposed to Cather in the blue carbon draft described earlier in this chapter:

> The period is the middle of the nineteenth century. Sapphira, a rather willful, haughty, and attractive child of the Tidewater aristocracy had "broken away from her rightful station" to marry Henry Colbert a sober, hard-working miller. Together they had moved to the uplands, to live among poor people who had no liking for Sapphira's fashionable Anglican creed and even less for her cavalier attitude toward slavery.
>
> On the whole the Colberts, who rank with Miss Cather's finest character creations, lived well together—until the slave girl, Nancy,

came between them. How the conflict that then arose is resolved and how the resolution influenced Sapphira and Henry, form the heart of the novel. It is a dramatic and moving theme;

This proposed copy, while true enough to the book, scarcely earns the conclusion toward which it moves: "It is a dramatic and moving theme." By contrast, Cather's new description probes what the book is about in ways that only she could know. She begins with its larger theme, comments in telling detail on the way its opening chapter establishes this theme, and calls attention to the novel's cast of "unusual characters." The resulting description not only captures the novel's unique quality but also suggests why it is indeed "moving and dramatic," the words from the blue carbon draft with which Cather ends her revised copy. It is also fascinating to know that Cather herself wrote both the statement that the African slaves "are, and doubtless were meant to be, the most interesting figures in the book" and the description of herself—now late in her career—as "a sympathetic artist who is neither reformer nor sentimentalist."[29]

While we lack similar documentary evidence for other blurbs, the typescript for this final jacket, in concert with the rest of what we have seen, including Cather's anonymous composition of other promotional copy, gives reason to believe that language on her books' jackets normally bears at least her imprimatur and may often be her own. Accordingly, the copy transcribed in this chapter offers important glimpses into *how Cather wished to present herself and her work at different stages of her career.* For with this jacket material, as with the biographical vignettes, we must always remember that Cather's purpose is not only to provide insight into her books and herself but also to attract readers and buyers. One suspects that such motivations help explain why an author who was soon to eschew the Wharton-James model permitted her *Troll Garden* stories to be called "fit companion to the stories of Mrs. Wharton" on the jacket to *Alexander's Bridge*, and why an author who had expressly turned from writing novels in the traditional mode was willing at the time of their first publication to have *O Pioneers!* billed as "[a] stirring romance" and *My Ántonia* as "a love story."[30]

Given that by the time she published *Youth and the Bright Medusa* Cather had already composed the 1903 and 1915 promotional biographies, one turns with particular interest to the biographical blurb inside the jacket of this 1920 book (fig. 11). Although it resembles those earlier pieces in its occasional bending of the truth (e.g., that she "wrote her first short story some fifteen years ago"—that is, in 1905, by which time she had in fact written and published well over twenty stories), this blurb also contains valuable new insights.[31] Its comment that a *McClure's* trip to London "found an echo" in *Alexander's Bridge* predates by eleven years what Cather writes about this novel in her 1931 essay, "My First Novels [There Were Two]."[32] The mention that "it was in Italy . . . that she wrote her first story about the prairie country of the West" is even more revealing, referring as it must to her 1908 Italian trip and "The Enchanted Bluff," which appeared in April 1909. Not only does the language suggest the importance Cather attached to this particular story, but that she wrote it in Italy is new information.[33] Moreover, if she wrote it while in Italy, she apparently did so in advance of Sarah Orne Jewett's famous comment that one day Cather would "write about your own country."[34] Even the astonishing typo "Alexandra's Bridge" seems to suggest Cather's own hand. It is hard to see why either a drafter of jacket copy or a typesetter would make this error, but one can easily imagine Cather doing so on her typewriter. If so, does the fact that she made it, and failed to correct it, further support the connection she felt between the hero of *Alexander's Bridge* and the heroine of *O Pioneers!*, a richly suggestive Freudian slip?[35]

Similarly intriguing is the same jacket's comment on the four stories from *The Troll Garden* that are included in *Youth*: "In finish and execution Miss Cather has travelled a long way, but the same ardor and restless energy of imagination which give her work the stamp of genius, flame out amazingly in these earlier tales." The *My Ántonia* jacket describes her in similar terms (she has "the rare quality of being able to put into her books the flame and driving force of unconquerable youth"), as does that on *One of Ours* ("the passion of her daring, impatient mind"). In contrast, later jackets describe her writing in language that is darker and more introspective: "a melancholy beauty, a thrilling pathos" that "underlie the easy brilliance of the writing" (*A Lost Lady*); "sympathetic but honest" (*The Professor's House*); "astounding and profound" (*My Mortal Enemy*); "the sensitiveness and imagination of a master," "the calm dignity of her beautiful style" (*Sapphira*).

I conclude with three general observations on Cather's promotional activities, which have been the focus of the first two chapters. First, from *My Ántonia* through *Death*, jacket descriptions become progressively shorter, moving to the terse compression of the *My Mortal Enemy* blurb and the absence of any blurb on *Death Comes for the Archbishop*.[36] In the same way, Cather's 1926 sketch is shorter than its 1915 counterpart and far less overt in its self-promotion, and the 1926 Knopf pamphlet hypes Cather and her career largely through articles and reviews by others. Cather's mixed feelings about her promotional activities are implicit in her decision not to attach her name to the biographical sketches, and her attack on the addictive nature of the "lecture-bug" in the 1926 interview, a piece also intended for anonymous publication, contains intimations of Cather's weariness with courting public favor. That Cather apparently paid scant heed to the *Professor's House* jacket in 1925 points the same way.

Second, the jackets on Cather's books published in the teens play variations on youthful courage and ambition winning through to success. Jacket copy in the midtwenties strikes very different notes, with the *Lost Lady* jacket speaking of "melancholy beauty" and "thrilling pathos," the *My Mortal Enemy* jacket of "tragic passion" and "a profound study of a human heart." Jackets on the intervening books, *Youth and the Bright Medusa* and *One of Ours*, focus on youth's confrontation with the "many-colored Medusa of art" in the one, on "a young Hamlet of the prairies" and "the haunting story of his struggle with life and fate" in the other. The sequence is both coherent and noteworthy: youthful ambition and fire in the teens, older figures coming to terms with life's dark realities in the midtwenties, the young and ambitious confronting the barriers to their dreams in the books at the turn from the teens into the twenties: "Youth and the Bright Medusa" indeed!

Third, after 1926 Cather writes no more independent promotional pieces about herself. The jackets of her later books progress from no blurb on *Death* and short comments only on *Shadows* (with nothing about the novel's characters) to more substantial blurbs on *Obscure Destinies* and *Sapphira*. Not only are the comments on these latter books longer, but they move beyond setting (the focus of the *Shadows* blurb) to focus on theme, character, and mood, as did the jackets on so many of the early novels. The *Obscure Destinies* jacket speaks of the "tragic human meanings" beneath the "apparently careless and light-hearted mood" of "Old Mrs. Harris" and "the old riddle of human relationships." The *Sapphira* jacket identifies "the keynote of the whole story, in which strong feelings and bitter wrongs are hidden under the warm atmosphere of good manners and domestic comfort," and describes the "unusual characters" who people "the beautiful Virginia countryside." Cather herself appears in emotionally complex roles in each of these two books—as Vickie in "Old Mrs. Harris" and as her childhood self in the epilogue of *Sapphira*—and the corollary to this literal involvement in the stories seems to be a deeper investment in writing advertising copy about them, something we know she did for *Sapphira* and that seems likely in the case of *Obscure Destinies*. That the blurb of *Lucy Gayheart* is both short and generic may, in contrast, suggest Cather's ambivalent feelings about both the novel and its heroine.

Albeit oversimplified and lacking nuance, these observations both survey where we have come and lead into what follows, in which we view these activities against the larger context of Cather's artistic aspirations and the books she wrote.

Part II
Entering the Kingdom of Art

The materials in the first two chapters give us two different Willa Cathers. Both are keenly ambitious, but the objects of their ambition are distinct.

One Willa Cather yearns to become a great writer, and a consistent focus of her publicity pieces is on her long quest to achieve that artistic goal, and on the steps that led her toward it. The "Literary Note" accompanying her first book speaks of the "voracious reading" in French and English that she did during her university years, of the deep acquaintance with both literatures that resulted, of the "craving for expression" that first motivated her to write. In her 1915 "Development of an American Novelist" she quotes her mentor, Sarah Orne Jewett: "Write it as it is, don't try to make it like this or that. You can't do it in anybody else's way—you will have to make a way of your own," advice that led to the "truthfulness and simplicity" of *O Pioneers!* In the 1926 "Biographical Sketch" she stresses the importance of the time she had spent in Lincoln and Pittsburgh: "These were the years when she was learning to write, doing all that work and experimenting that every writer and painter must do at some time or other to find and perfect his medium."

These same documents, however, also reveal her determination to garner applause. The 1903 statement cites the "remarkably discriminating" and "clever" criticism she did for papers in Lincoln and Pittsburgh, the 1915 brochure hails the "consummate art" of *O Pioneers!* and calls it a "novel of moment," and the 1926 sketch notes the attention accorded the *Troll Garden* manuscript by "that most discerning of American editors, S. S.

McClure" and concludes with Cather's "rapidly growing European reputation." Similar phrases dot the dust jackets as well: "[A] new exhibition of the writer's power and remarkable artistry" (*Youth and the Bright Medusa*); "the magic of Miss Cather's subtle and flexible style, all the passion of her daring, impatient mind" (*One of Ours*); "this winner of the Pulitzer prize" (*The Professor's House*). Even at the time of *Sapphira and the Slave Girl*, when Cather has surely won her place, the jacket promotion continues: "the sensitiveness and imagination of a master"; "the calm dignity of her beautiful style" that is "matchless among those of writers of today."

Such language may feel awkwardly self-congratulatory, but it matches the reality of Cather's achievement. Elsewhere, though, her ambition reaches beyond the facts. When the *Song of the Lark* brochure asserts that Cather is in "the front rank of American writers," among "the little group of novelists that count, the novelists that present American life with full knowledge and convincing reality," it is claiming more than her reputation at the time could justify, even granting the success of *O Pioneers!* Most critics would also have found excessive the claim on the jacket of *Youth* in 1920: "There are not many living writers from whom a new book commands the mixture of excitement, anticipation, and curious respect with which each successive volume of Miss Cather's is now awaited." And in 1931, when Cather's reputation was under attack from several quarters, the jacket of *Shadows on the Rock* clearly overreached when it asserted that "few would challenge" Cather's "title to first and foremost of living, if not of all, American novelists."[1]

That said, hyperbole of this sort is a staple of advertising, and few will fault Cather for indulging in it. But when an author who in both her essays and her fiction puts such store on truthfulness herself crafts advertising copy that is false, the issue becomes more complicated. This is a Willa Cather whose overwhelming interest is in selling books, in being "successful," and who is willing to do whatever it takes to win the public she wants: in 1903 to portray herself as three years younger than she is so that her first book of poetry will come from an author still in her twenties; in 1915 to stretch all manner of facts about herself—her childhood in Nebraska, her schooling, her graduation from the university, her move to Pittsburgh—so as to enhance her élan as author of *The*

Song of the Lark; to quote herself in both her 1915 brochure and her 1926 "Biographical Sketch" as if the writer of the piece in hand were someone else; and in 1926 to concoct an interview of herself to be circulated to the press as the real thing, as indeed it was.[2]

The complexities in Willa Cather that emerge from the advertising materials she helped craft correspond to the complexities in the woman herself. She was indeed supremely ambitious, but in two quite different, albeit related, directions. On the one hand, she was passionately committed to becoming as great a writer as she possibly could, to serving her highest vision and understanding of what great art could be. On the other, she was determined to be successful in more worldly terms—to gain public recognition for her accomplishments, and to garner financial rewards commensurate with her merits.[3] Two words she associates with herself and her art, preeminence and excellence, are appropriate to this dichotomy. Both words immediately evoke inherent quality, but as Cather the Latinist would have known, both also have strong competitive connotations: to be preeminent is to "stand out" (*eminere*) "before" (*prae*), to be more conspicuous than others; to excel is to "out-heighten" (*ex-cel-*), to stand taller than others. The ambivalence of the words fits Cather's dual ambitions. She worked tirelessly to create works that qualified as "consummate art," in the words of the *O Pioneers!* jacket, but she also worked tirelessly to position herself competitively—to be more conspicuous, to stand taller than others, to be hailed by the public as what she claimed on the *Shadows on the Rock* jacket: "first and foremost of living, if not of all, American novelists."

Part 2 explores some ramifications of this dichotomy in Cather's early work. In chapter 3 Cather ponders the varieties of ambition as she writes about art and artists for the Lincoln and Pittsburgh papers. In chapter 4 she confronts in Mary Baker Eddy a woman of modest talents but boundless ambition who has attained extraordinary preeminence. In chapter 5 we see Cather charting a course that honors the contrasting models of both Eddy and Sarah Orne Jewett—and, in her first novel, *Alexander's Bridge*, placing her title character at the crossroads between success as the world sees it and success that satisfies the spirit.

CHAPTER THREE

The Quest to Excel

Contrasting, even contradictory, facets of artistic ambition are a constant theme in what Cather wrote from 1890 to 1906 in Lincoln and Pittsburgh, the period she would describe in her 1926 "Biographical Sketch" as "the years when she was learning to write." In her many essays and reviews from this time we find the origins of the thinking that would shape, perhaps to a degree she herself did not realize, both her image of herself as an artist and also the ways in which she would portray the artist in her fiction.

From early on she associates the artist with ambition both soaring and aggressive. "Willa Cather," writes Bernice Slote, quoting Cather on Sarah Bernhardt, "thought of the artist as a conqueror. Images of combat, heroes, and victory charge her pages with the power and the glory of the strong arm or the winner of souls. 'O yes, art is a great thing when it is great, it has the elements of power and conquest in it, it's like the Roman army, it subdues a world'" (KA 54). Cather uses just such language of Mary Anderson, an actress she admired: "To aspire and create and conquer, to strike fire from flint, to compel the worship of an indifferent world, to make the blind see and the deaf hear whether they will or no, to win the world's highest honors and noisiest fame, that is great" (KA 155). Elsewhere she speaks of the artist's "intellectual passions" as "personal, intense, selfish," as "more violent than the loves of Helen . . . . They are not to be acquired by any labor, any worth, any effort, and once possessed they are not to be lost" (KA 71).[1]

Such passages stress conquest, winning the world's accolades, *excelling*, but they touch also on the more intrinsic capacities of art—"to make the blind see and the deaf hear"; "once possessed they are not to be lost." During her university years, as she strove to understand what it meant to be an artist, Cather frequently focused on these more transcendent aspects. In an essay inspired by news of John Ruskin's imminent death, she described his "creed" in language that both echoes her admiration for Keats and also anticipates her later reflections on Sarah Orne Jewett and the theme of truthfulness: "That beauty alone is truth, and truth is only beauty; that art is supreme; that it is the highest, the only expression of whatever divinity there may be in man. That the highest end of an individual life is to create, or, at least, to see and feel beauty; . . . that beauty and its handmaiden, art, were the only things worthy of the serious contemplation of men, the only things which could satisfy the 'immortal longings' within them" (*KA* 402). Even Yvette Guilbert, a singer from the demimonde, evokes similar motifs of truth and the quest for perfection: "[H]ere is a singer who is a realist, who simply knocks the varnish off, who tells the truth, and the most brutal form of the truth at that. She sings of the streets and cafes and dance halls, of drunkenness and vice and dishonor. Not a very noble thing to do, perhaps, but she does it well, and that, once and for all, is the *raison d'être* of art. No artist does a thing because it is noble or good; he does it because he can do it well, because his mind is so made that perfection in something or other is his chiefest need" (*KA* 226).

In these early writings Cather repeatedly emphasizes the distinction, and the gulf, between the artist's pure quest and the quest to win the world's approval. She colors one description of the artist with language borrowed from marriage vows: "The further the world advances the more it becomes evident that an author's only safe course is to cling close to the skirts of his art, forsaking all others, and keep unto her as long as they two shall live. An artist should not be vexed by human hobbies or human follies; he should be able to lift himself up into the clear firmament of creation where the world is not. He should be among men but not one of them, in the world but not of the world. Other men may think and reason and believe and argue, but he must create" (*KA* 407). Elsewhere she compares the artist to a pilgrim, again stressing the uncompromising quest for truth: "In the kingdom of art there is no God, but one God, and his service is so exacting that there are few men born of woman who are strong enough to take the vows. There is no paradise offered for a reward to the faithful, no celestial bowers, no houris, no scented wines; only death and the truth. 'Thy truth then be thy dower'" (*KA* 417).[2] She also recognizes from the start that many artists fall short of these ideals. Thus she writes of one American novelist,

> Well, Mr. [Marion F.] Crawford is a true American; he has made a "good thing" out of literature, he is what we call "a success." He publishes a new novel every few months and writes countless "articles" beside. He is a very rich man. In each of his bulky volumes there is evidence of his talent, talent that if it had been treated with reverence might have been invaluable to the world.... But I suppose the curse of having sold one's self is that one is always branded with a trade mark and can never escape from the habits of his vice. Truth once betrayed tracks the betrayer to his grave, he had better go out at once like Judas and hang himself. Like Midas, the Phrygian, when he seeks for beauty he will find only gold, gold that cannot buy perfection. (*W&P* 261–62)[3]

It is against this dichotomy—creating pure art on the one hand, selling oneself on the other—that Cather places many of the artists about whom she writes. She marvels at Poe's ability to hold fast to his ideals in the face of a hostile world: "I have wondered so often how he did it. How he kept his purpose always clean and his taste always perfect.... He died without the assurance that he was or ever would be understood. And yet through all this, with the whole world of art and letters against him, betrayed by his own people, he managed to keep that lofty ideal of perfect work" (*KA* 385–86). She notes that actress Helena Modjeska "has done no advertising except upon her play bills. She has seen no reporters.... She has gone about her work with the dignity of a woman and the reserve of an artist" (*W&P* 194). In contrast, she finds that Oscar Wilde has betrayed his native gifts: "To every man who has really great talent there are two ways open, the narrow one and the wide, to be great and suffer, or to be clever and comfortable, to bring up white pearls from the deep or to blow iris-hued bubbles from the froth on the surface. The pearls are hard to find and the bubbles are easy to make and they are beautiful enough on a sunny day, but when a man who was made for the deep sea refuses his mission, denies his high birthright, then he has sinned the sin." She specifically criticizes *Lady Windermere's Fan* for its specious "cleverness" and "insincerity" and writes that Wilde "thwarts the truth and tricks it, buys it and sells it until he loses all perspective, moral and artistic . . ." (*KA* 391, 390).[4]

Cather recognizes that many artists navigate "the two ways open, the narrow one and the wide," by living two lives, in one preserving their ideals, in the other making the compromises necessary to survival. She describes Poe's "wandering, laborious life, bound to the hack work of the press and crushed by an ever-growing burden of want and debt," calls him "a liar and an egotist," but emphasizes that "[w]hat he suffered never touched or marred his work . . . . [H]ad he not had the insane egotism and conviction of genius, he would have broken down and written the drivelling trash that his countrymen delighted to read" (*KA* 382, 386). While Poe refused to write the "trash" that his public wanted, Stephen Crane capitulated even in this regard, writes Cather: "He gave me to understand that he led a double literary life; writing in the first place the matter that pleased himself, and doing it very slowly; in the second place, any sort of stuff that would sell. And he remarked that his poor was just as bad as it could possibly be" (*W&P* 776).

In her comments on Sarah Bernhardt, Cather explores both sides of the divide. She recounts how Bernhardt, then in her sixties, responded when she saw that a rival, Eleonora Duse, was threatening her preeminence on the London stage: "She rented the biggest theatre and began playing her rival's plays in her rival's very teeth. She had none but the kindest feelings and the most appreciative words for and of Signora Duse, but she had been challenged and came for war. It was simply a duel of genius, not pique or vanity, but an artist's defense of her self-respect and her art" (*KA* 118). Cather admits that Bernhardt "has given herself body and soul to the public," contrasting her in this respect with Duse, whose "relations with her public are of the most self-respecting and platonic character" (*KA* 154). But she also praises Bernhardt's devotion to her art, its mix of genius and hard work: "What do you know of the sea till you have seen it, what can you know of Bernhardt till you have heard her? Who can tell you of the meaning in one gesture, of the anguish in one cry, of the longing in one look, of the love song in one tone, of the power of life and living that is in the woman? It is all a thing of feeling, you cannot apprehend it intellectually at all . . . ; and under it all there is that perfect art, the result of the most rigorous training of the most rigorous masters of France, technique that in itself is enough when for a moment her inspiration fails . . ." (*KA* 120–21).

Though Cather stresses the split between Bernhardt as conqueror and as artist, she finds a certain symbiosis between these two roles. She does not minimize Bernhardt's unattractive qualities: "Very few of the world's great artists have been desirable acquaintances. I would ask no greater boon of heaven than to sit and watch Sarah Bernhardt night after night, but heaven preserve me from any very intimate relations with her" (*W&P* 49). But she portrays Bernhardt's actions in her private life as inevitable corollaries to her artistry, and to the artistic domination she sought. Cather describes the moment when Bernhardt in Paris learned of Duse's triumph: "She read those London papers through and when she had finished her cigarette she telephoned for her manager. She cancelled her Paris engagement, sent her fond adieux to her despairing creditors, packed up her son and grandson and boa constrictors and in a week was in London." After putting Duse in her place, "Bernhardt went back to Paris to her wine cellar and her creditors" (*KA* 118). In Cather's vignette, Bernhardt does what she must do to be preeminent. Great actress that she was, she realized that to be what she wanted to be entailed playing different roles at different times. Along the same lines, Cather liked to quote her operatic idol, Olive Fremstad, who acknowledged that though a mezzo-soprano by nature and training, she also sang soprano roles: "What voice is necessary for the part I undertake, I will produce."[5]

In her early essays and reviews about artists and their art, Cather was reading into others what she was discovering about herself. On the one hand were her evolving vision of what art can be and her evolving determination "to take the vows." On the other was her fierce urge to achieve recognition and success of a more worldly sort. Bernice Slote, who has written so eloquently about Cather's artistic quest, calls her "smart, advanced, eager to achieve," and Cather's friend Elizabeth Sergeant comments that when Cather "had made her mind up, she wanted to prevail."[6] The manifold successes of her university years attest to her will to succeed, and when in later years her classmates were asked to describe her, they used words such as "assertive," "energetic," "outspoken," "individualistic," "superior," "independent," "forceful," "strong," "self-confident," and "egotistical."[7] Leon Edel traces Cather's competitive spirit to her early days in Nebraska: "In this period of her girlhood the only hint of her later aesthetic idealism might have been found in her addiction to reading. What we discover in Miss Cather's personal life . . . is that in Nebraska, amid the pioneers, she was caught up in the very heart of the 'American dream': opportunity, equality, competition for achievement, above all the idea of 'success.' One *had* to succeed. One could not be a failure. And if one's individuality and courage were not appreciated in the home town, then success was the way to conquest."[8]

In an 1894 article Cather wrote, "[T]he artist, poor fellow, has but one care, one purpose, one hope—his work. That is all God gave him; in place of love, of happiness, of popularity, only that. He is not made to live like other men; his soul is strung differently. He must wander in the streets because the need of his work is with him; he must shun the parlors of his friends and seek strange companions, because the command of his work is upon him" (*KA* 142). Over the course of her career Cather never lost sight of her "one care, one purpose, one hope—[her] work," and the proof of her steadfastness is the consistent splendor of what she wrote. That said, the road she followed was scarcely as austere as her description suggests, and her dedication to the quest by no means ruled out pursuit of more immediate and worldly forms of "excelling." At the university she not only threw herself into her studies with fierce energy but also sought involvement in dramatic productions and college publications, and these last in turn led to influential and visible positions with the Lincoln papers.[9] In Pittsburgh she used an unpromising starting point—editing a women's magazine, the *Home Monthly*—as springboard to better positions as reporter and critic at Pittsburgh's foremost paper, *The Leader*.[10] When she left journalism to teach, she began as a temporary fill-in teaching a variety of subjects but soon established herself as a respected (and well-compensated) full-time English teacher.[11]

The ways in which Cather effected her rapid journalistic progress in Pittsburgh are instructive. Though initially appalled by what she found at the *Home Monthly* ("the contents, she thought, were great rot—home and fireside stuff, all about babies and mince pies"), she quickly adapted herself to the challenge and made the compromises necessary to success, producing, as she would write of Stephen Crane a few years later, "any sort of stuff that would sell."[12] She told friends back in Lincoln that "if it was trash they wanted and trash they paid for, then trash they would have—the very best she could produce."[13] She also described her work "in terms of struggle, conquest, and victory," indicating she wanted "to triumph over her enemies and give satisfaction to her friends."[14] In the process she made full use of "the parlors of friends" she had shunned in the 1894 passage: her rapid rise in Pittsburgh owed much to the contacts she made in the women's clubs of which she soon became a habituée, the business leaders she came to know in the course of her work, the good words that Isabelle McClung's father occasionally put in for her.[15] The whole Pittsburgh sojourn exemplifies Cather's willingness to make the compromises needed to get ahead. Indeed, the route she followed has its similarities to that of the popular women writers whose work she so deplored: they too tailored what they wrote to their audiences, wrote trash when trash was what would sell, and often hid behind pseudonyms, as did Cather in many of her *Home Monthly* pieces.[16] Like Sarah Bernhardt and Olive Fremstad, Willa Cather in these Pittsburgh years showed herself both willing and able to play whatever role, adopt whatever voice, was necessary and expedient.

Louise Pound, Cather's close friend at the university, used to say that "there was a good deal of myth about Willa Cather" (KA 3), and the materials considered in part 1 show Cather herself shaping and even creating the myth. Here too her early years had prepared her well. Her 1900 essay "When I Knew Stephen Crane" is a good example. Crane had visited Lincoln in February 1895 to write an article on the drought-stricken Nebraska, and Cather may have met him during that trip. Nonetheless, the article she wrote five years later "is fictional in a number of details," as Bernice Slote puts it: not only does it change the time at which Crane's visit took place from the bitter cold of February to the arid late spring, but it portrays Crane "as a romantic but indigent wanderer, with no mention of his serious, even demanding, assignment in Nebraska."[17] The report of a visit with the painter Edward Burne-Jones that Cather sent back to the *State Journal* in Lincoln two years later, part of the series on her 1902 European travels, strays even further from the truth. Not only does Cather report a conversation with a nonexistent valet, but Burne-Jones himself had in fact died in 1898, four years before Cather's trip to England.[18] Cather plays further variations on this episode in her story "The Marriage of Phaedra," which is what we expect of a writer of fiction, but it is revealing that she should play so free with facts in a report to a newspaper, purportedly of an actual visit, coming as it does from a writer who had proclaimed "Thy truth then be my dower" as the artist's credo, who had scorned R. Marion Crawford for abandoning that calling ("Truth once betrayed tracks the betrayer to his grave"), and who had written that "[o]ne may lie to one's self, lie to the world, lie to God, even, but to one's pen one cannot lie."[19] Good storytellers embellish their writing, but in these two "interviews" Cather goes far beyond mere embellishment, and for an obvious reason: the accounts she gives unmistakably suggest her close familiarity with the famous, her prestige as a journalist—precisely the impression she wanted to create.

Just as Cather puts her fictional talents to promotional purposes in these two articles, so she writes the different sides of herself into some of her early fictional characters. The heroine of an 1896 story, "Tommy the Unsentimental," who—like Cather in her own childhood—prefers a masculine name to her given feminine name, suggests in her keen and "unsentimental" business acumen the practical, acquisitive Cather we have seen at several points in this chapter.[20] "Nanette: An Aside," written a year later, focuses on a great singer who has devoted her life to "classical art, art exalted, art deified" (*CSF* 408) and who frees her maid and companion to marry and find a happiness she knows she herself will never experience. Cather would repeatedly in her later work use singers as embodiments of her own artistic quest, and the Tradutorri of this tale surely reflects the Cather who has been contemplating just how lonely can be the life of the artist who "takes the vows"; that the singer's name unmistakably suggests "betrayal" is also revealing.[21] In "The Professor's Commencement" (1902), written when Cather was teaching school in Pittsburgh, the professor seeks in his final address—as he has always done in his teaching—to warn his students against the hypnotic "glitter of yellow metal" (*CSF* 287). His theme recalls Cather's awareness of the dangers that worldly temptations pose for the artist, but the professor's manifest ineptness, the degree to which he has lost touch with the "real world," even the forgetfulness that makes him unable to complete his public recitations of "Horatius at the Bridge," again suggest Cather's musings on the impotence and isolation faced by the intellectual and the artist. The glitter of Mammon is yet more central to "Paul's Case" (1905), also written during Cather's Pittsburgh years, and here one cannot miss her own attraction to the wide way as well as the narrow, for she shapes the story so as to reveal her understanding of, even empathy for, Paul's attraction to wealth and luxury and station.[22] The story is even more to the point in its focus on the two lives Paul is leading—one the life of mundane reality, the other that of his fertile imagination.[23] The division mirrors the two lives Cather herself was leading in her Pittsburgh years: working for the press and teaching school on the one hand, jobs that supported her well and that she took very seriously; on the other, trying to keep alive the goal of becoming a writer, a quest to which her work in these mundane, repetitive jobs represented as great a barrier as Paul's life on Cordelia Street did to his attainment of the life of his imaginings.

The different roles Paul plays, and that Cather was living, recall Cather's use of pseudonyms during this time. Although signing stories or columns with a pseudonym was a common practice among writers of the period, with Cather it takes on added significance from the frequency with which her early writings focus on the different lives the artist must live, the diverse roles the artist must play. It is a theme that recurs often in fictional characters she creates in the decades to come, and that will come into sharp focus in the next two chapters, where Cather encounters in Sarah Orne Jewett and Mary Baker Eddy two women who reflect the divergent ambitions Cather saw in herself. Additionally, in Eddy Cather would encounter a woman manifestly divided, a woman who in her public persona was dedicated to serving "the Truth" but who, in private, was obsessed with furthering her ambitions for power and prestige, often with a "truth be damned" attitude.[24]

CHAPTER FOUR

Cather Caught in the Eddy

Soon after S. S. McClure lured Willa Cather to New York to join the
McClure's staff, he sent her to Boston on a muckraking mission typical of
his magazine, and it was in the course of this assignment that Cather met
Sarah Orne Jewett. Cather repeatedly wrote that the resulting friendship
was the turning point in her career. We have seen the emphasis she places
on Jewett in the 1915 brochure, and seven years later, in the preface she
writes for a reissue of *Alexander's Bridge*, she cites Jewett's advice that "[of]
course, one day you will write about your own country" as "[o]ne of the
few really helpful words I ever heard from an older writer."[1] In November
1908 we can see Jewett already exerting her influence in a letter she writes
Cather about her story "On the Gulls' Road," in which Jewett suggests
that women can best write about women, that "when a woman writes in
the man's character,—it must always . . . be something of a masquerade."[2]
And Cather from this time on begins to give women greater prominence
in her fiction, a progression that peaks in *O Pioneers!*, *The Song of the Lark*,
and *My Ántonia*, the great novels of the teens in which Cather first puts
Jewett's counsel on this and other topics fully to work.

The Boston assignment that facilitated Cather's 1908 meeting with
Jewett, however, concerned a very different sort of woman, Mary Baker
Eddy, the founder of Christian Science. In January 1907 *McClure's* published the first installment of Georgine Milmine's *The Life of Mary Baker
G. Eddy*, a series that would run through June 1908 and appear in book
form in 1909. Even as S. S McClure was readying this first installment
for publication in late 1906, he chose Cather as the member of his staff

best able to handle the remainder of the project, which involved turning Milmine's extensive notes and documents into an accurate and cohesive account. Cather ended up spending close to a year and a half in Boston—from December 1906 until May 1908—checking Milmine's research and writing the articles that became a book of almost five hundred pages.[3]

The chronology speaks for itself: when Cather first met Sarah Orne Jewett in February 1908, she had already spent more than a year in Boston in effect living with Mary Baker Eddy. The phrase is scarcely too strong, for though she did not meet Eddy, working on her consumed Cather's waking hours. In a 1922 letter to Edwin H. Anderson, director of the New York Public Library, Cather bluntly admits that she wrote all but the first installment of the series.[4] She stressed, though, that her letter was confidential, and in public she repeatedly minimized her role, treating the project as an assignment completed conscientiously but neither wanted nor enjoyed. Most critics have followed her lead, portraying her involvement with Eddy as a detour that depleted her creative energies and, in her writing, at most influenced the portrayal of an occasional fictional character.[5] In fact, however, the time Cather spent working on Eddy had a profound impact on her writing—perhaps as great as that of Jewett, though very different in kind. To say this is in no way to downplay Jewett's contribution, and if in what follows my emphasis is on Eddy, it is only because Jewett's influence is already well understood, while Eddy's is not.

Later chapters explore Eddy's impact on Cather's novels of the teens and twenties—indeed, her presence remains palpable in Cather's last novel, *Sapphira and the Slave Girl*. This chapter focuses on the more immediate ways in which Cather's exposure to Eddy intersected with her own evolving views of art, the artist, and the artist's life, including her own. For in Eddy Cather found constant reminders of themes that had been on her mind for years. Ambition, the will and drive to succeed, had been central to her reading of the artist's life; in Eddy she encountered a woman whose life embodied aggressive, even violent ambition, and who had succeeded to an almost unbelievable degree. Another theme of Cather's early writing had been the tension between the artist's lofty pilgrimage and the need to make a living; in Eddy she encountered a woman who cast her life as spiritual quest but who was in fact consumed by material concerns. Cather had portrayed many artists as living double lives; in Eddy she found an almost complete divide between public image and private reality. At the very time when Cather was moving toward her great female protagonists of the teens—Alexandra, Thea, Ántonia—a shift that gained impetus from her contact with Jewett, in Eddy she met a woman who had risen from humble origins to a position of national prominence, and who dominated the men around her. Finally, in Eddy Cather found not only much that she deplored but also much that reminded her of herself—as if one were to see a grotesque image in a distorting mirror only to realize that the reflection was of oneself.

"An Inharmonious and Violent Nature"

Both in the series of *McClure's* articles and in the book version, Cather's attitude toward Eddy comes across as decidedly ambivalent, a mix of penetrating and often scathing criticism with considerable, albeit at times grudging, praise.[6] Of particular interest is the final *McClure's* installment, much of which did not find its way into the book. In both tone and substance this June 1908 section goes well beyond the book in both its criticism of Eddy and its recognition of her achievement, and it may well represent Cather's most candid assessment.[7] On the critical side, it attacks Eddy's theology, science, history, and economics with a vigor and specificity not matched in the parallel passages of the book, and has this to say about Eddy's writing: "[*Science and Health*] was a book of 564 pages, badly printed and poorly bound; a mass of inconsequential statements and ill-constructed, ambiguous sentences which wander about the page with their arms full, so to speak, heedlessly dropping unrelated clauses about as they go" (*McC* 180). Eddy's idiosyncratic writing evokes similar derision elsewhere—at one point Cather notes Eddy's "difficulties with punctuation, which was always a laborious second thought with her" (*MBE* 132).[8]

While sardonic amusement colors her comments on Eddy's writing,

Cather was truly horrified by what she found elsewhere in Eddy: "Her foolish logic, her ignorance of the human body, the liberties which she takes with the Bible, and her burlesque exegesis, could easily be overlooked if there were any nobility of feeling to be found in 'Science and Health'; any great-hearted pity for suffering, any humility or self-forgetfulness before the mysteries of life. Mrs. Eddy professes to believe that she has found the Truth, and that all the long centuries behind her have gone out in darkness and wasted effort, yet not one page of her book is tinged with compassion" (*McC* 185–86). In the same conclusion to the *McClure's* series, she has this to say about Eddy's view of science: "It is 'matter' that is our great delusion and that stands between us and a full understanding of God; and matter exists, or seems to exist, only because we have invented it and invented laws to govern it . . . . The more we know about the physical universe, the heavier do we make our chains; our progress in the physical sciences does but increase the dose of the drug which enslaves us" (*McC* 185). That such tenets of Eddy's system should trouble Cather, who had so strong an attachment to the land, such reverence for nature, such respect for human inquiry, is no surprise. And given her lifelong probing into the fact of evil, it is also no surprise that she was appalled by Eddy's proposal that sickness and death do not actually exist but are just forms of "error," the result of faulty thinking by "mortal mind." In just one of many passages in which Cather questions this basic tenet of Eddy's Christian Science, she writes: "No philosophy which endeavors to reduce the universe to one element, and to find the world a unit, can admit the existence of evil unless it admits it as a legitimate and necessary part of the whole. But the very keystone of Mrs. Eddy's Science is that evil is not only unnecessary but unreal" (*MBE* 227–28).[9]

On the other hand, Cather's concluding *McClure's* essay also pays tribute to Eddy's accomplishment. It accepts Christian Science's central article of faith: "That the mind is able, in a large degree, to prevent or to cause sickness and even death, all thinking people admit" (*McC* 183). It acknowledges that "Mrs. Eddy and her followers have given a demonstration too great to be overlooked, of the fact that many ills which the sufferer believes entirely physical can be reached and eradicated by 'ministering to a mind diseased'" (*McC* 187). Above all, it recognizes that Eddy, for all her flaws, is one of those people who make things happen:

> New movements are usually launched and old ideas are revivified, not through the efforts of a group of people, but through one person. These dynamic personalities have not always conformed to our highest ideals; their effectiveness has not always been associated with a large intelligence, or with nobility of character. Not infrequently it has been true of them—as it seems to be true of Mrs. Eddy—that their power was generated in the ferment of an inharmonious and violent nature. But, for practical purposes, it is only fair to measure them by their actual accomplishment and by the machinery they have set in motion. (*McC* 189)[10]

David Stouck notes that the Eddy book is Cather's "first extended piece of writing, . . . and at 495 pages it would be surpassed in length only by *The Song of the Lark*. . . . [F]or readers and students today it presents an important profile of Cather's developing voice . . . . As the strange drama of Mrs. Eddy's life unfolds in the narrative, we become aware of Willa Cather, the burgeoning novelist with a powerful and sympathetic interest in human psychology."[11] These qualities are especially apparent in the book's second half, where Cather traces how, in the years after the death of Asa Eddy, her third husband, Mary Baker Eddy led to national prominence a church that had become almost defunct. It is an oft-riveting account filled with vivid pictures of Eddy and the people, largely men, who surrounded her. The more one reads it, the more one detects Cather's distinctive voice, at once sardonic and admiring, and the more one becomes convinced that despite all her assertions to the contrary, she found both the project and its "heroine" deeply absorbing.

Reflections in the Mirror?

The picture of Eddy that emerges, though built around Milmine's research, is very much Cather's own, and what is particularly interesting is that the woman portrayed so closely resembles Willa Cather herself. The similarities begin with the two women's childhoods. Willa Cather's propensity for calling attention to herself, for distinguishing herself from her contemporaries, is familiar, whether by her frequent adoption of masculine dress or hairstyle, her express interest in activities usually associated with boys rather than girls, or her uncommon facility with words. Albeit in very different ways, Mary Baker also constantly sought attention, strove to be conspicuous: "[W]hatever the cause, Mary always seemed to be 'showing off' for the benefit of those about her . . . . In speaking she used many words, the longer and more unusual the better, and her pronunciation and application of them were original" (*MBE* 16).[12] Here is Mildred Bennett's description of the young Cather: "When Willa Cather . . . first came to Nebraska in April, 1883, she was a pretty nine-year-old with reddish-brown curls, fine skin and dark blue eyes. Her positive personality was apparent even at this age, and friends remember the little girl dressed in a leopard-skin fabric coat and hat, sitting on the base shelf in Miner Brothers' General Store . . . and discoursing, with some prompting from her father, on Shakespeare, English history, and life in Virginia."[13] And here is a former classmate describing Mary Baker: "I remember what a pretty girl she was, and how nicely she wore her hair. She usually let it hang in ringlets, but one day she appeared at school with her hair 'done up' like a young lady. She told us that style of doing it was called a 'French Twist,' a new fashion which we had never seen before. In spite of her backwardness at books she assumed a very superior air, and by her sentimental posturing she managed to attract the attention of the whole school" (*MBE* 17). In later years Cather often talked about the books she had read as a child, and about her early study of Latin; Eddy in later years similarly recalled her study of "Greek, Latin, and Hebrew," adding that she was "at ten years of age . . . as familiar with Lindley Murray's Grammar as with the Westminster Catechism" (*MBE* 17).

If their memories of their early studies were similar, the realities were not: we know that Willa Cather read voraciously as a child and began Latin early, while there is no evidence that Mary Baker ever studied any of the languages she mentions. As for Eddy's familiarity with Murray's *Grammar*, her writing speaks for itself. In other respects, however, the two women exercised their "memory" of the past in similar ways. Mary Baker Eddy in later years regularly adjusted the date of her birth. She dated her admission to the Congregational Church to her twelfth year (probably to parallel the story of Jesus debating the wise men in the temple), whereas church records show she was seventeen; and at the time of her marriage to Asa Eddy she indicated that she was forty (rather than fifty-six) so that she would be the same age as her new husband (*MBE* 19–20, 175). As Cather wrote about these episodes in Eddy's life, she cannot have forgotten that just a few years before, in her 1903 "Literary Note," she too had adjusted her date of birth to make herself three years younger. It is also hard to believe that as she described the various ways in which Eddy mythologized her childhood—indeed her whole life—Cather did not think of the ways in which she herself, with her 1903 statement, was well embarked on a romanticizing of her childhood that would take fuller form in later years.[14] Finally, as Willa Cather sketched the "little low-ceiled room on the third floor, lighted by one window and a skylight," in which Eddy completed the manuscript of *Science and Health*, may she not have recalled the third-floor room in Isabelle McClung's home which had been her study for the five years immediately prior to her move to New York—and her work on Eddy?[15]

There are as well larger and more significant similarities that Cather must also have recognized—after all, it was she who wrote them into the *McClure's* articles. We have seen that in her Lincoln and Pittsburgh years Cather frequently described the artist in quasi-religious terms: the artist is a pilgrim who "is in the world but not of the world"; the artist's quest is a taking of vows in the exacting service of the "one God" of the "kingdom of art." The language Cather uses of Eddy is similar. Her followers too were embarked on a sacred quest, inspired by a lofty vision. The book reports that Eddy's students—even those who subsequently broke with her—described what they received from her as "beyond equivalent in gold and silver. They speak of a certain spiritual or emotional exaltation which she was able to impart in her classroom; a feeling so strong that it was like the birth of a new understanding and seemed to open to them a new heaven and a new earth." Students "came out of her classroom to find that for them the world had changed. They lived by a new set of values; the colour seemed to fade out of the physical world about them ..." (*MBE* 156).[16] Cather portrays the artist-pilgrim as in the world but not of the world, as forsaking all others for art and resisting the world's enticements; Cather's Eddy uses similar language of the gulf between the spiritual quest and the material trappings of organized religion: "Church rites and ceremonies have nothing to do with Christianity ... they draw us toward material things ... away from spiritual Truth. ... The man of sorrows was not in danger from salaries or popularity" (*MBE* 197–98).

But just as Cather notes that many artists stray from the narrow way, attracted by wealth and prestige, so she points out that Eddy was far from immune to the material rewards she identified as barriers to the life of the spirit:[17] "[H]owever incoherent Mrs. Eddy became in other matters, she was never so in business. Through hysteria and frantic distress of mind, her shrewd business sense remained alert and keen" (*MBE* 217).[18] Cather's book describes the manifold ways in which Eddy attained wealth and power for herself, among them exacting steep tuition payments from her students, obliging all Christian Scientists to buy each of the many new versions of her books, doing a brisk trade in jewelry and mementos associated with herself, and, in her later years, acquiring under extremely favorable circumstances the land for the Mother Church in Boston.[19] The book pays particular attention to Eddy's skill at advertising, at one point remarking, "Never, since religions were propagated by the sword, was a new faith advertised and spread in such a systematic and effective manner" (*MBE* 370).[20] Elsewhere it stresses Eddy's early recognition that "the most important task before her was to advertise and push [the] sale" of *Science and Health*, commenting that throughout her career "Mrs. Eddy always displayed great ingenuity in stimulating the demand for her books." Cather notes also that Eddy made a particular point of vetting all articles and essays that described herself.[21]

These last items strike close to home, for Cather too, as we have seen, thought promotion of her books an "important task" and throughout her career "displayed great ingenuity in stimulating the demand for her books." Not only did she vet articles about herself—she even wrote them.

And though Cather frequently criticizes Eddy as a writer, she notes the impressive royalties Eddy earned. Cather kept close track of her own royalties and took considerable pride when they were flourishing, a fact that adds edge to her comment that Eddy's royalties "have now reached a figure which puts all other American authors to financial shame" (*MBE* 420).[22] It is also worth recalling that at the very time when Cather was writing about Eddy she herself was trying to juggle a demanding and well-compensated job at *McClure's* with her ongoing commitment to writing—witness her exchanges with Jewett in these very years. While Cather draws attention to the gulf between Eddy's spiritual mission and her material ambitions, she must as well have marveled at Eddy's deft handling of a balancing act that had its counterpart in her own life.

Cather also detects inconsistencies that undermine Eddy's repeated emphasis on "Truth," the word that lies at the heart of Eddy's whole system. "For years we had tested the benefits of Truth on the body," writes Eddy at one point in *Science and Health*; at another she comments that the driving of Adam out of Eden is "a clear and distinct separation of Adam, error, from harmony and Truth." Elsewhere Eddy defines her mission as "emancipat[ing] the race from the terrors which had imprisoned it for so many thousands of years. 'Ye shall know the Truth,' she said, 'and the Truth shall make you free.'"[23] Cather shows, however, that in practice Eddy constantly distorted the "truth"—indeed, her adjustments of her age pale in comparison to other lies she told. Of her only son, whom she had neglected and then virtually given away, she concocted a tale of how he had been wrested from her, and of how she had sat up all night by his side the night before his departure (*MBE* 36–37). Of her second husband, a dentist named Patterson who for years had stood by her until he could stand it no longer, Eddy published a fictional claim that he had "eloped with a married woman" (107). After largely lifting her doctrine of "Science" from P. P. Quimby, Eddy proceeded not only to claim it as wholly her own but also to accuse Quimby of all manner of wrongdoing.[24] She fabricated similar lies about former students and colleagues who had left her, or whom she had turned against.[25] Her falsehoods extended to the size of her church, as Cather points out: "There is an impression today that the Christian Science church numbers its members by hundreds of thousands; and this impression was created and is continued by the exaggerated statements of Mrs. Eddy herself . . ." (481). And this is the woman who in 1895 had the gall to visit the following pieties upon a former student who, in Eddy's view, had strayed: "Now, dear student try one year not to tell a single falsehood . . . . But this I warn you, to stop falsifying, and living unpurely in thought, in vile schemes, in fraudulent money-getting, etc." (434).

Once again, though, one wonders whether Cather could have documented and described these inconsistencies in Eddy without feeling some discomfort as to her own behavior. In 1896 she had praised Ruskin's credo "[t]hat beauty alone is truth, and truth is only beauty; that art is supreme" (*KA* 406), and in her conversations with Jewett that began during the time when she was working on the Eddy articles, truthfulness emerged as a central touchstone. And yet she herself in 1903 had not only falsified her date of birth but had in the years immediately preceding 1903 published interviews with Crane and Burne-Jones that were full of fabrications. Can she have failed to recognize that the harsh words she had leveled in 1895 at F. Marion Crawford—"Truth once betrayed tracks the betrayer to his grave . . ." (*W&P* 262)—were as relevant to herself as they were to Mary Baker Eddy?

Cather notes that Eddy's inconsistencies did not escape those around her. When eight of her most loyal followers reluctantly broke away in 1881, they cited the dichotomy between "the understanding of Truth imparted to us by our Teacher, Mrs. Mary B. G. Eddy," and the "frequent ebullitions of temper, love of money, and the appearance of hypocrisy" (*MBE* 276). A former neighbor who had known Eddy in the years when she was still Mrs. Patterson contrasted her "ungovernable temper and hysterical ways" in that former life with the adulation she was winning in later years, commenting that "this is a sort of Mr. Hyde and Dr. Jekyll case . . ." (*MBE* 35–36). Cather herself describes Eddy as a "curiously duplex personality" (219) and leaves a lasting impression of the double lives she led: a professed devotee and conveyor of "the Truth," yet an inveterate liar; a woman devoted to fostering health and yet herself constantly ill;

a proclaimer of lofty and even ascetic religious ideals but someone who constantly pushed others aside in her rush to wealth and dominance.[26] At one point Cather comments explicitly on Eddy's role-playing ability: "But the stage did not exist that was so mean and poor, nor the audience so brutal and unsympathetic, that Mrs. Glover could not, unabashed, play out her part" (*MBE* 120).

Once again, however, Cather's descriptions of Eddy recall herself, so devoted to the stage as both child and adult, so adept a player of roles, and, in these very years, so much a "duplex personality" herself. Indeed, when it comes to role-playing, Cather herself was playing, in the Eddy project, one of the great roles of her life, for well over a year writing a much-read series of articles for a prominent national magazine but masking her contribution under the name of Milmine, who had written not a word of them. Cather's role in this book can in fact be seen as one more refraction of her subject, as a negative image of sorts: Eddy had in *Science and Health* claimed credit for writing a book that was in large part the work of another person—just as Cather in this biography claimed no part in a book of which she had written almost every word. Two years before she began the Eddy project, Cather had in the hero of "Paul's Case" created a brilliant player of roles; Paul, however, is nothing compared to the two role-players Cather confronts in Boston in 1906–8—on the one hand, Mary Baker Eddy, and in the mirror, Willa Cather herself.

Heroic Womanhood

Beneath the critical cast of Cather's biography is an important subtext, Cather's recognition of Eddy's extraordinary success. She identifies Eddy's initial meeting with Quimby as "her first great experience, the first powerful stimulus in a life of unrestraint, disappointment, and failure," and explores with characteristic psychological insight the catalytic effect of this crucial moment: "Up to this time her masterful will and great force of personality had served to no happy end. Her mind was turned in upon itself; she had been absorbed in ills which seem to have been largely the result of her own violent nature—lacking adequate outlet, and, like disordered machinery, beating itself to pieces. Quimby's idea gave her her opportunity, and the vehemence with which she seized upon it attests the emptiness and hunger of her earlier years" (*MBE* 57). Of Eddy's second meeting with Quimby, Cather writes, "The desire became actually a purpose, perhaps an ambition—the only definite one she had ever known. She was groping for a vocation. She must even then have seen before her new possibilities; an opportunity for personal growth and personal achievement very different from the petty occupations of her old life. . . . [T]here is this new note of aspiration and resolve" (62–63). Subsequent pages track Eddy's rise to dominance: "[H]er imperative need was to control the immediate situation; to be the commanding figure . . . . [S]he must be exceptional at any cost" (119–20). One of her most successful students, Richard Kennedy, left her to pursue his own practice because "her grim ambition rather repelled him," but Cather uses a conversation between Eddy and this same student to describe Eddy's meteoric ascent: "She began in these days to sense the possibilities of the principle she taught, and to see further than a step ahead. She often told Kennedy that she would one day establish a great religion which would reverence her as its founder and source. 'Richard,' she would declare, looking at him intently, 'you will live to hear the church-bells ring out my birthday.' And on July 16, 1904, they did—her own bells, in her own church at Concord. The feeling of at last having her foot in the stirrup seemed to crystallise and direct Mrs. Glover's ambition as adversity had never done. She had something the world had waited for, she told Kennedy, and she meant to make the world pay for it. . . . During these early years in Lynn she becomes in every way a more commanding and formidable person. . . . People who were afraid of her complained that her 'hawk-eye' looked clear through them, and persons who admired her compared her eye to an eagle's. . . . Her power was one of personality, and people were her material" (152, 138–39). In its final summation, the book comments both on Eddy's goals and on her success in achieving them: "For herself, she has won what has always seemed to her most valuable, and what has been from the beginning a crying necessity of her nature: personal ease, an exalted position, and the right to exact homage from the multitude" (482).

Cather does not hesitate to compare Eddy's efforts to a military campaign, noting that her rivals "were certainly not her equals in generalship. Mrs. Eddy was a good fighter, and she knew it." She relates such language to Eddy's own words, pointing out that in later years Eddy spoke of battles she'd won, of "survey[ing] the fields of the slain and the enemy's losses" (352). By the time Cather came to Boston to work on this project, Eddy was, as the jacket of Cather's book proclaimed, the "Absolute Mental Ruler To-day of Over 60,000 Christian Scientists."[27] Her vast Mother Church, whose governance and finances she ruled completely, rose on a prime piece of land in Boston. A window in the Mother Church reflected Eddy's proclamation that she represented the fulfillment of a prophecy in Revelation: "And there appeared a great wonder in heaven; a woman clothed with the sun, and the moon under her feet, and upon her head a crown of twelve stars" (MBE 344). A Chicago preacher declared that "Christian Science is the Gospel according to Woman. . . . We are witnessing the transfer of the gospel from male to female trust. . . . Eighteen hundred years ago Paul declared that man was the head of the woman; but now, in 'Science and Health,' it is asserted that 'woman is the highest form of man'" (MBE 345). And the cover of the *Christian Science Sentinel* cited a Longfellow poem without attribution—and with the obvious expectation that readers of the *Sentinel* would apply it to Eddy (MBE 441):[28]

A Lady with a Lamp shall stand
In the great history of our land,
A noble type of good,
Heroic womanhood.

I have quoted at length these passages from Cather's portrait of Eddy because they have so many points of contact both with Cather's writings, future as well as past, and with herself. We recall first that in her early writings she frequently associates the artist with conquest, power, and possession, precisely the language in which she describes Eddy's rise to preeminence.[29] Thus she speaks of the "kingdom" of art; compares art to the world-subduing Roman army; writes of the artist's power "to aspire and create and conquer . . . to win the world's highest honors and noisiest fame"; and describes artistic pursuits as "personal, intense, selfish . . . more violent than the loves of Helen."

To these resonances we may add others that relate more directly to Cather herself. Here again is Cather on Eddy's second meeting with Quimby: "She was groping for a vocation. She must even then have seen before her new possibilities; an opportunity for personal growth and personal achievement very different from the petty occupations of her old life. . . . [T]here is this new note of aspiration and resolve" (*MBE* 62–63). How well these words fit Willa Cather in 1906, who for ten years in Pittsburgh had been, if not quite "groping for a vocation," at least marking time so far as a career was concerned; who had just left Pittsburgh to follow the inspired, charismatic S. S. McClure; who clearly saw in her new position "an opportunity for personal growth and personal achievement very different from the petty occupations of her old life"; and who—witness the Eddy project itself—was obviously bringing to this job "a new note of aspiration and resolve."

Not least, one phrase from the account of Eddy's triumph must catch the ear of anyone familiar with Cather's writing in the years following the Eddy book: "A noble type of good, heroic womanhood." Despite the presence of strong, even heroic, female role models in Cather's own family background, it is a type largely absent from her writing prior to 1908, though in figures like Aunt Georgiana in "A Wagner Matinée" and Katharine Gaylord in "A Death in the Desert" there are feints in that direction.[30] By the time of "The Bohemian Girl" in 1911, however, Cather not only gives the title role to a female character but has her male protagonist identify heroic qualities in the women who prepare the feast for a barn-raising: "[H]e fell into amazement when he thought of the Herculean labors those fifteen pairs of hands had performed."[31] Within the next decade Cather will create in Alexandra Bergson, Thea Kronborg, and Ántonia Shimerda three of American fiction's greatest instances of "the noble type of good, heroic womanhood." Sarah Orne Jewett's advice that a woman can best get inside the skin of another woman undoubtedly played an important role in Cather's creation of these heroines. As we shall see, however, each of them also displays qualities that grow out of Cather's lengthy exposure to Mary Baker Eddy and that recall Eddy's fierce, even heroic, will to succeed.

CHAPTER FIVE

Two Alter Egos

Willa Cather felt that her contact with Sarah Orne Jewett in 1908–9 enabled her to find the "real me."[1] And it is true that themes Jewett stressed became the heart of Cather's developing esthetic. Write from experiences long lived with—"the thing that teases the mind over and over for years, and at last gets itself put down rightly on paper—whether little or great, it belongs to Literature."[2] You will one day write about your own country, but "[i]n the meantime, get all you can. One must know the world *so well* before one can know the parish."[3] "Write it as it is, don't try to make it like this or that. You can't do it in anybody else's way—you will have to make a way of your own. . . . [W]rite the truth, and let them take it or leave it." Remember that a woman will always write more naturally in a woman's character. The *Song of the Lark* brochure acknowledges Jewett's role in the creation of Cather's first mature novel by quoting Cather's own words from a 1913 interview: "I dedicated my novel *O Pioneers!* to Miss Jewett because I had talked over some of the characters in it with her one day at Manchester, and in this book I tried to tell the story of the people as truthfully and simply as if I were telling it to her by word of mouth."

But if, as Sharon O'Brien writes, in Sarah Orne Jewett Cather "met part of herself," in Mary Baker Eddy she met other parts, some of which were uncomfortable enough as to explain why in later years Cather worked as hard to distance herself from Eddy as she did to associate herself with Jewett.[4] In Eddy Cather recognized someone as "ferociously competitive" as herself, someone as determined to loom larger than others, to win—

one recalls Cather's veneration for Napoleon, Alexander the Great, Sarah Bernhardt.[5] And as with Eddy, one side of Cather wanted not just to win but to savor the accoutrements of success—influence, power, wealth: think of her determined rise to prominent positions during her Lincoln and Pittsburgh years, of the pride with which she describes these successes in her 1903 and 1915 statements. Cather rightly credits Jewett with pointing her in directions that led to *O Pioneers!*, but we shall see that Alexandra's fierce ambition, like that of Thea and Ántonia in Cather's next two novels, owes a great deal to Eddy.

One further trait that Cather saw in Eddy, and must reluctantly have recognized in herself, again leaves its traces in Cather's writing. Cather often describes, with at least tacit distaste, the way Eddy used people for her own ends, often sacrificing them after they had served her purposes. Cather herself was not immune to this same tendency. Some eighteen months before she began her work on Eddy, Cather had set off a major row with Dorothy Canfield by her plan to include in her forthcoming *Troll Garden* a story, "The Profile," whose central character was modeled on a mutual friend who was badly scarred. Canfield pleaded with Cather to omit the story, arguing that to publish it would hurt their friend deeply. Cather finally yielded to her entreaties—but then opened the published *Troll Garden* with "Flavia and Her Artists," a story that many readers, with good reason, read as a parody of Dorothy's mother, Flavia Canfield.[6] Another *Troll Garden* story, "A Wagner Matinée," raised similar concerns among friends and family in Nebraska, since they thought, again with some reason, that in it Cather had used Nebraska in general and her Aunt Franc in particular as grist for her fictional mill, and had done so in a manner insensitive to the feelings of those involved.[7]

Eddy's callous use of people for her own ends is precisely the sort of trait that Cather saw as typical of the contradictions in Eddy's life: on the one hand, high-sounding pronouncements about spiritual mission and helping others; on the other, sordid actions motivated by the drive to get ahead, often at the cost of leaving others behind. Here again it is hard to imagine that someone with Cather's "intense drive to know herself" would not, as she wrote her articles on Eddy, have fastened on the similar divide in herself.[8] She too had identified lofty goals for herself, had even invested such goals with quasi-religious overtones, but in most respects her life for the past ten years had been shaped not by these high purposes but by her drive for success. Indeed, as she began her work on Eddy, Cather's presence in Boston bespoke her recent decision to accept a position with the ambitious and entrepreneurial S. S. McClure, a step that meant at the very least deferring her goals as a writer, as she told Jewett in a 1908 letter: "With her energy absorbed by work she didn't want to be doing, after a day in the office she simply didn't have the resources to write fiction . . . and she knew that she had not progressed artistically since *The Troll Garden*."[9] If in Eddy Cather saw someone who had lived a double life, she must have seen that she herself was doing so also: the split between Cather the artist and Cather the entrepreneur that was well on its way in Lincoln and Pittsburgh was widening even as she worked on the Eddy project. It would continue to gape in the years immediately ahead.

While Sarah Orne Jewett in these years became "the mirror of Cather's artistic self," Mary Baker Eddy emerged as a mirror both of Cather's ambitious and competitive self and of the gulf between that side of her and her "artistic self."[10] What made the reflection the more uncomfortable was that Cather saw in Eddy not just reminders of some sides of herself that she might prefer to forget but also tempting intimations of their positive potential. If a woman of such modest gifts as Eddy could achieve such extraordinary success, what could a woman of Willa Cather's huge talents not accomplish? If so pathetic an author as Mary Baker Eddy could sell so many copies of *Science and Health* and her other books, could reap annual royalties in the tens of thousands of dollars, what could a brilliant young author—with similar business acumen and promotional savvy—not do? And while Cather's biography impugns the double life Eddy was living, Sarah Bernhardt and others had shown Cather that the quest for the artistic heights often had as its corollary the willingness to do whatever was necessary to complete the ascent.

Cather directed readers and interviewers to Sarah Orne Jewett as an important key to understanding her fiction. To suggest—as Cather did not do—that we need also to understand the role Eddy played in the years after Cather came to know both women is in no way to minimize Jewett's impact. It is simply to recognize that fully to appreciate Cather's fiction, and her life, one needs to understand the contrapuntal ways in which these two paradigmatic alter egos played on her view of herself and on her imagination.

1907–1908

The impact of these contrasting models, and the cross-currents between them, are already apparent in the short stories Cather writes in 1907–8, the years in which she came to know both Eddy and Jewett, though in these early years the counterpoint is predictably unbalanced. Throughout Cather's portrait of Eddy, including even those sections where she pays tribute to Eddy's accomplishments, one senses an instinctive antipathy that was no doubt exacerbated by the fact that this project was both long-lasting and not of Cather's own choosing. By contrast, Cather's contact with Jewett early in 1908 was profoundly positive—a breath of fresh air, a vision of new vistas, amid Cather's long focus on a woman whom she found deeply troubling. It is accordingly no surprise that stories written in these years reflect radically different responses to these two women: three stories published in 1907 suggest Cather's strongly negative initial reactions to Eddy, while two written early in 1908 breathe the sense of release and renewal she felt in the early months of her friendship with Jewett. Cather never fully overcomes her revulsion for Eddy, but when in the teens she begins to build her fiction around heroic women, those qualities that enabled Eddy to achieve such success will come more clearly into focus.

Cather's "The Willing Muse," a story published in August 1907, tracks the marriage of Kenneth Gray, a slow-working and meticulous author, to Bertha Torrence, a woman who turns out two popular novels each year (as so often with Cather, one suspects name games: Bertha Torrence—"birth of torrents"?—as against her lackluster, "gray" husband). Though friends hope the wife's example will inspire the husband to become more efficient in completing what he starts, the opposite happens: feeling totally eclipsed by her, he stops writing altogether and becomes, in effect, her secretary. Sharon O'Brien reads the story as reflecting Cather's fear that working for the energetic and charismatic S. S. McClure would sap her own creative energies.[11] Another source, however, was nearer at hand—Cather's growing grasp of Eddy's effect on the often insecure young men who flocked to her. Eddy would draw such men into her service, then suck them dry and either drop them or turn against them; and just as many of Eddy's young men eventually chose flight as their only salvation, so Kenneth Gray ends up fleeing his wife's overwhelming presence. The story—including its gender relationships—mimics what Cather describes as a recurrent pattern in Eddy's life, and it dates from the period when she was first working on Eddy in Boston.[12] Lending support to this reading is another Cather story that also focuses on a strong woman's hold over a weaker man. In "Eleanor's House," published in October 1907, the title heroine retains her powerful influence over her former husband long after her death, sapping any energy he may have for new interests and activities. That she also exerts a "mesmeric" power over her husband's second wife is yet one more tie to Eddy, who for much of her later life was obsessed with "malicious mesmerism."[13]

Stewart Hudson has persuasively suggested the impact of Eddy on a third story that Cather published in 1907, "The Profile."[14] The story tracks a painter's relationship to a young woman whose beauty is marred by a horrible scar on one side of her face. When the painter is invited to paint her portrait, she turns her face so that he can paint her in profile, with the scar hidden. Moved by the courage with which she confronts her disfigurement, he falls in love and marries her. Once they are married, however, the young woman reveals a different side of herself, one that is egotistic, unfeeling, even vicious toward those around her, including her husband. When a daughter is born, the mother shows no interest, abandoning the child and attending dress balls where she can flaunt the elegance and extravagance of her clothing. When at the end a niece comes to help care for the child, the wife, jealous over what she sees as the young woman's attractiveness to her husband, contrives an explosion that leaves the niece as scarred as she is herself.

As Hudson suggests, several motifs in this story suggest Eddy. Above all, there are the dualities of the young wife, Virginia, whose mix of beauty and disfigurement mirrors her character. Like Eddy, she is two-faced, a woman who can appear beautiful to those whom she wants to impress but in private reveals a side of herself that is ugly, even deformed. The way Virginia ignores her child echoes the way Mary Glover abandoned hers, and her revenge on the woman she perceives as a rival recalls Eddy's obsession with getting back at those she saw as her enemies. Virginia's blithe insouciance toward her scar, treating it as if it didn't exist, seems to parody Eddy's belief that physical impairment does not exist, is merely a product of "error." The start of the story, which describes a painting of monstrous, half-bestial figures, gestures in the same direction when it brands such "freakish excesses" as not the proper subject for art: rather, "they are all errors," a phrase that parrots the word Christian Science used to describe physical ailment or deformity.

Although at many points "The Profile" seems closely to reflect Cather's troubled reactions to Eddy and Christian Science, the chronology is problematic: the story was first published in June 1907, but we have seen that Cather had completed at least a version of it by late 1904, when Dorothy Canfield persuaded her to omit it from *The Troll Garden*.[15] The connections to Eddy and Christian Science, however, are close enough to tempt surmise that before Cather published the story in 1907 she revised it to enhance these links, perhaps adding the first part, which sets up the theme of distorted appearances, and their origin in "error," motifs that run through the whole piece. Even absent such revision, as Cather worked on the Eddy articles in 1906–7 she must have recognized how closely a story written in 1904 foreshadowed her emerging view of this woman: may not her awareness of these eerie similarities have encouraged her at last to publish a story that had taken on new meaning?

If these three 1907 stories reflect in their different ways Cather's early, and negative, reactions to Mary Baker Eddy, two 1908 stories suggest her immediate, and positive, response to Sarah Orne Jewett. "On the Gulls' Road," written during her spring 1908 European trip, soon after she first met Jewett, seems the first Cather work clearly to reflect Jewett's impact. In the warmth and wisdom of Alexandra, the older woman who responds so generously to a young writer who falls under her spell during an Atlantic crossing, one hears echoes of how Cather felt accepted by Jewett. That Alexandra bears the name of the eventual heroine of *O Pioneers!*—one of the characters Cather recalls discussing with Jewett—reinforces the connection, as does the fact that this older woman, like Jewett at the time, is seriously ill. In addition, Cather had Jewett in mind when she wrote the story, for she sent her a copy of the proofs prior to its publication. Jewett responded favorably, writing Cather that she felt "very near to the writer's young and loving heart" and indicating that the story made her "the more sure that you are far on your road toward a fine and long story of very high class. . . . [O]h, how close—how tender—how true the feeling is! the sea air blows through the very letters on the page."[16]

Reflecting even more the influence of Jewett is Cather's wonderful story "The Enchanted Bluff," which she wrote during the same 1908 trip to Europe (though it was not published until 1909).[17] Short but unforgettable, the story tells of a group of boys who camp for the night on a sandbar in the middle of what must be the Republican River, which flows just to the south of Red Cloud. The boys swim, kindle a fire, watch the stars and moon, and one of them tells the tale of the "Enchanted Bluff," a sheer mesa on the top of which a small tribe of Native Americans once lived cut off from the world—the first appearance in Cather's fiction of a motif that will figure significantly in several later works.[18] As Sharon O'Brien has commented, the story draws an implicit contrast between the easygoing, collaborative atmosphere shared by the boys and the competitive, conquest-oriented heroes they talk about—Columbus, Napoleon, Coronado—a contrast echoed later in the story when the peaceful lifestyle of the dwellers on the bluff is set against the violence of the tribes who eventually bring about their demise.[19] It is a dichotomy that also suggests both the contrasting personalities of Jewett and Eddy and the two different sides of Willa Cather herself, one of them strongly drawn to conquerors of just the sort named. Noteworthy in this story is that Cather here "writes about her own country" on her own initiative, apparently well before Jewett first encouraged her to do so.[20] That

Cather had intuitively taken this new tack even before Jewett suggested it may be reflected in the way she singles out this story—and this turning point—in 1920 on the jacket of *Youth and the Bright Medusa*: "It was in Italy curiously enough, that she wrote her first story about the prairie country of the West, where she spent her childhood, and which has since become so much her field."[21]

These five stories, all published during the years when Cather was coming to know Eddy and Jewett, suggest the very different values she soon came to associate with them. A central theme of both "The Willing Muse" and "Eleanor's House" is the way one person can take over and control another, precisely what Cather saw Eddy doing with so many of those around her. In contrast, the Jewett-like heroine of "On the Gulls' Road" draws out the story's young narrator and responds to the ways in which he in turn draws her out. The heroine of "The Profile," like the Eddy Cather was coming to know in 1907, carefully controls the image she conveys to the world, an image radically different from the reality, whereas Alexandra in "On the Gulls' Road" allows the narrator to see her as she is, with all her limitations and vulnerability. In the same way, the open camaraderie of the boys on the island in "The Enchanted Bluff" contrasts with Virginia's obsession in "The Profile" with being conspicuous, and with her resentment toward anyone who stands in her way. The "Eddy stories" take place largely indoors and feel claustrophobic, especially when set against the open-air settings of the "Jewett stories"— the wide skies and open seas that, as Jewett noted, feel so real in "On the Gulls' Road," the starry skies and prairie vistas so vividly evoked in "The Enchanted Bluff." The Eddy stories focus on people set on making things happen, the Jewett stories on people willing to let things happen, a theme reflected in the ever-shifting, ever-new sandbanks of the river in "The Enchanted Bluff."

1911–1912

The fiction Cather writes in 1911–12 continues to suggest the influence of both women, but the echoes are more submerged. By the time Cather writes her first novel in 1912, the counterpoint between them has become yet more complex. Cather will take the next step in her novels of the teens, where even as she continues to cite Jewett as her model, she increasingly begins to write Eddy-like qualities into her heroines.

Three stories that Cather published in 1911–12 reflect issues that were very much on her mind as she moved toward what was planned as a temporary leave from *McClure's* but turned into her permanent departure. One detects Sarah Orne Jewett's impact on "The Joy of Nelly Deane" and "The Bohemian Girl," in both of which, as in "The Enchanted Bluff," Cather returns to the Nebraska of her childhood for setting and subject. Both also respond to Jewett's suggestion, made in response to Cather's use of a male narrator in "On the Gulls' Road," that she focus her narrative voice on women.[22] Thus Nelly's story is told by a female narrator, and in "The Bohemian Girl" the character who, like Cather, is contemplating a decisive break in her life is a woman. Indeed, both stories reflect, albeit in opposite ways, Cather's longing to break free of the competitive business scramble in which she found herself, and which Jewett had warned her she must escape if she were to become the artist she could be.[23] The opening scene of "Nelly Deane" establishes Nelly's strong resistance to marrying the successful, pietistic, and acquisitive Scott Spinny, but circumstances conspire to beat her down and she finally acquiesces. The disturbing scene in which she is baptized by immersion prior to her wedding powerfully suggests the spiritual drowning that this marriage, in which she will die in childbirth, represents, and the way Scott Spinny complements greed with conspicuous religiosity has its clear—and still negative—echoes of Mary Baker Eddy.[24] "The Bohemian Girl" reverses the progression, with the lively and imaginative Clara, at one point a piano student in Chicago but now married to the prosperous and ambitious Olaf Ericson (again an Eddy-like combination), in the end leaving him to seek a better and freer life with Olaf's younger brother, Nils.

If these two stories suggest both the freedom to which Jewett had beckoned Cather and the Eddy-like barriers that stood in its way, in "Behind the Singer Tower" Cather uses the metaphor of New York's skyscrapers to evoke the masculine competitiveness that threatens both of these young women: "Our whole scheme of life and progress and profit was perpendicular. There was nothing for us but height," says the narrator (*csf* 46). Embodying the way this world of ambition, advertisement, and aggressiveness entraps its workers is the deep, hell-like cavern in which the story's central episode takes place, an episode in which the builder's callous disregard for human life ends up killing several of his workers. Though the male milieu of the story is far from that of Mary Baker Eddy, this city in which every effort is made "to swell its glare, its noise, its luxury, and its power" (53) is of a piece with Eddy's mania for conquest and control, and evocative of everything that Jewett had urged Cather, then enmeshed in her New York job, to escape.[25] While this powerful desire to rise ever higher was something Cather deplored in others, it was also an Eddy-like trait she could see in herself: indeed, this yearning had been the driving force behind her rapid rise to prominence—in New York—at *McClure's*.[26]

Cather's first novel, *Alexander's Bridge*, published in 1912, resembles these 1911 stories in both the themes it sounds and the variations it plays on them. As in these stories, the presence of Jewett and Eddy is less overt than in the stories of 1907–8, something "felt upon the page without being specifically named there," to use words Cather would write some ten years later.[27] That the novel's primary setting is Boston, the city where Cather came to know both women, makes these echoes the more fascinating.

The 1915 *Song of the Lark* brochure gives the following description of the novel's hero:

> Bartley Alexander was a builder of bridges. A man of elemental, restless force, he realized that the success which had made him famous had forced upon him exactly the kind of life he had determined to escape. Confronted by the possibility of a calm, secure middle age, he felt as if he were being buried alive. At this critical period he met again a girl whom he had known in his struggling student days at the Beaux Arts. She was like his youth calling to him. Yet he could respond only through deception and he was not the sort of man who could live two lives.

Alexander the Great had long been among Cather's favorite heroes, and she must have chosen this name because of its heroic connotations. The achievements of Bartley Alexander, her "warder/conqueror of men" (the root meaning of "Alexander" in Greek, as Cather would have known from her study of Homer), resemble Cather's own during the *McClure's* years: recognition within one's profession, generous financial rewards, a comfortable lifestyle. But just as Cather too was fearful of being "buried alive" by her work at *McClure's*, as she had told Sarah Orne Jewett as early as 1908, so Bartley feels trapped by all that goes with this life—its busy-ness, its endless round of meetings, its implicit social expectations, its need to maintain appearances.[28] Further, when Bartley rediscovers in Hilda Burgoyne, a girl from his student days, a figure who is "like his youth calling to him," there are again reminders of the course Cather herself was pursuing at this very time, as she turned away from the successful life that was swallowing her to return to writing—and, in response to Jewett's advice, began writing stories that, like Hilda, were calling to her from her youth.[29] Finally, Cather resembles Bartley Alexander in that during the years leading up to this novel, and even as late as 1911–12, she herself was, like her hero, caught between two lives, in one of them playing the role of dynamic managing editor of a famous magazine, in the other feeling her artistic self being smothered and her life slipping away.[30] Significantly, she had concluded a 1908 letter to Jewett "by observing that she must have something like a split personality."[31]

"I am not a man who can live two lives" (*AB* 104), says Bartley as he feels his life becoming a "masquerade" in which he can never truly be himself (Cather's title for the novel's serial publication in *McClure's* was "Alexander's Masquerade").[32] The most important bridge this great builder of bridges must build—and the one at which he most conspicuously fails—is a bridge to join his two increasingly divided selves.[33] The very names of Alexander's bridges reflect his situation. The bridge he is building at the time the novel takes place is the Moorlock Bridge, a name that suggests the degree to which he feels trapped in his current life—moored, locked in, without hope of escape.[34] In contrast, the first bridge he had built was the Allway Bridge—the bridge of youth from which all ways open, the bridge that had led to his subsequent successes. Cather uses Bartley's two contrasting bridges to limn a basic human dilemma: we long to succeed, to prove ourselves as adults, but in doing so we lock ourselves into fixed patterns, moor ourselves to our very success. In our youth, all ways are open, but until we choose among the many alternatives, our potential remains unrealized. To make that choice is to grow up and succeed, but to do so is also to look back on doors once open but now closed.

"Moorlock" and "Allway" reflect Cather's situation as well. At this stage of her career she too found herself locked into her success, moored to a life she no longer found satisfying; she too sought to recover her earlier aspirations as a creator, to return to that youthful time when all ways are open, and to draw on those early years as a resource for her writing. At a climactic moment in the novel Cather deftly underscores her close relationship to Alexander. As he rides a train to survey his faltering Moorlock Bridge, he sees below, by the bank of the river, a group of boys around a fire on the riverbank. It is a scene that immediately takes him back to the freedom of his childhood—and indeed, right after he sees the boys he catches sight of his earlier Allway Bridge; just as immediately, the sight of the boys by the river takes us back to Cather's youth, for it inescapably recalls the opening pages of "The Enchanted Bluff," the story that Cather herself identifies as her first real return to the West, and to the scenes and stories of her youth.[35]

The novel's tangled resonances of Jewett and Eddy reflect the complexities of both Alexander's and Cather's situations. On the one side, the elegance, graciousness, and warm hospitality of Bartley's Boston house—and its oft-mentioned view of the Charles River—recall the home of Annie Fields, where Cather first met Sarah Orne Jewett; on the other, Bartley's Boston house is associated in the novel with the competitive and constraining life that he seeks to escape, a lifestyle more like that of Mary Baker Eddy than that of Jewett. Similarly, in turning from this organized, constrained life of success to someone who represents freedom, imagination, new possibilities—his youth—Alexander is pursuing a course not unlike what Jewett had recommended to Cather, but the result in the novel is that he finds himself living two lives in conflict with each other, one of which he is ashamed of and must hide from the public—a double existence similar to what Cather had so clearly seen in Eddy.

Adding to the complexity is the fact that in this novel Cather assigns to a male the role that parallels her own flight from *McClure's*, her own search for a freer life, a role that in "The Bohemian Girl" she had given to Clara. It seems a step back toward what Jewett had counseled against, and Cather's original title, "Alexander's Masquerade," strongly recalls Jewett's comment that "when a woman writes in the man's character,—it must always, I believe, be something of a masquerade."[36] Gender issues of the sort that Cather would surmount in her next three novels seem here still at play: with Clara she had returned to her Nebraska roots and had used a woman to embody her own longing to break free, but though Clara sheds the shackles of marriage to Olaf Ericson and finds with Nils a "utopian and cosmopolitan marriage" characterized by "shared mobility and nonrestrictive housekeeping," she remains in a conventional female role.[37] In creating in her first novel an exemplar for her own situation and her own ambitions, Cather has in mind something more heroic and, at this stage, consequently more masculine—hence her choice of Alexander as protagonist. That in his brilliance, charisma, and success Bartley has much in common with S. S. McClure, the very boss whom Cather was trying to escape, further suggests the complexity of Cather's feelings, as does the fact that Alexander knows that to abandon his marriage means to abandon forever his ambitions for worldly success, something that remains dear to him, as indeed it did to Cather.[38]

The ultimate irony is that Cather herself was to experience the same sort of difficulty in connecting her divided selves as Bartley Alexander experiences in her novel.[39] In leaving *McClure's* to return to writing, she was hoping to give up one of these lives and to concentrate on the other. But the divisions in her own soul were not to be so easily bridged.[40] She could relinquish the aggressive, competitive life of *McClure's* fairly easily, but escaping her own innate drive to succeed and to conquer was far more difficult. Her later novels, especially those of the teens, suggest that the competitive, acquisitive side of herself that she had seen mirrored in Mary Baker Eddy remained very much alive even as she strove to give herself fully to art and to the generous paradigm of Sarah Orne Jewett. She too sought a return to the openness of Allway, but she too found it impossible to escape the restraints of Moorlock. In light of all this, it is all too appropriate that while the Clara of "The Bohemian Girl" does escape, does find a new life, albeit in a conventional female role, the quest of Cather's "heroic" Alexander to escape the "Moorlock" of success ends up materially contributing to the collapse of his bridge and the loss of his life.[41]

Part III
At Home on the Divide

The lack of self-confidence implicit in Cather's decision to build her first novel around a male protagonist, a step backward from the role given Clara Vavrika in "The Bohemian Girl," seems implicit also in the novel's dust-jacket copy, which compares the stories of *The Troll Garden* to those of Edith Wharton and sticks to generalities in describing *Alexander's Bridge* itself. We know that this jacket copy comes largely from Ferris Greenslet, Cather's editor at Houghton Mifflin. In contrast, the description of *Alexander's Bridge* in the 1915 *Song of the Lark* brochure confidently focuses on the novel itself and gives the vivid description of its hero quoted in the last chapter, and we know that Cather herself played a major role in shaping that brochure. In her comments about "On the Gulls' Road," Jewett advised Cather to let the woman speak for herself: in the 1915 brochure, in contrast to the 1912 jacket, Cather does just that.

The same forward momentum is evident in the three novels of the teens, where Cather moves beyond both "The Bohemian Girl" and *Alexander's Bridge*, sustaining from the latter her commitment to building her fiction around individuals of heroic magnitude but placing in these roles not men but women—and women, moreover, who, unlike Clara Vavrika, transcend the roles conventionally assigned them in a male-dominated society. It is a step that again owes much to Sarah Orne Jewett, implicitly honoring as it does the woman who had pointed the way for Cather as a writer and explicitly heeding her counsel that women are the characters about whom a woman can write best. Mary Baker Eddy is also part of this progression, however, for as Cather begins to create these heroines who forge their own way and approach epic stature, she imbues them with qualities that strongly recall Eddy—drive, toughness, a fierce will to succeed. By this time Cather has apparently accepted that these are characteristics she herself shares with Eddy, and that just as they were critical to Eddy's success, so they will be to her own. So what if these qualities rendered Eddy repugnant? Cather had noted similar qualities in Sarah Bernhardt as well, but look where they got Bernhardt as an artist! And so in these novels of the teens, and in their heroines, Cather dares to embrace "heroic womanhood" with all the flaws, all the ambivalence, that regularly attend heroic character and achievement—a mix that she had studied closely in her work on the flawed, and near-mythic, Mary Baker Eddy.

Complementing the enhanced roles Cather gives to women in these novels is the enhanced role she herself plays in their promotion. This is most obvious in her direct participation in creating the *Song of the Lark* brochure, but one detects her voice also in the *O Pioneers!* jacket blurb, whose vividness contrasts so markedly with the generalities on the *Alexander's Bridge* jacket. Cather's role in the creation of such copy again reflects the impact of both Jewett and Eddy: like Eddy, she clearly understands the importance of aggressive self-promotion, but, as Jewett had advised, she increasingly makes sure that it is her own voice that sounds in the advertising copy.

As Cather the drama critic knew well, heroes and heroines regularly complement their great strengths with great weaknesses, and every one of the heroic individuals she creates in this period—Bartley Alexander, Alexandra Bergson, Thea Kronborg, Ántonia Shimerda—exhibits this duality. It is most obvious in *Alexander's Bridge*, where Cather crafts a close parallel between Alexander and his bridges, especially his fatally flawed final bridge. He himself has shoulders that look "strong enough in themselves to support a span of any one of his ten great bridges," but his friend Wilson has long feared "that there was a weak spot where some day strain would tell. . . . The more dazzling the front you presented, the higher your façade rose, the more I expected to see a big crack zigzagging from top to bottom" (*AB* 11, 15). Later, when the Moorlock Bridge falls, the language describing its disintegration closely echoes this latter passage: "It lurched neither to right nor left, but sank almost in a vertical line, snapping and breaking and tearing as it went, because no integral part could bear for an instant the enormous strain loosed upon it" (*AB* 158). The three novels that follow avoid such overt symbolism, but each of their heroic women also displays "weak spot[s] where one day strain would tell."

Indeed, like *Alexander's Bridge*, all three of these novels are very much about things divided, and the divisions extend beyond the pairing of strength with weakness in their central characters. In *O Pioneers!* there is the division between Alexandra and Marie, a division that is rooted in the different stories with which the novel began and that gapes wide in the novel's climactic tragedy. In *The Song of the Lark* there are the huge and varied tensions Cather traces within Thea herself. Though the internal strains within Ántonia yield by the end to wholeness and harmony, the novel itself remains riven by the divided focus between its narrator, Jim Burden, and its heroine. As if embodying these central divisions of character and plot, we feel behind the creation of these novels both the divergent influences of Jewett and Eddy and the deep divisions within Willa Cather herself. The questions posed in *Alexander's Bridge* remain focal, though in very different ways, in all three of these novels of the midteens: How does one bridge a divided soul? Which of the lives open to me should I choose? Which road is better?

CHAPTER SIX

O Pioneers! and *My Autobiography*

One way to approach the divisions within *O Pioneers!* is to listen again for the contrasting voices of the two strong women whom Cather had come to know just a few years before. For while the liberating, generous presence of Sarah Orne Jewett is felt throughout *O Pioneers!*—in its wide open spaces, the warmth of its central female characters, the simplicity and resonance of its language—one cannot miss the insistent reminders of Mary Baker Eddy, which bubble up as if from an obsessive subconscious, shaping characters and themes so that they recall Eddy even as they resist her influence.

It is the impact of Jewett that one feels most immediately. Instead of the eastern setting of *Alexander's Bridge* and so many of the early stories, we find ourselves in the broad plains of Nebraska: Cather is, as Jewett had urged, writing of her own country. And instead of the contrived setting and character of so many of the early works, and a voice that for all its richness still recalls James and Wharton, the tone, setting, and especially the voice feel like Cather's own. In a retrospective essay written in 1931, "My First Novels [There Were Two]," Cather herself emphasized these changes (*WCOW* 92–94):

> ... I began to write a book entirely for myself; a story about some Scandinavians and Bohemians who had been neighbours of ours when I lived on a ranch in Nebraska, when I was eight or nine years old. ... [T]here was no arranging or "inventing"; everything was spontaneous and took its own place, right or wrong. This was like taking a ride through a familiar country on a horse that knew the

way, on a fine morning when you felt like riding. . . . *O Pioneers!* interested me tremendously, because it had to do with a kind of country I loved, because it was about old neighbours, once very dear, whom I had almost forgotten in the hurry and excitement of growing up and finding out what the world was like and trying to get on in it.

Not only does the passage recall Jewett's advice to write about "[t]he thing that teases the mind over and over for years" (*NUF* 76), but its reference to "finding out what the world was like" implicitly acknowledges Jewett's counsel that Cather needed to know the world before she could know and write about her own parish. In the 1913 interview quoted in the *Song of the Lark* brochure, an interview that dated from soon after the publication of *O Pioneers!*, Cather's tribute to Jewett is explicit—and worth hearing again:

> Then I had the good fortune to meet Sarah Orne Jewett, who had read all of my early stories and had very clear and definite opinions about them and about where my work fell short. She said, "Write it as it is, don't try to make it like this or that. You can't do it in anybody else's way—you will have to make a way of your own. If the way happens to be new, don't let that frighten you. Don't try to write the kind of short story that this or that magazine wants—write the truth and let them take it or leave it."

The very quotation of Cather's 1913 interview in the 1915 brochure, however, is typical of the subtle ways in which Mary Baker Eddy's influence makes itself felt: the passage is about Jewett, but Cather's clever citation of herself in a puff piece that she herself is helping to create owes much to what she had learned from Eddy about promoting oneself and one's books. Moreover, though in speaking about *O Pioneers!* Cather always stressed Jewett's influence, Eddy's impact on the novel itself is in fact pervasive.

To begin with, Alexandra, the first "heroic woman" Cather creates after her work on Eddy, shows some striking resemblances to the founder of Christian Science. Not only do both Eddy and Alexandra begin in relative poverty and rise to great wealth, but in both cases their keen business instincts are essential to their success: "Before Alexandra was twelve years old she had begun to be a help to [her father], and as she grew older he had come to depend more and more upon her resourcefulness and good judgment. . . . It was Alexandra who read the papers and followed the markets, and who learned by the mistakes of their neighbors" (OP 22–23).[1] Compare Cather's comment, cited earlier, that "however incoherent Mrs. Eddy became in other matters, she was never so in business" (MBE 217). In keeping with their business acumen, Cather portrays both Eddy's and Alexandra's minds as prevailingly practical, and finds similar limitations in both: "What Mrs. Eddy has accomplished has been due solely to her own compelling personality. She has never been a dreamer of dreams or a seer of visions, and she has not the mind for deep and searching investigation into any problem. Her genius has been of the eminently practical kind, which can meet and overcome unfavourable conditions by sheer force of energy . . ." (MBE 482). Here is Alexandra: "Her mind was slow, truthful, steadfast. She had not the least spark of cleverness" (OP 61). And as with Eddy, the flip side of Alexandra's genius in practical matters is a lack of vision in others: "If Alexandra had had much imagination she might have guessed what was going on in Marie's mind, and she would have seen long before what was going on in Emil's. But that, as Emil himself had more than once reflected, was Alexandra's blind side, and her life had not been of the kind to sharpen her vision" (OP 203).[2] In keeping with their natures, when Eddy and Alexandra do dream, their visions take physical, material form. We recall Eddy's promise to Richard Kennedy that he would "live to hear the church-bells ring out [her] birthday," and Cather's comment that on July 16, 1904, they did just that, "her own bells, in her own church at Concord" (MBE 138). Alexandra may "dreamily" watch her brothers swim in a "shimmering pool," but she can't keep her eyes from drifting "back to the sorghum patch south of the barn, where she was planning to make her new pig corral" (OP 46).[3]

Alexandra resembles Eddy also in her strong will, her ambition, and the pleasure she takes in the material success she achieves. Like Eddy, she is shrewd when it comes to acquiring land (OP 57–71, 167–73) and willing to brandish the threat of the law when necessary. "Go to town and ask your lawyers what you can do to restrain me from disposing of my own property," she tells her brothers. "And I advise you to do what they tell you; for the authority you can exert by law is the only influence you will ever have over me again" (172).[4] The way Alexandra dominates both her brothers and the other men of her household itself recalls Cather's description of Eddy: "Her business assistants and practitioners were, most of them, young men whose years had need of direction. In the nature of the case, they were generally young men without a strong purpose and without very definite aims and ambitions" (MBE 305). Carl sees his relationship to Alexandra as part of a similar pattern: "What a hopeless position you are in, Alexandra! . . . It is your fate to be always surrounded by little men. And I am no better than the rest" (OP 181). Even when Alexandra and Carl marry, it is a marriage of a strong woman to a younger and weaker man, a marriage with affinities to that between Mary Baker Glover and the considerably younger, and far less strong, Asa Eddy: "People who knew [Mr.] Eddy well in Lynn describe him as a quiet, dull little man . . ." (MBE 172).[5]

Finally, the accomplishments of both women inspire Cather to comment on the impact a single person can have—indeed, to suggest that important things happen only through such persons: "New movements are usually launched and old ideas are revivified, not through the efforts of a group of people, but through one person," writes Cather of Eddy at the close of her final *McClure's* article. "Then the Genius of the Divide, the great, free spirit which breathes across it, must have bent lower than it ever bent to a human will before. The history of every country begins in the heart of a man or a woman," she writes as she describes Alexandra heading back to the Divide, certain now that her future, in which she will make such a mark, lies there and not in the river lands she has just visited with Emil (OP 65). As we shall see, Cather sets Alexandra apart from Eddy in significant ways, but the fact remains that to a great degree Alexandra owes her heroic achievements to her Eddy-like qualities. Perhaps without quite realizing it, Cather has breathed into this first of her three great heroines of the teens a host of qualities that recall the woman whose character she found so troubling—but whose accomplishments she could not help but admire.[6]

The "charismatic" side of Eddy, which will leave its mark also on Thea and Ántonia, appears in *O Pioneers!* not in Alexandra but in Marie Shabata. The correspondences between Eddy and Marie are again close, and they are underscored by the women's virtually identical first names. Of Mary Baker Eddy Cather writes, "[L]ife in the society of this woman was more intense and keen than it ever was afterward," of Marie (and women like her), "People come to them as people go to a warm fire in winter" (*MBE* 65, *OP* 304). Cather constantly evokes Marie's presence through vivid colors, as in this first description of her: "She was a dark child, with brown curly hair, like a brunette doll's, a coaxing little red mouth, and round, yellow-brown eyes. Every one noticed her eyes; the brown iris had golden glints that made them look like gold-stone, or, in softer lights, like that Colorado mineral called tiger-eye" (*OP* 11).[7] As for Mary Baker Eddy, "She was like a patch of colour in those gray communities.[8] She was never dull . . . and never commonplace. . . . There was something about her that continually excited and stimulated, and she gave people the feeling that a great deal was happening" (*MBE* 122–23). The effect of Eddy's words was "that of the wind stirring the wheat-field"; Marie too is a force of nature: "People couldn't help loving her" (*MBE* 314, *OP* 305).

These similarities between Mary Baker Eddy and the two central women of *O Pioneers!* are striking, given the severe reservations Cather had felt and expressed about Eddy just a few years earlier. It is accordingly not surprising that Cather also invests these two women with other qualities that sharply differentiate them from Eddy, and that recall Sarah Orne Jewett: warmth, generosity of spirit, steadfastness, humanity. These are the very qualities Jewett had shown Cather during the short period of their friendship, and that must so sharply have distinguished her from the Eddy Cather had been coming to know in her Boston sojourn. They are also the qualities Cather must have heard and felt in the wonderful words Jewett wrote in her last long letter to her younger friend: "[Y]ou must write to the human heart, the great consciousness that all humanity goes to make up."[9]

In contrast to the Eddy of Cather's biography, who repeatedly deserts her friends when it fits her personal agenda, Alexandra is Jewett-like in the way she stands by hers, be it Ivar, so attacked by members of her own family; Mrs. Hiller, who so angers Frank Shabata; or Frank himself after he has committed the murders. From the novel's first scene, Alexandra serves as surrogate mother to Emil, a role she maintains throughout the book, and a role that contrasts sharply with Eddy's callous abandonment of both her natural and her adopted sons.[10] One thinks too of the mentorlike role Jewett soon assumed toward Cather, and it can be no accident that the heroine of O Pioneers! has the same name as the older, Jewett-like woman who was the heroine of "On the Gulls' Road," the 1908 short story Jewett had praised so warmly. And while there may be similarities between the women's marriages to younger, initially weaker men, there are also significant differences. Asa Eddy becomes ever more his wife's pawn after their marriage, and even his premature death provides her with a readily grasped lever by which to attack her enemies.[11] In contrast, Carl grows into the role he assumes at the end of the book, and despite the open-ended nature of the final page, we suspect his marriage to Alexandra will gain in strength and reciprocity as the years pass: "She took Carl's arm and they walked toward the gate. 'How many times we have walked this path together, Carl. How many times we will walk it again! . . . I think we shall be very happy'" (OP 308).[12]

Cather's biography constantly shows Eddy living off those around her, draining their energies and resources, and often paying them inadequately or not at all. In contrast, Alexandra pays her help well (too well, her brothers feel), is unfailingly generous both to her neighbors and to less well-off members of her own family, and makes her home a center of good will. While Eddy constantly uses the law to attack others or to protect her own interests, Alexandra turns to the law only when she is attacked by her brothers and when at the end she promises to use every legal means to gain pardon for Frank Shabata. There is a similar opposition in the ways Eddy and Alexandra use their savvy about land. On the maneuvers by which Eddy took over (at favorable cost) the land on which the Mother Church was to be built, then gave it back, but only so as to guarantee her total control, Cather acidly comments, "The members of the Boston church were dazzled by Mrs. Eddy's lavish gift, and very few of them had followed the legerdemain by which the church had gone into Mrs. Eddy's hands a free body and had come out a close corporation" (*MBE* 404). In contrast to Eddy's power play to gain sole possession, Alexandra recognizes that any human ownership is but temporary: "The land belongs to the future, Carl .... We come and go, but the land is always here. And the people who love it and understand it are the people who own it—for a little while" (*OP* 307–8). In both their spacious vision and their autumnal sadness, her words recall the generosity with which the dying Sarah Orne Jewett gave of herself and her wisdom to the young Willa Cather.

Finally, as Cather laments in her last *McClure's* installment, Eddy sees all of nature as but a barrier to our freedom: "The earth, the sun, the millions of stars, says Mrs. Eddy, exist only in erring 'mortal mind'.... All phenomena of nature are merely illusory expressions of this fundamental error" (*McC* 181). In contrast, this same world of nature, and the stars in particular, feed Alexandra's very being: "[She] drew her shawl closer about her and stood leaning against the frame of the mill, looking at the stars which glittered so keenly through the frosty autumn air. She always loved to watch them, to think of their vastness and distance, and of their ordered march. It fortified her to reflect upon the great operations of nature, and when she thought of the law that lay behind them, she felt a sense of personal security" (*OP* 70–71).[13] It is a responsiveness to nature that once again recalls Jewett, as in her reaction to Cather's "On the Gulls' Road": "[H]ow true the feeling is! the sea air blows through the very letters on the page."[14]

The counterpoint between Marie and Eddy, so alike in their magnetic impact on others, so different in their personalities, is equally instructive. Throughout Cather's book Eddy displays a dearth of warmth, compassion, or love, and we have seen how appalled Cather was by her lack of human feeling. It is no surprise, then, to find these very qualities richly embodied in Marie, be it in her readiness to love—first Frank, then Emil; her continuing care for Frank and her efforts to comfort him, even when he behaves abominably to her and to others; her anguish over the five ducks that Emil has shot for her; or the firelike glow that draws everyone to her. Marie's sheer animal vitality, exemplified in the speed with which she moves ("But can't she walk?" asks Carl. "[D]oes she always run?" [OP 136]), contrasts with Eddy's chronic sickliness, her frequent need to be carried from place to place. And while Cather endows Marie with a powerful and earthy sexuality, she portrays Eddy as deeply ambivalent about marriage and procreation, a stand consonant, of course, with her distrust of the whole physical side of nature.[15]

Eddy deploys her charismatic powers in a calculating fashion, and so as to line her own pockets, enhance her own power, and—frequently—destroy or weaken those around her. Marie's magnetism is an inevitable outgrowth of her vitality, warmth, and love of life, and it destroys both herself and others despite her best efforts: "It happens like that in the world sometimes," Carl tells Alexandra. "I've seen it before. There are women who spread ruin around them through no fault of theirs, just by being too beautiful, too full of life and love. They can't help it" (OP 304).[16] Eddy too spread ruin in her wake, as Cather constantly shows, but scarcely "by being too beautiful, too full of life and love." Despite the comparison of her oratory to "the wind stirring the wheat-field" (MBE 314), Eddy's impact in Cather's biography usually comes across as sinister, warped, at war with nature. In contrast, the tragic fate toward which Marie draws both Emil and herself partakes of the grandeur—and beauty—of nature at its most appealing, and most terrifying: "[I]t was something one felt in the air, as you feel the spring coming, or a storm in summer. . . . [W]hen I was with those two young things, I felt my blood go quicker, I felt—how shall I say it?—an acceleration of life" (OP 305).

Of Evil, and of Divided Souls: Still Caught in the Eddy

Eddy's persistent hold on Cather's imagination is felt not only in the central characters of O Pioneers! but also in its thematic texture, and here again one senses both Cather's ongoing obsession with Eddy and her acute discomfort. There is, to begin with, Cather's continuing resistance to what she saw as Eddy's foolish theory of evil, Eddy's idea that sickness and death do not actually exist but are just forms of "error," her belief that "evil is not only unnecessary but unreal" (*MBE* 227–28). That Cather still has these matters much in mind seems apparent from the way she shapes the story of Emil and Marie, rooting her telling in the quintessential parable of evil, the story of the Garden of Eden, something she will do frequently in later works, but never more explicitly than here. The overtones are inescapable, given the similarities of Marie to Eve, the episode where she and Emil meet in the orchard and together eat of the fruit, and even the specific mention of the threat of snakes (*OP* 151).[17] Emil, as he moves toward his fatal meeting with Marie/Eve, again in the orchard, entertains imaginings that could come right out of Eddy's writings on how mind can transcend evil: "He felt as if a clear light broke upon his mind, and with it a conviction that good was, after all, stronger than evil, and that good was possible to men. He seemed to discover that there was a kind of rapture in which he could love forever without faltering and without sin" (*OP* 255). Emil's Eddy-like and Edenic vision shatters as Ivar tells Alexandra of Emil's and Marie's deaths: "'Mistress, mistress,' he sobbed, 'it has fallen! Sin and death for the young ones! God have mercy upon us!'" (*OP* 271). Could there be a clearer refutation of Eddy's faulty theology, of her belief that evil and sin can just be wished away, than the way Cather tells this story of her doomed Adam and Eve in their Garden of temptation?

The way Marie and Emil come together so irresistibly only to suffer the ultimate separation leads naturally into a second theme, that of division and dividedness, where Eddy's presence is again unmistakable. It is a theme that Cather repeatedly sounds in her Eddy biography, and in the divisions she saw in Eddy's life—public image against private reality, high-minded leader against calculating self-promoter—she can only have sensed reminders of gulfs in herself and her own life. Cather had focused on divisions and dividedness in *Alexander's Bridge*, but the theme is no less present in *O Pioneers!* For though the novel ends in the union of Alexandra and Carl, it is dominated by separations: between Alexandra and her brothers; between Alexandra and Marie, from whom

Alexandra feels increasingly separated as the novel moves toward its tragic climax; between Alexandra and Emil, whom she realizes too late she has failed to understand; between Marie and her husband; between the novel's central pairs, Alexandra/Carl and Marie/Emil—so different in character and outcome, and so poised against each other in the structure of the novel (as in their genesis as separate novellas);[18] between the goodness of the land—and of most of the novel's people—and the reality of evil, which is embodied not only in the story of Emil and Marie but also in that of Amédée and Angélique, whose "made-in-heaven" marriage (with Amédée, "beloved of god," marrying Angélique—"angelic") is so senselessly destroyed.[19]

Most important, the gulf between the novel's central figures, Alexandra and Marie, takes us back to the divisions focal to *Alexander's Bridge*, and to those in Willa Cather herself, who has strong resemblances to each of these women. Like Alexandra (and Eddy), Cather was a woman of sound business sense—shrewd, steady, practical, capable of keeping her mind on the bottom line; like Alexandra, she was the oldest child in the family, a child who helped her father with his business, and who in both her physical build and her interests often resembled men more than women; and Cather's age at the time she wrote the novel was the same as Alexandra's in the body of the novel—forty.[20] Cather is also, however, very much like Marie, as we see from the early pages of the novel. The opening scene in the general store, with Marie an object of adoration, strikingly recalls a similar episode, recounted earlier, when Cather found herself in the same position.[21] And in her imaginative energy, her ability to tell stories, the rapidity with which she moves and thinks and lives, her delight in acting a part (e.g., her success as a fortune teller), Marie resembles Willa Cather far more than does Alexandra.

Charismatic, irresistible, enchanting, a creature of whim and passion who acts as she does because she can only be who she is, Marie pulls against not only the common sense of Alexandra but also against basic moral and societal norms, pulling Emil with her—exactly as Hilda Burgoyne draws Bartley Alexander in similar directions in *Alexander's Bridge*. The parallel is not accidental, for the qualities in Hilda that so appeal to Bartley are precisely those we meet again in Marie: beauty, perennial freshness, and above all youth, as the book's jacket blurb reminds us: "the beautiful Bohemian whose love story is the very story of Youth." In many respects *O Pioneers!* is unlike anything Willa Cather had ever written before, a harbinger of yet greater breakthroughs in the future, but its central thematic dichotomy is familiar. On the one side is Alexandra, established, successful, an artist of the land, but a woman who in her mature achievement feels by the end a strong sense of loss, of longing for earlier days and better times—very much what the similarly named hero of *Alexander's Bridge* also feels. On the other is Marie, embodying warmth, imagination, youth—as Hilda does in *Alexander's Bridge*—but, again like Hilda, offering these only as a second, hidden life, one at odds with society and, in Ivar's words, associated with "sin and death." For all its differences in setting and tone, *O Pioneers!* continues to explore the central divide that Bartley Alexander faces in *Alexander's Bridge*: as one option, mature success attended with narrowing options for the future— "Moorlock"; as the other, youthful freedom with its attendant risks, but "all ways" still open.[22] It is a divide Cather herself faced when she left *McClure's* in 1911, and that she was still facing in 1912–13 as she wrote and published *O Pioneers!* That there is so much of Willa Cather in both Alexandra and Marie, the contrasting heroines of her novel, and that this novel reveals so clearly the influence of both of Cather's diverse alter egos, is telling evidence of the continuing divisions in her own soul.

Unity Found? S. S. McClure's *My Autobiography*

In Bartley Alexander and Alexandra Bergson Cather creates two figures whose significant success remains incomplete, less than fully satisfying. Bartley feels that his success has tied him up in business obligations he does not enjoy and distanced him from the passion, creativity, and breadth of possibility he relished in his youth. Alexandra is proud of what she has accomplished on the Divide, but she cannot help feeling that her all-consuming attention to the farm is in part responsible for the tragedy of Emil and Marie. Carl's return brings comfort and companionship, but Alexandra's life will always be shadowed by what she has lost, will always lack the passion and imagination so apparent in Marie Shabata. And just as Marie suggests what is missing in Alexandra's successes, and in Alexandra herself, so the Marie-like Hilda draws Alexander away from all that he has achieved, opens up the fatal gulf that he cannot bridge. Despite their names, neither Alexander nor Alexandra is fully a "conquering hero/ine."

In Willa Cather's next project, her ghosted autobiography of S. S. McClure, she is working with a hero who in many ways does seem all-conquering, who despite his success still feels youthful and finds in his work the challenge and adventure that Bartley now misses, and that Alexandra feels passing from her life. As written by Cather, the book traces the literally rags-to-riches story of McClure, moving from the tiny hut where he grew up in the north of Ireland to his leadership of a powerful and financially successful publishing empire. Like Bartley Alexander and Alexandra Bergson—and like Mary Baker Eddy—McClure was a man of keen ambition who set high goals for himself and achieved them. The speech he gave upon graduating from Knox College proposed "that the men who start the great new movements in the world are enthusiasts whose eyes are fixed upon the end they wish to bring about—that to them the future becomes present":

> When I wrote my oration I had one clear picture in mind, though I did not use this figure at all in the oration. It was that of a man out in the open on a dark night, and before him, on a hilltop, a light shining. Between this man and that light there were woods and brambles and sloughs and marshes and deep rivers. But the man was so unconscious of all this that it seemed to him he could already put out his hand and touch the light. This kind of man, I felt, would in some fashion get what he started out for. (139)

McClure's words, so eloquently shaped by Cather, describe what he would in fact achieve.[23] Having migrated at nine to America, which he calls "a young country for Youth" (34), he works his way through college, finds work as an editor in Boston, creates the first company to syndicate stories to papers throughout the country, and founds *McClure's*, which within three years has a circulation of 250,000 and monthly net profits of five thousand dollars.

In a passage inescapably reminiscent of *Alexander's Bridge* (and written by the same hand, of course), McClure speaks of his feelings as he first entered his office on Boston's Washington Street to become editor of the *Wheelman*, a new publication of the Pope Manufacturing Company, which turned out bicycles:

> It was just at that crook in the street that I said good-by to my youth. When I have passed that place in later years, I have fairly seen him standing there—a thin boy, with a face somewhat worn from loneliness and wanting things he couldn't get, a little hurt at being left so unceremoniously. When I went up the steps, he stopped outside; and it now seems to me that I stopped on the steps and looked at him, and that when he looked at me I turned and never spoke to him and went into the building. I came out with a job, but I never saw him again, and now I have no sense of identity with that boy; he was simply one boy whom I knew better than other boys. He had lived intensely in the future and had wanted a great many things. It tires me, even now, to remember how many things he had wanted. He had always lived in the country, and was an idealist to such an extent that he thought the world was peopled exclusively by idealists. But I went into business and he went back to the woods. (151–52)

One cannot read these words without recalling the passage from the novel Cather had published just two years earlier in which Bartley Alexander walks alone on the Embankment in London:

> [H]e walked shoulder to shoulder with a shadowy companion—not little Hilda Burgoyne, by any means, but some one vastly dearer to him than she had ever been—his own young self, the youth who had waited for him upon the steps of the British Museum that night, and who, though he had tried to pass so quietly, had known him and come down and linked an arm in his.

It was not until long afterward that Alexander learned that for him this youth was the most dangerous of companions. (*AB* 52)

Differentiating the two heroes is that McClure says a firm goodbye to this figure of his youth, so filled with the idealism and open-endedness of the future, while Alexander goes back to him. In doing so, he opens the fatal gulf between his present adult life and the youth he tries to recapture in his affair with Hilda, a gulf as broad and threatening as the stormy ocean he must cross each time he visits her in London, and as unbridgeable. And as the passage implies, once he has taken the first step back, he finds he cannot escape.

Cather's *My Autobiography* suggests that the reason McClure can bid his other self so final a farewell is that his adult professional life, unlike Alexander's, still gives play to his youthful idealism and zest for adventure. His innate wanderlust continues to find outlets in trips to Europe and elsewhere in search of authors to write for his publications. His swift movement from one business to another—printer in Boston, syndicate owner in New York, founder of *McClure's*—satisfies his long-ing for ever-new challenges and opportunities. The pleasure he found when as a Knox student he traveled the Midwest as a peddler transmutes into the delight of creating new ways to make money for his publishing house. He finds the work he is doing stimulating—and when it ceases to be such, he explores new vistas. To put it differently, he is still at Allway, not facing Moorlock. At one point he comments, "I usually forgot my financial anxieties, even when we were in the direst straits, in the pleasure I always got out of the editorial end of my work—hunting new ideas and new writers, and, as it were, introducing them to each other" (212). Not least, the business he builds both brings success and also provides an outlet for his ideals, a complementary mode for which he thanks the printers and publishers with whom he worked in his early years: "[T]hese men had made fortunes, but they had also made great names. They were all men who could inspire a young man, who valued ideas above the price they brought in the market, and who were not ashamed to have ideals" (166).

Cather's shaping of McClure's autobiography speaks to questions she had raised in her portrayals of Bartley Alexander, Alexandra Bergson, and Mary Baker Eddy: Is mature, worldly success compatible with personal satisfaction? Can one attain such success without giving up one's youthful dreams, as Bartley had done? Without sacrificing imagination and attention to those around one, as Alexandra had done? Without treating others horribly to bolster one's own cause, as Eddy had done? Can one be successful without living a double life, as both Eddy and Alexander had done? The S. S. McClure of Cather's autobiography seems to suggest positive answers to all these questions.

These questions bore on Cather herself, for she too had faced many of these same issues as she tried to reconcile her highly successful career at *McClure's* with the writing career she still sought, and as she balanced her lofty artistic goals with her strong ambition for success, recognition, and material comfort. That the autobiography so often conveys such brio in the telling of McClure's story, and that Cather never denied her authorship of it—a sharp contrast to her repeated denials as to her role in the Eddy biography—suggests that in McClure she found a model far closer to her tastes than she did in Eddy. The similarities that existed between McClure's story and her own no doubt encouraged her to see him this way: he had migrated from Ireland to America at nine, her age at the time of her family's move to Nebraska; as a publisher, he shared her strong interest in literature, and with special fondness for two authors who were also among her favorites, Stevenson and Kipling; both McClure and Cather had set high goals for themselves—his commencement image of setting one's sights on a far-off light on a hill seems in keeping with the way Cather saw herself (no doubt in part because she penned it); and from childhood and college years in the Midwest they had both found their way to New York.[24] There is also the fact that McClure, at least as Cather draws him, seems not to suffer from those negative character traits that she identifies in Eddy—and that she saw also in herself. In this respect, Cather may be more ready to acknowledge a relationship with McClure than she is with Eddy precisely because his model strikes a bit less close to home.[25]

As she began work on *The Song of the Lark*, Cather clearly had McClure in mind, even if only because she had just been working on his autobiography. And in fact, her heroine, Thea Kronborg, has much in common with the publisher—energy, drive, clarity of purpose. Unlike McClure, however, Thea ends up living a double life—one as the triumphant diva the public sees, the other as the private individual known only to herself and her close associates; and unlike McClure, at least as he is portrayed by Cather, Thea wins the triumphs of her public life only through an unflagging ambition that has its decidedly unpleasant corollaries. Despite Cather's deep admiration for McClure, and her equally deep distaste for Eddy, it is the latter who in many ways will most shape the heroine of what has been called Cather's "portrait of an artist as a young woman."[26]

CHAPTER SEVEN

The Song of the Lark

"I only want impossible things.... The others don't interest me."
—THEA KRONBORG, *The Song of the Lark* 243

In *The Song of the Lark* Cather replaces the two heroines of *O Pioneers!* with a single dominant figure, Thea Kronborg. Like Bartley Alexander, Thea is an "elemental, restless force," and as so often in Cather, her name fits her character: Thea, "goddess, divine female," a step beyond even the man-conquering Alexander/Alexandra, and a name in keeping both with the heights that Thea scales and with the role in which she does so, as a "diva," a word that carries the same "divine" connotations as Thea.

Thea Kronborg owes much to Cather's fascination with the Wagnerian soprano Olive Fremstad, whom she had written about and come to know in the years before she wrote *The Song of the Lark*.[1] During the period when she was becoming acquainted with Fremstad, Cather commented on the delight she took in "finding a new type of human being and getting inside a new skin," calling it "the finest sport she knew."[2] Even more important in the creation of Thea, however, was Cather's willingness to get inside her own skin, for the artist's "awakening" that she identifies as this novel's theme is above all her own.[3] Emphasizing the self-referentiality of Cather's heroine is the fact that the first part of the novel, "Friends of Childhood," is "the most autobiographical fiction she ever wrote."[4] Thea's town of Moonstone, though nominally in Colorado, is so similar to Cather's Red Cloud that one can still use the novel's descriptions as a town map.[5] The house in which Thea grows up is modeled on the home to which the Cather family moved in September 1884, and Thea's second-story room is Cather's, even down to the distinctive wallpaper Thea puts on the wall. Thea's mother closely resembles Cather's, including the rawhide whip she uses to keep her children in line; Thea's slightly dotty Aunt Tillie is based on a Cather cousin; and the key figures of Thea's childhood—Dr. Archie, Spanish Johnny, Ray Kennedy, Mr. and Mrs. Kohler—all have their counterparts in Cather's childhood.[6] Cather headed off to the university late in her seventeenth year; Thea leaves Moonstone to study music in Chicago when she is "barely seventeen" (151). And just as Cather felt that her 1912 western trip had released her creative powers, so a similar trip to Panther Canyon is the catalyst for Thea's artistic blossoming, with an eagle she sees flying above the canyon a powerful image of the ambitions she identifies in herself: "O eagle of eagles! Endeavour, achievement, desire, glorious striving of human art!" (321).[7]

Once again the contrasting pulls of Jewett and Eddy make themselves felt. As with *O Pioneers!*, Jewett's influence is immediately evident, especially in contrast with most of what Cather wrote prior to 1912. Not only has Cather again returned to people and places that have long teased her mind, but she also imbues Thea's story with her own experience of places beyond Nebraska—New York, Chicago, the far West, Europe—again honoring Jewett's advice to write about one's own parish from knowledge of the world. And just as Jewett had urged Cather to write in her own voice, thus avoiding the masquerade of a woman trying to write as a man, so Thea's immersion in the female landscape of Panther Canyon both frees her as a woman and helps her discover her own artistic voice:

> Here she could lie for half a day undistracted, holding pleasant and incomplete conceptions in her mind—almost in her hands. . . . She was singing very little now, but a song would go through her head all morning, as a spring keeps welling up . . . . Music had never come to her in that sensuous form before. . . . And now her power to think seemed converted into a power of sustained sensation. She could become a mere receptacle for heat, or become a

color, like the bright lizards that darted about on the hot stones outside her door; or she could become a continuous repetition of sound, like the cicadas. (299–300)[8]

As we have already seen, Cather in her description of Thea's climactic operatic triumph sounds yet another theme strongly associated with Jewett—truthfulness:

> Artistic growth is, more than it is anything else, a refining of the sense of truthfulness. The stupid believe that to be truthful is easy; only the artist, the great artist, knows how difficult it is. . . . While she was on the stage she was conscious that every movement was the right movement, that her body was absolutely the instrument of her idea. Not for nothing had she kept it so severely, kept it filled with such energy and fire. All that deep-rooted vitality flowered in her voice, her face, in her very finger-tips. She felt like a tree bursting into bloom. (477–78)

This release of Thea's natural powers, and of her capacity for truth, not only provides the climax of the novel but also evokes "the artist's awakening" that Cather herself was experiencing in the novels of the teens as she dared to take Jewett's counsel to heart. In her long letter of December 13, 1908, Jewett had told Cather, "You must find a quiet place near the best companions . . . and you need to dream your dreams and go on to new and more shining ideals, to be aware of 'the gleam' and to follow it . . . ."[9] In Cather's telling of the Panther Canyon episode, she celebrates through Thea the fulfillment of Jewett's words in her own life and in her writing: she too had found her Panther Canyon, had become the instrument of her ideas, had learned to write fiction so natural and truthful that it feels like a tree bursting into bloom.

If Jewett's catalytic impact on Thea/Willa is felt at the deepest level of *The Song of the Lark*, the presence of Mary Baker Eddy is also ubiquitous, especially in the shaping of its heroine. The similarities are everywhere. Mary Baker as a child had a temper that separated her from her siblings, and that her family feared (*MBE* 20–23). Thea's temper does not reach the hysterical level of Mary's, but it is described in similar ways: "Thea, from the time she was a little thing, had her own routine. She kept out of every one's way, and was hard to manage only when the other children interfered with her. Then there was trouble indeed: bursts of temper which used to alarm Mrs. Kronborg" (*SOL* 65).[10] Cather's biography repeatedly describes Mary Baker Eddy as unique, a creature unlike others: "The one thing she could not endure was to be thought like other people. . . . [S]he must be exceptional at any cost" (*MBE* 119–20). Thea's piano teacher, Andor Harsanyi, uses similar language of Thea: "She will do nothing common. She is uncommon, in a common, common world" (*SOL* 212). Cather's biography frequently points out that Eddy's idiosyncratic nature made her hard to live with. So did Thea's, as Mr. Harsanyi remarks: "I don't know what I think about Miss Kronborg, except that I'm glad there are not two of her" (*SOL* 192).[11] Just as Cather's biography stresses Eddy's awareness of her uniqueness, so Thea too understands that she is and must be different: "She realized that there were a great many trains dashing east and west on the face of the continent that night, and that they all carried young people who meant to have things. But the difference was that *she was going to get them.* That was all. Let people try to stop her!" (218).

This last passage suggests the greatest similarity between Thea and Eddy, their indomitable drive to prevail, a trait that Cather can capture so well because she knows it from herself. Thea's drive becomes yet more evident as the same passage continues: "Let people try to stop her! She glowered at the rows of feckless bodies that lay sprawled in the chairs. Let them try it once! Along with the yearning that came from some deep part of her, that was selfless and exalted, Thea had a hard kind of cockiness, a determination to get ahead. Well, there are passages in life when that fierce, stubborn self-assertion will stand its ground after the nobler feeling is overwhelmed and beaten under" (218). The combative tone persists throughout the Chicago episode as Thea faces up to the competitive nature of art and artists. She had encountered this challenge as a child in the Christmas Eve concert in Moonstone, where Lily Fisher had outmaneuvered her; in Chicago she learns to hold her own. She now sees such rivals as her "enemy," as people "lined up against her," determined "to take something from her. Very well; they should never have it" (201). When she returns to Moonstone after her year in Chicago, she stuns Dr. Archie by what she has become: "[A]bout this tall girl . . . he knew nothing. She was goaded by desires, ambitions, revulsions that were dark to him. . . . To-night a very different sort of girl . . . had let him see the fierceness of her nature" (245). During the train trip back to Chicago Thea recognizes what lies ahead: "Thea remembered how she had gone away the first time, with what confidence in everything, and what pitiful ignorance. Such a silly! She felt resentful toward that stupid, good-natured child. How much older she was now, and how much harder! She was going away to fight, and she was going away forever" (246).[12]

Once back for her second year in Chicago, she develops the toughness that will enable her to fight her way to the top. Thea comments to Mr. Harsanyi's wife, "[I]t seems to me that what I learn is just to *dislike*. I dislike so much and so hard that it tires me out" (257).[13] Mrs. Harsanyi notes that "there had come a change in her face; an indifference, something hard and skeptical" (255), and fellow students in the rooming houses see her as "cold, self-centered, and unimpressionable" (260). Thea's transformation reflects the impact of her teacher, Madison Bowers, who "flattered himself that he had made her harsher than she was when she first came to him" (252). Although she instinctively dislikes Bowers, "[u]nconsciously she began to take on something of his dry contempt. . . . His cynicism seemed to her honest, and the amiability of his pupils artificial. She admired his drastic treatment of his dull pupils. The stupid deserved all they got, and more" (266). These qualities moderate as Thea begins to rise above Bowers's model, but she does not forget what she has learned from him. When she goes to sing for a wealthy Chicago couple who will become her supporters, her hostess notes "that hard glint in her eye" and comments, "The people won't matter much, I fancy. They will come and go. She is very much interested in herself—as she should be" (278).[14] During the episode in Panther Canyon, Fred Ottenburg, the friend who has made this trip possible, and who will become Thea's lover, remarks on her calculating mind, her willingness to use people: "Do you know, I've decided that you never do a single thing without an ulterior motive. . . . You ride and fence and walk and climb, but I know that all the while you're getting somewhere in your mind. All these things are instruments; and I, too, am an instrument" (315).

Every feature noted in Cather's Thea has its counterpart in her portrayal of Mary Baker Eddy. Eddy too was keenly competitive, determined to win. She too saw the world as a battlefield, her opponents as enemies lined up against her; she too was always ready to fight, and took delight in defeating her adversaries. Thea has that "hard glint in her eye," Eddy her "hawk-eye" that looked clear through people. Thea's Moonstone piano teacher notes Thea's dogged delight in meeting hard challenges, Cather comments that Eddy is "never so commanding a figure as when she bestirs herself in the face of calamity" (*SOL* 96, *MBE* 292). Hard, cold, stubborn, fierce, resentful, self-centered—the adjectives Cather uses of Thea line up with those she uses of Eddy. If Thea is "very much interested in herself," so—unfailingly—was Eddy. Fred Ottenburg's comment that Thea knows where she wants to go and is willing to use people to get there is just what Cather tells us about Eddy. Indeed, in realizing their ambitions, both Eddy and Thea draw upon and use the weaker people, and in particular the weaker men, who surround them. Cather repeatedly emphasizes Eddy's penchant for attracting such men and turning them to her own purposes, while the *Song of the Lark* jacket calls the book a "story of aspiration and conflict, of the magnificent courage of young ambition, and of the influence of four men upon the singer's career." Wealth was high among Eddy's priorities, and a goal she attained in great measure. The same is true of Thea, who comments to Fred that being rich is "the only thing that counts. . . . To do any of the things one wants to do, one has to have lots and lots of money" (242). And like Eddy, she ends up with just that—witness Aunt Tillie's delight in reminding Moonstone friends that Thea makes one thousand dollars a night (484).

Eddy and Thea resemble each other also in that for both a sudden revelation clarifies their future and spurs their ambition. For Eddy the contact with Quimby provided "her first great experience, the first powerful stimulus in a life of unrestraint, disappointment, and failure," and led directly to a "new note of aspiration and resolve." She now "had something the world had waited for, and she meant to make the world pay for it ..." (*MBE* 57, 63, 138). Thea's recognition that her future lies in her voice, not the piano, is similarly catalytic, and soon after the session where Harsanyi points her in this direction she feels in herself a "full, powerful pulsation" and with it "the natural contempt of strength for weakness, with the sense of physical security which makes the savage merciless" (*SOL* 217–18).

As she does with Alexandra and Marie in *O Pioneers!*, Cather gives Thea many qualities that differentiate her from Mary Baker Eddy, but the similarities nevertheless run deep. And despite the negative overtones of many of these Eddy-like characteristics, Cather portrays them as integral to the success Thea achieves—just as many years before she had found much to admire in the way Sarah Bernhardt took on the competitive challenges of her profession and did what she needed to do, repugnant and petty as her actions might seem. In both her biography of Eddy and her novel about Thea, Cather is, as when she writes about Bernhardt, focusing on a prima donna, a diva, a woman who rises to extraordinary heights by extraordinary means—indeed, Thea is Cather's supreme example of "heroic womanhood."[15] In her student years Cather had described Bernhardt's combination of genius and will, and more recently she had seen a similar combination at work in Olive Fremstad, but it was above all her work on Mary Baker Eddy that for an extended period brought Cather face to face with ambition at both its ugliest and its most resourceful. In Thea Kronborg she gives us a woman who triumphs because she combines what Cather had learned so well, and so gladly, from Sarah Orne Jewett with what she had learned equally well, though less gladly, from Mary Baker Eddy. Cather's portrait of Thea is unimaginable without Jewett's inspiration: both Thea's artistic awakening and the magnitude of her accomplishment evoke the woman who had told Cather to "dream your dreams and go on to new and more shining ideals." But Thea is also impossible to imagine without Cather's extended exposure to Eddy.

Cather's recent work on S. S. McClure also enriches the portrayal of her heroine. Thea displays the same steadfastness that Cather finds in

McClure, the same clarity about where she is going and how she will get there. Most notably, Thea squarely faces what it means to become a mature artist and, like McClure, consciously bids farewell to childhood innocence. The moment comes on the train ride back to Chicago, in a passage quoted earlier but worth hearing again: "Thea remembered how she had gone away the first time, with what confidence in everything, and what pitiful ignorance. Such a silly! She felt resentful toward that stupid, good-natured child. How much older she was now, and how much harder! She was going away to fight, and she was going away forever." These words immediately recall the passage, penned by Cather not long before she wrote *The Song of the Lark*, in which McClure bids farewell to his youth: "I never saw him again, and now I have no sense of identity with that boy; he was simply one boy whom I knew better than other boys. He had lived intensely in the future and had wanted a great many things." Thea relinquishes her childhood less easily than does McClure, but unlike Bartley Alexander, she never turns back, never seeks that child again. She cries all night on the train, "[b]ut when the sun rose in the morning, she was far away. It was all behind her, and she knew that she would never cry like that again" (246). Like the ugly traits of Eddy that Cather writes into Thea, Cather transposes this painful liminal moment from McClure's autobiography into her account of Thea's journey to artistic maturity.

Another harsh fact of Thea's life again takes us back to Eddy. In her biography, Cather repeatedly emphasizes the duality—indeed, the duplicity—of Eddy's life, the gulf between her public persona and the realities of her private life. Thea, like any great diva, ends up in a similar situation. A passing comment early in *The Song of the Lark* notes that once Thea got her own room she "began to live a double life" (58), and at one point during her first year in Chicago Thea herself expands on the same theme:

> Her voice, more than any other part of her, had to do with that confidence, that sense of wholeness and inner well-being that she had felt at moments ever since she could remember. . . . She had always believed that by doing all that was required of her by her

family, her teachers, her pupils, she kept that part of herself from being caught up in the meshes of common things. She took it for granted that some day, when she was older, she would know a great deal more about it. It was as if she had an appointment to meet the rest of herself sometime, somewhere. It was moving to meet her and she was moving to meet it. (216)[16]

Although her work in Chicago ultimately draws her closer to that hidden side of herself, this passage also foreshadows the gulf that opens as she develops into the triumphant diva we encounter in "Kronborg."[17] This final section of the novel at point after point draws attention to the private realities of Thea's life, and to how distant they are from the image her audiences see on the stage.[18] We learn of her years spent in Germany, taking what roles she can get, even forgoing a visit home to see her dying mother in order to sing a role important to her career. In Dr. Archie's first meeting with her we see how drained and self-critical she is after a performance, and in a subsequent scene how terrified she is when she agrees to step in at the last moment, unprepared, for a singer who has taken ill in midperformance.[19] Fred Ottenburg notes that when she is not performing her manner can become "a little cold and empty, like a big room with no people in it" (442). We witness the pettiness Thea endures from other singers, the threat of illness and insomnia that haunts her in the week before what turns out to be her triumphant appearance as Sieglinde in *Die Valkyrie*.

The pervasive doubleness of Thea's life is an aspect of the novel on which Cather elaborated at length in the preface she wrote for a 1932 reissue of *The Song of the Lark*:

> The life of nearly every artist who succeeds in the true sense (succeeds in delivering himself completely to his art) is more or less like Wilde's story, "The Portrait of Dorian Grey." As Thea Kronborg is more and more released into the dramatic and musical possibilities of her profession, as her artistic life grows fuller and richer, it becomes more interesting to her than her own life. As the gallery of her musical impersonations grows in number and beauty, as that

perplexing thing called "style" (which is a singer's very self) becomes more direct and simple and noble, the Thea Kronborg who is behind the imperishable daughters of music becomes somewhat dry and preoccupied. Her human life is made up of exacting engagements and dull business detail, of shifts to evade an idle, gaping world which is determined that no artist shall ever do his best. Her artistic life is the only one in which she is happy, or free, or even very real. It is the reverse of Wilde's story; the harassed, susceptible human creature comes and goes, subject to colds, brokers, dressmakers, managers. But the free creature, who retains her youth and beauty and warm imagination, is kept shut up in the closet, along with the scores and wigs.... [I]n an artist of the type I chose, personal life becomes paler as the imaginative life becomes richer....[20]

A fascinating feature of this passage is that it highlights a duality that is in fact written into the novel's final section but that strikes home to most readers far less acutely than Cather's 1932 description would suggest. The use of the single name "Kronborg" as the title for this section, implicitly conferring iconic status such as we associate with "Heifetz," "Toscanini," "Flagstad," imbues Thea's operatic appearances, and especially her performance as Sieglinde, with such brilliance that we, like the Met audience, are swept away by the aura that surrounds her.[21] We too remember the public persona so vividly evoked and unconsciously downplay the mundane and less attractive aspects of Thea's private life even though they are there for us to see.

Even more interesting is the degree to which this 1932 description calls to mind Cather herself—indeed, its language fits a writer at least as well as it does an opera singer, and not least the Willa Cather of 1915. This was a time when Cather's artistic life too had become "fuller and richer," when her "gallery of impersonations" had "grown in number and beauty," when she was mastering a "style" (a writer's "very self") that was "becoming more direct and simple and noble." But it was also a time when "her human life" was becoming "dry and preoccupied, made up of exacting engagements and dull business detail, of shifts to evade an idle, gaping world which is determined that no artist shall ever do his best." In 1915 Cather too could well have said of herself, "In an artist of the type I chose, personal life becomes paler as the imaginative life becomes richer."

If the way Thea moves open-eyed beyond her childhood recalls Cather's account of S. S. McClure at the same stage of his life, in other respects his model does not work for Thea, or for Cather herself. For one thing, for all his love of literature, McClure remains a businessman, not an artist; to put it differently, the art he pursues is that of business. In tending to the details of advertising, of building a company, of making money, he is practicing his "art," and his autobiography captures the satisfactions he finds in that pursuit. In contrast, Thea's art, or Cather's, leads in one direction, their involvement in the business of their careers in a different one. Where McClure can lead a single life, their lives end up double. McClure also seems largely free of the negative qualities that Cather found in Eddy, saw in herself, and builds into Thea. In part this reflects the radically different conditions under which Cather wrote the two books, a ghosted autobiography of a friend and colleague on the one hand, a muckraking exposé of a controversial icon on the other. But important too is that McClure did not face the cutthroat conditions an Eddy faced if she, a woman, were to succeed as she did—or that are givens in the competitive world of the arts. Cather does not describe McClure as cold, harsh, self-centered, cynical—but he did not need these qualities to succeed, while Eddy, Thea, and Cather did.[22] Years before, Cather had identified similar qualities as essential to Bernhardt's success, and she was increasingly seeing them as corollaries to her own ambitions.

In *The Song of the Lark* Cather tries to bridge the gulfs that loomed in *Alexander's Bridge* and *O Pioneers!* by focusing on a single heroine, one single-minded in her artistic ambition, but the novel ends up with its own divisions. Not only does her heroine achieve preeminence by a combination of what Cather had absorbed from the radically divergent Jewett and Eddy, but in casting her own artistic awakening as the story of an operatic diva Cather embraces a life even more divided than that of Bartley Alexander. In doing so she is but mirroring the facts, for in these very years Cather was both seeing herself in iconic terms, as the triumphant artist, and also, in her efforts to advance her career, taking on the sorts of exacting engagements that characterize the private life of her operatic heroine.

The divide is implicit in the advertising brochure crafted to accompany this novel, whose purpose was to establish Cather's place in "the front rank of American writers ... the little group of American novelists that count," but which by its very nature involved her in the nitty-gritty of self-promotion. While the brochure honors Jewett for the advice and inspiration she had imparted, simultaneously it puts to work the practical lessons Cather had learned from studying and writing about Eddy. The theme of truthfulness seals the point. The brochure places truth at the heart of Jewett's counsel to Cather, and the climactic moment of the novel being advertised identifies artistic growth as "more than anything else ... a refining of the sense of truthfulness." At the same time, in writing copy to promote this very novel, Cather does not hesitate to stretch and distort the truth repeatedly—just as Mary Baker Eddy had done in promoting herself and her books.

The role Thea plays in her climactic appearance in *Die Valkyrie* is also apt. Sieglinde, like her brother Siegmunde, is a Volsung, a child of the god Odin and a human mother, and hence a mix of divine and mortal. The same mix fits Thea: her name suggests her divine side, as does her professional title, "diva," and we recall that many years before Cather had written that art "is the highest, the only expression of whatever divinity there may be in man" (*KA* 402). In her private life, however, and in what she has had to do and become to succeed, Thea is very human—flawed, limited, mortal. It is a mix that Cather understood well from looking at herself and her own career, and a mix that, as we shall see, will become focal in the fiction she writes in the 1920s.

In a passage quoted earlier, Fremstad commented to Cather that in her ambition to sing the greatest operatic roles the question of whether she was a contralto or a soprano became insignificant: "I do not sing contralto or soprano. I sing Isolde. What voice is necessary for the part I undertake, I will produce."[23] Her words fit both Cather and Thea. Thea finds, as Sarah Bernhardt found, that to reach her artistic goals she must in her private life play certain parts that don't appeal to her, and that once she has reached these goals a wide gulf opens between the roles she plays in public and in private. In the same way, in this novel Cather sets her sights higher than ever before, but she knows that for her novel to win the readers, the recognition, and the royalties it deserves, she must play her role in advertising and promoting it, and must do so by whatever means will best achieve her ends. That Thea Kronborg contains so much of Mary Baker Eddy is not entirely comfortable, nor is the fact that Cather herself in promoting her novel so vigorously is emulating Eddy's model. That said, Eddy had been supremely successful, as is her Thea. As for herself, Cather knows the book she has written belongs to a different world from anything Eddy ever wrote, and to reach the kingdom of art, she—like Thea—will do what she must: "What voice is necessary for the part I undertake, I will produce."

CHAPTER EIGHT

My Ántonia

Near the end of "The Pioneer Woman's Story" Jim Burden and Ántonia see the moon rising as the sun sets: "For five, perhaps ten minutes, the two luminaries confronted each other across the level land, resting on opposite edges of the world" (364). This haunting image not only resonates with the reunion of Jim and Ántonia but also evokes the significance of this moment, standing as it does between their past, which they have recalled in their conversation, and the adult lives which both are now beginning, and of which we will soon learn in "Cuzak's Boys." The same image also fits the place of *My Ántonia* in Cather's career: like the setting sun, the novel marks an ending, a point of arrival and summation for themes Cather has been pursuing in her last three novels. At the same time, in its intimations of themes that will occupy Cather in the stories and novels of the coming decade, *My Ántonia* also looks ahead, like the rising moon.

Among the recapitulations is Cather's return to the theme of evil that had so fixed her attention in her work on Eddy, and that she weaves so vividly into *O Pioneers!* Once again, as she had done there, she underscores this theme with imagery drawn from the Garden. The early pictures of Jim and Ántonia, like the early scenes of Emil and Marie in *O Pioneers!*, have an Edenic cast. We have Jim's early experience of the garden, where he settles into the warm sun: "... I did not want to be anything more. I was entirely happy"; Ántonia and Jim at her place, "so deep in the grass that we could see nothing but the blue sky over us and the gold tree in front of us"; Ántonia and Jim on a late fall afternoon: "That hour always had the exultation of victory, of triumphant ending, like a hero's death . . . . It was a sudden transfiguration, a lifting-up of day. How many an afternoon Ántonia and I have trailed along the prairie under that magnificence!" (20, 29, 44–45).[1] And we recall that these Eden-like scenes are framed by snakes that do no harm—the rattlers that Jim's grandmother keeps at bay with her rattlesnake cane, the harmless bull snakes Jim learns to live with ("I sat down in the middle of the garden, where snakes could scarcely approach unseen"), and especially the giant rattler that Jim slays at the prairie-dog town, a snake Jim describes as "the ancient, eldest Evil" (19, 53).[2] But Cather knew what she was doing in ordering her episodes, and it is no accident that this triumph over "the ancient, eldest Evil" immediately precedes mention of the "evil bird" that seems to settle on Peter and Pavel's house, and the telling of their horrific tale of humans throwing humans to wolves. In the chapters that follow, evil of every sort flowers: the death of Mr. Shimerda, the episode with the tramp and the threshing machine, Ántonia's narrow escape from the sexual designs of Wick (as in "wicked"?) Cutter, Ántonia's jilting and pregnancy.[3]

My Ántonia moves beyond *O Pioneers!* in its treatment of this theme, for while Marie and Emil's story ends in their death, here Ántonia's jilting by Larry Donovan—what seems her "paradise lost"—is not the end of the story. Instead, the language and imagery of the novel's final section repeatedly take us back to the innocent days before Ántonia's "fall." Not only do its descriptions of Ántonia's farm and her children's lives there recall shared moments and scenes from Ántonia's and Jim's childhoods, but the lead-in to this final book is the passage at the end of "The Pioneer Woman's Story" in which Jim imagines himself and Ántonia once again playing together as they did so many years ago. Even the names of Ántonia's children—Ambrosch, Yulka, Anna, Nina—bring back the children of the early parts of the novel, as Ántonia herself remarks: "'She's Nina, after Nina Harling,' Ántonia explained" (377). Reinforcing the theme of rebirth is the repeated mention that Leo is "an Easter baby" (376, 378–79), and it cannot be accidental that one of the roles Leo plays is that of a bull snake—a deft reminder of the bull snake, also benign, that Jim confronts in his grandmother's garden (Cather no doubt knew that snakes are associated with rebirth as well as with the Fall). Despite its undercurrent of sadness, the final book powerfully evokes the good life Ántonia has achieved after the Fall: this may not be paradise regained, but its portrayal of Ántonia and her children recapitulates enough childhood motifs to have its own Edenic cast, and appropriately, Wick Cutter is now dead.

The goodness of Ántonia's life in this final book stands out the more clearly in comparison to the way Alexandra's and Thea's lives play out. It is true that Ántonia shares a number of qualities with Thea, including some of those essential to Thea's success, and some of those that link Thea to Mary Baker Eddy: Ántonia too is ambitious, tough, resilient; she too knows what she wants and goes after it fiercely; she too can annoy people by the airs she puts on ("Much as I liked Ántonia," says Jim, "I hated a superior tone that she sometimes took with me" [48]); she can, like Eddy, be grasping and greedy, a trait she shares with her mother ("Nowadays Tony could talk of nothing but the prices of things," says Jim soon after Mr. Shimerda's death [144]); she too can turn against her friends, one of the traits Cather emphasizes in her picture of Eddy (compare Ántonia's swift reaction during the quarrel between her brother and Jake: "I never like you no more, Jake and Jim Burden . . . . No friends any more!" [148]). But if these traits link her with Eddy and with Thea, she notably escapes the double life that awaits both of them. As with S. S. McClure, Ántonia's life and work are by the end of the novel happily meshed, so that striving to better her farm, her children, her husband, and herself is simultaneously living as she wishes to live, doing what she most enjoys doing. At no point does Ántonia end up living two lives, as Eddy and Thea do; indeed, one of the reasons she gets taken in by Larry Donovan is that she is so open and honest that she cannot believe anyone could be so two-faced as he turns out to be (Edenic innocence once again).[4] Her winning openness is possible in part because she is so different from Thea, and her goals so much less rarefied. But if Ántonia never reaches Thea's lofty heights, there is also no hint of the negative elements that accompany Thea's triumph—the fatal split between her public and private lives, the pale existence with its myriad intrusions and anxieties where

Thea must spend most of her hours and days. Ántonia's life is her art; not only does she herself live it well and find deep satisfaction in it, but her "art" enriches the lives of her children and her husband.

The fullness and wholeness of her life become even more apparent when we compare her with Alexandra. Like Alexandra, Ántonia emerges by the end of the book as the iconic pioneer woman: courageous, undaunted, resilient—like Alexandra, a survivor. But where Alexandra at the end looks back on better days and knows that she will never get over the tragedy of Marie and Emil, Ántonia constantly looks ahead to the future that awaits herself and her family. In addition, we have seen that Alexandra lacks Marie Shabata's innate charisma—by no stretch could one describe Alexandra, as the jacket does Marie, as "a creature so warm and palpitating with life." In contrast, Ántonia from the start has the quickness, the charm, the imagination, the color that Alexandra lacks, and that we associate with Marie. "I remembered what the conductor had said about her eyes," says Jim in an early description of Ántonia. "They were big and warm and full of light, like the sun shining on brown pools in the wood. Her skin was brown, too, and in her cheeks she had a glow of rich, dark color. Her brown hair was curly and wild-looking" (26). His words, with their emphasis on Ántonia's hair and eyes and color, strongly recall Marie Tovesky as we first meet her: "a dark child, with brown curly hair, like a brunette doll's, a coaxing little red mouth, and round, yellow-brown eyes. Every one noticed her eyes; the brown iris had golden glints that made them look like gold-stone . . ." (*OP* 11). Furthermore, the Ántonia Jim meets in the final book still has Marie-like qualities—her "fire of life," her "inner glow," her capacity to "fire the imagination," to "stop one's breath for a moment" (379, 398). For all the warmth of its conclusion, *O Pioneers!* leaves us with a woman who never had, and never will have, those Cather-like qualities that animate Marie. Part of the wholeness and harmony we feel in Ántonia is that she unites Marie's warmth and vivacity with those more stern, more heroic qualities that give Alexandra her greatness.

Further contributing to the sense of unity projected by the final book of *My Ántonia* is that at every level it is about people coming together. Most obviously, there is Jim's account of how he and Ántonia come together after so many years, and his discovery that despite all that has intervened, there remains so much that still binds them to each other. But there are many other reunions as well. Our first glimpses of Ántonia's children are of one or two at a time, in different places; soon we begin to see more of them together, and the movement peaks in the marvelous pictures of Ántonia introducing them one by one, of them rushing together from the cellar, and of the family sitting down to dinner at the huge table. Cuzak and his oldest son are away when we begin; during the course of the final book they too return, reuniting the family. We also sense that this union of Ántonia with Anton is right and good. Their marriage, like Alexandra's with Carl at the end of *O Pioneers!*, has its Eddy-like overtones, pairing as it does a strong woman with a weaker man; as Cuzak himself admits, Ántonia is the dominant force, a wife who outshines her husband, and beside whom he seems small (Jim describes him on their first meeting as "a crumpled little man" [401]). But Ántonia has succeeded where her mother failed, in leading a city-minded husband to become a successful farmer, and this is a marriage in which both parties take pride and pleasure: "The two seemed to be on terms of easy friendliness, touched with humor. Clearly, she was the impulse, and he the corrective. As they went up the hill he kept glancing at her sidewise, to see whether she got his point, or how she received it" (403). Even the "hired girls," so much a group earlier in the novel but now so divided by time and distance, come together again as Ántonia brings out her pictures of "the three Bohemian Marys" and talks about them, then displays the picture of Lena Lingard that she received from San Francisco the previous Christmas. Comings together also frame this final book: shortly preceding "Cuzak's Boys," near the end of the previous book, is the marvelous image of the sun and moon appearing simultaneously, and this leads in short order to Jim's picture of Ántonia and himself "laughing and whispering to each other in the grass" (365); balancing this lead-in to the final book are Jim's famous words at its close about the ties between Ántonia and himself that transcend the years and the miles: "Now I understood that the same road was to bring us together again. Whatever we had missed, we possessed together the precious, the incommunicable past" (419).

There is also in *My Ántonia* a fuller coalescing of what Cather had learned from Jewett and Eddy. In *The Song of the Lark* she draws on both, but the heroine she leaves us with in "Kronborg" remains edgy, uneasy, divided, with one side of her resembling Jewett in her quest for the truthfulness of art, the other embodying the tough lessons about getting ahead that Cather had learned from Eddy. In contrast, the reminders of these two women feel complementary in *My Ántonia*, and at the end of the novel they leave us with a heroine who seems whole and unified to a degree that is rare in Cather's fiction.

My Ántonia marks the point in Cather's artistic awakening where she attains the "refining of the sense of truthfulness" that she ascribes to Thea. In this respect the novel is Cather's ultimate tribute to Sarah Orne Jewett, for its truthfulness goes beyond returning to figures remembered from childhood, beyond weaving into the whole her own growing up. Cather had done that, wonderfully, in both *O Pioneers!* and *The Song of the Lark*. In *My Ántonia* she transmutes these old experiences into something with its own internal coherence and logic, something so fresh and vivid that it feels like a world created anew.[5] Cather's description of what she had learned from Jewett, what she finds in Jewett's own writing, precisely matches what she herself achieves in *My Ántonia*: "The shapes and scenes that have 'teased' the mind for years, when they do at last get themselves rightly put down, make a much higher order of writing, and a much more costly, than the most vivid and vigorous transfer of immediate impressions. . . . The design is, indeed, so happy, so right, that it seems inevitable; the design is the story and the story is the design. The . . . sketches are living things caught in the open, with light and freedom and air-spaces about them. They melt into the land and the life of the land until they are not stories at all, but life itself."[6]

At the same time, however, this same novel also reveals Cather's respect for what she had seen in Mary Baker Eddy, a woman who, like Alexandra and Ántonia, is a survivor, a pioneer, an accomplisher, someone who, despite her huge flaws, has over a long and challenging life achieved remarkable things, and who at her best has had a transforming impact on her followers—the same effect Ántonia has on anyone who comes to know her. Indeed, Cather evokes Ántonia's impact in language similar to that she had used ten years before of Eddy: "[L]ife in the society of this woman was more intense and keen than it ever was afterward"; Eddy's words had the effect "of the wind stirring the wheat-field"; "[t]here was something about her that continually excited and stimulated, and she gave people the feeling that a great deal was happening." Contrast her language in *My Ántonia*: "Ántonia had always been one to leave images in the mind that did not fade—that grew stronger with time.... She was a battered woman now, not a lovely girl; but she still had that something which fires the imagination, could still stop one's breath for a moment by a look or gesture that somehow revealed the meaning in common things" (397–98). The fragment from Longfellow associated with Eddy on the masthead of the *Sentinel* could well be about Ántonia: "A lady with a lamp shall stand in the great history of our land, a noble type of good, heroic womanhood." And indeed, as the family heads into the parlor after dinner in "Cuzak's Boys," Ántonia goes "first, carrying the lamp" (391).[7]

These two complementary influences here lead Cather to a new level of artistry, but they do so in characteristically diverse ways. Jewett's way encouraged Cather to focus on the realities of life, on people and places and actions that she knew intimately, and over time to draw from these experienced realities a higher order of truthfulness, one in which such particulars "melt into the land and the life of the land until they are not stories at all, but life itself." In contrast, at her best Eddy inspired her followers to look beyond the gray minutiae of everyday life, to imagine a life lived more intensely and in which more important things could happen. One can see Cather's heroic women of the teens as products of these two processes. Following Jewett's way, she begins with real women she had known as a child and works from them to universal figures who reflect the heroic qualities common to so many of these women. Her work on Eddy, and her gradual recognition of the mythic stature Eddy had attained among her followers, led Cather in the opposite direction—to begin with Christian Science's idealized image of "heroic womanhood" and from there to work back to the qualities appropriate and necessary to female heroism, qualities that Cather clearly differentiated from those she saw in Christian Science's "heroic woman"—Eddy herself. Like Ántonia, Cather leaves images in the mind that do not fade, that grow stronger with time, but she arrives at these images by these two contrasting ways, one inductive, starting with particulars and working toward universals, the other deductive, starting from an imagined archetype and working back to its human realizations.

That my language carries overtones of Plato's theory of forms is not accidental, for it appears that in this novel Cather herself had Plato, and especially his most famous image, in mind. She describes Ántonia's children tumbling up from the cellar as "a veritable explosion of life out of the dark cave into the sunlight. It made me dizzy for a moment": the language clearly echoes Plato's Cave, with its humans dizzied as they emerge into the light of the sun (382).[8] In addition, it is Jim's memory of the children rushing from the cave into the light that evokes his comments on Ántonia's capacity to leave images in the mind that do not fade, that capture "immemorial human attitudes which we recognize by instinct as universal and true"; her capacity to stop one's breath "by a look or gesture that somehow revealed the meaning in common things" (398). In what Jim sees in Ántonia there is again the move toward unity that makes itself felt at so many levels of this novel, for what is the progression from "common things" to the "universal and true" but the search for underlying unity? And like the images of Ántonia's life that Jim remembers in this passage—"Ántonia kicking her bare legs against the sides of my pony when we came home in triumph with our snake; Ántonia in her black shawl and fur cap, as she stood by her father's grave in the snowstorm; Ántonia coming in with her work-team along the evening sky-line"—the images that Cather leaves in our minds also grow stronger with time, strike us as universal and true, reveal the meaning in common things: the plow against the sun, "heroic in size, a picture writing on the sun," comparable in magnitude and meaning to the heroic figures Cather evokes in these novels of the teens; the sun and moon facing each other "on opposite edges of the world," and by their "singular light" lending deeper significance to the particulars of the world: "[E]very little tree and shock of wheat, every sunflower stalk and clump of snow-on-the-mountain, drew itself up high and pointed; the very clods and furrows in the fields seemed to stand up sharply" (279, 364).[9]

Still on the Divide

Although on so many levels *My Ántonia* moves toward unity, Cather, as always, weaves in contrapuntal lines that pull in different directions, in this instance countering the surge toward unity and helping create the novel's strong undercurrent of separation and loss.[10] It is easy, for instance, to see the final book focusing on Ántonia alone, casting her as the sole and quintessential model of heroic womanhood. In fact, however, implicit in this very section is Ántonia's—and Cather's—awareness of diverse models of female achievement that differ from but complement Ántonia's own. As Janis Stout has commented, Jim Burden may see Ántonia primarily as wife and mother, an embodiment of the teeming fertility of the land, but Cather and Ántonia herself clearly suggest other models of female fulfillment.[11] During Jim's visit, the photographs of Lena Lingard and Frances Harling receive special attention. Both are women who have their own professional lives, and Frances is expressly identified "as a heroine in the family legend" (394).[12] As if to foreshadow the emphasis on these two women in "Cuzak's Boys," a good portion of "The Pioneer Woman's Story" is devoted to another woman and another paradigm: Tiny Soderball and her entrepreneurial success in Alaska. In addition, Ántonia has her own keen business instincts (compare Jim's comment at one point that she "could talk of nothing but the prices of things"), the fruit of which we see in her management of the farm; and Ántonia herself notes her intention to give her daughters what she did not have—the opportunity to pursue lives that reach beyond the usual female stereotypes.[13]

While the inclusion of these alternative paths for women complicates the overall surge toward unity, it also contributes to the sense of fulfillment and wholeness projected by Ántonia: though she herself has chosen one route, she brings into her house, and imagines for her daughters, other and different possibilities. But "Cuzak's Boys" contains one other professional model, one in fact implicit on every page of the novel, that pulls against the momentum of convergence so strongly felt in this final book. Central to this momentum is the reunion of Ántonia and Jim, but we cannot forget that after Jim's joyous scenes with Ántonia and her family he does not see her again. Instead, he heads back to New York, leaving Ántonia in Nebraska, a fact that shadows the climactic reunion with a sharp reminder of the central division that Cather has built into the whole novel.

Ántonia embodies one side of Cather's personality, and the life she attains at the end of the novel—undivided, fulfilled, at peace with herself—is one in which the author is clearly invested, even envies; that said, it is Jim Burden with whom Cather associates herself in the novel's introduction. She and Jim are "old friends" who both grew up in Nebraska: "We agreed that no one who had not grown up in a little prairie town could know anything about it." They have both left Nebraska and now "both live in New York." Not only do Jim's childhood and his university years at point after point recall Cather's own, but the similarities extend into his adult life: he too is a storyteller, someone involved in the competitive whirl of life in New York, someone who finds himself dissatisfied, thinking back to a better time, being drawn—imaginatively at least—into that earlier life.[14] In a very real sense, both Cather and Jim find themselves where Bartley Alexander was in Cather's first novel: successful, busy, prospering, but longing for the openness and freedom and youth represented by a woman vividly remembered from years long past. That in her energy, verve, and slightly exotic beauty Ántonia resembles Hilda Burgoyne strengthens the analogy, as does the fact that, like Bartley, Cather/Jim in writing about Ántonia are both seeking a lost youth. Jim boldly writes "My" before "Ántonia" when he delivers his manuscript in the introduction, and Cather calls her novel by the same name, asserting her ownership as well: *My Ántonia*.[15] But the fact is that Ántonia belongs to neither of them. They may long for the unity and harmony she has found, may take her to themselves in what they write, but their lives are separated from hers by time and distance, and her life is theirs only in the telling. Indeed, the starting point for the jacket blurb on the novel is the distinction between the New York teller of the story and the Nebraska woman who is his subject: "A New York lawyer, whose worldly and successful career has been shaped by a brilliant marriage, tells the story of the one woman who has most influenced his inner life and stirred his imagination,—a Bohemian girl, Ántonia Shimerda, whom he first knew in his boyhood on the Nebraska prairies."[16]

The two passages cited from Virgil's *Georgics* in "Lena Lingard" capture this central divide. Jim's professor, Gaston Cleric, interprets one of them as Virgil's "hope, at once bold and devoutly humble, that he might bring the Muse ... not to the capital, the *palatia Romana*, but to his own little 'country'; to his father's fields, 'sloping down to the river'...": *Primus ego in patriam mecum ... deducam Musas* ("for I shall be the first, if I live, to bring the Muse into my country" [*MA* 299]).[17] It is a reading that suggests Cather's own sense of what she had accomplished in her three novels of the teens: by immersing herself in the lives of people she had known as a child, as Cleric's Virgil also had done, she had brought the Muse to her own country, to her own fields sloping down to the river, one more act of bringing together, and one achieved with particular success in *My Ántonia*, her great novel of comings together. And there is great pride in the *primus*: I did this first. But the same word figures also in the second *Georgics* passage quoted on the same page, a passage that suggests not fulfillment but loss, not arrival but separation: *optima dies ... prima fugit* ("the best days are the first to flee"). Like the first, this passage too evokes Cather's relationship to this novel, and to Ántonia herself. For the "best days" that she so powerfully evokes here, through Jim, have indeed fled: *optima dies ... prima fugit*. And these words, with their evocation of irremediable loss, are the ones Cather chooses as epigraph for her novel.

The choice is appropriate, for at the very time she was creating in Ántonia a heroine who embodied a wholeness and harmony that Thea could never approach, Cather herself was living a life far more similar to Thea's—striving on the one hand for the sort of transcendent artistic achievement she achieves in this novel, but on the other wrestling daily with the challenges and frustrations that came with being a writer amid the competitive whirl of New York City. Indeed, as we shall see in the next chapter, at the time she was writing *My Ántonia*, she was also writing stories that focused on this very world, a world from which she, like Jim, flees toward Ántonia, but one to which she very much belonged. What's more, when she mentions in her introduction that Jim Burden's wife "finds it worthwhile to play the patroness to a group of young poets and painters of advanced ideas and mediocre ability," she is describing types among whom she herself was living in New York.

No reader of *My Ántonia* ever forgets the plow seen against the sun, or the sun and the moon facing each other across the land at sundown; like Ántonia's images, these do not fade with time but grow stronger. What we may forget, but what Cather writes into these archetypal moments, is that in both cases the sun soon sets.[18] The plow sinks back to its littleness somewhere on the prairie, and in the other scene darkness comes so fast that soon Jim must look hard even to see Ántonia's face: *optima dies . . . prima fugit.*[19] And as the light disappears, so does the magical conjunction of sun and moon—just as in both this scene and in the novel itself Jim and Ántonia soon separate. In the same way, Willa Cather can never achieve the unified life Ántonia has fashioned for herself; like Thea, she is destined instead to live a double life inside a divided soul. That said, Cather has in *My Ántonia*—like Thea in her triumphant performance— so fully breathed herself into her heroine that she becomes part of what Ántonia has found. As the book's final lines remind us, Cather/Jim with Ántonia "possess together the precious, the incommunicable past." And the miracle of this novel is that, faithful to the memory of Sarah Orne Jewett, Willa Cather keeps forever alive that past which she and Ántonia shared. *Primus ego in patriam mecum . . . deducam Musas*: "for I shall be the first, if I live, to bring the Muse into my country."

Part IV
Confronting Medusa

In her three novels of the teens Cather moves from division to unity and then back toward division. Central to *O Pioneers!* is the sharp contrast between the stories of Alexandra and Marie, a contrast that echoes both the two lives between which Bartley Alexander is torn in *Alexander's Bridge* and the divisions in Cather's own life, for she writes herself into both women, as she does into the divided Bartley. In Thea Kronborg Cather explores both transcendent artistic achievement and the mundane realities behind such achievement, a mix that reflects the life Cather herself was living at the time. Though it is an uneasy amalgam, at least with both Kronborg and Cather the two lives are joined in a single person. The wholeness evoked in Ántonia is far more complete: in particular, the heroic image Ántonia projects at the end of the novel comprehends both Alexandra's stamina and ambition and Marie's imagination and charisma. As we have seen, though, Cather here returns to reading herself into two characters, for although she shares much with Ántonia, she shares yet more with Jim Burden. Ántonia's integrity of life is insulated from the competitive pressures that Thea faces, that Jim knows so well, and that were so much part of Cather's life in the years when she was writing this novel. One side of her returns to New York with Jim, leaving what Ántonia is and has achieved on the Divide.

Cather's New York side comes to the fore in several stories she writes in 1916–19. Four of them revolve around singers, but in contrast to the way Cather shapes Thea's story in *The Song of the Lark*, her focus here is not on these singers' transcendent artistry but on the spirited resourcefulness with which they handle the challenges of their careers. And when Cather includes these four stories in *Youth and the Bright Medusa*, her first Knopf book, she underscores their focus on the nitty-gritty of the artist's life by combining them with four stories from her earlier collection, *The Troll Garden*, which in different ways evoke the loftier goals to which art and artists can aspire. By 1919, when she is writing "Coming, Eden Bower," the longest and finest of these four stories, she is already embarked on a novel that takes her back to Nebraska and whose hero is seeking the sort of heroic achievement that had been central to the novels of the teens, and that simply seems out of mind in the stories of 1916–19. The very alternation between these different foci of her writing suggests the multiple worlds Cather inhabited in these years.

CHAPTER NINE

"Hard and Dry"

My Ántonia conveys the same sense of artistic arrival as does Cather's description of Thea Kronborg's climactic performance: "[T]his afternoon the closed roads opened, the gates dropped. What she had so often tried to reach lay under her hand. She had only to touch an idea to make it live." That this novel breathes this aura of natural, almost foreordained artistry is the more remarkable in that during the years in which Cather was planning and writing it, the daily concerns and frustrations of the writer's life were very much on her mind. In her relations with Houghton Mifflin she was dealing with a host of business issues—creating advertising copy to promote *The Song of the Lark*, protesting what she saw as Houghton Mifflin's reluctance to make use of positive reviews, trying to make sure that her books were available in bookstores.[1] She was outraged at one point by a bill she received for typesetting changes in *The Song of the Lark*, and as she moved forward with *My Ántonia*, she found herself fighting about the illustrations she wanted included, their placement in the book, and their cost.[2] Exacerbating these concerns was her nagging sense that she was short on funds and needed to write and sell magazine stories to support herself, and the stories that date from 1916–17 reflect these pressures.[3] Although these stories do not explore the artistic heights that Thea scales, three of them focus on opera singers and on issues central also to *The Song of the Lark*: the nature of art and the artist; the gulf between artists' public and private lives; the financial pressures that are never far from an artist's mind. Implicit, though more by what is missing than what is present, are additional questions as to what is the artist's goal:

To create immortal masterpieces and give transcendent performances? To win public recognition and acclaim—and the concomitant material rewards? Simply to put bread on the table?[4]

The Stories of 1916–17

My Ántonia began to take shape during 1915–16, was well underway by the spring of 1917, and began—in sections—to reach Ferris Greenslet at Houghton Mifflin in November 1917.[5] The following stories date from the same period: "The Bookkeeper's Wife" (written spring 1916, published May 1916); "The Diamond Mine" (written spring 1916, published October 1916); "Scandal" (written summer–fall 1916 but not published until August 1919); "A Gold Slipper" (written summer–fall 1916, published January 1917); "Ardessa" (written by fall 1917, published May 1918); and "Her Boss" (written by fall 1917 but not published until October 1919).

A quick overview of these stories immediately suggests the dominance of issues largely distant from *My Ántonia* but central to Cather's life during these years. "The Bookkeeper's Wife" deals with the financial pressures a young bookkeeper faces, and their tragic consequences; "The Diamond Mine," "Scandal," and "A Gold Slipper" revolve around opera singers and their dealings, often commercial and unsavory, with the people who surround them; "Ardessa" and "Her Boss" concern the complex relationships between secretaries and their superiors; all six stories have as their backdrop the busy, ambitious, and sophisticated world of the city, another sharp contrast to *My Ántonia* (except, of course, for Jim Burden's role, and the occasional glimpses of his New York life).

The central figures of the stories that concern opera singers reflect models less heroic in cast than Olive Fremstad, the Wagnerian soprano who was the model for Thea Kronborg: Lillian Nordica for Cressida Garnet in "The Diamond Mine," Mary Garden (and probably Geraldine Farrar) for Kitty Ayrshire in "Scandal" and "A Gold Slipper."[6] The change in Cather's prototypes does not, however, explain the gulf between Thea Kronborg on the one hand, Cressida Garnet and Kitty Ayrshire on the other; indeed, while Cather especially admired Fremstad, she thought highly as well of Nordica, Garden, and Farrar.[7] It is rather that Thea's quest to reach the "kingdom of art" is simply not what these stories are about. Both Cressida and Kitty have devoted years to becoming fine singers and have achieved successful, even brilliant, careers, but on neither does Cather lavish a hint of the transcendent language that Thea evokes in *The Song of the Lark*. Cressida's achievement is defined by far more mundane qualities: "Cressida was always living up to her contract," always "singing reliably, and satisfying the management."[8] Her triumph was not—as with Thea—that she could touch an idea and make it live, plumb the depths of the music she sang, but that "[a] great voice, a handsome woman, a great prestige, all added together made 'a great artist,' the common synonym for success" (YBM 122–23). Kitty Ayrshire has some awareness of the heights to which art can soar, as she indicates in a conversation about Tolstoy, but that is not the way she chooses to go: "In some miraculous way a divine ideal was disclosed to us, directly at variance with our appetites. . . . I can understand that. It's something one often feels in art" (YBM 161). She adds that the topic is central to the greatest of all operas—which she loves because she can never hope to sing it (the opera in question is probably *Tannhäuser*, an opera closely associated with Thea in *The Song of the Lark*).[9] In contrast, her own artistry resides in knowing how to please an audience, even when, as in the Pittsburgh recital she gives in "A Gold Slipper," it is initially chilly: "Kitty studied her audience with an appraising eye. She liked the stimulus of this disapprobation. As she faced this hard-shelled public she felt keen and interested; she knew that she would give such a recital as cannot often be heard for money" (145). By the end she is triumphant, and for her final encore she gives the audience "what she of course knew they wanted"—a popular aria from an opera with which she is especially associated. "This brought her audience all the way. They clamoured for more of it . . ." (148). The concert displays her vocal mastery and her skill as a performer, but it takes place in a different world from Thea's triumph in *Die Valkyrie*.

In addition, while in the final section of *The Song of the Lark* Thea's sublime music-making overshadows all else, so much so that we tend to overlook the offstage existence that is its corollary, the opera stories of 1916 focus far less on their heroines' musical activities than on their offstage lives. Dominating "The Diamond Mine" is the bevy of hangers-on for whom Cressida Garnet is a primary source of support—her family, her former husband and her husband-to-be, her accompanist, her greedy son: "They regarded her as a natural source of wealth; a copper vein, a diamond mine" (137). "Scandal" revolves around a wealthy admirer's successful attempt to make the public believe that he is having an affair with Kitty Ayrshire, a scandal that she grudgingly admits will probably stimulate valuable attention among her public. "A Gold Slipper" concerns another older man, one who initially finds Kitty off-putting and artistically lightweight but who by the end has yielded to her charm (and to the gold slipper she tucks into his berth as she leaves the train on which they are both traveling to New York).

Central to all three stories is the place money holds in the lives of these singers.[10] Cressida comments that somehow her "relations with people always become business relations" (93), noting that what people want of her, and what she has to give, tends to boil down to what they need from her. At another point she asks, "Why is it? I have never cared about money, except to make people happy with it, and it has been the curse of my life. It has spoiled all my relations with people" (134). Given these perpetual demands, she never forgets that she must keep herself in the public eye, cultivate a smile that she can flash at a moment's notice, and (like Cather) always watch for advertising opportunities. "She was too much an American not to believe in publicity. All advertising was good," remarks the narrator on the first page of the story, using a phrase from Cather's McClure autobiography (145)—which he repeats at the end when he explains why Cressida chose to sail on the *Titanic*: "[S]he still believed that all advertising was good" (135). Her very name suggests her plight: "Garnet," a jewel for others to acquire ("[S]he appealed to the acquisitive instinct in men," comments the narrator [95]), and "Cressida," the name of a woman willing to sell herself, something this Cressida ends up having to do.

The selling instinct is even stronger in Kitty Ayrshire, as she muses to herself on the eve of her concert for that hostile Pittsburgh audience: "She had every reason to believe, from experience and from example, that to shock the great crowd was the surest way to get its money and to make her name a household word. Nobody ever became a household word of being an artist, surely; and you were not a thoroughly paying proposition until your name meant something on the sidewalk and in the barber-shop" (144–45). Like Cressida Garnet, she sees herself as a "diamond mine" ("[A]t present I am supporting just eight people, besides those I hire," she says, referring in the first group to the "cripples and hard-luckers" of her family [159]). The atmosphere is yet more tawdry in "Scandal." Kitty is suffering from an illness that makes the world itself look base, and from which she seeks respite by having a mockingbird sing her to sleep. She is more than willing to believe "that everything for sale in Vanity Fair [is] worth the advertised price" (171), and when she realizes that her illness is causing an extended absence from the stage, her first thought is that she is "losing a great deal of money" (169). A friend who visits her while she is ill reminds her that the gossip swirling around her name is precisely what her public wants: "Those people are like children; nothing that is true or probable interests them. They want the old, gaudy lies" (189–90). In the "scandal" at the heart of the story, a man hires a girl who resembles Kitty to masquerade as his mistress, then lures Kitty herself into a situation where she will appear to have played that role herself. It is a world where rich men rent singers for their pleasure and where Kitty and her double are commodities to be exploited; not only does Kitty, like Cressida, have an "electric" smile she can flash from the stage, not only does she too live in two worlds—the glamour of the stage and the tawdriness of her daily life—but she even has this "counterfeit" double masquerading as herself.

These stories remain in the world of opera, but they are distant from Thea and *The Song of the Lark*. Thea may realize that "to do any of the things one wants to do, one has to have lots and lots of money," but money represents for her not an end in itself but a means to reach her artistic goals. Despite the differences, however, there is an important way in which Cressida and Kitty do resemble Thea, and Alexandra and

Ántonia as well: they too are survivors, women who keep alive the vital spark when the nastiness of the world would put it out. Here is Cressida: "For twenty years she had been plunged in struggle; fighting for her life at first, then for a beginning, for growth, and at last for eminence and perfection; fighting in the dark, and afterward in the light . . . ." More than even her furs or her fortune, her family covet "her personal effectiveness, her brighter glow and stronger will to live" (90–91). As for Kitty, she speaks of giving to her best students "my *wish*, my desire, my light" (160); she imagines her fans waiting in the rain and cold to hear her sing "because they loved to believe in her inextinguishable zest" (171–72). When confronting her skeptical Pittsburgh businessman on the train she reminds him that she is "neither a coward nor a shirk" and that she could hold her own if shipwrecked with him on a desert island (163). For all the tawdry world they live in, for all the ways they have to sell themselves, Cressida and Kitty again reflect much of what Cather had learned from both Eddy and Jewett. Like Eddy, their focus is on worldly success and self-promotion, but also like Eddy, they pursue their ends with perseverance, resourcefulness, and courage, leaving the inferior men who cluster about them in their wake. As for Jewett, these stories show Cather bringing her knowledge of the world to the artistic milieux of New York and Pittsburgh, parishes she knew well from her own experience, portraying them with a raw truthfulness that is the ultimate tribute to her mentor, and continuing to build her stories around female protagonists, as Jewett had encouraged her to do.

"Her Boss" and "The Bookkeeper's Wife," both dating from the same period, also feature dominant, ambitious women who have their eye on material rewards, but these women lack the redeeming qualities that mark both Cressida and Kitty. In "Her Boss," Mr. Wanning, a businessman who has just found that he is dying of cancer, recognizes without malice that "it was his wife's way of following things up, of never letting the grass grow under her feet, that had helped to push him along in the world. She was more ambitious than he,—that had been good for him. He was naturally indolent, and Julia's childlike desire to possess material objects, to buy what other people were buying, had been the spur that made him go after business."[11] The portrait of his daughter Roma is less balanced: "The elder daughter had often been told that her name suited her admirably. . . . Her head was massive, her lips full and crimson, her eyes large and heavy-lidded, her forehead low. At costume balls and in living pictures she was always Semiramis, or Poppea, or Theodora. Barbaric accessories brought out something cruel and even rather brutal in her handsome face. The men who were attracted to her were somehow afraid of her" (*UV* 121). Although the younger daughter escapes such damning description, she too is callous in her treatment of her father. On the night after he has learned of his cancer, all three women downplay his disease, ignore him during dinner to pursue their own concerns, and leave him home alone for the evening. When summer comes a few weeks later, each heads off on vacation to pursue her own expensive interests, returning only for his last few days.

In their selfishness and their willingness to use Mr. Wanning, these women recall the worst of what Cather had seen and portrayed in Mary Baker Eddy, and the way they respond to an illness he has told them is mortal suggests that the reminiscence is more than accidental. "You are not going to let this upset you, Paul?" says his wife. "If you take care of yourself, everything will come out all right." Roma tells her father that someone she has met that day "wants to tell you about some doctor he discovered in Iowa, who cures everything with massage and hot water." Later, when she urges her father to seek out this doctor, she adds, "New discoveries are often made by queer people" (120–21, 122–23).[12] Harold, the son, is even more dismissive: "So awfully sorry you've had this bother, Governor . . . . No question about its coming out all right, but it's a downright nuisance, your having to diet and that sort of thing" (126). In contrast to the family's Eddy-like inclination to wish and talk his illness away, two relative outsiders take Mr. Wanning's disease seriously: his black servant, Sam, and the young secretary at the office, Annie, who transcribes the memoirs he dictates over the summer and gives him companionship and sympathy during his family's absence. In theme, tone, and even its characters, the story looks ahead to *The Professor's House*, with Annie in several ways foreshadowing the Augusta of that novel.[13] But while Augusta helps the professor to accept the diminished years that lie ahead, the ending of "Her Boss" is even bleaker: Mr. Wanning dies, and his business partner and his son cheat Annie out of the one-thousand-dollar bequest Wanning has left her.

"The Bookkeeper's Wife" is yet more cynical. Percy Bixby, a young, romantic bookkeeper, steals one thousand dollars from his company to enable him to marry Stella, a woman with "a hard, practical mouth," and one who even before his marriage Percy knows is "much too handsome and expensive and distinguished for him . . ." (*UV* 90). Early in their increasingly unhappy marriage they meet Percy's boss, Mr. Remsen, and his wife at a theater. When Mrs. Remsen asks, "Is that little man afraid of you, Oliver?" her husband answers, "I half believe it's his wife. She looks pitiless enough for anything" (92). An impending audit obliges Percy to confess his theft to Mr. Remsen, who agrees to lend him the seven hundred dollars still outstanding and deduct ten dollars a week from his already paltry salary. When Percy gets home and tells Stella of his dilemma, she is pitiless. She taunts him with "playing solitaire with the books" (95), expresses her hatred for Mr. Remsen, and deserts her husband to take a job under a dashing but notorious young rake. At the end of the story even Mr. Remsen turns against the broken Bixby, recognizing that though he'd thought of helping the young man, "one never did do anything for a fellow who had been stung as hard as that" (97). Underscoring the story's utter cynicism is the absence of anyone—like Sam and Annie in "Her Boss"—who brings a measure of compassion. Whether Eddy was again in Cather's mind is impossible to say, but in her self-absorption, callousness, and greed Stella certainly resembles Eddy, and the way she dumps a husband who no longer meets her needs is yet more reminiscent. What is certain is that the heartless women of these two stories reflect the cutthroat world in which Cather found herself living during these years.

Women hold center stage also in a more attractive story from the same period. "Ardessa" is set in the offices of the energetic and restless Mr. O'Mally, a publisher unmistakably modeled on S. S. McClure. (O'Mally too believes in advertising, runs a journal whose articles unmask societal wrongdoing, and has discovered a brilliant English mystery writer—just as McClure had discovered Arthur Conan Doyle.)[14] Its principal characters are Ardessa, an executive secretary who for years has been coasting on past accomplishments, and Becky, a young and initially diffident secretary who rapidly proves her mettle—and exiles Ardessa to a job where she will have to earn her salary. Cather's picture of Ardessa is sardonic, and her portrait of the publisher's office has its dark sides, but the overall mood is benign and amusing, its women far more appealing than those in "Her Boss" and "The Bookkeeper's Wife," and its picture of the business world far less cutting.[15] One suspects that the difference owes much to Cather's memory of her years with McClure, and that in this story his model supplants that of Eddy. Although McClure was certainly as ambitious as Eddy, and could be as infuriating to work for, he characteristically drew the best from his employees and gave them a sense of working together on projects that were important. Not least, strong women were always prominent on his staff, among them Ida Tarbell, Viola Roseboro', and Willa Cather herself. (It seems likely too that the gentle and generous figure of Annie in "Her Boss" reflects Cather's 1913 experience of taking notes for his autobiography from a badly shaken S. S. McClure—a service similar to that which Annie performs for the dying Mr. Wanning.)[16]

Though these last three stories are less germane to Cather's charting of her artistic evolution than are the Cressida Garnet and Kitty Ayrshire stories, their very existence is a reminder of the harsh New York scene that Cather came to know so well in these years. It is a world often glimpsed in *The Song of the Lark*, but there it is balanced and upstaged by Thea's artistic success. Significantly, too, while one detects echoes of Cather's experience with Eddy and McClure in these three cynical tales, Jewett is conspicuously absent.

"Coming, Eden Bower!" (1919)

The last story that Cather wrote in the teens (though it did not appear until August 1920) was "Coming, Eden Bower!," a story more familiar as "Coming, Aphrodite!," the title under which it appeared in *Youth and the Bright Medusa* the next month.[17] One of her longest stories, it is also among her most memorable.[18] It explores themes that have been on her mind ever since *The Song of the Lark*: art and the artist, with again a singer in a central role; ambition, whether for artistic merit, public recognition, or financial reward; the different routes to a career—through connections, advertisement, "selling oneself"; the different roles an artist plays, including the gulf between one's public and private personae.

Its central characters are both artists: Eden Bower, a glamorous and ambitious young singer, and Don Hedger, a painter who in his brusque manner, scruffy dress, and highly conceptual approach to art exemplifies a familiar Greenwich Village type. The two meet when Eden moves into the rooms adjacent to Don's studio. After some early and largely hostile encounters (she objects when she finds his dog's hairs in the hall bathtub they share!), matters take a sudden turn when he happens upon a knothole in the back of his closet and becomes obsessed with watching her as she exercises each day in the nude. Eventually they come to know each other and become lovers, a relationship shattered abruptly when he scorns the fashionable painter she has identified to help advance his career. The end of the story briefly glimpses them many years later. Eden is now a highly successful singer who has returned to appear at the Lexington Opera House, bringing her orchestra leader with her. Don Hedger has become "one of the first men among the moderns," someone who "is decidedly an influence in art," though the dealer whom Eden questions adds that "one can't definitely place a man who is original, erratic, and who is changing all the time" (*UV* 175–76).

Among the story's chief interests is the sharp contrast drawn between Eden Bower and Don Hedger. Hedger is treated with enough respect to lead one critic to describe him as "the serious artist," Eden Bower as but "an entertainer."[19] But Cather's depiction of Hedger has a satiric undertow from the start: "He was absorbed in a picture of paradise fish at the Aquarium, staring out at people through the glass and green water of their tank. It was a highly gratifying idea; the incommunicability of one stratum of animal life with another—though Hedger pretended it was only an experiment in unusual lighting" (144). A bit later we learn that "he had already outlived a succession of convictions and revelations about his art. Though he was now but twenty-six years old, he had twice been on the verge of becoming a marketable product," but both times he chose to veer in different directions. When he needs money he works as a draughtsman; "[t]he rest of his time he spent in groping his way from one kind of painting into another, . . . and he was chiefly occupied with getting rid of ideas he had once thought very fine" (146). As we have seen, the comments the art dealer makes on Hedger many years later stress the same restlessness.

While Don Hedger is a loner who flees popularity and dresses to suit himself, Eden Bower constantly seeks others out (especially those who can help her career), courts the public, and pays careful attention to her appearance. As a singer she is determined to become successful, famous, and rich, and she is ready to do whatever it will take to get where she wants to go. "She was like someone standing before a great show window full of beautiful and costly things, deciding which she will order. She understands that they will not all be delivered immediately, but one by one they will arrive at her door . . . ." She has figured out that certain people can open doors for her, and she is willing to pay the price to encourage them to do so: "She already knew some of the many things that were to happen to her; for instance, that the Chicago millionaire who was going to take her abroad with his sister as chaperon, would eventually press his claim in quite another manner. He was the most circumspect of bachelors, afraid of everything obvious . . . [b]ut she knew that he would at last throw all his precautions to the winds" (157). While Hedger is happy when for days he talks "to nobody but his dog and the janitress and the lame oysterman" (147), Eden Bower seeks always to attract attention and advertise herself (it is no accident that her name recalls Madison Bowers, Thea's voice teacher in Chicago, who, like Eden, is always on the watch for the useful connection, the chance to be noticed). On a Sunday jaunt to Coney Island, Eden angers Don when she contrives to change places with a young woman who periodically goes up in a balloon as a stunt—something that appeals to both Eden's exhibitionist tendencies and her instinct for self-advertisement.

Eden invites comparison with another Cather singer, Thea Kronborg. Indeed, the final chapter of the story begins with "Coming, Eden Bower!" shining from the marquee of the Lexington Opera House, a moment that recalls Dr. Archie's delight in seeing Thea's name on the notices outside the Metropolitan Opera House. And while Eden seems shallow, a mere "artiste" when set beside Thea, the two have much in common. Both come to New York from Illinois; both possess an earthy strength and energy; both are determined to succeed, and certain that they can and will do so. Like Thea, Eden knows the price of success and the masks a performer must wear, motifs sounded at the end when we see her in her carriage after her inquiries about Hedger: "Leaning back in the cushions, Eden Bower closed her eyes, and her face, as the street lamps flashed their ugly orange light upon it, became hard and settled, like a plaster cast; so a sail, that has been filled by a strong breeze, behaves when the wind suddenly dies. Tomorrow night the wind would blow again, and this mask would be the golden face of Clytemnestra. But a 'big' career takes its toll, even with the best of luck" (176).

Both also radiate a powerful sexuality. The sensuous description of Thea in the river at Panther Canyon evokes a goddess in her sacred spring: "When Thea took her bath at the bottom of the canyon, in the sunny pool behind the screen of cottonwoods, she sometimes felt as if the water must have sovereign qualities, from having been the object of so much service and desire. . . . Thea's bath came to have a ceremonial gravity. The atmosphere of the canyon was ritualistic" (*SOL* 304). The description of Eden when Don first sees her nude through the knothole has the same aura: "Yonder, in a pool of sunlight, stood his new neighbor . . . . The soft flush of exercise and the gold of the afternoon sun played over her together, enveloped her in a luminous mist which, as she turned and twisted, made now an arm, now a shoulder, dissolve in pure light . . ." (*UV* 151). For both Thea and Eden, their sexuality opens the door to their subsequent careers, but in very different ways. Though Thea's sexual awakening in Panther Canyon involves Fred, its real function is to release her latent but powerful artistic energies and individuality, that whole side of her that has become stifled and stunted during her study in Chicago with Madison Bowers (cf. the description in the 1915 brochure: "for the first time in her life, she grew all at once into a powerful and willful young creature, got her courage, and began to find herself"). In contrast, Eden consciously uses her sexual attractions to advance her career, as in her calculated seduction of the Chicago millionaire. The threat implicit in Eden's sexuality is suggested elsewhere as well. One passage of the text links her to Diana, who destroys Actaeon when he stumbles upon her nude (as Don does with Eden).[20] In the original version of the story the golden mask Eden wears for her performance is that of the man-slaying and sexually voracious Clytemnestra (replaced in the later version by that of Aphrodite, who also represents a threat to her lovers, as in the stories of Anchises and Adonis); and shortly before Don and Eden make love for the first time, he tells her the grisly story of an Aztec princess who seduces, then destroys some forty lovers. As always in Cather, names are revealing. Thea—"goddess"—suggests the Olympian heights to which her artistry will climb; "Eden Bower," which would seem to carry overtones of paradisiacal bliss, instead takes us back to both Eve and Lilith, as in the Rossetti poem from which Cather took the name, and to the Garden and its tale of temptation.[21]

That Thea's sexual awakening opens the way to the artistic heights while Eden uses her sexuality to advance her career is an index of the gulf between *The Song of the Lark* and "Coming, Eden Bower!" In the novel Cather explores the process by which an artist discovers and brings to fruition her artistic potential, something she herself was on the way to accomplishing as she wrote this novel in the midteens. In "Coming, Eden Bower!," by contrast, her theme is the artist's ability to use every means available to achieve public recognition and success, precisely what she found herself doing in the years leading up to the composition of this story.[22] For "Coming, Eden Bower!" is once again highly self-referential, set as it is in the early years of the twentieth century in a building on the south side of Washington Square, a time and place that closely fit Cather herself, who arrived in New York in the early 1900s and had her first apartment in this very location.[23]

As the association suggests, there is a good deal of Cather in both

Eden Bower and Don Hedger. Cather resembles the latter in her oft-expressed scorn for the philistine values of the public, in her dislike of crowds and public occasions, and in her aversion to artists who prostitute themselves to the public. Even Hedger's habit of always changing artistic tacks, which Cather satirizes in the story, has its counterpart in herself: one of her most frequent claims—as in the 1915 brochure—is that she never repeats herself, is always trying something new.[24] There is, however, even more of Willa Cather in Eden Bower, for as we have seen, there was a side of Cather that craved success and acclaim and material reward, that believed profoundly in advertisement, and that was willing to go to great lengths to make the connections, and create the éclat, that would draw people to herself and her work; indeed, Eden's cadged balloon ride feels like something Cather herself might have done! Though Cather clearly distinguishes between the artistry of a Thea and the entertainment offered by an Eden, she too, like Eden, wanted to create art that would draw an audience, she too believed in knowing what one wants and going after it. In her energy and vitality, to say nothing of her attention to what she wore, Cather again resembles Eden Bower more than she does Don Hedger. Even Eden's choice of restaurant when she and Don first go out together is revealing: the Brevoort, a restaurant up Fifth Avenue from Washington Square that was stylish, expensive, and a favorite Cather haunt.

That Cather is closer to Eden than to Don says a lot about where she has come since *The Song of the Lark*. In that novel she embodied her own artistic quest in the story of a great opera singer. Though this singer ends up living a double life similar to Cather's own, at least the persona that dominates the final book of the novel, and that defines Thea, is that of the transcendent artist. Eden too lives a double life, but what marks her success is not her artistry but her brilliance in imagining and promoting her career, in getting her name onto the Madison Square marquee lights: "Before she was out of short dresses she had made up her mind that she was going to be an actress, that she would live far away in great cities, that she would be much admired by men and would have everything she wanted" (157). If in Thea's climactic triumph Cather honors the truthfulness she had so admired in Jewett, in Eden she honors the promotional genius she had marveled at in Eddy and McClure. By 1919 it is Eden's voice, not Thea's, that is closest to Cather's own. It is the voice of a brilliant self-advertiser, and we recall that in 1921 Cather will move permanently to Alfred A. Knopf, who promised her full freedom to use this voice in writing her own advertising copy. Even before that, Knopf will publish her *Youth and the Bright Medusa*, which begins with Eden's story, followed by the three stories about Cressida Garnet and Kitty Ayrshire, singers who, like Eden, are also experts in the art of self-advertisement.

CHAPTER TEN

Youth and the Bright Medusa

Youth and the Bright Medusa, Willa Cather's first book with Alfred A. Knopf, was published in September 1920. Although its stories had all appeared previously, its combination of four stories from *The Troll Garden* with four written since 1916 creates such provocative interplays that the collection as a whole feels like something fresh and new. As the lead story Cather chose her most recent work, "Coming, Eden Bower!," revising its title to "Coming, Aphrodite!" and, in keeping with this change, at some points using more sensuous language than had been possible for its publication in *Smart Set*.[1] In organizing the collection, Cather placed the new stories first, the *Troll Garden* stories later, creating in the process a loose but artful parallelism between its two halves:

1916–19 Stories	*Troll Garden* Stories
"Coming, Aphrodite!"	"Paul's Case"
"The Diamond Mine"	"A Wagner Matinée"
"A Gold Slipper"	"The Sculptor's Funeral"
"Scandal"	"A Death in the Desert"

The arrangement highlights important differences between the two sets of stories. Although the four 1916–19 stories contain no heroines who approach Thea or Ántonia in stature, all do feature women—indeed, women singers—in central roles. In contrast, males are focal in the four stories from *The Troll Garden*. They dominate the cast in "Paul's Case" and "The Sculptor's Funeral," and although Aunt Georgiana and Katharine Gaylord are important figures in "A Wagner Matinée" and "A Death in the Desert," the one is life-weary, the other dying, and men take the initiative in both stories—the young narrator in the one, Everett Hilgarde in the other. Furthermore, although the heroines of Cather's four new stories fall short of Thea in their artistic aspirations, all resemble Thea in their determination, their will to succeed, and their sheer animal energy: all are women who wrest what they need from life.

And it is life that wins out in these four new stories, whereas death dominates the four from the earlier collection. Eden Bower in the first story and Kitty Ayrshire in the third may be worn down by the drudgery of their profession, but they remain very much alive at the ends of their stories; and even in the fourth story, where Kitty is ill, she outshines those around her, and we sense that this survivor will soon be singing again. In contrast, the stories that are their counterparts in the second half all end in death: Paul kills himself at the close of the fifth; the subject of the seventh is Merrick's funeral; and Katharine Gaylord's illness in the eighth, unlike Kitty's in the fourth, culminates in her death. As for the second stories in each half, Cressida Garnet dies on the *Titanic* at the end of "The Diamond Mine," but the impression she leaves is of a life force who has supported those around her; Aunt Georgiana too is a life force for those around her in "A Wagner Matinée," and it is to that role that she will return, but the impression she leaves is of a woman ravaged by her years on the prairie (compare her comatose state when she arrives in Boston) who must now return to a "life" far worse than Cressida's death: "She burst into tears and sobbed pleadingly. 'I don't want to go, Clark, I don't want to go!' I understood. For her, just outside the concert hall, lay the black pond with the cattle-tracked bluffs; the tall, unpainted house, with weather-curled boards, naked as a tower . . ." (*YBM* 247).

The passage highlights one more contrast between the two sets of stories: initiative as against dependency. Not only do the new stories focus on women and on life, but these are women who act, who make things happen. Eden is fully aware of where her ambitions will lead her, and fully willing to accept the compromises needed to get there. Cressida knows that she is a "diamond mine" for those around her, doesn't especially like it, but accepts her role as important and necessary and plays it with energy and style. Kitty too realizes that others depend on her, as well as that she herself depends on the comforts her career provides, and she accordingly accepts what comes with that career, whether it is playing the stage games that make audiences love her in "A Gold Slipper" or putting up with the lies and gossip that swirl around her in "Scandal." In contrast, the central figures of the *Troll Garden* stories are, at least as we see them, victims. The heroines of both "A Wagner Matinée" and "A Death in the Desert" are women whose lives have been built around others, and who are now dependent upon the men who narrate their stories, a fact made the more poignant in that we get clear glimpses of earlier periods in which both Katharine Gaylord and Aunt Georgiana exerted considerable control over their lives. With Harvey Merrick too we get tantalizing glimpses of a past in which he was a dynamic and influential artist, but by the time we see him in "The Sculptor's Funeral," he is a defenseless corpse surrounded by his former townspeople: whether they ridicule him thoughtlessly and callously, or, in the lonely case of the lawyer Laird, defend him bravely, he is at their mercy. As for Paul, he may engineer both his escapade and his death, but the story projects a strong aura of determinism, of environment and character shaping destiny, and its final line underscores this impression of Paul as a victim of "the infernal machine": "Then, because the picture making mechanism was crushed, the disturbing visions flashed into black, and Paul dropped back into the immense design of things" (234).[2]

In the new stories, then, dominant women, life, doers and shapers; in the *Troll Garden* stories, subordinate women, death, and victims. Once again, though, the full picture is more complex. The heroines of the four new stories may shape their fate, may wrest a living from "successful" careers, but none of them comes close to Cather's earlier description of what it means to be an artist: "An artist should not be vexed by human hobbies or human follies; he should be able to lift himself up into the clear firmament of creation where the world is not. He should be among men but not one of them, in the world but not of the world" (*KA* 407). Eden Bower, Cressida Garnet, and Kitty Ayrshire have made their way in the world of art by going in precisely the opposite direction—by making the adjustments and compromises that enable them to adapt to the world and to achieve the "worldly" success they need and crave. In contrast, the *Troll Garden* stories contain several figures who come far closer to Cather's ideal. Aunt Georgiana may be a victim, but her response to Wagner, the composer so closely associated with Thea Kronborg, is profound: unlike the people who flock to see and hear Eden Bower, this woman, and the nephew who hosts her as well, recognize the divide between real art and mere entertainment. "A Death in the Desert" gives us in Adriance Hilgarde a musician who is severely flawed, who in his self-absorption can treat those around him cruelly and thoughtlessly, but the story leaves no doubt that he is a composer of surpassing talent, as in the powerful piano sonata ("deeper and nobler" than his "early lyric vein" [295]) that he sends his brother to play for the dying Katharine. Harvey Merrick's art may remain a closed book to most denizens of his hometown, but again the story leaves no question as to his greatness as an artist—indeed, the language used of him foreshadows that by which Cather will describe Thea Kronborg: "Surely, if ever a man had the magic word in his finger tips, it was Merrick. Whatever he touched, he revealed its holiest secret; liberated it from enchantment and restored it to its pristine loveliness" (261–62; cf. Cather's comment that Thea "had only to touch an idea to make it live"). As for Paul, Cather lets us know that he lacks what it takes to be an artist ("He had no desire to become an actor, any more than he had to become a musician . . ." [217]); nevertheless, there is in his response to art an element of transport and surrender that is similar to what Aunt Georgiana feels as she listens to Wagner: "It was not that symphonies, as such, meant anything in particular to Paul, but the first sigh of the instruments seemed to free some hilarious spirit within him; something that struggled there like the Genius in the bottle found by the Arab fisherman. He felt a sudden zest of life; the lights danced before his eyes and the concert hall blazed into unimaginable splendour" (205–6). It is language for which there is no counterpart in the four stories that begin the volume, in all of which the arts have become disciplined, difficult professions in which one can with ambition, talent, persistence, and savvy gain deserved acclaim and reward—but in which there is no hint of the transcendent artistry of a Hilgarde or a Merrick, or of the transport of an Aunt Georgiana, or even a Paul.

If the four final stories of *Youth and the Bright Medusa* reveal by contrast the limitations as well as the strengths of the artists in its four new stories, comparison of these artists with Thea Kronborg is even more telling.[3] It is a contrast Hermione Lee captures when she describes Eden Bower as the "coolly ballooning heroine, quite happy to be the cynosure of all eyes, in a pantomime version of Thea's eagle-like climb on the cliffs . . . ."[4] Not until *Lucy Gayheart* in 1935 will Cather focus another book so explicitly on the arts, and the gulf between the singers in the 1916–19 stories of *Youth* and Thea Kronborg speaks worlds about where Cather herself has traveled in the years since *The Song of the Lark* appeared.[5]

Both the title she chooses for her 1920 collection and the new title she gives to its lead story are also instructive, for Medusa and Aphrodite are goddesses who attract their victims irresistibly and then destroy them.[6] Eden Bower is the Aphrodite who invades Don Hedger's life, enticing him into her arms despite his knowledge of the dangers that lurk in a woman's sexuality (of which he reminds both her and himself in his story of the Aztec princess), and who then abandons him for her Chicago millionaire, who we know will also succumb to her allure. It is significant that on the jacket for this novel Cather uses the new leeway she has from Knopf to call special attention to this story and its theme: "*Coming, Aphrodite!* the first story in the book is perhaps the most interesting from an artistic point of view. Its savage and purely pagan theme loses nothing from being set to an accompaniment of New York asphalt streets and studio skylights. This story of a young painter, drawn by accident under the overwhelming obsession of a woman's beauty, has both the grace and the naked ruthlessness that one expects to find only in a fragment of Greek art." As noted earlier, Cather's portrayal of Hedger is highly ironic, but he still projects an artistic seriousness that Eden Bower lacks, and Cather's jacket précis of his story comes close to describing her own experience of the past five years. She too had been a serious, hard-working Greenwich Village artist—indeed, had herself once lived on Washington Square South; she too had been seduced by an "Eden Bower," so much so that she even aligns herself more with Eden than with Don as she tells their story. The echo in Eden's name of Madison Bowers, Thea's cynical and self-promoting voice teacher, is significant, for it is self-promotion and selling that are both Eden's great strengths and also increasingly Cather's preoccupation by this time. And as we have seen, "Eden" takes us back once more to the Garden, to temptation and the loss of the good and simple life, all relevant to what happens to Don Hedger when he encounters his "Eden," and to Cather when in the years after 1915 she begins to become more Eden than Thea.

The theme Cather identifies as relevant to all the stories, "Youth's adventure with the many-colored Medusa of art," is also apt, for this Medusa lures the central figures of all eight stories into her clutches, then turns them, if not into stone, at least into something not anticipated. Eden Bower as a young woman clearly imagines her future, but there is no suggestion that she foresees just how steep a toll her "big" career will exact—one thinks of the stonelike plaster cast to which her face is reduced at the end, the comparison of it to a sail that has lost its wind. The same is true of Cressida and Kitty, both of whom feel the best years of their careers passing and fear where this Medusa will lead them in the future. The Medusa of art snares the youths of the *Troll Garden* stories as well. It lures the young Paul to his death and sows in the young Georgiana a longing for beauty that will haunt her as the years pass and her youth recedes from sight and even from mind. We get glimpses of the early pull that art exerted upon Harvey Merrick and Katharine Gaylord, including the miseries it inflicted on both, but we see them only at the end, when their youth too has become a distant memory—and they themselves are also stonelike in their dependency.

We have seen that the time and setting of the book's first story, Washington Square in 1906, recall those of Cather's own first years in New York, and that this adventure of Youth with the Medusa of art refracts upon herself. Like so many of the characters in these stories, she too had responded in her youth to this goddess's allure only now to discover that this goddess has led her in directions she could not have foreseen. Like the women in the first four stories, she has achieved very considerable success but, again like them, now finds elements of this success both uncomfortable and inescapable. Like Cressida and Kitty and Eden, she has had to devote a great deal of energy to advertising herself and in doing so has made some conscious sacrifices of her integrity. And like these singers, she finds herself living a private life far less satisfying and glamorous than the image the public has of her—or the image her own publicity creates for her, whether in the 1915 brochure or the *Youth* dust jacket itself. Like so many figures in *Youth*, she feels her dreams receding, and with them her youth. Just five years earlier she had modeled Thea Kronborg largely on herself, and though the final section had acknowledged the paler private life behind the brilliant public image, Cather had, as she herself admits, structured the novel so as to conclude on a strong note of artistic and personal triumph.[7] By 1920 she is far closer to the singers in the first four stories of *Youth*, with Thea a dream almost as distant as Aunt Georgiana's musical studies in "A Wagner Matinée."[8] Her new book breathes a truthfulness that expresses her continuing debt to Sarah Orne Jewett—one reviewer, in words that would have pleased Jewett, spoke of "truth . . . attained with simplicity" and "freshness of feeling."[9] At the same time, her actual life in these years is increasingly devoted to selling herself and her writing—in short, to activities that must have reminded her of Mary Baker Eddy, and with the added irritant that despite her efforts, her books were still returning royalties paltry in comparison to those Eddy had garnered year after year.[10]

The thematic texture of *Youth and the Bright Medusa* suggests how deeply Cather, like many characters in her collection, feels the gulf between the kingdom of art and the philistine world in which artists live, that world to which, if they are to survive, they must sell their work and themselves. The first four stories show admiration for the resilience, resourcefulness, and bravado with which Eden, Cressida, and Kitty do what they must do, maintaining—or at least projecting—not only composure but even a measure of good cheer (e.g., Kitty's pleasure in confronting, and besting, McKann in "The Gold Slipper"). But the stories suggest also the weariness and strain these heroines feel, and that Cather herself was feeling in these years; like Paul, she must frequently have longed for a world insulated from everyday tawdriness. It is a theme she will explore in depth in her next novel, where allied to it are questions that are implicit throughout *Youth* and that will, in different ways, animate her novels of the 1920s: Are there values that transcend the world's focus on material possessions and mere survival, "something splendid" that can justify and motivate heroic striving, be it of the artist or the ordinary human being? Is it possible to be a Thea, not just an Eden or Cressida or Kitty? Even if we can imagine and respond to such transcendent values, as Aunt Georgiana, Katharine Gaylord, Harvey Merrick, and others in the *Troll Garden* stories do, where does it all lead? What comes of these dreams as we age and sicken and die? What remains when these intimations of immortality, like Paul's visions, flash into black and we drop back into the immense design of things?

CHAPTER ELEVEN

One of Ours

It is worth recalling the diverse directions in which Cather was moving during the years when she was writing *One of Ours*. Fresh from the completion of *The Song of the Lark*, and even as she is working on *My Ántonia*, with its Nebraska setting and its ultimately heroic theme, she is also writing a number of stories, largely set in New York, that focus on what people must and will do to make money—the same motivation that in good part is leading her, also in New York, to write these stories. In the same way, even as she is writing "Coming, Eden Bower!" in 1919, another story of the same ilk, and again set in New York, she is well into *One of Ours*, with its Nebraska setting and its idealistic hero. And in the middle of the period in which she is working on *One of Ours* (1918–22), she puts together *Youth and the Bright Medusa* (1920), in it juxtaposing four cosmopolitan stories of 1916–19 with four earlier stories far different in tone and setting.[1] Her ability to juggle such disparate projects bespeaks her versatility and energy, but it also suggests the degree to which her daily life, and her writing, were divided among different models and visions. On the one hand are heroic strivers like Thea and Ántonia and Claude, all of whom, albeit in differing ways, give voice to her own quest for "something splendid"; on the other, highly professional artists bravely dealing with a philistine world—Cressida, Kitty, Eden, women who go about their business in ways that Cather knew all too well, not least at this very time, when she was involved not only in these major writing projects but also in constant promotional efforts on behalf of her books and stories.

The young hero she creates in *One of Ours* is similarly torn, caught as he is between a growing realization of what life is for most people and a strong but vague longing for something better. Claude Wheeler takes us back to such questers as Bartley Alexander and Thea Kronborg, but his nearest counterpart may well be Paul, whose story was on Cather's mind during these very years as she prepared it for inclusion in *Youth and the Bright Medusa*. Like Paul, Claude feels trapped in a world that is tawdry and dull, surrounded by people who are lackluster and petty: "Platitudes, littleness, falseness . . . . His life was choking him . . ." (220). His friend Gladys uses similar language of what awaits if he marries Enid Royce, as he will do: "Claude would become one of those dead people that moved about the streets of Frankfort; everything that was Claude would perish, and the shell of him would come and go and eat and sleep for fifty years" (154–55).

The object of Claude's aspiration, though, is something more intrinsic than the ersatz glamour Paul courts in the Pittsburgh theatre and concert hall and in his New York escapade. And unlike Paul, Claude is willing to work for his ideal. When he discovers at the university a professor who offers him a glimpse of "a subject which seemed to him vital, which had to do with events and ideas, instead of with lexicons and grammars" (37), he throws himself into his work, and when in the second half of the novel he decides that joining the Allied war effort will give his life meaning, he takes on his new responsibilities with similar passion. But there is in him as well a congenital discontent with both his world and himself that fits his jacket description—a "young Hamlet of the prairies" (fig. 12). Although later he finds in the war a cause that satisfies him, in the first part of the book his cravings are inchoate and undefined, the product more of what he knows he loathes than of any clear vision of what he wants, a fact emphasized in the description of him heading off to college: "He is not so much afraid of loneliness as he is of accepting cheap substitutes; . . . of waking up some morning to find himself admiring a girl merely because she is accessible. He has a dread of easy compromises, and he is terribly afraid of being fooled" (34). The halting words in which he voices his discontent to a friend are similarly revealing, suggesting as they do the degree to which he intuits a goal in life mainly from its felt absence: "[I]f we've only got once to live, it seems like there ought to be something—well, something splendid about life, sometimes" (52). When the topic arises in a later conversation with the same friend, Claude is still groping: "Claude knew, and everybody else knew, seemingly, that there was something wrong with him. He had been unable to conceal his discontent. . . . [T]he old belief flashed up in him with an intense kind of hope, an intense kind of pain,—the conviction that there was something splendid about life, if he could but find it!" (103).

Claude finds this "something splendid about life" in his enlistment in the Allied Expeditionary Force. From this moment on, both his language and the language used to describe him change: "There is only one thing we ought to do, and only one thing that matters; we all know it," he tells Gladys when he returns from training camp (231). His assurance remains unshaken as he prepares to leave, as he heads off to war, and as he fights and dies in France, a sharp contrast to the vague longings he has felt and voiced earlier. As he says to his friend David Gerhardt shortly before they both die in combat, "I never knew there was anything worth living for, till this war came on. Before that, the world seemed like a business proposition" (419). A bit later he muses to himself about the war and his role in it: "Ideals were not archaic things, beautiful and impotent; they were the real sources of power among men. As long as that was true, and now he knew it was true—he had come all this way to find out—he had no quarrel with Destiny" (420).

In both his belief that there are values that transcend the ordinariness of everyday existence and his willingness to give his all for them, Claude contrasts sharply with the lead figures in the first four stories of *Youth and the Bright Medusa*, all of whom have come to believe that success entails making peace with the world as it is, accepting the compromises necessary to survival. This is precisely what Claude is unwilling to do, as Gladys remarks before he leaves for France: "If you'd been like all the rest, you could have got on in their way" (259). In turn, the distance Claude maintains between himself and this world of just "getting on" recalls the gulfs between the transcendent and the ordinary that mark the stories in the second half of *Youth*—between Aunt Georgiana's life in Nebraska and the world she reenters in her afternoon with Wagner, between the artistry of Harvey Merrick and the narrow-mindedness of the town that spawned him, between Adriance Hilgarde's mysterious, other-worldly music and his own flawed humanity, between Paul's visions of grandeur and his life on Cordelia Street. There is, however, another crucial similarity between Claude and Paul: just as Cather reveals the delusional character of Paul's quest, so in *One of Ours* she undercuts the "something splendid" that Claude has discovered in life.[2]

The first person at home to whom Claude reveals his plan to enlist is Mahailey, the simple-minded servant who so loves him. She is overjoyed by his decision: "Before he could stop her, before he knew what she was doing, she had caught and kissed his unworthy hand" (233–34). The "unworthy" which Cather drops into this sentence foreshadows the ironic authorial touches we will meet everywhere.[3] There is the description of Claude, on leave before going to France, in love with the nobility of the cause: "He was still burning with the first ardour of the enlisted man. He believed that he was going abroad with an expeditionary force that would make war without rage, with uncompromising generosity and chivalry" (248). There are the comments that follow the soldiers' departing salute to the Statue of Liberty as they head for war: "[T]he scene was ageless; youths were sailing away to die for an idea, a sentiment, for the mere sound of a phrase . . . and on their departure they were making vows to a bronze image in the sea" (274). The irony is yet more marked when they get to France. "Deeper and deeper into flowery France!" is the line that keeps going through Claude's head as the troop train makes its way toward the horrific trenches (339), and Vachel Lindsay's "Bidding the eagles of the west fly on" the patently cynical epigraph to the whole section.[4] In Rouen he and his companions view the Seine and imagine what the river must be like upstream where it passes Paris—"spanned by many bridges, all longer than the bridge over the Missouri at Omaha. There would be spires and golden domes past counting, all the buildings higher than anything in Chicago, and brilliant . . ." (341). Even when he arrives at the trenches, he wishes his mother could know the happiness he feels

(364). In retrospect we recall early hints of Claude's romanticizing cast of mind: the comparison of him to Hippolytus, Euripides' chastity-obsessed (and destruction-bound) youth (56), or his history professor's certainty that Claude would have sided with Joan of Arc in his thesis on her trial (63). When his French host comments that his name, Claude, is "un peu romanesque," even he catches the note of bemusement (351).

Complementing this consistent undercutting of Claude's idealism is the rhythm of disillusionment that Cather has built into the book.[5] She establishes the pattern in the novel's first pages. Claude wakes early to a glorious Nebraska morning: "The sun popped up over the edge of the prairie like a broad smiling face . . . . It was a fine day to go to the circus at Frankfort, a fine day to do anything; the sort of day that must, somehow, turn out well" (2), with "somehow" hinting again at the irony. Claude immediately begins washing the car so that he can drive to the circus. No sooner has he begun than he sees Dan and Jerry, the two hired men, "shambling down the hill," men whom Claude detests. We hear that Jerry's carelessness has injured the faithful old mare, Claude's favorite, and over breakfast Claude's father informs him that he will go to town not in the car he has just washed but on the mule cart, which he hates, and that he will carry in it not only a bunch of smelly hides but also Dan and Jerry. So much for "fine days" that "must turn out well."[6]

Wherever we look, this rhythm persists, whether on the small scale or the large. In Lincoln, Claude finally manages to escape from Temple, the small Bible college he dislikes, and to find at the university a professor whom he admires and friends he enjoys. When he comes home for the summer, his father tells him that the following year he will supervise the farm instead of returning to Lincoln. An attractive girl gives him a ride in Denver, but his good fortune sours when Claude has her drop him at a hotel far more elegant than the one where he is staying, only to reveal his artifice by blushing. Claude walks through the countryside, where it seems there is "a lark on every fencepost" (120), to the Royces' mill, one of his favorite places. No sooner does he arrive than we learn that the water wheel, which Claude loves, is no longer working; that the mill is no longer profitable; and that Mrs. Royce, though she can bake the best cake in the county for a church supper, never serves her husband a meal he can enjoy—an omen of how her daughter Enid will treat Claude after they are married.

The rhythm becomes yet more marked in the portions of the novel that deal with the war. As the troops are riding toward New York, the train stops, they crowd to the side, and suddenly they see spectral hulls of wooden ships, "skeleton vessels," under construction. Though the ghost ships eerily foreshadow their whole future, Claude characteristically gives them a romantic reading: "Wooden ships! When great passions and great aspirations stirred a country, shapes like these formed along its shores to be the sheath of its valour" (267–68). When he arrives at the dock in New York he finds instead that his ship is the aging *Anchises*, aptly named after Aeneas' decrepit father. Once the troops are aboard, their early halcyon days—the "gold curtain" of the sky (283), "fresh-blowing hills of water" (285), "those first long, carefree days at sea" (290)—soon turn to storm, cold, disease: to a soldier's body being "lowered into the cold, leaping indigo ridges that seemed so destitute of anything friendly to human kind" (292); to waves that "had a malignant, graceful, muscular energy, were animated by a kind of mocking cruelty" (293); to a "sinister sunset," clouds that "came up out of the sea,—wild, witchlike shapes that travelled fast and met in the west as if summoned for an evil conclave" (293).[7]

Toward the end of the voyage, Claude again begins to revel in his escape from Frankfort, his newfound feeling of "fateful purpose," only in the next episodes to face the same sort of financial sharpers he thinks he has left behind—the venal steward of the ship, whom Claude must help blackmail to gain the food that will save a fellow officer's life; a French shopkeeper from whom Claude manages with his fledgling French to get cheese for his men only to find that he has been badly cheated. In France, Claude and his men glory as they go "through every village in march step, colours flying, the band playing. . . . They were bound for the big show . . ." (358). But the "big show" quickly turns to the muck of the battlefield and to a French family whose widowed mother is dying even as she nurses her child, himself the product of her rape by a German soldier. Claude and David pay a visit to a family whose son studied music along with David in Paris; we soon learn that this son is now dead, and David tells how his own violin was smashed. Claude speaks of having at last found in this war something "worth living for," only to be drily reminded by David, "You'll admit it's a costly way of providing adventure for the young" (419).

This rhythm's incessant downward pull, woven as it is into page after page of the novel, achieves a powerful cumulative effect, especially as it mirrors the similar disillusionments that occur on the larger scale. The primary such disillusionment in the first half of the novel comes in Claude's marriage. As Enid Royce nurses him after an accident, he begins to imagine that in love and marriage he may find something to make life in Frankfort worth living: "Enid was meant for him and she had come for him; he would never let her go" (145). But then reality strikes. Enid's father warns him that he will "find out that pretty nearly everything you believe about life—about marriage, especially—is lies" (150). Enid accepts his proposal and lets him kiss her for the first time; immediately after, "[a] terrible melancholy clutched at the boy's heart. He hadn't thought it would be like this" (154). En route to Denver his wife locks him out of their stateroom on their wedding night; his "storm of anger, disappointment, and humiliation" fades, but he cannot forget the "peculiarly casual, indifferent, uninterested tone of his wife's voice" as she sent him away (196–97). Later, as he ponders the marriage for which he had held such high hopes, Claude admits to himself, "It's the end of everything for me" (210).[8]

Balancing the collapse of Claude's dreams for love and marriage in the first part of the novel is the undermining of his idealized vision of war in the second. While Claude himself never quite recognizes the folly of his dreams, never fully faces the war's ugly refutation of his romanticized imaginings, Cather leaves the reader in no doubt. Again and again she confronts us with the horror of war. There are Claude's own soldiers being brought wounded into the hospital after the first battles: "Their skin was yellow or purple, their eyes were sunken, their lips sore. Everything that belonged to health had left them, every attribute of youth was gone. . . . To shed bright blood, to wear the red badge of courage,—that was one thing; but to be reduced to this was quite another. Surely, the sooner these boys died, the better" (335). There is the horror of the English "Pal Battalion," young men who had known each other as students and of whom, when they are sent into battle, seventeen out of one thousand survive. There is the French town that has been fought over by both sides, where even Claude for a moment sees war for what it is: "Ruin was ugly . . . . There was nothing picturesque about this, as there was in the war pictures one saw at home. . . . The place was simply a great dump-heap . . ." (380). There is the horror of the final trench battle, with the bodies of those who have recently died grotesquely reaching from the mud, and from the lime in which they have been buried, as if to grasp the living and pull them down.[9] Claude dies bravely, but his mother's comments leave no doubt as to how we are to interpret his death. As she reads of those brave soldiers who did not die, and who kill themselves on their return, she is thankful that Claude did not come back: "[A]s she reads, she thinks those slayers of themselves were all so like him; they were the ones who had hoped extravagantly,—who in order to do what they did had to hope extravagantly, and to believe passionately. And they found they had hoped and believed too much. But one she knew, who could ill bear disillusion . . . safe, safe" (458–59).[10]

One of Ours gives us a hero who dreams of great deeds, believes in great possibilities, and follows his dreams—quests that Eden Bower, Cressida Garnet, and Kitty Ayrshire have long since surrendered, if they ever thought of them. But the novel repeatedly casts doubt on Claude's accomplishment, undercutting his idealism by revealing its lack of purpose in the first half of the novel and, in the second, when he finds his life's meaning in the war, consistently coloring his story with an irony that tempers whatever respect we may feel. In addition, at every level the novel's ubiquitous rhythms raise hopes only to puncture them, project dreams only to reveal how foolish they are, and how destructive when realized. We are instinctively drawn to Claude's courage and idealism, but we are left with a world in which human aspiration proves hollow and humans themselves are doomed to failure and death. It is a world far darker than that of the first stories in *Youth*, where artistic ideals are faded but the talented singers at least know what they are doing, and why, and go about doing it with persistence and panache.

Underscoring the darkness is the fact that the portion of the country which was so integral to the heroic achievement of Cather's great women of the teens—and which she, with Jewett's encouragement, had seen as so rich a source for her own writing—in *One of Ours* is itself in decline. Claude's father had come to Nebraska "when the Indians and the buffalo were still about, remembered the grasshopper year and the big cyclone, had watched the farms emerge one by one from the great rolling page where once only the wind wrote its story" (6).[11] In his place—again the rhythm of decline—are people like his oldest son, Bayliss, "a narrow-gauge fellow," "thin and dyspeptic, and a virulent Prohibitionist; he would have liked to regulate everybody's diet by his own feeble constitution" (7–8). As Claude drives to town, he ponders the diminished life of farmers in his time: "The farmer raised and took to market things with an intrinsic value . . . . In return he got manufactured articles of poor quality . . . . With prosperity came a kind of callousness; everybody wanted to destroy the old things they used to take pride in" (101–2). Instead of the West providing the locus for heroism, in *One of Ours*, as Guy Reynolds puts it, "Claude's idealistic sense of the 'something splendid' explicitly shifts from its American context to a setting in France." Claude even thinks of buying a farm in France: as Reynolds remarks, the Eden once to be found in America, whether by Cather or her heroic figures, is no longer there.[12]

Frankfort instead represents for Claude everything he wishes to flee— "platitudes, littleness, falseness" (220); rubbish, junk; people more concerned with machines than with people, people whose overwhelming concern is with money: "One of [Claude's] chief difficulties had always been that he could not make himself believe in the importance of making money or spending it. If that were all, then life was not worth the trouble" (38).[13] This life he is fleeing is eerily reminiscent of that which we meet in the first four stories of *Youth and the Bright Medusa*, and the singers in those stories are just the sort of people with whom Claude does not wish to spend his life—compromisers, people whose concern is with making the best of life, with getting on, people who enjoy having things.

We have seen that Cather herself in these very years was increasingly concerned with just such matters, was increasingly seeing herself as similar to the brave but life-worn singers of these first stories in *Youth*. In *One of Ours* she writes a book in which her hero is a Nebraska boy imbued with the idealism she herself had once felt and who flees both the sort of life she is now living and the sort of person she is now becoming.[14] That not only does he die in the search but that even the object of his quest proves profoundly tainted underscores the pessimism of the novel. At least the alternatives represented by Thea on the one hand, the singers of the 1916–19 stories on the other, both offer much that is positive. *One of Ours* projects a far bleaker choice: on the one hand, life in Frankfort, with all its pettiness and meaninglessness and smallness of spirit; on the other, Claude's large-hearted, courageous quest—but with our knowledge that it is in vain, and for an empty, even evil cause. It is easy to understand why Cather in retrospect identified 1922, the year in which *One of Ours* appeared, as the year in which "the world broke in two."

Given all this, it is no surprise that one more movement Cather builds into the novel is that of division, of things and persons broken apart. Claude ends up torn from his family, from his wife, from his home, and at the end from David, his closest friend, who also dies. His ideals also shatter, miss their mark. As soon as he finds something worth doing, it is taken from him: he meets a woman who he thinks will bring companionship and love only to find instead that living with her is the ultimate loneliness; he believes that he has found in his service in France the "something splendid" he has sought for so long, but Cather makes us see it instead as tainted, ugly, and worse than meaningless.

In keeping with this rhythm of division, Claude himself lives that double life so common in Cather heroes and heroines. His mother imagines the "inner kingdom" of his mind (69); as he tries to come to terms with the misery of his marriage, he recognizes that "[i]nside of living people, too, captives languished" (207), prisoners like the one now penned inside himself that he must hide from his wife and the world. Under these circumstances, he finds his only solace among the ash trees of his timber claim, where he can lie in the sun and let his imagination play with life:

"His thoughts, he told himself, were his own. He was no longer a boy. He went off into the timber claim to meet a young man more experienced and interesting than himself, who had not tied himself up with compromises" (212). Earlier in the book a passing line describes Claude and his mother watching a snowstorm, "together in the pale, clear square of the west window, as the two natures in one person sometimes meet and cling in a fated hour" (87). When Claude heads off to war, it seems that at last his two sides have come together, that he can finally devote his external life to seeking his inner ideal. It seems a union like that which Thea achieves: despite the dualities of her existence—the glamour of the stage uneasily paired with the dreariness of her daily round—she is at least devoting her life, all of it, to fostering her ideal. But whereas Thea's union of these two sides leads to glorious accomplishment, to a life that at least touches "something splendid," Claude's comparable "union" leads not only to his death but to a life wasted for an empty ideal.[15]

Just how empty becomes clear in his mother's final comments.[16] As she reads the papers about the war and ponders Claude's death, "it seemed as if the flood of meanness and greed had been held back just long enough for the boys to go over, and then swept down and engulfed everything that was left at home. When she can see nothing that has come of it all but evil, she reads Claude's letters over again and reassures herself; for him the call was clear, the cause was glorious. Never a doubt stained his bright faith. . . . He died believing his own country better than it is, and France better than any country can ever be" (458).

Her comment that "nothing . . . has come of it all but evil" suggests that Cather's theme goes beyond Claude's personal tragedy. Early in the book, when his mother has just read him Milton's description of Hell, Claude makes a comment that suddenly recalls Mary Baker Eddy—and Cather's concern with Eddy's view of evil: "It just struck me," he says, "that this part is so much more interesting than the books about perfect innocence in Eden" (86). The irony of his remark is that Claude himself, like Eddy, is someone who minimizes evil's ubiquity and power—indeed, in one Eddy-like moment he even imagines that he might escape death: "[H]e sometimes felt sure that he, Claude Wheeler, would escape; that he would actually invent some clever shift to save himself from dissolution" (50). We know how Willa Cather felt about such foolish optimism, be it Claude's or Eddy's, and the rest of *One of Ours* both refutes his notion that he might escape death and provides a reductio ad absurdum for his notion that life is more interesting in hell than it is in Eden. The whole second half of the novel surrounds him with death, and with evidence of evil's omnipresence. When Claude's mother at the end speaks of "nothing coming of it all but evil," she is echoing an earlier passage describing the spread of the war and "the destruction of civilian populations. Something new, and certainly evil, was at work among mankind" (167). We can only compare this "something new, and certainly evil," with the "something splendid" that Cather's hero sought, and for which he loses his life.

There are other troubling echoes of Mary Baker Eddy as well. Though Claude is very different from Eddy in his generosity of spirit, he has a violent temper, his strength often asserts itself "inharmoniously," and "[t]he storms that went on in his mind sometimes made him rise, or sit down, or lift something, more violently than there was any apparent reason for his doing" (17).[17] Violent, inharmonious, the storm of the mind—and in a child who felt, and was, out of tune with those around him: all of this, not least the language itself, strongly recalls what Cather had written about Eddy. So does the fact that Claude, like Eddy, is adrift until he suddenly finds his calling, his ideal, in "the final adventure which releases the baffled energy of the boy's nature," as the novel's jacket puts it—language similar to that which Cather had used to describe Eddy's discovery of her mission. And once he finds his "mission," Claude serves it with the same unthinking certitude that Eddy brought to hers. Given the ravages of war that fill the second half of this novel, and the role of "noble ideals" in motivating this war, we recall the question Cather at one point asks about Mary Baker Eddy—"whether there is anything else in the world that can be quite so cruel as the service of an ideal" (*MBE* 324). It is a cruelty in which Claude is doubly implicated, for he both serves this ideal and becomes its victim.

If echoes of Eddy implicitly impugn Claude's quest, so does Cather's jacket description of him as "a sort of young Hamlet of the prairies," words we know are her own.[18] Shakespeare's play was a frequent topic of Cather's essays during her college years, and from those essays two recurrent themes emerge. First, *Hamlet* was to Cather not only Shakespeare's greatest play but a "Holy Thing," something comparable to the ark with its censer of fire in the lives of the early Israelites: "That play and the Magna Charta are the two most worthy things that the Anglo-Saxon people has done from its beginning" (*KA* 306). Second, Hamlet himself, for all his soaring language and rich humanity, is clearly mad: "The madness of Hamlet is the highest point in tragedy which Shakespeare ever reached," Cather wrote in an 1891 essay. Three years later she went yet further in resisting the idea that Hamlet's madness is merely feigned: "Give Hamlet one grain of common sense and you have no play at all. Everything depends upon his being beautifully but unreasonably stupid" (*KA* 431, 303). Cather commented that these last words were overstated for emphasis, and carried a grain of humor, but the fact remains that she insists from the start on the reality of Hamlet's delusions, and this fact must certainly color our response to her description of Claude as a "Hamlet of the prairies." His devotion to the cause of the war may, in the jacket's words, "release the baffled energy of the boy's nature," but at every level *One of Ours* raises questions as to the uses he makes of this released energy. That Cather associates Claude with Hamlet in her description of the novel but underscores the validity of such questions.

The Garden of The Heart

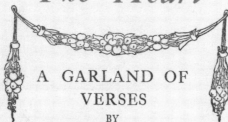

A GARLAND OF
VERSES

BY

Ethelwyn Wetherald
Edith M. Thomas
Harriet Prescott Spofford
Hattie Horner Louthan
Clifford Lanier
Roy Farrell Greene
Marian Douglas
Herman Montague Donner
Virginia Woodward Cloud
James Courtney Challiss
Willa Sibert Cather
Mary M. Adams

BOSTON
RICHARD G. BADGER
1903

Figure 1. *The Garden of the Heart*, containing Willa Cather's poem "Paris" (Richard Badger, 1903).

LITERARY NOTE.

MISS WILLA SIBERT CATHER, whose first book, a delightful volume of poems entitled *April Twilights*, will be published at once, was born near Winchester, Va., in 1876. When she was ten years old, the family moved to a ranch in Southwestern Nebraska, and for two years the child ran wild, living mostly on horseback, scouring the sparsely-settled country, visiting the Danes and Norwegians, tasting the wild-plum wine made by the old women, and playing with the little herd girls, who wore men's hats, and were not in the least afraid of rattlesnakes, which they killed with clods of earth. Even when the family moved later to Red Cloud, she still kept up her friendship for the Norwegian farmer folk, whose business brought them often to her father's office During the ranch period and for some time after going to Red Cloud, Miss Cather did not go to school at all, and her only reading was an old copy of Ben Jonson's plays, a Shakespeare, a Byron, and *The Pilgrim's Progress*, which latter she said she read through eight times in one winter. The first two years of her course at the University of Nebraska, where she graduated in 1895, were spent in the hardest kind of study, but then she discovered herself and began to write a little, mostly for her own pleasure and to satisfy the new craving for expression. She edited a creditable college magazine, and did remarkably discriminating dramatic criticism for the *Nebraska State Journal*. With all this she read voraciously, both in French and in English, and laid the foundation of her wide acquaintance with both literatures. Every vacation she went back to the sunflowers and the Norwegians, where she says she found her real life and her real education. After graduation she wrote for the *Lincoln* (Neb.) *Courier*, and in 1896 she came to Pittsburg, where she was for several years on the staff of the *Leader*, doing clever dramatic and literary criticism in addition to her regular work.

Figure 2. (left) Order form for Cather's *April Twilights* (Richard Badger, 1903).

Figure 3. (above) "Literary Note," written by Cather to accompany order form for *April Twilights* (Richard Badger, 1903).

THE SONG OF
THE LARK

By
WILLA
SIBERT
CATHER

The story of a singer, her childhood
in the Colorado desert, her early
struggles in Chicago, her romantic
adventures among the ruins of the
Cliff Dwellers in Arizona, her splendid
triumphs on the operatic stage.

Figure 4. Brochure promoting Cather's *The Song of the Lark* (Houghton Mifflin, 1915).

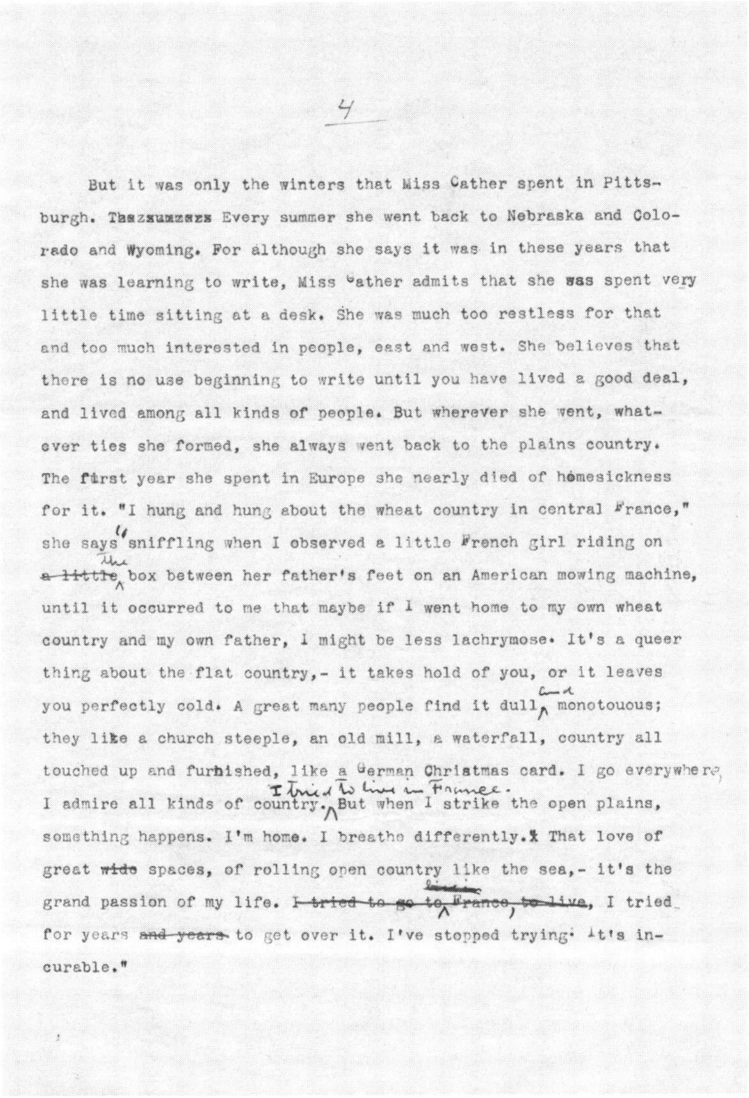

But it was only the winters that Miss Cather spent in Pittsburgh. Thezxumzsrs Every summer she went back to Nebraska and Colorado and Wyoming. For although she says it was in these years that
she was learning to write, Miss Cather admits that she was spent very
little time sitting at a desk. She was much too restless for that
and too much interested in people, east and west. She believes that
there is no use beginning to write until you have lived a good deal,
and lived among all kinds of people. But wherever she went, whatever ties she formed, she always went back to the plains country.
The first year she spent in Europe she nearly died of homesickness
for it. "I hung and hung about the wheat country in central France,"
she says sniffling when I observed a little French girl riding on
a little the box between her father's feet on an American mowing machine,
until it occurred to me that maybe if I went home to my own wheat
country and my own father, I might be less lachrymose. It's a queer
thing about the flat country,- it takes hold of you, or it leaves
you perfectly cold. A great many people find it dull and monotouous;
they like a church steeple, an old mill, a waterfall, country all
touched up and furbished, like a German Christmas card. I go everywhere,
I admire all kinds of country. I tried to live in France. But when I strike the open plains,
something happens. I'm home. I breathe differently.% That love of
great wide spaces, of rolling open country like the sea,- it's the
grand passion of my life. I tried to go to France, to live, I tried
for years and years to get over it. I've stopped trying. It's incurable."

Figure 5. Typescript of Cather's "A Biographical Sketch," 1926. Used by
permission of the Caspersen Collection at Drew University.

"Oh, that remains to be seen! My train is called."

"One general question on the way down, please. What do you consider the greatest obstacle American writers have to overcome?"

"Well, waxx what do other writers tell you?"

"Some say commercialism, and some say Prohibition."

"I don't exactly agree with either. I should say it was the lecture-bug *but*. In this country a writer ~~can get on at all only by being rude to womens clubs and colleges. He,her she,~~ has to hide and lie and almost steal *in order to get* time to work in¬and peace of mind to work with. Besides, lecturing is very dangerous for writers. If we lecture, we get a little more owlish and self-satisfied all the time. We hate it at first, if we are decently modest, but in the end we fall in love with the sound of our own voice. There is something insidious about it, destructive to ones finer feelings. All human beings, apparently, like to speak in public. The timid man becomes bold, the man who has never had an opinion about anything becomes chock full of them the moment he faces an audience. A woman, alas, becomes even fuller! Really, I've seen people's reality quite destroyed by the habit of putting on a ra rostrum front. It's especially destructive to writers, ever so much worse than alcohol, takes their edge off. ~~Why? Certainly I~~

~~ZWixxxx~~ "But why, why?"

"Certainly, I can't tell you now. He's calling 'all aboard'. Try it out yourself; go lecture to a Sunday School or a class of ~~help-~~

~~less~~

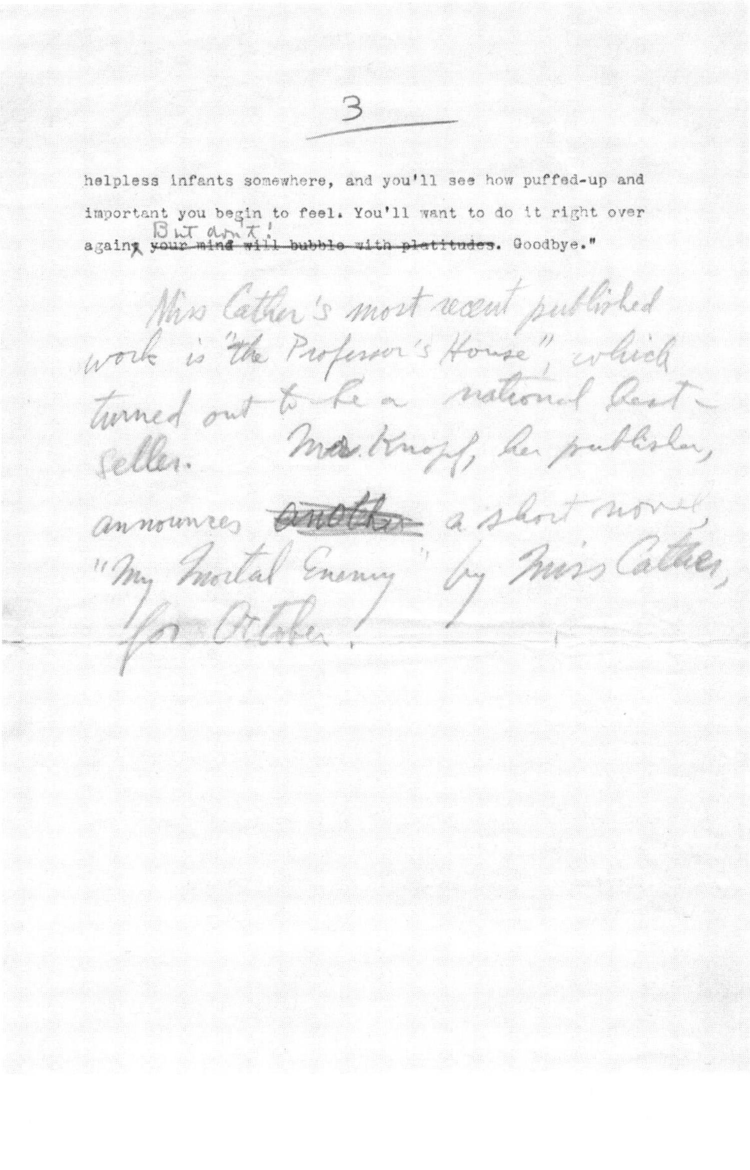

helpless infants somewhere, and you'll see how puffed-up and
important you begin to feel. You'll want to do it right over
again, ~~your mind will bubble with platitudes~~. Goodbye."

But don't!

Miss Cather's most recent published
work is "the Professor's House", which
turned out to be a national bestseller. Mrs. Knopf, her publisher,
announces ~~another~~ a short novel,
"My Mortal Enemy" by Miss Cather,
for October!

Figure 6. Typescript, untitled, of Cather's "Interview at Grand Central," 1926.
Used by permission of the Caspersen Collection at Drew University.

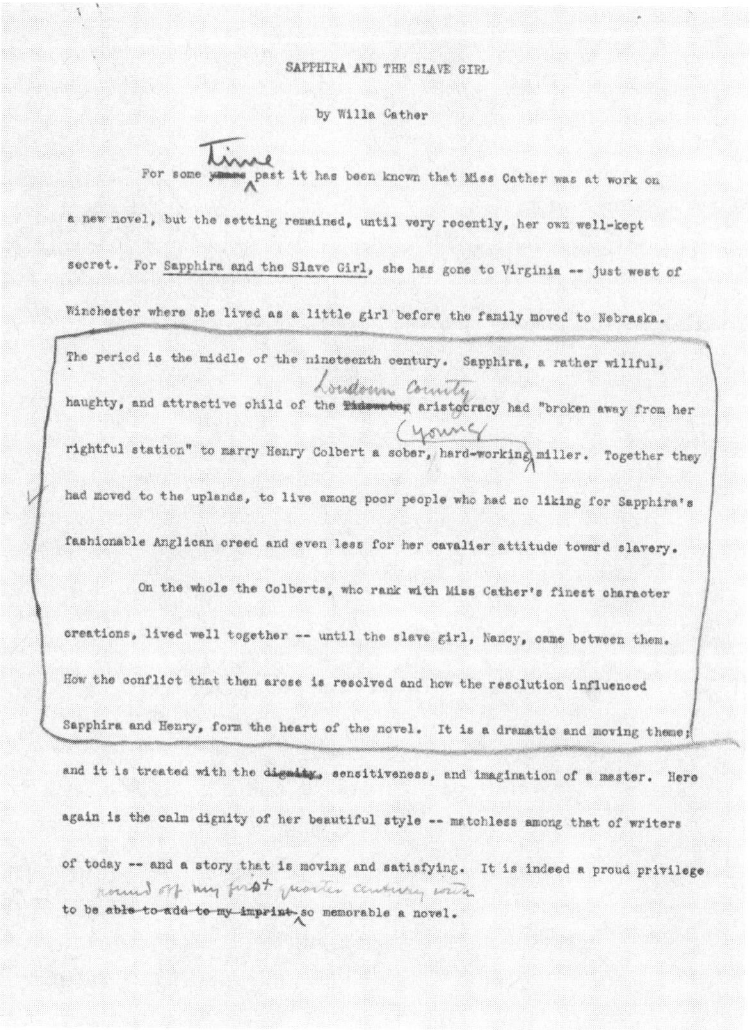

SAPPHIRA AND THE SLAVE GIRL

by Willa Cather

For some ~~years~~ *Time* past it has been known that Miss Cather was at work on

a new novel, but the setting remained, until very recently, her own well-kept

secret. For Sapphira and the Slave Girl, she has gone to Virginia -- just west of

Winchester where she lived as a little girl before the family moved to Nebraska.

The period is the middle of the nineteenth century. Sapphira, a rather willful,

haughty, and attractive child of the ~~Tidewater~~ *Loudoun County* aristocracy had "broken away from her

rightful station" to marry Henry Colbert a sober, hard-working *(young)* miller. Together they

had moved to the uplands, to live among poor people who had no liking for Sapphira's

fashionable Anglican creed and even less for her cavalier attitude toward slavery.

On the whole the Colberts, who rank with Miss Cather's finest character

creations, lived well together -- until the slave girl, Nancy, came between them.

How the conflict that then arose is resolved and how the resolution influenced

Sapphira and Henry, form the heart of the novel. It is a dramatic and moving theme;

and it is treated with the ~~dignity,~~ sensitiveness, and imagination of a master. Here

again is the calm dignity of her beautiful style -- matchless among that of writers

of today -- and a story that is moving and satisfying. It is indeed a proud privilege

to be ~~able to add to my imprint~~ *round off my first quarter century with* so memorable a novel.

Figure 7. Draft (not by Cather) of jacket copy for *Sapphira and the Slave Girl*. From the David and Helen Porter Collection.

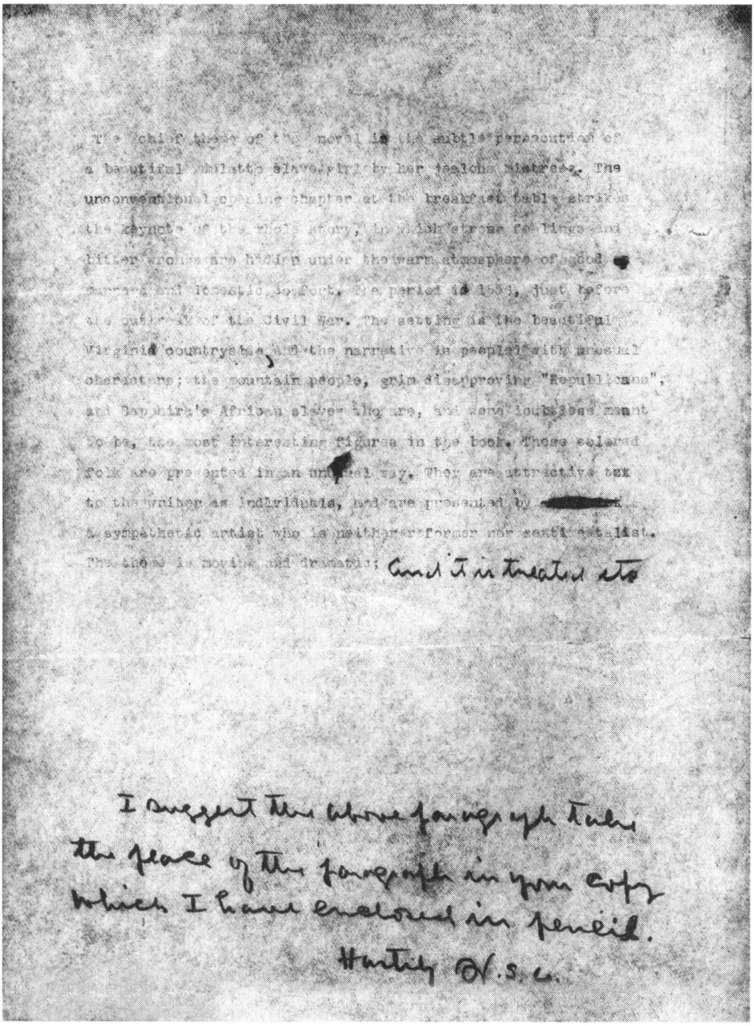

Figure 8. Cather's revision of jacket copy for *Sapphira and the Slave Girl*. From the David and Helen Porter Collection.

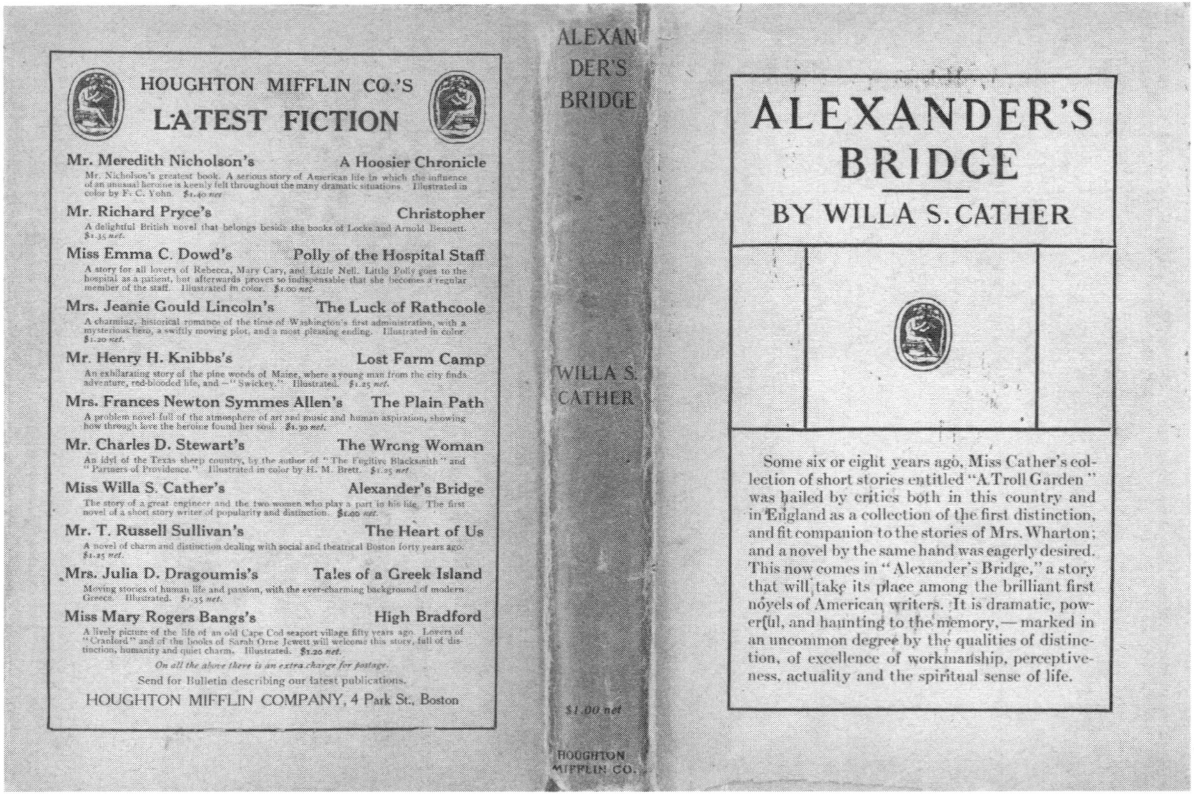

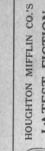

Figure 9. Dust jacket from *Alexander's Bridge* (Houghton Mifflin, 1912).

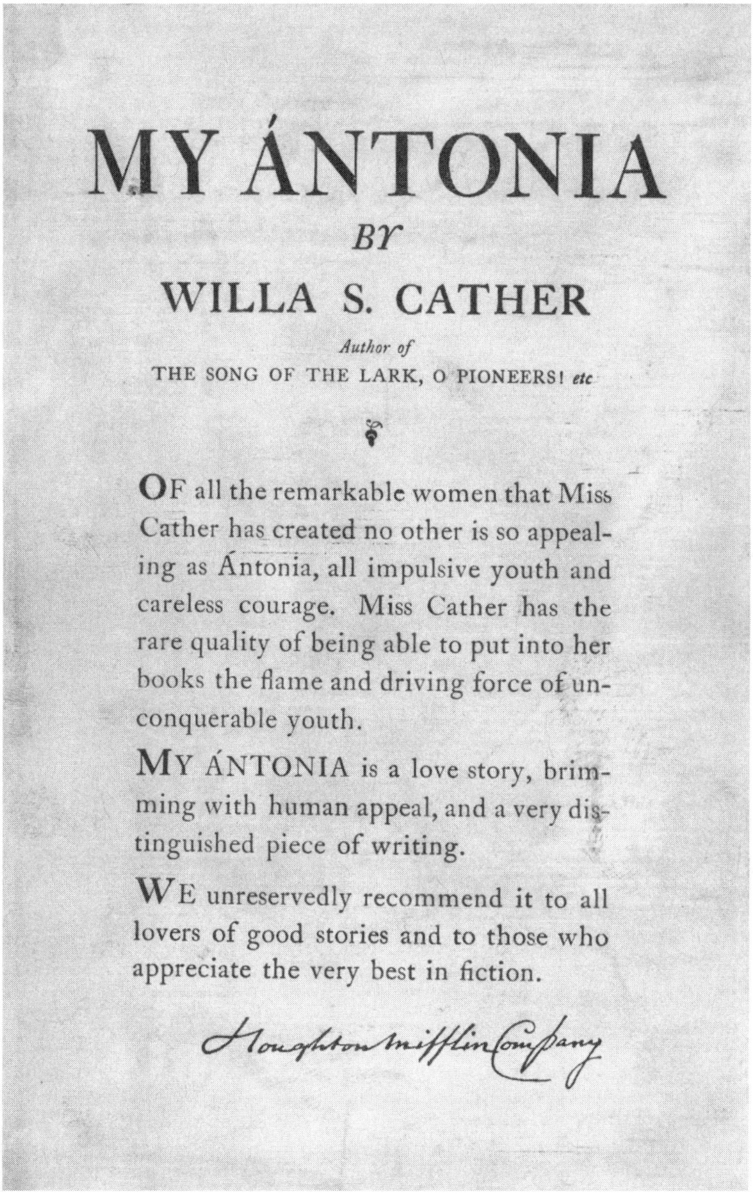

MY ÁNTONIA

BY

WILLA S. CATHER

Author of
THE SONG OF THE LARK, O PIONEERS! *etc*

❦

OF all the remarkable women that Miss Cather has created no other is so appealing as Ántonia, all impulsive youth and careless courage. Miss Cather has the rare quality of being able to put into her books the flame and driving force of unconquerable youth.

MY ÁNTONIA is a love story, brimming with human appeal, and a very distinguished piece of writing.

WE unreservedly recommend it to all lovers of good stories and to those who appreciate the very best in fiction.

Houghton Mifflin Company

Figure 10. Dust jacket from *My Ántonia* (Houghton Mifflin, 1918).

[continued from front of jacket]

human experience and emotion, the daring play of her imagination, that make each of these stories stand out as a separate new discovery about character and life.

Coming, Aphrodite! the first story in the book is perhaps the most interesting from an artistic point of view. Its savage and purely pagan theme loses nothing from being set to an accompaniment of New York asphalt streets and studio skylights. This story of a young painter, drawn by accident under the overwhelming obsession of a woman's beauty, has both the grace and the naked ruthlessness that one expects to find only in a fragment of Greek art. *The Diamond Mine,* the story of a great singer's life, is a whole novel resolved into its elements and foreshortened with an ironic simplicity.

The last four stories in the volume are republished from Miss Cather's early work. *The Sculptor's Funeral* and *Paul's Case* are the stories that first won a reputation for their author. *Paul's Case* has been studied, imitated, plagarized by young writers as perhaps only O. Henry's "The Unfinished Story" has been. In finish and execution Miss Cather has travelled a long way, but the same ardor and restless energy of imagination which give her work the stamp of genius, flame out amazingly in these earlier tales.

ALFRED A.
K N O P F

$2.25 net

A New Book of Stories by the Author of

"My Antonia"

By WILLA CATHER

T HERE are not many living writers from whom a new book commands the mixture of excitement, anticipation, and curious respect with which each successive volume of Miss Cather's is now awaited.

This collection of eight stories is a new exhibition of the writer's power and remarkable artistry. The theme on which all the stories more or less loosely hang—youth's adventure with the many-colored Medusa of art—is in itself fascinating; but it is the writer's quick, bold cutting into the very tissues of

[continued on back of wrapper]

ALFRED A. KNOPF PUBLISHER, N.Y.

WILLA CATHER

wrote her first short story some fifteen years ago. It was published in *McClures*, having been accepted by correspondence with the author, who was in the West. She was also asked to come east as a member of the magazine's staff. For several years she devoted herself to editorial work in New York and abroad. It was in Italy curiously enough, that she wrote her first story about the prairie country of the West, where she spent her childhood, and which has since become so much her field. The next summer, which she spent in London on magazine business, found an echo in her first novel, "Alexandra's Bridge," published in 1912.

"My Antonia" was her last published work prior to the present one.

Figure 11. Dust jacket from *Youth and the Bright Medusa* (Alfred A. Knopf, 1920). Used by permission of Alfred A. Knopf, a division of Random House, Inc.

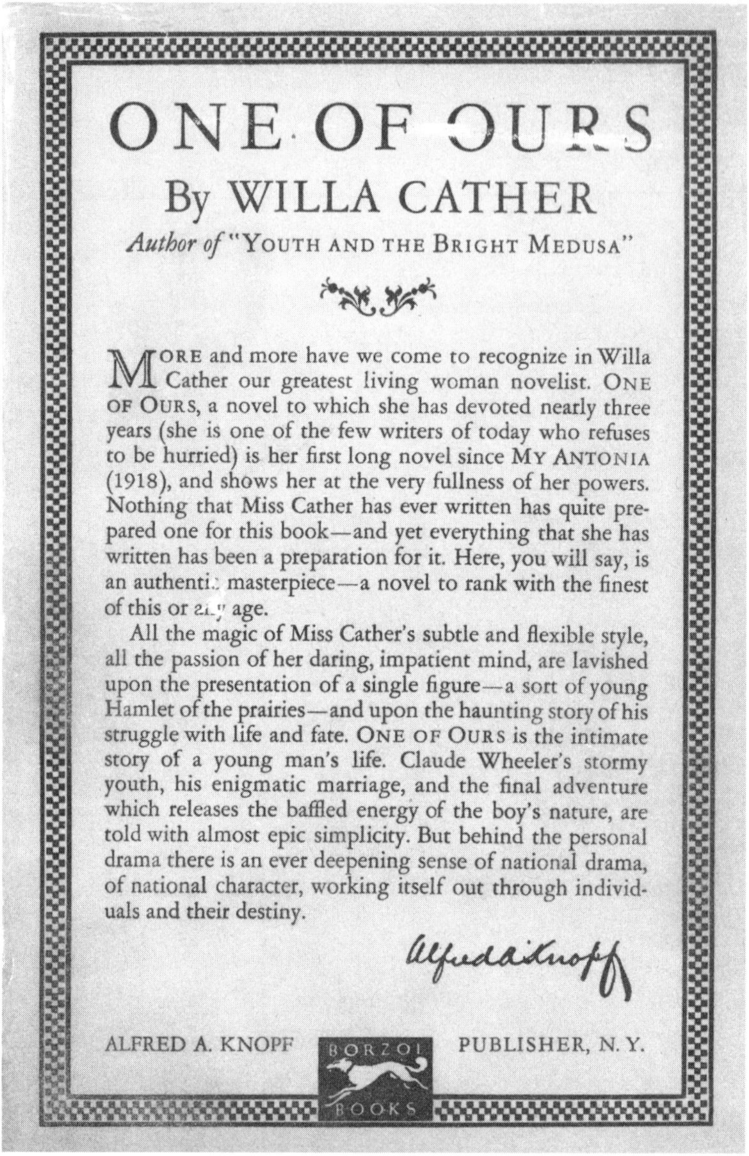

ONE·OF OURS
By WILLA CATHER
Author of "YOUTH AND THE BRIGHT MEDUSA"

MORE and more have we come to recognize in Willa Cather our greatest living woman novelist. ONE OF OURS, a novel to which she has devoted nearly three years (she is one of the few writers of today who refuses to be hurried) is her first long novel since MY ANTONIA (1918), and shows her at the very fullness of her powers. Nothing that Miss Cather has ever written has quite prepared one for this book—and yet everything that she has written has been a preparation for it. Here, you will say, is an authentic masterpiece—a novel to rank with the finest of this or any age.

All the magic of Miss Cather's subtle and flexible style, all the passion of her daring, impatient mind, are lavished upon the presentation of a single figure—a sort of young Hamlet of the prairies—and upon the haunting story of his struggle with life and fate. ONE OF OURS is the intimate story of a young man's life. Claude Wheeler's stormy youth, his enigmatic marriage, and the final adventure which releases the baffled energy of the boy's nature, are told with almost epic simplicity. But behind the personal drama there is an ever deepening sense of national drama, of national character, working itself out through individuals and their destiny.

Alfred A. Knopf

ALFRED A. KNOPF   PUBLISHER, N.Y.

Figure 12. Dust jacket from *One of Ours* (Alfred A. Knopf, 1922). Used by permission of Alfred A. Knopf, a division of Random House, Inc.

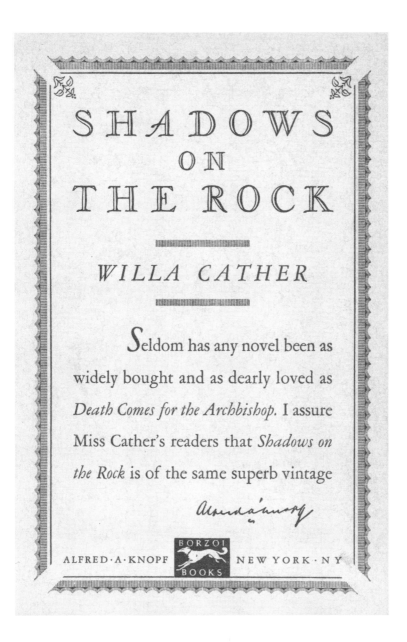

SHADOWS ON THE ROCK

WILLA CATHER

Seldom has any novel been as widely bought and as dearly loved as *Death Comes for the Archbishop*. I assure Miss Cather's readers that *Shadows on the Rock* is of the same superb vintage

Alfred A. Knopf

ALFRED·A·KNOPF   BORZOI BOOKS   NEW YORK·NY

Figure 13. Dust jacket from *Shadows on the Rock*, first edition (Alfred A. Knopf, 1931). Used by permission of Alfred A. Knopf, a division of Random House, Inc.

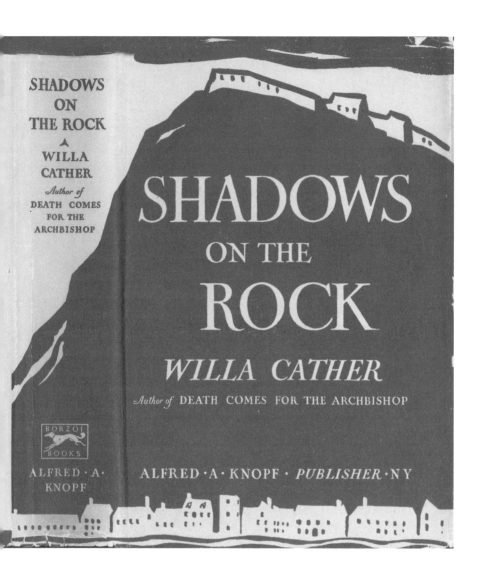

Figure 14. Dust jacket from *Shadows on the Rock*, first edition, fifth printing
(Alfred A. Knopf, 1931). Used by permission of Alfred A. Knopf, a division of
Random House, Inc.

Part V
"The Seeming Original Injustice"

In *The Song of the Lark* Cather's heroine attains her extraordinary success by combining artistic genius with determination, savvy, and toughness. Though these two sides pull in different directions and leave Thea living two lives, both sides are essential to her success. In the stories Cather wrote immediately after this novel, and especially in the four that focus on singers, the heroines have Thea's professional drive and know-how, often to an admirable degree, but little of her transcendent artistry. *One of Ours* moves in the opposite direction, giving us a hero who devotes his energies to fleeing the everyday rat race in order to pursue a transporting vision. Although we admire his idealism, Cather makes us aware that what he sees as glorious is anything but that. To put it differently, while she explicitly associates Thea's quest with truthfulness, an association that honors what Cather so admired in Jewett, in *One of Ours* she makes us realize, as Claude's mother realizes, that Claude's quest seems good to him only because he does not see its ugly truth.

The next three novels Cather writes also focus on figures who, like Claude, seek to rise above the mundane and grasping world around them, and again she shapes their stories in such a way as to test the validity of their quests. But while in *One of Ours* Claude seeks "something splendid" primarily as an alternative to the tawdriness of the surrounding world, the next three novels add to this focus a pervasive emphasis on another feature of the world we inhabit—mortality itself. The threat posed to Marian Forrester, to Godfrey St. Peter and Tom Outland, and to Myra Henshawe is not only the greed and small-mindedness of the surrounding society; it is also the fact that they themselves, for all their courage and aspiration, are mortal. Like all humans, they too will age, sicken, and die.[1]

The two choices that occupied Cather's mind in the teens, and on which her fiction plays constant variations, were the quest for the ideal on the one hand, the reality of making one's way, earning a living, and garnering success on the other. At their best, as in Thea, these choices complemented each other, albeit uneasily; at their worst they pulled against each other, but at least the focus of both was on life. In the twenties this tension transmutes into something both darker and more profound: on the one hand there is now the human capacity to dream immortal dreams, to devote our lives to "something splendid," on the other the erosive downward pull not only of everyday life but of our very mortality. When in her 1931 essay "Escapism" Cather evokes this central dichotomy, she uses language that suggests a redefinition of evil itself: "the seeming original injustice that creatures so splendidly aspiring should be inexorably doomed to fail; the unfairness of the contest in which beings whose realest life is in thought or endeavour are kept always under the shackles of their physical body . . ." (WCOW 22). While life was the presupposition of the choices focal in the teens, death becomes the central given in the twenties, a fact already implicit in the death of the idealistic young hero of One of Ours.[2] This given now colors both choices, just as the quest for life colored the choices focal to the fiction of the teens. One may still dream immortal dreams, but as Claude's story shows, our dreaming them in no way negates our mortality, and the dreams themselves may be horribly flawed. If our dreams are both evanescent and misguided, may it not be a better choice to accommodate oneself to the realities of the world and at least wrest the most out of living while one can?

Once again, these themes in the novels of the twenties have their counterparts in Cather's life, for it is a period in which she was both reaching new artistic heights and also, as she passed the age of fifty, becoming all too aware of the encroachments of mortality. Her novels are coming ever closer to the ideals she has set for herself, are winning ever more recognition, are even at last earning substantial royalties, but what good does all this do her as she battles fatigue, chronic sickness, loss of energy and patience, and as she sees ever more clearly that her youth and her best years lie behind her, with death the one certainty ahead? She has since her university days embraced the lonely quest to write immortal masterpieces. That quest continues—indeed, the period that begins with *A Lost Lady* and stretches through *Death Comes for the Archbishop* represents perhaps the greatest creative surge of her career— and one side of her takes deep satisfaction as she sees herself creating fiction that will surely outlive her. At the same time, the stresses and strains of her career, including the act of writing itself, daily remind her of the mortal world in which she lives, and of the mortality to which she herself is bound: if this is the "something splendid" to which she has given her life, is it all that splendid? Does creating immortal art salve the fact of one's mortality or compensate for the drudgery this activity entails? These questions, implicit in *One of Ours*, rise ever closer to the surface in the novels of the midtwenties, *A Lost Lady*, *The Professor's House*, and *My Mortal Enemy*, and it is on a related note that Cather ends her preface to the Jewett stories she edits in 1924–25.

CHAPTER TWELVE

A Lost Lady

Niel Herbert, the narrator in *A Lost Lady*, shares with Claude Wheeler a distaste for the smallness of spirit and outlook, the lack of generosity, and the obsession with material success that he sees around him. While Claude discovers a purpose that rises above the surrounding tawdriness only when he leaves Nebraska and goes to fight in France, from the early pages of *A Lost Lady* Niel finds in Marian Forrester, in his own town, someone who represents much of what he is seeking: "How strange that she should be here at all, a woman like her among common people! Not even in Denver had he ever seen another woman so elegant. . . . Compared with her, other women were heavy and dull; even the pretty ones seemed lifeless,—they had not that something in their glance that made one's blood tingle . . ." (41). And Niel recalls that even when he first met her as a child "he had recognized her as belonging to a different world from any he had ever known" (42).

In many ways *A Lost Lady* is about the fading of his bright vision. Its very title suggests from the start that this will be a story of loss, and Cather underscores the theme by using as an epigraph Ophelia's tragic farewell (*Hamlet* is still on her mind!): "Come, my coach! Good night, ladies; good night, sweet ladies, Good night, good night." Claude identifies his ideal belatedly, lives the rest of his short life serving it with pride, and dies without seeing it crumble; in contrast, Niel has his "ideal" close at hand from the beginning but over the course of the novel witnesses its relentless decline. Similarly, Claude's brother Bayliss, who in his grasping, sanctimonious narrowness so embodies all that Claude detests, fades from sight in the second half of *One of Ours*, while Niel must watch his bête noire, the shyster Ivy Peters, not only acquire ever more land and money as *A Lost Lady* progresses but even extend his poisonous influence over Marian Forrester herself.

As she had done in *One of Ours*, so in *A Lost Lady* Cather uses as backdrop the decline of the West, a topic that meshes with the novel's downward pull. Early on we are reminded that "the town of Sweet Water was changing. Its future no longer looked bright. Successive crop failures had broken the spirit of the farmers" (32). In the second half the decline takes on more spiritual overtones as Niel ponders Ivy's rise to power: "The Old West had been settled by dreamers, great-hearted adventurers who were unpractical to the point of magnificence; a courteous brother-hood.... Now all the vast territory they had won was to be at the mercy of men like Ivy Peters, who had never dared anything, never risked anything. They would drink up the mirage, dispel the morning freshness, root out the great brooding spirit of freedom, the generous, easy life of the great land-holders.... All the way from the Missouri to the mountains this generation of shrewd young men, trained to petty economies by hard times, would do exactly what Ivy Peters had done when he drained the Forrester marsh" (106–7).[1] In the book's last chapter Niel recognizes that "[h]e had seen the end of an era, the sunset of the pioneer.... It was already gone, that age; nothing could ever bring it back" (168–69). Janis Stout has also shown that the movement of the novel, and the relationship between its two halves, suggest not only the decline from an idealized past to a deteriorating present but even a questioning of that past itself: "The narrative perspective of the novel ... reflects not only [Cather's] sense of severance from a time that was good but her severance from an assurance that it really was."[2]

Paralleling this fall of the West is the decline of the Forrester place itself, the "house" that is celebrated in the book's first sentence, that was built in a location Captain Forrester saw as especially beautiful, and that was known throughout the West for its hospitality and elegance. From its legendary aura at the start we witness the stages of its decline: Marian leaving her aging husband in the house to make love with Frank Ellinger by the river; Ivy Peters draining the marsh; Ivy and his doltish companions sitting around the table, shoveling down the dinner that Marian has prepared for them—so different a party from those we have seen earlier; Ivy and his wife buying the house itself. The decline comes sharply into focus during the Captain's final illness, when the women of the town swarm over the house "like ants, the house where they had never before got past the parlour; and they found they had been fooled all these years. There was nothing remarkable about the place at all! The kitchen was inconvenient, the sink was smelly. The carpets were worn, the curtains faded, the clumsy, old-fashioned furniture they wouldn't have had for a gift, and the upstairs bed-rooms were full of dust and cobwebs" (138).

Like the persistent rhythm of disillusionment in *One of Ours*, a rhythm of decline defines *A Lost Lady* at every level.[3] There is the movement of part 1, which begins with the power the Captain once exerted and his creation of this handsome house but ends with the impoverishing losses he accepts in Denver, and his debilitating stroke. There are the contrasts between parallel chapters of parts 1 and 2: in chapter 1, part 1, the house and the Captain in all their glory, in chapter 1, part 2, the Forresters in such poverty that they need Ivy's rent money, and the Captain, in Ivy's words, "only about half there" (105); in chapter 2, part 1, Marian Forrester deftly barring the pushy Ivy from her bedroom, in chapter 2, part 2, Marian carrying on her affair with Frank Ellinger with the full knowledge of her husband; in chapter 3, part 1, Niel hearing Marian's "soft, musical laugh which rose and descended like a suave scale" as she climbs to the Judge's office (34), in chapter 3, part 2, Niel hearing "her naughtiest laugh" as she listens to Ivy telling her an "improper" story (119). Individual chapters reflect the same pattern, not least the first four: chapter 1, part 1, moves from the brilliant past, when Marian was still young and the Captain still in his prime, to their retirement in "the house on the hill. He grew old there,—and even she, alas! grew older" (13). Chapter 2, part 1, begins with a fairytale evocation of a "summer morning long ago, when Mrs. Forrester was still a young woman, and Sweet Water was a town of which great things were expected" (14), but moves from the jolly picnic of its early pages to Ivy Peter's arrival, his sadistic mutilation of the bird,

Niel's fall from the tree, and, at the end, the death of Niel's mother (30). Early in chapter 3, part 1, Niel and the Judge hear Mrs. Forrester's "light footsteps coming rapidly down the outside corridor" (34), but her light, assured step yields later in the chapter to the Captain's heavy fall: "There was no ice, he didn't slip. It was simply because he was unsteady. He had trouble getting up. I still shiver to think of it. To me, it was as if one of the mountains had fallen down" (41). Chapter 4, part 1, begins with the Captain and Marian together welcoming guests to their home but ends with her taking off her rings and slipping down to the living room for a drink with her lover, Frank Ellinger.[4]

The most tragic decline is that of Cather's "lost lady" herself. In contrast to Marian's elegant, flirtatious bearing with the boys at the picnic, her brave acceptance of the Captain's devastating losses, there is her collapse in the second part—her loss of self-control during her phone call with Frank, her inability to deal with the Captain's second stroke ("Mrs. Forrester quite went to pieces" [137]).[5] Balancing the fourth chapter of part 1, where Frank is virtually her slave and Constance Ogden a love-struck guest whom they both ridicule, is the fourth chapter of part 2, where Marian learns that Frank has abandoned her for this very woman. Echoing Niel's early vision of Marian rising above "common people" (41) is his comment near the end that her house has become a place "where common fellows behaved after their kind and knew a common woman when they saw her" (170).[6] We watch her fall into drinking too much, the very failing that earlier she has noted in her husband, and as she declines, so do the men with whom she associates: the Captain, a man of such integrity and strength at the beginning but who steadily fails; then Ellinger, physically impressive, but a philanderer and social climber at heart; finally Ivy Peters—"Poison Ivy"—whom Marian keeps at a distance when he is a boy but whom Niel later glimpses embracing her, his hands casually folded over her breast as if he owns her.

Her decline is implicit in the first description of the Forresters' home as "a house well known" (9) to railroad men across the West, a phrase that subtly suggests a brothel.[7] These connotations come to mind when we hear later of Frank's affair with Nell Emerald, a madame "who conducted a house properly licensed by the Denver police" (50), and by the middle of the second part Marian Forrester lives up to them as she virtually sells herself to Ivy Peters.[8] Critics have noted the novel's apparent acceptance of white supremacy (e.g., the way Cather portrays Black Tom), its implicit approval of manifest destiny (both Captain Forrester and Ivy Peters assume their right to cheat the natives out of their land), and its prevailing, though not absolute, assumption that society works best when ruled by a stable upper-middle class, with the lower classes knowing their place.[9] At the same time, in her portrayal of the slow deterioration of both Marian's values and those of the society around her, Cather clearly identifies and impugns the root cause of so many of these very ills: the all-consuming quest for money and the attendant willingness to sacrifice one's principles to that quest—to sell oneself—flaws from which Marian is far from immune.

As she does with the story of Emil and Marie in *O Pioneers!*, Cather colors Marian's decline with echoes of the biblical Fall, with sexual attraction again serving as catalyst. In the early scene by the creek Marian gamely laughs off her dislike of the snakes in the water. Already lurking in the background, however, is Ivy Peters, with his small eyes and an absence of eyelashes, which "gave his pupils the fixed, unblinking hardness of a snake's or a lizard's" (21–22), a foreshadowing of the role he will later play. When Frank arrives, Niel instinctively senses "something evil" (46). The scene in which Frank and Marian make love by the creek has strong reminiscences of Marie and Emil in their grove, and over the course of the scene Marian changes from the courteous, caring hostess who asks Niel to take care of her guest, Constance, to the "fallen woman" who, as Frank cuts the cedar branches after their lovemaking, shivers softly at each of his axe strokes and tells him at the end, "It doesn't matter if we are late for dinner. Nothing matters" (67).

Reminiscences of the Garden become unmistakable in the scene where Niel carries roses up to the house, hoping to surprise Marian with a fresh bouquet before Ellinger arrives.[10] He awakes "with that intense, blissful realization of summer which sometimes comes to children in their beds." As he walks up the Forresters' road on this "cloudless summer dawn," he notes the "almost religious purity about the fresh morning air, the tender sky, the grass and flowers with the sheen of early dew upon them. There was in all living things something limpid and joyous—like the wet, morning call of the birds, flying up through the unstained atmosphere.... Niel wondered why he did not often come over like this, to see the day before men and their activities had spoiled it, while the morning was still unsullied, like a gift handed down from the heroic ages.... He would make a bouquet for a lovely lady" (84–85). Cather's language, which recalls Emil's as he heads for the fatal meeting in his "Garden," everywhere evokes a prelapsarian dawn, a cruel setup for what Niel hears when he reaches the window where he is going to leave the roses: "a woman's soft laughter; impatient, indulgent, teasing, eager. Then another laugh, very different, a man's" (86). After he has run from the house to the foot of the hill, Niel realizes that "[i]n that instant between stooping to the window-sill and rising, he had lost one of the most beautiful things in his life. Before the dew dried, the morning had been wrecked for him; and all subsequent mornings, he told himself" (86).[11] The final stage comes when Marian takes up with the snakelike Ivy Peters. In Marian's "fall" and its frequent intimations of the Garden it is hard not to suspect once again echoes of Mary Baker Eddy and her blithe attitude toward evil. But Cather's theme is yet darker here, for Marian's flaw, and the evil into which she is tempted, belong to the inexorable rhythm of decline that defines human life in the novel. In 1922 Cather noted to Dorothy Canfield her concern over "the disappearance from the world of a conception of sin"; as if in response, the downward pull of the Fall dominates every aspect of the novel she writes that year.[12]

The trajectory of Marian's life diverges sharply from those of the great heroines of the teens, all of whom, though in very different ways, trace a rising curve from humble beginnings to iconic, heroic endings. In contrast, Marian begins the book as the Lady of the Castle, with overtones of Maid Marian in her Forest (cf. Mr. "Forrester," with his Robin Hood–like concern for the poor), and appropriately with men in thrall to her—her husband, the boys at the picnic, the powerful Frank Ellinger, Niel Herbert (whose name suggests his vassal-like willingness to kneel before his Lady).[13] By the end she has fallen, and as this happens she becomes increasingly dependent on the men around her. She realizes when she recites the story of her husband's literal fall how much she has depended on him; she cannot resist drawing to herself Ellinger's strength, and before long she has become as addicted to him as she is becoming to alcohol. By the end she is dependent, as she herself admits, on the pathetic Ivy, whom once she had barred even from her room.

As always there are cross-currents, and in this case they pull against the novel's downward spiral. To begin with, we must remember that just as Ántonia's story is shaped by Jim Burden, so Marian's is told by the naive Niel Herbert, who has a romantic image of her that he wants to protect (just as he would have kept that fateful morning as pure as it felt when he awoke). But as Cather stresses in her Eddy biography, evil and sex are realities that humans must confront. And when set against Claude, who fails to see the evil that is so woven into the dream he is living and the ideal he is pursuing, Marian comes off well: for like Cather's great heroines of the teens, she faces the truth and deals with it.

She recalls also the singers in the first four stories of *Youth and the Bright Medusa*. Like them, she evinces a powerful will to live and a willingness to do what she must in order to survive. She does so, moreover, despite lacking what they have, the independence that comes from having a career and an income of one's own. She is by her station dependent on the men around her, a fact suggested by the way the Captain first carried her when she was injured. He has, to recall her words, since then been her mountain, someone solid, supporting, and of unswerving moral strength, as the dust jacket reminds us: "this story of an incorruptible man and the beautiful woman who was his wife." As he begins to fail, she turns, out of both choice and necessity, to other men—Frank, Ivy, the Judge, Niel himself. Despite living a role defined by dependence—the wife of a great man, the Lady of his house—she nonetheless shows, when she must, a gumption and resourcefulness that recall Eden Bower, Cressida Garnet, and Kitty Ayrshire. She is devastated when she realizes that the Captain's losses will completely change their lifestyle, but she rises gamely to the challenge, as she does when he suffers a devastating stroke immediately thereafter. And though the Captain's integrity in making good his debts even at the expense of reducing himself to poverty elicits both the Judge's admiration and Marian's, the reader cannot help asking where the Captain's idealism leaves his wife, especially given that he is her sole support, is twenty-five years older than she, and is no longer strong.[14] It is a question that Marian herself soon confronts, without his idealism, but with more pragmatism and common sense (compare again those shrewd singers in *Youth*). She recognizes honestly and openly that money is important—indeed, something without which she cannot live.[15] When Niel asks if she doesn't miss the marsh that Ivy has drained, she answers, "Not much. I would never have time to go there, and we need the money it pays us. And you haven't time to play any more either, Niel. You must hurry and become a successful man. . . . Money is a very important thing.[16] Realize that in the beginning; face it, and don't be ridiculous in the end, like so many of us" (113–14). Her affair with Frank Ellinger is scarcely admirable, but she is a woman for whom a sexual relationship— something she no longer has in her marriage—is important, and she makes sure that during this ongoing affair she takes loving care of her husband. In short, Marian is a woman who recognizes that sex, evil, and the snake exist, that we do not live in Eden, and who opts for action and for life.[17] The jacket description captures both her flaws and her unique, indomitable spirit: "Marian Forrester, full of feminine mystery and charm, inscrutable in her weakness and her reckless courage."

While we share with Niel a sense of loss as we watch her inexorable descent, we can but admire the way she not only accommodates herself to her circumstances, wrests a life from a harsh world, as Eden and Cressida and Kitty do, but even manages to preserve something of her unique aura, including her zest for life: "Perhaps people think I've settled down to grow old gracefully," she says to Niel, "but I've not. I feel such a power to live in me . . . ." She proceeds to tell him of a recent visit to the home of old friends: "I looked happier than any woman there. They were nearly all younger, much. But they seemed dull, bored to death. . . . I accepted the Dalzell's [*sic*] invitation with a purpose; I wanted to see whether I had anything left worth saving. And I have, I tell you!" (125–26).

In retrospect we see that if Cather has built into her novel a persistent rhythm of loss, as counterpoint she has also built in Marian's resurgent will to live, and to live with zest. In the next to last chapter of part 1 she is already talking about how she and the Captain will manage life after his stroke, and as she speaks, Niel hears again, despite all he has witnessed, something of the magic he had always found in her: "In her voice there was the heart-breaking sweetness one sometimes hears in lovely, gentle old songs" (97). Part 1 ends with Marian and her husband wishing Niel "Happy days," the Captain's traditional toast, and with the two of them standing at the door bidding Niel farewell. The upward thrust at the end of part 2 is even more marked. The next to last chapter tells of the party in which Marian, in her words, tries "to do something for the boys in this town . . . . I hate to see them growing up like savages" (155). Early in the party they are just that—awkward, unappreciative, boorish—but at the end she wins them over by telling the story of how she and Captain Forrester first met, beginning with the words "[O]nce upon a time . . . ," which themselves evoke her aura of romance. By the end, the boys are genuinely moved, and Niel realizes that she is "still her indomitable self" (163, 166–67). Early in the final chapter Niel is disappointed that "she [is] not willing to immolate herself, like the widow of all these great men, and die with the pioneer period to which she belonged; that she preferred life on any terms" (169). But Marian is not one to die with the past, and before the book ends Niel learns that after selling the house she moved to Buenos Aires, remarried, and lived well with her new husband—and that "[a]fter she left Sweet Water, wherever she was, she always sent a cheque to the Grand Army Post every year to have flowers put on Captain Forrester's grave" (174). At the end, despite all the disillusionment he has felt, Niel is "very glad that he had known her, and that she had had a hand in breaking him in to life. He has known pretty women and clever ones since then,—but never one like her, as she was in her best days. Her eyes, when they laughed for a moment into one's own, seemed to promise a wild delight that he has not found in life" (171).

It is a conclusion in tune with the way Jim feels at the end about Ántonia—that for all they have lost, they "possess together the precious, the incommunicable past." It is a great possession, and precisely what Cather herself achieves in this book. Just as Marian by her story, against all odds, captures the imaginations of her swinish audience at the end of the party for Ivy and his friends, so Cather, true to the advice of Sarah Orne Jewett, returns to a woman and a place that she had loved, that had teased her mind for years, and creates this haunting, resonant tale that in the very act of tracing Marian's decline captures and preserves the unique loveliness that once was hers.[18] And just as Marian herself once more rises above the men around her, and Niel realizes that what she has lost matters less than what remains, so by the end he realizes also that though the West is no longer what it was, that "nothing could ever bring it back," nonetheless "[t]he taste and smell and song of it, the visions those men had seen in the air and followed,—these he had caught in a kind of after-glow in their own faces,—and this would always be his" (169).

Despite its title and its pervasive downward pulls, *A Lost Lady* projects far more affirmation than does *One of Ours*. Claude may believe that his life has found a purpose and that he will die for a noble cause, but his mother, and the reader who follows Cather's clear signs, know better. In contrast, Marian manages to survive both her own folly and the cruelties of the world. At the end she is not just a survivor, someone who does what it takes to muddle through, but someone who, like Thea and Ántonia, combines this will to live with the ability to transcend the ordinary, and to lift others with her. Once again, as in the novels of the teens, the focal character is a woman, and by the end she is, like Ántonia, someone battered by life but still able to leave powerful images on the mind. As the jacket puts it, "Through the whole story one figure stands out with irresistible fascination—the figure of Marian Forrester. . . . She is one of Miss Cather's greatest triumphs."[19]

"Even she, alas! grew older"

Common also to *A Lost Lady* and *My Ántonia* is a focus on the passage of time, a motif that will become increasingly important in the two novels that follow *A Lost Lady*. Here the theme is stressed from the very first chapter, which begins with the glory days of "thirty or forty years ago" but ends with the Captain growing old, and even Marian growing older. And whereas in *My Ántonia* the theme relates above all to the passing of youth—*optima dies . . . prima fugit*—in *A Lost Lady* Cather traces the stages of this decline across Marian's whole lifetime. In the early chapters we are reminded that she is twenty-five years younger than the Captain, and the descriptions of her evoke an almost girlish image—"the gay challenge in her eyes," "the droll word of greeting on her lips," "her long black hair rippling over her shoulders," (12), the freckles on her cheeks in the summer (18). The first chapter ends with its ominous warning that "even she, alas! grew older," however, and subsequent chapters trace the continuing process. When Niel pays a visit to the Forresters during the first winter they spend in town, a concession to the Captain's advancing age, Marian comes down for tea "looking very pale," with "dark shadows under her eyes," and Niel imagines she has been losing sleep (73). When he visits them after the Captain's first stroke, he notices "that her skin was no longer like white lilacs,—it had the ivory tint of gardenias that have just begun to fade . . ." (112). When she comes to make her late-night call to Ellinger, Niel notes "the singular frown of one overcome by alcohol or fatigue . . . , the black shadows under her eyes" that make her look "as if some poison were at work in her body" (131), and during her call she herself alludes to her "dead face" (134). After Mr. Forrester's second stroke she becomes "so exhausted that she was dull to what went on about her" (138), and at the party she gives for Ivy and his friends, Niel notes that despite the rouge on her face she looks "pinched and worn as he had never seen her" (161). After Niel has left town, he hears that "her health is failing," and a last description mentions both her enhanced use of cosmetics as she ages and her death (170, 173–74). Her decline is also constantly set against the flow of time—the aging of the Captain and herself (13); her anxiety over the passing of the years as she winters in Sweet Water so as to tend her husband, and her brave jest that she will become "the waltzing grandmother" (77); her puzzlement at her husband's fixation on his sundial ("How can anybody like to see time visibly devoured?" [111]); her description of the Dalzells' party as an occasion where she can regain her youth, and Niel's reaction that "[w]hen women began to talk about still feeling young, didn't it mean that something had broken?" (125–26). When Niel finds Marian asleep in the hammock, he runs up and lifts her: "How light and alive she was! . . . If only he could rescue her and carry her off like this,—off the earth of sad, inevitable periods, away from age, weariness, adverse fortune!" (110).

As Cather in 1923, the year *A Lost Lady* was published, faced her fiftieth year, she clearly was asking the same questions that are implicit throughout this novel: as time passes, taking with it so much of what we had and of what we were, what remains? What can we hold on to? What place is there for pursuing dreams such as Claude's, for reaching beyond the merely mundane, as Marian does? The theme will be central in both *The Professor's House* and *My Mortal Enemy* and will indirectly lead to the very different tack Cather takes in *Death Comes for the Archbishop*. As for *A Lost Lady* itself, in it Cather creates a heroine who by her willingness to accommodate herself to a flawed world, to face open-eyed the erosions that accompany time's passing, preserves something of her own unique splendor. Her bravery is her ultimate tribute to her husband and the philosophy she liked to hear him voice: "Well, then, my philosophy is that what you think of and plan for day by day, in spite of yourself, so to speak— you will get. You will get it more or less. . . . [A] thing that is dreamed of in the way I mean, is already an accomplished fact" (54–55).

Cather voices the same philosophy in writing this book. She too can still think and plan, day by day, can still dream. As her world breaks in two, and as she faces her own mortality, she creates a novel that bridges a broken world and rises above our mortal Fall.

CHAPTER THIRTEEN

The Best Stories of Sarah Orne Jewett

More than any other Cather novel, *A Lost Lady*, with its genesis in memories of Lyra Garber apparently evoked by news of her death, embodies Sarah's Orne Jewett's familiar words about "[t]he thing that teases the mind . . . and at last gets put down on paper." This is not surprising, for Jewett was in fact very much on Cather's mind during this period. In 1922, at the same time as Cather was working on *A Lost Lady*, she also wrote and published a review of *Memories of a Hostess*, M. A. De Wolfe Howe's edition of Annie Fields's diaries, in which Cather described her first meetings with Jewett at Mrs. Fields's home, 148 Charles Street. And early in 1924, just months after the appearance of *A Lost Lady*, Cather indicated to Ferris Greenslet her willingness to edit a selection of Jewett stories for Houghton Mifflin, and the preface Cather wrote for this collection begins by recalling Jewett's words about "the thing that teases the mind."[1]

In turn, that preface reveals the degree to which another 1922 essay, "The Novel Démeublé," also dating from the time when Cather was writing *A Lost Lady*, is in both substance and language very much in tune with Jewett's spirit. "The Novel Démeublé" speaks of "the overtone divined by the ear but not heard by it, the verbal mood, the emotional aura of the fact or the thing or the deed, that gives high quality to the novel or the drama . . ." (*NUF* 50); Cather's preface to *The Best Stories of Sarah Orne Jewett*, written in 1924, expands on this same idea, speaking of a story's capacity to "leave in the mind of the sensitive reader an intangible residuum of pleasure; a cadence, a quality of voice that is exclusively the writer's own, individual, unique. A quality that one can remember without the volume at hand, can experience over and over again in the mind but can never absolutely define, as one can experience in memory a melody, or the summer perfume of a garden" (*Best Stories* xi). "The Novel Démeublé" condemns "the novel manufactured to entertain great multitudes of people," likening it "to a cheap soap or a cheap perfume, or cheap furniture" (*NUF* 44); in her Jewett preface Cather suggests that "[i]f a writer's attitude toward his characters and his scene is as vulgar as a showman's, as mercenary as an auctioneer's, vulgar and meretricious will his product remain forever" (*Best Stories* xvii–xviii). "The Novel Démeublé" describes the contemporary novel as "overfurnished" and the "higher processes of art" as "processes of simplification" (*NUF* 43, 48–49); the Jewett preface compares great writing to a "modern yacht, where there is no ornamentation at all," and speaks of Jewett's best stories as "tightly built and significant in design. . . . The design is the story and the story is the design" (*Best Stories* xviii, x). Both "The Novel Démeublé" and the Jewett preface pay particular tribute to Hawthorne's *The Scarlet Letter* (*NUF* 49–50; *Best Stories* xviii).

That in taking on the Jewett project Cather was returning to Houghton Mifflin is itself significant, for in doing so she was moving from the aggressive, ambitious Alfred A. Knopf, whose offer of full leeway in promotional activities had helped win Cather over, back to the very firm she had abandoned because she thought it recalcitrant in promoting her books.[2] There are intimations of a similar progression in the fiction Cather was writing in this same period. In 1920 she had in the first four stories of her first Knopf book, *Youth and the Bright Medusa*, focused on women who were, like Knopf, adept at self-promotion, at achieving a certain éclat and reaping the attendant benefits. In contrast, her next two novels, published in 1922 and 1923, respectively, turn against people obsessed with such things: Claude Wheeler, the hero of *One of Ours*, explicitly rejects his society's focus on wealth and its accoutrements, and Niel Herbert, the narrator of *A Lost Lady*, indicts contemporary society for similar reasons, contrasting its greed with the nobler motives of earlier generations. And we have seen that even Cather's 1922 essay "The Novel

Démeublé" attacks fiction written merely to amuse and to sell. We may go a step further: in her writings of the early 1920s we sense Cather both moving back toward the qualities that she associated with Jewett and also resisting the Eddy-like qualities that had characterized the ambitious and successful singers she had been writing about in the late teens, and whose stories occupy the first half of *Youth and the Bright Medusa*.

The progression is, of course, not without its complexities and contradictions. Marian Forrester, for all her Jewett-like refinement and sensitivity, displays—not least as she encounters the difficult times that attend her husband's decline and death—a dogged determination and a willingness to compromise that recall the singers of *Youth* and that pay their own tribute to Mary Baker Eddy; and like Eddy, Marian well knows the importance of money. As for *One of Ours*, its hero may flee the commercialism and competition of contemporary society, but Cather herself took delight in the novel's astonishing sales, its popularity with the general public (in contrast to the critics), and the Pulitzer Prize it won for her, just the sort of successes for which she had worked so hard, and for which she had envied Eddy.

Cather's compilation of Jewett's "Best Stories" has its own sharp tensions. The collection purports to showcase an author who, in the words of Cather's preface, set modest goals for herself: "To note an artist's limitations is but to define his genius.... [A] creative writer can do his best only with what lies within the range and character of his talent. These stories of Miss Jewett's have much to do with fisher-folk and seaside villages; with juniper pastures and lonely farms, neat gray country houses and delightful, well-seasoned old men and women" (*Best Stories* xv). In her 1936 expansion of this preface, Cather goes still further: "She was content to be slight, if she could be true.... She wrote for a limited audience, and she still has it, both here and abroad" (*NUF* 89, 92).

When Cather compiled her collection of Jewett's stories, however, she brought to the project her own keen promotional instincts. One obvious manifestation of Jewett's willingness "to be slight" was the diminutive format of many of her books. Cather indicates her own liking for these "dumpy little ... books" but opts in *her* edition for something more substantial. Noting that librarians have told her that Jewett's child-sized books often turn modern readers from them, she recommends to Greenslet "that they be reissued in standard-size volumes with good clear type—and she suggests that a type like that used in *My Ántonia* would be appropriate . . . ."[3] In addition, as many critics have pointed out, Cather includes in the text of Jewett's masterpiece, *The Country of the Pointed Firs*, three stories that were not in Jewett's original version. In doing so she was, from one standpoint, merely following precedents already established by her publisher in this project: Houghton Mifflin had—with the approval of Jewett's sister, Mary—in its 1910 version of the book added two of these stories, "The Dunnet Shepherdess" and "William's Wedding," and in a 1919 edition had added the third, "The Queen's Twin." That said, Cather in taking on the project had emphasized her intention to begin with Jewett's original versions, so the retention of the three stories represents her conscious decision (a fact underscored by her further decision to alter the order of these three stories so that "The Queen's Twin" now falls between, rather than after, the other two).[4] It is, in the words of Ann Romines, an editorial judgment that "fractur[es] the formal unity of the 1896 version of *The Country of the Pointed Firs*" and "that seems to violate the ethic of sympathy that she describes as central to Jewett's art"—and this from an editor who in her preface has praised Jewett's capacity to create a design "so happy, so right, that it seems inevitable."[5] In her emphasis on packaging the Jewett collection to sell and her somewhat magisterial approach to materials that in her preface she seems to hold sacred, Cather in many ways treats Jewett with a freedom that reveals her kinship to her other Boston alter ego, Mary Baker Eddy. In her Eddy biography, Cather had emphasized Eddy's aggressive willingness to plunge into the competitive rat race, while she had typically associated Jewett with serenity and seclusion—the peaceful setting in which she first met Jewett in Boston, the serenity she finds in Jewett's writing, the seclusion that Jewett had recommended as essential to a writer: "[Y]ou must find your own quiet centre of life."[6] While Cather's preface to *Best Stories* eloquently honors the quiet waters of Jewett's art, the collection she puts together is roiled by Eddy-like cross-currents.[7]

Cather's work in 1924–25 on Jewett's *Best Stories*, which at first glance might seem a passing diversion from her work as a novelist, in fact proves an important catalyst for much that follows. Jewett's spirit is strongly felt in the fiction of the next decade, from *My Mortal Enemy* through *Lucy Gayheart*. Cather returns to Jewett herself in her 1936 collection *Not Under Forty*, expanding her 1925 preface into a far more ambitious essay, "Miss Jewett," which she makes both the physical and the thematic centerpiece of the whole collection. And Cather's last novel, *Sapphira and the Slave Girl*, comes fully into focus only when we pay attention to the ongoing contrapuntal dance of the two women who had so teased Cather's mind during her 1906–8 Boston sojourn.

We shall return to all of these topics in later chapters. More immediately, as we shall soon see, *The Professor's House*, which Cather begins to write in the same year as she embarks on the Jewett story project, reveals the same tension we have noted in *Best Stories*—that between the quest to find one's "own quiet centre" on the one hand, the pull of ambition and worldly success on the other. In addition, even more central to that novel will be the thematic divide with which Cather ends her Jewett preface, the tension between the immortality of art and the ravages of time:

> I like to think with what pleasure, with what a sense of rich dis-
> covery, the young student of American literature in far distant
> years to come will take up [*The Country of the Pointed Firs*] and say,
> "A masterpiece!" . . . It will be a message to the future, a message
> in a universal language, like the tuft of meadow flowers in Robert
> Frost's fine poem, which the mower abroad in the early morn-
> ing left standing, just skirted by the scythe, for the mower of the
> afternoon to gaze upon and wonder at—the one message that even
> the scythe of Time spares.[8]

One other way in which the Jewett project exerts its influence also de-
serves mention here, for its impact too is immediate. In her letter to Cather about "On the Gulls' Road," Jewett had many years earlier commented that a woman speaks most naturally when she speaks in a woman's voice. One result of Cather's return to Jewett through the Houghton Mifflin

project seems to be that in the following years she finally takes this advice to heart. In both Cather's "Uncle Valentine," a story published in March 1925, and in *My Mortal Enemy*, her novel published in 1926, she for the first time in her mature fiction specifically gives her narrator a woman's voice ("a girl of sixteen" in the one [*UV* 4], Nellie Birdseye in the other).[9] It is a step with important consequences for the works Cather will write in the 1930s, particularly *Not Under Forty* and *Sapphira and the Slave Girl*, in both of which she serves as both narrator and participant. This new direction is subtly foreshadowed in Cather's 1925 Jewett preface, where in both the first and the last paragraphs she allows herself briefly to come on stage and to speak in her own person: the preface begins with Cather reading over a package of letters from Jewett and ends with her musing, in her own person, on the long life that lies ahead for *The Country of the Pointed Firs*. It is a significant move toward what Jewett had recommended about letting the woman speak for herself, and a tribute, perhaps, to Jewett's own practice of both narrating her stories and often appearing in them as one of the characters.

CHAPTER FOURTEEN

The Professor's House

A closer look at the growing gulf between Cather's public successes in the early 1920s and the private dismay and discouragement she was feeling in the same years makes tangible the broken world in which she was living at this time. *One of Ours*, despite mixed critical reception, received the Pulitzer Prize in 1923 and achieved booming sales from the start. *A Lost Lady* received excellent reviews and also sold very well, as would *The Professor's House*. Cather's letters from these same years, however, suggest little corresponding satisfaction. In a February 1923 letter to her friends Achsah and Earl Brewster, she rebuts the critics of *One of Ours* by pointing to its excellent sales but immediately laments that she receives so much correspondence about the book that she has had to hire a secretary to deal with it.[1] She is glad she has not had this sort of success before—all it brings is "bother and fatigue," words that in many ways capture these years. She notes that her secretary must also deal with all the unwanted invitations to give lectures, complains that such lectures keep her from writing, and as she tries to complete *The Professor's House* tells Blanche Knopf that she has gone into hiding to avoid such engagements.[2] A portrait of her by Leon Bakst becomes another annoyance, both in Paris, where she has to handle logistical details and make numerous sittings, and back home, where there is the awkwardness of unveiling a painting that pleases neither her nor those in Omaha who commissioned it.[3] Her impatience with these endless demands comes out in the testiness of many of the letters she writes during these years, and one suspects that feeling beleaguered contributes to her frequent medical problems, among them a tonsillectomy, appendicitis, neuritis of her arm, back problems and a cold, ringworm, and a stiff neck.[4] At one point she admits that she is ill in bed partly to avoid having to see people, and on another occasion she explicitly blames her chronic neuritis on the activity of writing.[5] In a 1924 letter she longs to drop everything and escape to England. "Mustn't get weighed down by routine, but leave the day-to-day chores . . . [to] others and get away while she can, before she is utterly exhausted."[6] Edith Lewis describes Cather's struggle during these years "to preserve the integrity of her life as an artist, its necessary detachment and freedom," and the concomitant "exertion of her will against the will of the public."[7]

Given all this, it is not surprising that in September 1924, as she begins work on *The Professor's House*, Cather writes Zoë Akins that her new novel will be rather sour, not very pleasant.[8] The tone she ascribes to the novel mirrors her own mood at the time, and the connection between her lead character, Professor Godfrey St. Peter, and herself is also close. He too is in his early fifties, has completed eight books, and has recently won a major prize. Just as Cather in these years is editing the works of her revered mentor Jewett, so in the novel the professor is editing a manuscript that his beloved student, Tom Outland, left when he died.[9] Most important, he too is experiencing not the joy of accomplishment but malaise with where his success has brought him and anxiety over what lies ahead.[10]

Dominating the book is the same tension that had shaped Cather's portrait of Claude Wheeler a few years earlier. On the one hand there is the search for "something splendid," the aspiration to attach one's life to some transcendent cause or creation. St. Peter has imagined his eight-volume history of the Spanish adventurers in North America as "this dazzling, this beautiful, this utterly impossible thing!" (25), and thinks that "[d]esire is creation, is the magical element in that process" (29). In a lecture we overhear, he tells his class that "[a]rt and religion . . . are the same thing, in the end, of course," and notes that what makes humans happy, be they kings or beggars, is "believing in the mystery and importance of their own . . . lives" (68–69). Tom Outland's quest is also for transcendent values, whether in the ancient city he discovers on the Blue Mesa, which he associates with "immortal repose," "the calmness of eternity" (201), and "religious emotion" (251), or in his decision to follow the lead of his former teacher, Father Duchene, and, like Claude, join the allied cause in the Great War, where he dies on Flanders Field. On the other side are the mundane concerns that dominate most people's lives: getting ahead, making money, building new and bigger homes, motivations of the sort that Claude found so unsatisfying. Godfrey's wife, Lillian, and his daughter Rosamond are more openly caught up in this race for worldly possessions, but even his younger daughter Kathleen, who appears less obsessed with such matters, keenly envies what her sister has—and she herself does not have. Tom captures this element of society when he speaks of his friend Roddy as one of the few people who "aren't trained by success to a sort of systematic selfishness" (185). The most obvious exemplar of these worldly goals would seem to be Rosamond's highly successful husband, Louie Marsellus, a name whose anomalous spelling highlights its central syllable: SELL. In fact, though, as St. Peter himself comes to realize, Louie proves to have a warmth and generosity that reach well beyond this easy stereotyping.

While in *One of Ours* Claude flees the family and hometown that embody the rat race he so abhors, in *The Professor's House* there is no such escape: money and the search for it destroy and undermine both the dreams of St. Peter and Tom Outland and the fabric of the professor's family. It is the five-thousand-pound prize the professor has won that enables the St. Peters to build a new and larger house, which in turn threatens to take the professor away from the old home, and especially the old study, that he associates with his book and with the dreams that spawned it. Louie Marsellus inherits the patent for one of Tom's scientific discoveries, and the riches that accrue from this patent become a constant source of tension within the family, and especially between the two sisters. One use for these funds is to build a magnificent house on the nearby lake. Not only does St. Peter perceive this project as a threat to a lake he associates with the purity of his childhood, but in naming their house "Outland," Rosamond and Louie Marsellus appropriate a name that both St. Peter and Kathleen feel is theirs and replace Tom's city on the mesa with an ersatz palace of their own.[11] A shopping junket with

Louie and Rosamond sends St. Peter home from Chicago feeling he has witnessed "an orgy of acquisition" (154). Finally, when Tom returns empty-handed from a trip to drum up interest and funds in Washington, he finds that during his absence Roddy has sold off most of the artifacts they had discovered, including even "Mother Eve," a young woman who had been murdered on the mesa, and whose mummified body they have found in the ruins.[12] Not only are these unique treasures gone, but the resulting quarrel destroys the friendship between Tom and Roddy. At one point in the novel St. Peter quotes Mark Antony's remark that his "fortunes have corrupted honest men" (150): it is a comment apt to the way in which Cather at every level of the novel identifies money and its allure as corrosive to both the individual and society.[13]

If society's obsession with material wealth here takes on even darker colorations than in *One of Ours*, so by the end does the other side of the equation—the quest for "something splendid." Both Tom and St. Peter associate the ideals that have captured their imaginations with lofty, shining images in the sky, images that have their own internal order. As Tom scans the mesa where he will soon find his city, he sees it "red with sunrise, and all the slim cedars along the rocks would be gold—metallic, like tarnished gold-foil" (192). When he discovers the city itself he senses its creators' "feeling for design": "It all hung together, seemed to have a kind of composition" (201).[14] As for St. Peter, it is on a Mediterranean voyage that he finds the key to the structure of his great history: "[E]verything seemed to feed the plan of the work that was forming in St. Peter's mind . . . . One day stood out above the others. All day long they were skirting the south coast of Spain; from the rose of dawn to the gold of sunset the ranges of the Sierra Nevadas towered on their right, snow peak after snow peak, high beyond the flight of fancy, gleaming like crystal and topaz. St. Peter lay looking up at them from a little boat riding low in the purple water, and the design of his book unfolded in the air above him, just as definitely as the mountain ranges themselves" (106).[15]

But there is another facet to the objects of both Tom's and St. Peter's fascination: they are in the past, frozen, no longer alive. Tom compares the city he has found to sculpture, speaks of it as "the city of some extinct civilization, hidden away in this inaccessible mesa for centuries, preserved in the dry air and almost perpetual sunlight like a fly in amber" (202). Even the body of Mother Eve is not a skeleton but a mummy, her mortal decomposition checked. Father Duchene, who visits Tom and Roddy and sees their city, imagines the tribe that built it as "isolated, cut off from other tribes" (220), and after Roddy has left him, Tom himself spends a summer alone atop the mesa in his city, also isolated and alone, and so happy that he virtually forgets about the friend he has so hurt. The professor's great work also deals with bygone ages, and he too finds the greatest happiness when he is isolated, alone, without having to worry about other people. His "city on the mesa" is his top-floor study in the old house, where he holes up for the summer apart from his family, with the sewing forms of the aging seamstress Augusta as his only companions— fit counterparts to the mummified Mother Eve which Tom and Roddy stash away with their other finds. If from one viewpoint Tom's and St. Peter's pursuits lift them above the everyday concerns of ordinary people, enable them to contemplate and create images of timeless order and beauty, these same pursuits also fix their gaze on past worlds, distance them from the living people around them, and focus their attention on inanimate realms that have their composed order precisely because they stand apart from the messiness—and reality—of life. The first sentence of the novel, "The moving was over and done," is a perfect lead-in to the world on the mesa that lures Tom into its clutches, and to the insulated world that the professor both creates in his books and tries to preserve for himself in his study: all are isolated from life, kept preternaturally stable, worlds where normal humans cannot exist.

Just as Tom's summer on the mesa enables him to forget Roddy— whom, as he already half knows, he has wronged horribly—so the professor's attic retreat embodies his disregard for those around him.[16] Prior to a dinner party early in the novel, his wife, noting his pleasure in having his own room in the new house, comments with a smile that he is growing "more intolerant all the time" (35). The next morning, after he has behaved uncivilly to virtually everyone at the party, she comments more sharply on his behavior: "Your disapproving silence can kill the life of any company"

(46). Over the course of the novel we learn that in fact his project has for years pulled him away from his family. We hear of his trips to the lake to spend days alone in his boat when his spirits lag; of the garden where he so loves working and sitting alone; of the leaves he has taken in Europe, also often alone, which he recalls as he spends Christmas Day alone in the study of his old house. Though during these years he has cared about and enjoyed being with his wife and daughters, the momentum has clearly been toward separation and seclusion, a movement that over the course of the novel pulls him ever more from his family and his new home, ever more toward his attic eyrie (compare Tom alone atop the mesa). After St. Peter returns from the shopping trip to Chicago, he tells his wife that he has been thinking about Euripides and "how, when he was an old man, he went and lived in a cave by the sea. . . . I wonder whether it was because he had observed women so closely all his life" (156). His wife, concerned by how he has changed, comments, "You're naturally warm and affectionate; all at once you begin shutting yourself away from everybody" (162). By the final chapters, he has become so obsessed with privacy that he can no longer imagine living with his family, and especially with his wife; even death itself has become vaguely appealing. And though he notes that in part his feelings reflect annoyance with ways in which his wife and daughters have changed, he also recognizes that his altered feelings toward them are as much the result of his own malaise as of these changes in them (see esp. 159–61).

Both Tom Outland and Father Duchene comment on the "feeling for design" that is reflected in the city on the Blue Mesa (204, 219), and the anomalous structure of the novel in turn reflects Cather's feeling for design. The book begins and concludes with sections set in the professor's hometown, Hamilton; in between is the remarkable "Tom Outland's Story," originally conceived as a separate piece, and in the completed novel functioning as a great shaft driven between the other two.[17] The resulting structure mirrors the divisions that obtain throughout the book: divisions within the professor's family—husband against wife, sister against sister; the rift between Tom and Roddy; the gulf between the lonely preoccupations of Tom and St. Peter and the mundane concerns of those around them.[18] The analogy extends yet further. It is Tom Outland, the writer of this story, who precipitates many of these divisions: it is he who drives a wedge between St. Peter and his wife; it is income from his invention that fuels Kathleen's jealousy toward Rosamond, along with the fact that though Rosamond became Tom's fiancée, Kathleen too had loved him.[19] Finally, Tom himself realizes that his proprietary obsession with the city on the mesa is responsible for the rift between Roddy and himself. The lonely Blue Mesa, surmounted by the ancient city and its great tower, looms tall in the middle of the book as the emblem both of Tom's lofty aspirations and of his divisive impact upon those around him.

The resulting structure, with the Blue Mesa towering above the surrounding landscape, also mirrors the cosmic rift that emerges in the novel between the transcendent aspirations humans entertain and the fact that the dreamers of these immortal dreams are mortal and flawed. Tom sees in the city he has discovered a world that is orderly, pure, and untainted by contemporary society.[20] He speaks of the "exaltation" of breathing in the pure air around the mesa, air different from that on the other side of the river, "though that was pure and uncontaminated enough" (200). Once in the city on the mesa, he discovers the "perpetual twilight" of a cavern, and within it a spring whose water is "as cold as ice, and so pure," water that looks like "liquid crystal, absolutely colourless . . . . It threw off the sunlight like a diamond" (209).[21] It is language strikingly similar to that in which Cather describes the pre-Fall morn when Niel gathers roses for his "Lady." And just as Niel's Eden soon perishes, so the "immortal repose" and "calmness of eternity" of Tom's city are soon invaded by everything associated with mortality and the Fall. Underscoring the connection are the name that Tom and Roddy give to the young girl whose body they find, "Mother Eve," and their reconstruction of her story: "We thought she had been murdered; there was a great wound in her side, the ribs stuck out through the dried flesh. Her mouth was open as if she were screaming, and her face, through all those years, had kept a look of terrible agony" (214).[22] The discovery of Mother Eve sets the stage for the first break in Tom and Roddy's good fortune. The change comes with the onset of "the little new moon, that looked so innocent" (216) and takes the form of a rattlesnake that kills their companion, Henry (innocence shattered and the snake: the Garden again). Tom, Roddy, and Father Duchene muse over what destroyed the city and its builders and conclude that "they were probably wiped out, utterly exterminated," by "brutal invaders" (221). And although Tom carves out for himself an Edenic interlude in his immortal city the following summer, this comes only after he has returned to discover that his friend has sold off their findings, and only after Tom has turned on this friend in a self-righteous rage that he soon regrets. And we already know the end of Tom's own story: this brilliant and visionary young man will die on Flanders Field.[23]

As St. Peter ponders Tom's short life, he perceives the gulf between his youthful idealism, his immortal longings, and the world he would have encountered had he returned from the war, and he concludes that Tom is better off having died young. His language unmistakably recalls the musings of Claude's mother after her son's death:

> [W]hat would have happened to him, once the trap of worldly success had been sprung on him[?] He couldn't see Tom building "Outland," or becoming a public-spirited citizen of Hamilton. What change would have come in his blue eye, in his fine long hand with the backspringing thumb, which had never handled things that were not the symbols of ideas? A hand like that, had he lived, must have been put to other uses. His fellow scientists, his wife, the town and State, would have required many duties of it. It would have had to write thousands of useless letters, frame thousands of false excuses. It would have had to "manage" a great deal of money, to be the instrument of a woman who would grow always more exacting. He had escaped all that. He had made something new in the world—and the rewards, the meaningless conventional gestures, he had left to others. (260–61)

In this passage the professor is clearly talking as much about himself as he is about Tom. When he mentions becoming the instrument of "a woman who would grow always more exacting," he is surely thinking of his own wife. His comment on "the rewards, the meaningless gestures," recalls the prize he himself has won, which has brought none of the satisfaction that came with writing his books, and the prize money that has caused so many problems. Tom, like Claude, escapes before grasping the degree to which idealism such as his own is incompatible with human life; the professor, in contrast, has lived on, and the planned move to the new house, along with his own advancing years, lead him to contemplate just what it means to be mortal. He recalls his once strong sexual attraction to Lillian, and where it has led: "Because there was Lillian, there must be marriage and a salary. Because there was marriage, there were children" (265). He confronts the double life he has had to lead, juggling his research with his intense teaching as well as dealing with the demands of his family and of an aging and imperfect house. His wife notes that he "is not old enough for the pose [he] take[s]," that from being an "impetuous young man" just two years ago (when he was still writing his book) he has become someone who "save[s him]self in everything." He answers with a candor that contrasts with his usual irony toward her: "I can't altogether tell myself, Lillian. It's not wholly a matter of the calendar. It's the feeling that I've put a great deal behind me, where I can't go back to it again—and I don't really wish to go back. The way would be too long and too fatiguing. Perhaps, for a home-staying man, I've lived pretty hard. I wasn't willing to slight anything—you, or my desk, or my students. And now I seem to be tremendously tired. One pays, coming or going. A man has got only just so much in him; when it's gone he slumps" (162–63). That there is a side of him that still longs for his youth becomes apparent later in the book—on the other side of the divide that is Tom's story—when he contrasts the young man he once had been, in "the realest of his lives," with what he has now become: "His career, his wife, his family, were not his life at all, but a chain of events which had happened to him. . . . He did not regret his life, but he was indifferent to it. It seemed to him like the life of another person" (264, 267). And as he looks back toward that boy Godfrey, his mortality suddenly comes into focus as well—"a conviction (he did not see it coming . . .) that he was nearing the end of his life. . . . [O]ne day, when he realized that all the while he was preparing for the fall term he didn't in the least believe he would be alive during the fall term, he thought he might better see a doctor" (267).

Although "Tom Outland's Story" includes its own hints of the Fall, its own tale of evil and the snake invading Eden, Tom himself never fully confronts the realities of the Garden, and as the professor notes, Tom dies before "life" brings these realities home to him (we recall St. Peter's observation that when Tom first lived with the professor's family "there were no shadows" in the stories he told the children [123]). In contrast, St. Peter, with his magnum opus behind him, and the loss of his study ahead, must suddenly face those realities, as must any human who lives long enough. He may have been able in his books to create a world of order, control, and permanence, but those are not the properties of the world in which he lives. Worst of all, the problem lies not with the world but in himself: the name Mephistopheles that his students attach to him because of his "wicked-looking eyebrows" (13) is apt: he, "mortal, subject to the chances," is himself the devil, himself the snake that poisons the Eden he can imagine.[24]

Willa Cather had in these years been daily confronting the evidence of her own mortal limitations, and the professor's words capture the tone of many of her letters from these years: "And now I seem to be tremendously tired. One pays, coming or going. A man has got only just so much in him; when it's gone he slumps." Perhaps the most despairing aspect of *The Professor's House* is that the ideal world Tom finds in his city, St. Peter in his history, is also the world of art—and, as Cather makes unmistakably clear, that of her own art. It is not just that she creates so close an identification between herself and the professor, one in which his books line up with her own, his prize with hers. Nor is it that Tom's discovery of the city on the Blue Mesa so closely echoes her own expedition to Mesa Verde in 1915, an expedition that fed directly into "Tom Outland's Story," which she drafted soon after that trip. It is rather that the qualities of Godfrey's and Tom's ideal worlds so closely match those that Cather sought in her own work: proportion, symmetry, design, immortal repose, the calmness of eternity, qualities reminiscent of Keats's Urn, which she had long held up as an image of art, and of her art. The professor as he views the Sierra Nevadas from his ship has a sudden sense of how his history will come together, attain wholeness: "[T]he design of his book unfolded in the air above him." Of his final summer in his city, Tom writes, "This was the first time I ever saw it as a whole. It all came together in my understanding . . . . Something had happened in me that made it possible for me to co-ordinate and simplify . . ." (250–51). As we read these passages we cannot fail to think of Cather comparing what she is trying to do in a novel with walking around an urn on the table and trying to see, and present, its wholeness.[25] Nor can we fail to remember what she had written in "The Art of Fiction" in 1920: "Art, it seems to me, should simplify. That, indeed, is very nearly the whole of the higher artistic process" (*wcow* 102).[26] In addition, the language of these passages of *The Professor's House* is strikingly similar to that which Cather in these very years was using to describe the art of Sarah Orne Jewett. In her preface to Jewett's collected stories, Cather describes "the almost flawless examples of literary art that make up these two volumes" as "tightly built and significant in design. The design is, indeed, so happy, so right, that it seems inevitable; the design is the story and the story is the design" (*Best Stories* x).[27]

The similarities between Cather's artistic vision on the one hand, St. Peter's history and Tom Outland's city on the other, cut two ways. They help us to see more clearly what Cather sought in her own work and, in particular, to identify in this novel itself the qualities that the professor and Tom seek: order, symmetry, balance, the coherence of the parts within a whole, a quality especially marked in this novel whose strangeness of form so precisely reflects its meaning, where "the design is the story and the story is the design." But the similarities also suggest that Cather here is casting art as an "outland" akin to Tom's city and Godfrey's history, something set apart from the living world, something that creates barriers with other people (as the Marselluses' "Outland" does in the novel), something at odds with life itself. "Immortal" means ageless, lasting, unfading, all qualities that artists seek in their creations; but humans are mortal, and to some extent anyone who fixates on the immortal pulls against life and living and one's fellow mortals, as St. Peter and Tom find in the novel, and as Cather herself was finding in her own life at this time. Words and phrases and images that describe St. Peter in the novel fit the Cather of these years, as she herself surely recognized: intolerant, impatient, ungracious to visitors; a loner who wants to shut others out, keep them at a distance; someone out of sorts with life, tired of the balancing act that Tom would have faced had he lived longer, in which one must "succeed" in the external world if one is to have the wherewithal to pursue one's ideals, but in which those ideals are eroded by all that is entailed in "succeeding."[28] Not least there is the strong, if paradoxical, association of immortality with death: the city Tom finds has its eternal order because it is dead, just as Mother Eve can project her emotions across the centuries precisely because she is mummified. Once the professor has woven his adventurers into the patterned whole of his history, they too are frozen forever, like the amber-embalmed fly to which Tom compares his city.[29] In both cases, "[t]he moving is over and done." And by the way Cather tells their stories, with Tom dying early, the professor finding himself obsessed with death, she pointedly asks whether devoting one's life to these "immortal" projects balances the price of turning one's back on life and on the living, surely a question she had in mind in 1924–25 as she watched the years slip by, and as she felt the fruit of her quest for artistic perfection to be the "bother and fatigue" she lived with daily. That Cather apparently chose not to devote much effort to the blurb advertising *The Professor's House* reflects both the weariness with life that she was feeling and the relative insignificance such efforts assume when weighed against the literally life-and-death issues that were on her mind and that find expression in the novels of this time, and especially in *The Professor's House*.

Equally wrenching is the fact that echoes of the language she was using of Sarah Orne Jewett at this very time become part of the same network. Just as the professor in his work, and Tom Outland in his city, had sought order and symmetry that were lasting, so Cather had long seen Jewett's works as exemplary of the way artistic achievement can survive its creator's passing, a point she makes at the end of her Jewett preface, where she describes the capacity of *The Country of the Pointed Firs* to "confront time and change so serenely" and "fairly to shine with the reflection of its long, joyous future. It is so tightly yet so lightly built, so little encumbered with heavy materialism that deteriorates and grows old-fashioned" (*Best Stories* xix). Cather's novel itself, however, suggests the degree to which these lasting properties, for all their order and beauty, are as mummified and dead as Mother Eve herself, a figure who one critic has suggested herself contains intimations of Cather's conflicted attitudes toward Sarah Orne Jewett.[30]

That even Cather's vision of Jewett and her art is swept into the pessimistic trajectory of *The Professor's House* is painfully appropriate to the end of the novel, where the professor, with Augusta's help, makes his peace with the future, accepting that it will be a future devoid of his former zest for life.[31] In the final scene in the study, St. Peter recognizes that the person he really was, the boy he has rediscovered, "seemed to know, among other things, that he was solitary and must always be so; he had never married, never been a father. He was earth, and would return to earth" (265). In the pages that follow, Godfrey faces his own return to earth. After seeing the doctor, he acknowledges that his premonition of death is probably his sole ailment, and in the subsequent scene he recalls lines from Longfellow's poem "The Grave," lines that suggest the different "house" that now awaits him—his coffin. Before falling asleep he acknowledges also that he has fallen out of love—"[s]urely the saddest thing in the world"—and that this "[f]alling out, for him, seemed to mean falling out of all domestic and social relations, out of his place in the human family, indeed" (275). Surely all this contributes to the questions he asks of himself when he awakes briefly to find his study window closed and the gas-leaking stove still on: "How far was a man required to exert himself against accident? How would such a case be decided under English law? He hadn't lifted his hand against himself—was he required to lift it for himself?" (276).

In the event, the professor rouses himself enough to stumble and fall, thus catching the attention of Augusta, who drags him to safety. The resolution she offers in the final pages is real but limited, something like what the psychiatrist Harcourt-Reilly offers the disillusioned Celia in T. S. Eliot's *The Cocktail Party*: "I can reconcile you to the human condition."[32] It is a reconciliation in which St. Peter accepts life rather than death, mortality with its limitations in place of his quest to create something immortal. He recognizes that he must learn to live without delight, something he has shunned in the past, and that during his brief unconsciousness he "had let something go—and it was gone; something very precious, that he could not consciously have relinquished, probably" (282). What the reconciliation achieves is that for the first time in months he longs for human company (compare his earlier sense of having "fallen out of the human family"). He can face his family's imminent return, and, for now, he is glad to be with Augusta: "Augusta was like the taste of bitter herbs; she was the bloomless side of life that he had always run away from,—yet when he had to face it, he found that it wasn't altogether repugnant" (280).

It is a bleak ending to a beautiful but despairing novel. St. Peter reconciles himself to the world in effect by abandoning both sides of the ambition that led to Thea's triumph, those two sides, at their best complementary, that Cather had identified in Sarah Bernhardt, and had striven for in her own life. Not only does he no longer entertain dreams of accomplishing anything that will rise above the dreary level of everyday human existence, but he also no longer has reason and motivation even to exert himself for the worldly goals that motivate the singers of Cather's 1916–19 short stories. It is a conclusion markedly darker than that of *A Lost Lady*. In that novel Marian too encounters the encroachments of mortality, sees them erode the good life she has enjoyed and eat away even at her own character; and she too gets drawn into dealing with the daily round, and with other people, in ways she had previously avoided. She does so, however, to assure that she will *not* live without delight, that despite any compromises she makes she will retain something of the zest and magic that are uniquely hers; and it is thus that Niel remembers her at the end of the novel. Cather's next novel, *My Mortal Enemy*, will end on a still bleaker note—with a heroine who not only forswears her youthful dream but also has no interest in reconciling herself to life itself. At the same time, however, she will seek in the way she dies something that reaches beyond the dim life St. Peter finds at the end of *The Professor's House*, a foreshadowing of directions Cather will pursue in *Death Comes for the Archbishop*.

CHAPTER FIFTEEN

My Mortal Enemy

For the gods there is Walhalla and forever and a day, but for mortals there is only the moment, and that is dying even while it is being born.
—LILLIAN NORDICA TO CATHER in the
   Lincoln Courier, June 10, 1899 (*W&P* 623)

A Lost Lady and *My Mortal Enemy*, both with titles that carry intimations of Ivar's "sin and death," have much in common. Both are par excellence novels démeublés, and both are tightly structured, with close parallels between each book's corresponding parts.[1] Unlike the novels they follow in Cather's oeuvre, *One of Ours* and *The Professor's House*, respectively, they both have women as their central figures, and the origins of these two vividly imagined figures may also be similar. We know that Cather modeled Marian Forrester on Mrs. Silas Garber, whose death in 1921 evoked such powerful memories that purportedly the entire novel came to Cather in a single afternoon.[2] Cather never revealed her prototype for Myra Henshawe, but she "wrote in 1940 that she had known Myra's real-life model very well, and the portrait drawn in the story was much as she remembered her."[3] If, as has recently been suggested, Cather's models for Myra and Oswald Henshawe were Hattie and Samuel S. McClure, Cather has once again, as in *A Lost Lady*, followed Jewett in taking as starting point something that has for years teased her mind.[4]

Both Marian and Myra rise above those around them, especially if they happen to be men, and both exude a fairytale aura.[5] Niel Herbert speaks of gathering flowers for "his lady," while Nellie Birdseye, the narrator of *My Mortal Enemy*, thinks of Myra's childhood home as "the Sleeping Beauty's palace" (*MME* 25). For Niel, Marian "belong[s] to a different world from any he had ever known" (*LL* 42), and Myra strikes Nellie the same way. As a child she has heard Myra described as a "brilliant and attractive figure" with a life "as exciting and varied as ours was monotonous" (10), and her Aunt Lydia has told her of the "thrilling night (probably the most exciting in her life)" when Myra fled home to marry Oswald Henshawe, giving up her inheritance to do so (23). Though at their first meeting Nellie finds Myra older than she expected, and decidedly prickly, she quickly falls under her spell. When she visits the Henshawes in New York, she notes the same sort of details that distinguish Marian Forrester—the style of Myra's home ("[e]verything in their little apartment seemed to me absolutely individual and unique" [37]); Myra's "extravagance . . . in caring for so many people, and in caring for them so much"; the way Myra's merely mentioning a name "invested the name with a sort of grace" (54–55). When a guest sings from *Norma* after dinner at the Henshawes', Nellie watches Myra and senses "something in her nature that one rarely saw, but nearly always felt; a compelling, passionate, overmastering something for which I had no name, but which was audible, visible in the air that night, as she sat crouching in the shadow" (60).[6] Like Marian, Myra retains this nameless "something" even when in the novel's second half she is living under straitened circumstances, and is mortally ill. Father Fay, who ministers to Myra in her last weeks, comments that she is "a most unusual woman, Mrs. Henshawe . . . . I wonder whether some of the saints of the early church weren't a good deal like her" (110–11).[7]

Again like Marian, Myra understands that to live the way she wants requires money, and she applies her energy and intelligence to helping her husband in his work. Just as Marian charms her husband's colleagues when they visit Sweet Water, so Myra on Sunday afternoons visits her "moneyed" friends—people she "cultivate[s] . . . on Oswald's account" (50–51). When her husband, like Marian's, falls upon hard times, she too tries to bear up but acutely feels "the cruelty of being poor. . . . Money is a protection, a cloak; it can buy one quiet, and some sort of dignity" (83).

After the Captain's stroke, Marian cares for him lovingly but also works to protect her own interests. Myra carries matters a step further. Aunt Lydia comments even in part 1 that "[e]verything is always for Myra," that Oswald "never gets anything for himself" (45), and it seems completely in character when in part 2 Myra reveals that amid the poverty in which she and Oswald live she has her own stash of gold tucked away in an old trunk. In a subsequent scene Myra contrasts herself with her husband: he can look back on their marriage and imagine that it was all as good as "the best of those days when we were young and loved each other," while she "was always a grasping, worldly woman; I was never satisfied" (104).

Marian's possessiveness, and her capacity for jealous rage, manifest themselves mainly in her telephone call to Frank Ellinger, after she learns that he has forsaken her for Constance Ogden. In contrast, envy and jealousy consume Myra throughout *My Mortal Enemy*. What Nellie describes as a "long, delightful afternoon alone with Mrs. Henshawe in Central Park" (51) suddenly turns sour when a carriage passes their hired cab and the woman within leans out and waves. "There, Nellie," Myra exclaims, "that's the last woman I'd care to have splashing past me, and me in a hansom cab!" When they arrive home, Myra complains, "[I]t's very nasty, being poor!" (52–53), and Nellie comments that the episode has given her a glimpse of Myra's "insane ambition." Shortly after, when they are together at a matinée, Nellie asks Myra about a young man she sees, who looks like a much-photographed writer. "Yes, it's he," says Myra. "He used to be a friend of mine. That's a sad phrase, isn't it? But there was a time when he could have stood by Oswald in a difficulty—and he didn't. He passed it up. Wasn't there. I've never forgiven him." Nellie realizes that from then on Myra's mind is on the young man: "[F]or the rest of the afternoon I could feel the bitterness working in her. . . . She was going over it all again; arguing, accusing, denouncing." As they leave the theatre, Myra says, "Oh, Nellie, I wish you hadn't seen him! It's all very well to tell us to forgive our enemies . . . . But oh, what about forgiving our friends? . . . [T]hat's where the rub comes!" (56).

Myra's capacity to turn on those she loves comes fully into the open in the final scenes of part 1, where she confronts Oswald with some cuff links a young woman has sent him at the office, and which he has tried to pass off as a gift from Aunt Lydia. Soon after, she attacks Lydia herself for her part in the plot, and in part 2 she suddenly turns on Nellie and sends her away because she senses Nellie is getting too close to Oswald (105–6). But even in their first meeting Nellie sees signs of Myra's savage side. Myra taunts Nellie for staring at her amethyst necklace, and in the conversation that follows Nellie feels her sarcasm: "so quick, so fine at the point—it was like being touched by a metal so cold that one doesn't know whether one is burned or chilled" (14).[8] After dinner Nellie's mother comments on "how good it is . . . to hear Myra laugh again," but Nellie immediately adds that she was later to find that Myra also "had an angry laugh . . . that I still shiver to remember" (17)—the angry laugh that will herald the cuff-links episode.

Myra's distinctive laugh is yet one more tie to Marian Forrester, whose inimitable laugh echoes throughout *A Lost Lady*.[9] But though Marian's laugh, and her laughing eyes, contain their own hint of mockery (cf. *LL* 35), Myra's laugh is symptomatic of her deeply divided nature. "Strong and broken, generous and tyrannical, a witty and rather wicked old woman," is how Nellie describes Myra when she rediscovers her in the dumpy San Francisco apartment (80). "She can't endure, but she has enough desperate courage for a regiment," says her husband at one point (92). Soon after the cuff-links contretemps and Myra's discovery of Lydia's role in it, Myra turns out to be on the same train as Nellie and her aunt, and once again Nellie comments on the oppositions within her: "All day Mrs. Myra was jolly and agreeable, though she treated us with light formality, as if we were new acquaintances. We lunched together, and I noticed, sitting opposite her, that when she was in this mood of high scorn, her mouth, which could be so tender . . . was entirely different. It seemed to curl and twist about like a little snake. Letting herself think harm of anyone she loved seemed to change her nature, even her features" (67).

The flawless formal mastery of *My Mortal Enemy* suggests the continuing impact of Sarah Orne Jewett, an impact renewed by Cather's work on Jewett in 1924–25. Indeed, no other Cather novel more closely approximates what Cather had written of Jewett in her preface to the 1925 collection of Jewett stories: "The design is the story and the story is the design." In addition, in *My Mortal Enemy* Cather not only again gives center stage to a woman but also for the first time in a novel introduces a "specifically female narrative voice—the voice in which Jewett wrote almost exclusively . . . ."[10] Cather's other alter ego, however, is yet more in evidence.[11] In numerous respects, as David Stouck has noted, Myra Henshawe recalls Mary Baker Eddy as Cather had portrayed her some twenty years earlier: greedy, grasping, tyrannical; obsessed with status and money and appearances; fiercely possessive; capable of intense jealousy against anyone she thought might be invading her turf; ready both to charm those she cared for and to turn upon them savagely; almost pathologically bimodal in her moods and behavior.[12] Given Cather's penchant for wordplay, it seems likely that in "Myra" she is playing a variation on "Mary"—same consonants and sequence, but with the vowels reversed as in a mirror; and, of course, it is in a mirror that Nellie first sees Myra.[13] In addition, there is the tie between "my mortal enemy," the repeated phrase that gives the book its title, and the enemy against which Eddy constantly inveighs, and which in Cather's biography of Eddy becomes the equivalent of Eddy's otherwise-missing principle of evil: "Mortal Mind" (*MBE* 228–29).

And indeed, Cather's echoes of Eddy in *My Mortal Enemy* herald yet one more probing into the persistent reality of evil, but the theme here takes on yet darker and more cosmic colors, for the evil identified is nothing less than what Cather in 1931 would describe as "the seeming original injustice that creatures so splendidly aspiring should be inexorably doomed to fail," a rift relevant not just to the individual but to all humans. Cather's very language, "the original injustice," recalls the Garden, and in the novels of the 1920s, above all in *My Mortal Enemy*, Cather fastens on this "original sin" of the race, the fatal divide between our "splendid aspiring" and our inexorably doomed mortal failings. The tension is implicit in *One of Ours*, where Claude's mother is grateful that his death prevented him from seeing his soaring visions shattered by life's realities. The theme comes further to the fore in *A Lost Lady*, where Niel watches Marian struggle to preserve her "something that made one's blood tingle" against the erosions and failings of mortality, including her own. And we have just seen how central to *The Professor's House* is the tension between the immortal worlds to which Godfrey St. Peter and Tom Outland aspire and the mortal realities to which they are reduced.

This quintessential human dichotomy reaches its apex in *My Mortal Enemy* and its heroine.[14] On the one hand, Myra is someone who, like Marian Forrester, "belongs to a different world." Like Claude, she dares in eloping with Oswald to stake all on the quest for "something splendid," and even in her waning days she remains, as Mr. Harsanyi says of Thea, "uncommon, in a common, common world." At the same time, for all the aura that surrounds her, we are constantly reminded that Myra is very human, very mortal. In contrast to Marian Forrester, who exudes an almost maidenly freshness when we first meet her with the boys in the pasture, Myra even in her first appearance breathes mature sophistication and even a touch of cynicism. We are specifically reminded of her age—forty-five—as we are of the fact that she is twenty-five years older than she was when she eloped; and we learn from her first gesture, the look in the mirror, that this is a woman who watches herself closely as the years pass, a hint underscored when Nellie surmises that one reason Myra holds her head high is to avoid showing her double chin. Her sarcasm, her sharp tongue, the way she fences with those around her, all remind us that though her home may evoke a fairytale princess, Myra is no Sleeping Beauty but a seasoned woman of the world. Further details emphasize the passage of the years, and their impact. Nellie senses with surprise that Myra and Oswald are still in love, but she also notices how Myra hectors her husband and detects signs of bitterness as well as of affection in his response to her.[15] Even Lydia, who has such romantic memories of Myra's elopement, undercuts Nellie's dreams when she answers her query about Myra and Oswald's marriage: "Happy? Oh, yes! As happy as most people" (25).

Such details are very much to the point. Myra is a woman who consciously chose a romantic quest over the riches the world treasures, and whenever we see her, we glimpse the aspiring mind and spirit that set her apart from ordinary mortals, and that make believable her willingness to take this bold step. What we also see, though, are all those aspects of mortality that eat away at her romantic dream as the years pass, and make her question its worth. We see love itself decline, become less satisfying: early scenes suggest that Myra and Oswald no longer sleep together, and he is clearly having some sort of dalliance with the young woman who sends the cuff links. We see age attack both Oswald and Myra—frequent hints of it in part 1, its reality front and center in part 2. We see the onset of disease, something Marian Forrester largely escapes but that becomes, in every sense of the word, a mortal presence in the second half of *My Mortal Enemy*.

Not only is the erosion of human aspiration by these mortal realities implicit in page after page of the novel, especially its second half, but its protagonists explicitly comment on this theme. As Nellie contemplates Myra's reduced circumstances in California, she thinks how this woman has always responded to the contrarieties of life: how she has "hated life for its defeats, and loved it for its absurdities," how she has always "greeted shock or sorrow with that dry, exultant chuckle which seemed to say: 'Ah-ha, I have one more piece of evidence, one more, against the hideous injustice God permits in this world!'" (80; cf. the phrase Cather will use in 1931 to describe our mortality, "the seeming original injustice"). Commenting on the savagery that is her one inheritance from her uncle, Myra remarks, "We think we are so individual and so misunderstood when we are young; but the nature our strain of blood carries is inside there, waiting, like our skeleton" (98–99). And as she thinks back on what she has given up to follow love, she admits that had she to do it over again, she would go back and "ask [her uncle's] pardon; because I know what it is to be old and lonely and disappointed" (98). She has already said as much to Oswald: "Oh, if youth but knew! . . . We've destroyed each other. I should have stayed with my uncle. It was money I needed. We've thrown our lives away" (90–91). And to Nellie she comments on how the passage of time erodes love itself: "A man and woman draw apart from that long embrace, and see what they have done to each other. Perhaps I can't forgive him for the harm I did him. . . . In age we lose everything; even the power to love" (105). After Myra's death, Oswald encourages Nellie to remember Myra at her best, including the happiness of their marriage in its earlier days: "Remember her as she was when you were with us on Madison Square, when she was herself, and we were happy. Yes, happier than it falls to the lot of most mortals to be" (120–21). Unfortunately, "happier than most mortals" is not good enough for a person who, like Myra, stakes her life on immortal aspirations.[16]

All those aspects of human nature that Cather felt Eddy foolishly ignored come to the fore in *My Mortal Enemy*. Sex, disease, and death, which Eddy preached were "errors" of "Mortal Mind" that we can transcend, all emerge in this novel as "mortal enemies": they are mortal in that they are inextricable parts of our human constitution, mortal as well in that they can destroy us. Such resonances of "mortal" inevitably color that moment when, on one of the long nights when Nellie and Oswald sit with her as she nears death, Myra says in a voice like that of "a soul talking," "Why must I die like this, alone with my mortal enemy?" (113). Willa Cather noted that in penning these words she thought of Myra's primary reference as being to her husband, but what follows in this very chapter invites broader interpretation. Nellie comments that she has "never heard a human voice utter such a terrible judgment upon all one hopes for," a phrase that suggests she understands Myra to be speaking more about herself than about anyone else.[17] What Nellie then adds not only points the same way but also places Myra in that group where Cather had placed Eddy many years before, people of a violent nature: "I began to understand a little what she meant, to sense how it was with her. Violent natures like hers sometimes turn against themselves . . . against themselves and all their idolatries" (113). Nellie's reference to "idolatries" nicely comprehends the full range of what Myra sees in herself—at one end of the spectrum her willingness to stake all on romantic aspirations, at the other her recognition of how desperately she wants and needs the material comforts of life.

Taken reflexively in this way, Myra's "my mortal enemy" also fits the snakelike qualities she reveals at balancing moments of jealousy—in the scene on the train already quoted, and when, at a parallel point in part

2, she suddenly turns on Nellie: "She was smiling, but her mouth curled like a little snake, as I had seen it do long ago" (106, cf. 67).[18] The image is telling, for Myra herself, so torn by internal contradiction, so pulled in opposite directions, *is* the snake, the "mortal enemy" in the Garden, "the original injustice," our fatal mix of immortal aspiration and mortal failing. We recall too St. Peter's nickname, "Mephistopheles," another "mortal enemy": it too is apt, for like Myra he carries within himself the same mark of the Fall, the same divide between yearning and frailty.

On the final page of the book Nellie returns to Myra's "terrible" words: "Sometimes, when I have watched the bright beginning of a love story, when I have seen a common feeling exalted into beauty by imagination, generosity, and the flaming courage of youth, I have heard again that strange complaint breathed by a dying woman into the stillness of night, like a confession of the soul: 'Why must I die like this, alone with my mortal enemy!'" (122).[19] It is a passage that casts Myra's words as response not only to her own mortality and her own conflicting idolatries but also to the universal divide between our immortal aspirations—"a common feeling exalted into beauty by imagination, generosity, and the flaming courage of youth"—and the human, mortal realities that limit those dreams: "Why must I die like this, alone with my mortal enemy!"

Like Mary Baker Eddy, both Marian Forrester and Myra Henshawe show the greatest strength when they seem the most beleaguered, and in their resilience and courage they recall the independent women Cather had created in her novels and stories of the teens.[20] The goals of the actions Marian and Myra take, however, are diametrically opposed. Marian tells Niel that she has within herself too much power to live for her to grow old gracefully, as people expect her to do, and at the end of *A Lost Lady* Niel learns that after leaving Sweet Water she has again forged a new and good life for herself. Myra's action is no less bold—indeed, it makes us recall Oswald's comment that she "has enough desperate courage for a regiment"—but its focus is on death, not life, on assuring that she dies in a manner that suits her wishes, and in the location that she has long since chosen.

When Nellie and Myra first discover this location, a great bare headland that overlooks the Pacific, Myra quickly identifies it as a place that offers "light and silence: they heal one's wounds." She also imagines returning there at dawn: "That is always such a forgiving time. When that first cold, bright streak comes over the water, it's as if all our sins were pardoned; as if the sky leaned over the earth and kissed it and gave it absolution. You know how the great sinners always came home to die in some religious house, and the abbot or the abbess went out and received them with a kiss?" (88–89). Several familiar notes sound in this passage: the purity of dawn, as in the morning when Niel gathers roses for Marian; the brightness of light shining over water, as when the professor visits his lake to feel the release offered by its silence, or sees the Sierra Nevadas across the sunny brilliance of the ocean; a great rock standing tall and alone, reminiscent of the enchanted bluff that so captivates the boys of Cather's early story, and of Tom Outland's Blue Mesa. These echoed passages, however, all look forward to action—to Niel taking flowers to his lady, to the professor returning to his work with new vigor and inspiration, to the lives the boys have ahead of them, to Tom's hopes for climbing the mesa and his discovery of the city that will transform his life. In contrast, Myra's Pacific bluff is from the start a retreat: it offers escape from one's wounds, and even at dawn it evokes not the innocence of the Garden—as with Niel—but the possibility of absolution for past sins. The difference is analogous to that between the goal of Marian's efforts, which is to give sway to her will to live, and the goal of Myra's flight to her bluff, which is to enable her to die as she wishes. In addition, Myra explicitly links the place to her newfound religious faith, carrying a substantial step further the Catholic roots of the comfort Augusta brings St. Peter in the final scene of *The Professor's House*. The motifs that Cather uses to such effect in this final scene of *My Mortal Enemy*—the strength of Catholicism, the Rock, its long and light-flooded vista—are ones she will invest with yet further meaning in her next book, *Death Comes for the Archbishop*.[21] In turn, the title of that next book suggests one further resonance of "my mortal enemy": Myra's final act is surely her way of shaping that final confrontation with death, in which she is indeed "alone with my mortal enemy."

We have traveled far from where Cather was a decade earlier. At that time her heroines were women bravely struggling either to survive or to attain some transcendent goal in life. Here we end with a woman who consciously gives up the struggle to live in favor of achieving her goal of a transcendent death. We are in both instances dealing with women of unusual courage and vision, but their orientations are radically different. Myra Henshawe's focus on dying well may be the natural next step from Godfrey St. Peter's reconciling himself to living without delight, but it is a major step. In the teens Cather had played variations on two divided ways, both focused on life: one way was devoted to the quest for an immortal ideal, the other to confronting with courage the daily duties that enable one to "live well." By the time of *My Mortal Enemy*, both ways are focused instead on death: the daily round is above all something that brings home to us our mortality, and the transcendent act of courage is to assure that one will die in a manner true to one's ideals. Cather is as much Myra as she is Godfrey St. Peter, and that she writes this book in which mortality looms as the essential fact of both ways says a great deal about the Willa Cather of these years.[22] At the same time, though, she, like Myra, remains a woman of paradox, someone always playing contrasting roles. For whatever the despair and discouragement of these years, in writing this very novel, as death-haunted as it is, Cather creates something so perfect in its form, so true to her vision of the novel démeublé, and so brimming with life, as itself to embody her continued search for the kingdom of art, her ongoing defiance of "our mortal enemy."[23] As suggested earlier, the formal mastery of *My Mortal Enemy* owes much to Sarah Orne Jewett—no other novel is, as Cather had written of Jewett in her 1925 preface, "so tightly yet so lightly built" (*Best Stories* xix). And, to add one more paradox, the Eddy-like Myra's final quest—for a place that offers "light and silence"—echoes what Jewett had told Cather in 1908: "You must find your own quiet centre of life."

Part VI
Recapitulation

In a recent novel Tobias Wolff comments eloquently on the gulf between a writer's "real" life and the imaginative life from which his or her writing springs: "The life that produces writing can't be written about. It is a life carried on without the knowledge even of the writer, below the mind's business and noise, in deep unlit shafts where phantom messengers struggle toward us . . . ."[1] Even with a writer who draws as heavily on her own experiences as does Cather, it would be wrong-headed and misleading to suggest any one-to-one correspondence between her fiction and her life. There inevitably remains, however, an ongoing and lively exchange of signs and signals between these areas, and this retrospective chapter reviews the oft-illuminating conversation that occurs between Cather's life and two different forms of her writing—her fiction and her promotional copy.

CHAPTER SIXTEEN

Cather Talks with Cather

The further the world advances the more it becomes evident that an author's only safe course is to cling close to the skirts of his art, forsaking all others, and keep unto her as long as they two shall live. An artist should not be vexed by human hobbies or human follies; he should be able to lift himself up into the clear firmament of creation where the world is not. He should be among men but not one of them, in the world but not of the world. Other men may think and reason and believe and argue, but he must create. (KA 407)

In the kingdom of art there is not God, but one God, and his service is so exacting that there are few men born of woman who are strong enough to take the vows. There is no paradise offered for a reward to the faithful, no celestial bowers, no houris, no scented wines; only death and the truth. "Thy truth then be thy dower." (KA 417)

Two Roads Meet: Through 1915

In keeping with these passages, Willa Cather from her university days on saw her artistic quest as a pilgrimage that brooked no compromise in its service of truth and beauty. She did so with full understanding of what it meant to be "in the world but not of the world." Her long and close study of artists and their lives had made her painfully aware of the temptation to bend standards so as to attract the public; of the danger of becoming enamored of fame and fortune and losing sight of one's artistic goals; and of the erosion of ideals as year in, year out, an artist struggles to make a living. These dangers came home to Cather during her ten years in Pittsburgh and her five subsequent years with *McClure's*, not least in the Mary Baker Eddy project: hard, complex work stretching over a long period, on a topic she often found repugnant, and with little time and energy left for her own writing.

It was just months after this project ended that Sarah Orne Jewett wrote the letter in which she reminded Cather of the danger she faced, and of her need to choose which road she would take: "I cannot help saying what I think about your writing and its being hindered by such incessant, important, responsible work as you have in your hands now. I do think that it is impossible for you to work so hard and yet have your gifts mature as they should—when one's first working power has spent itself nothing ever brings it back just the same, and I do wish in my heart that the force of this very year could have gone into three or four stories." Jewett also reminded Cather that she needed "still more to feel 'responsible for the state of your conscience' (your literary conscience . . .), and you need to dream your dreams and go on to new and more shining ideals, to be aware of 'the gleam' and to follow it . . . ." In words that uncannily recall what Cather herself had written in 1894, Jewett added, "To work in silence and with all one's heart, that is the writer's lot; he is the only artist who must be a solitary, and yet needs the widest outlook upon the world."[1]

Although the attractions of her work at *McClure's*—prestige, excitement, travel, money—were enough to keep her there well into 1911, even in 1908 Cather recognized the validity of the advice Jewett had given her. In "On the Gulls' Road," written in the first half of 1908, one senses already the impact of Jewett's generous spirit, and a second story from the same period, "The Enchanted Bluff," both feels like Cather's first breakthrough into the artistic space Jewett had encouraged her to explore and also, paradoxically, suggests how distant the artistic ideals— "the Enchanted Bluff"?—toward which Jewett was directing her gaze still were. Three works written in 1911–12, the years when she finally did break away, suggest Cather's confrontation of the choices she had to make, and of their attendant consequences. *Alexander's Bridge* places its hero where Cather herself stood at this time. Like Bartley Alexander, she is in young middle age, has a brilliant career in the making, but feels dissatisfied with her life and weary of the daily duties that come with success. Above all, she too feels the ideals she had sought in her youth receding from her grasp. One senses a yet more personal involvement in two stories of the same period, "The Joy of Nelly Deane" and "The Bohemian Girl," where, in contrast to *Alexander's Bridge*, Cather gives women lead roles as she explores choices similar to those she herself was facing: to accede to society's expectations, as Nelly does, a choice that leads to death both physical and spiritual; or to follow one's heart into a frightening unknown, as Clara does, abandoning societal support and approval but opening the door to a life closer to her dreams.

Cather chooses Clara's way, and in so doing she opens the door to three novels that feature heroines cut in Clara's daring mold. These novels also move ever closer to the artistic ideals Cather had set for herself, and that Jewett had held up for her as reasons to reach beyond her work, and her success, at *McClure's*. The sense of release is palpable both in the "heroic womanhood" of Cather's lead characters and in the spacious themes these novels explore—pioneer courage pitted against smallness of spirit, good against evil, the artist confronting the hurdles posed by society. Dark undercurrents are present in all three novels, but all three nonetheless conclude with heroines able to look back at achievements that fulfill youthful dreams and forward to futures that have their own satisfactions. The expansive sense of freedom and achievement, the equipoise between past and future triumphs, and even something of the epic scope of these novels sound also in the autobiography Cather ghostwrites for S. S. McClure during this same fertile period.

It is informative to revisit the unsigned publicity materials Cather wrote or helped write—the dust jackets for the novels and the copy for the 1915 brochure—against this backdrop of Cather's life from late 1906 (when she begins the Eddy project) to early 1918 (when she completes *My Ántonia*). In her December 1908 letter Jewett reminded Cather of what she had previously done, and of the as yet unfulfilled promises of those beginnings: "In the 'Troll-Garden' [*sic*] the Sculptor's Funeral stands alone a head higher than the rest, and it is to that level you must hold and take for a starting-point. You are older now than that book in general; . . . but if you don't keep and guard and mature your force, and above all, have time and quiet to perfect your work, you will be writing things not much better than you did five years ago."[2] The opening of the *Alexander's Bridge* dust jacket reads like a response to Jewett's words: "Some six or eight years ago, Miss Cather's collection of short stories entitled 'A Troll Garden' [*sic*] was hailed by critics both in this country and in England as a collection of the first distinction . . . ; and a novel by the same hand was eagerly desired. This now comes in 'Alexander's Bridge,' a story that will take its place among the brilliant first novels of American writers."[3] Unlike most of the *Alexander's Bridge* blurb, this passage does not come from Ferris Greenslet's house memo. Instead, one hears in it Cather's own voice, her own declaration that at last in writing this novel she has begun to meet Jewett's hopes and expectations. As mentioned earlier, her input seems likely also in the passage (again not in Greenslet's memo) where the jacket praises the novel as "haunting to the memory," language which echoes Jewett's advice that Cather write about what teases and haunts the mind and memory.

If the *Alexander's Bridge* jacket implicitly acknowledges Jewett's advice, the jackets on the three novels that follow suggest where that advice has now led Cather, for they convey a powerful sense of energy released, of breakthrough into new regions, of life lived at a different and higher level: "A stirring romance . . . embodying a new idea and a new country . . . the splendid Swedish girl, Alexandra, who dares and achieves . . . the beautiful Bohemian whose love story is the very story of Youth . . . a creature so warm and palpitating with life . . ." (*O Pioneers!*); "The story of a great American singer . . . splendid triumphs on the operatic stage . . . a story of aspiration and conflict, of the magnificent courage of young ambition . . ." (*The Song of the Lark*); ". . . Ántonia, all impulsive youth and careless courage . . . the flame and driving force of unconquerable youth . . . so burning with vitality that no disaster can crush her . . . Ántonia has the freshness and vitality of the new soil from which she springs, the vigor of the great prairies on which her vivid and enthralling personal drama unfolds" (*My Ántonia*). In concert, these words and phrases capture the epic sweep of these three novels; their focus on youth and life and vigor, on ambition and daring and conquest; the memorable individuals they place against the backdrop of the prairie and the nation. The language also points to Cather herself, for the writing of these novels, depending as it did on her relinquishing her position at *McClure's*, was also the act of someone who "dares and achieves," a story of "the magnificent courage of young ambition," a tapping into the "freshness and vitality of the new soil from which she [had sprung], the vigor of the great prairies."

That such language is self-referential, a reflection of Cather's own breakthrough in writing these novels, becomes yet more clear when one turns to the autobiographical sketch she wrote for the 1915 brochure, especially in comparison with the "Literary Note" she had written in 1903 to accompany *April Twilights*. Where the note gives approximately equal space to Cather's childhood on the prairie and her years at the university, the 1915 statement includes one passing sentence on her university years but devotes almost a fifth of the whole essay to Cather's childhood on the prairie, and its impact on her. And where the 1903 note emphasizes the role of reading in Cather's education—the three books she read and reread as a child, her "voracious" reading of French and English literature at the university—the 1915 statement mentions not a single book but credits her education to her life on the Divide and to the people whom she came to know there. And this education is all about excitement, adventure, new vistas. Cather describes the "stimulating change" from "the quiet and the established order" of life in Virginia to life on the prairie; she talks about the preponderance of foreigners on the Divide and her efforts to understand them, her delight in the stories they told her. Quoting herself, she says that she has "never found any intellectual excitement more intense than I used to feel when I spent a morning with one of these pioneer women," tells of "rid[ing] home in the most unreasonable state of excitement," and compares the experience of getting inside another's skin to "the story of the man-eating tiger—no other adventure ever carries one quite so far."

Daring and adventure in fact sound throughout the brochure, and again the theme often transfers from the characters of the novels to

Cather and her writing. The brochure cites Jewett's advice that Cather "will have to make a way of your own. If the way happens to be new, don't let that frighten you." As if in response, the brochure notes that in *O Pioneers!* "Miss Cather has departed from conventional lines" and casts each Cather book as a new adventure: "[O]ne book in no way prepares [the reader] for what is coming next." Phrases used to describe Cather's writing seem to grow out of the pioneer life that is her subject: "simplicity and truthfulness," "virility and art," "a ruthlessness in keeping with the country and the stark simplicity of its moral code." Conversely, the characters evoked in the brochure seem reflections of her own energy and ambition: Bartley Alexander, "[a] man of elemental, restless force," Thea Kronborg, "a powerful and willful young creature." Compare all this with the "delightful volume of poems" hailed in the 1903 note.

Jewett's impact extends well beyond the section of the brochure that explicitly quotes her. Take, for instance, the following passage about *Alexander's Bridge*: "Avoiding alike the Western backgrounds and the newspaper and magazine world, with which she felt she was still too closely connected to 'see them from the outside,' Miss Cather laid the scene of her story in Boston and London." The language mirrors—indeed, quotes without attribution—what Jewett had advised in 1908: "I want you to be surer of your backgrounds,—you have your Nebraska life,—a child's Virginia, and now an intimate knowledge of what we are pleased to call the 'Bohemia' of *newspaper and magazine*-office life. These are uncommon equipment, but you don't *see them* yet quite enough *from the outside* . . ." (italics mine).[4] The brochure's emphasis on Cather's broad background—her childhood in Nebraska, her recent trip to the cliff-dweller remains of southwest Colorado, her knowledge of New York and of "the old, fine culture and traditions of New England"—similarly echoes Jewett's comment on Cather's "uncommon equipment." Jewett had also told her, "You must write to the human heart, the great consciousness that all humanity goes to make up." In response, the brochure notes that "the experiences of pioneering, and the contact with people of strange languages and customs . . . inspired in her the broad, human understanding so essential to a writer of fiction." Finally, the brochure's description of Bartley Alexander echoes Jewett's warning to Cather about the dangers of success: "[H]e realized that the success which had made him famous had forced upon him exactly the kind of life he had determined to escape. Confronted by the possibility of a calm, secure middle age, he felt as if he were being buried alive."[5]

That throughout the 1915 brochure one hears echoes and overtones of Jewett's words reminds us of Cather's intimate involvement in writing it, and of that second life that is implicit in all the anonymous promotional copy she produced. And this second life, with its attendant responsibilities and drudgery, by nature pulls against Jewett's call to find "the time and quiet to perfect your work." It is a tension that the brochure itself suggests in its contrasting descriptions of Thea, in so many ways Cather's double: "... Thea Kronborg, not yet appreciating the possibilities of her voice, is spending all her money and almost more than all her strength for the sake of her lessons and the drudgery of choir work" (Chicago); "away from drudgery for the first time in her life, she grew at once into a powerful and willful young creature, got her courage, and began to find herself" (cliff-dweller ruins). This same tension between the drudgery of the daily round and the demands of high art is implicit also in the stark contrast between the brochure's second section, "Journalism and Editing," and its other five sections. As we have seen, the long opening section stresses the energy and excitement of Cather's childhood in Nebraska, and the relevance of those years to her subsequent writing career. The final four sections both sustain the sense of adventure and also stress the magnitude of her achievement: "great artistic skill, brilliant and sympathetic in its reflections of character and life" (section 3); "a virility and art that mark her book as a novel of moment" (section 4); "'The Song of the Lark'... places her definitely in the little group of American novelists that count ..." (section 6). In contrast, section 2, which covers more than two decades of her life (1890–1911), mentions her university years, tersely recounts her decade as an editor, critic, and teacher in Pittsburgh, notes of her first books only that *The Troll Garden* "attracted a good deal of attention," and has this to say about her years at *McClure's*: "The duties of this position, the demands of life in New York, and the claims of her new social and business connections occupied her entire attention and for four years she did no writing at all." In both style and content, this section, written by

Cather and covering twenty-one of the forty-two years she had lived by 1915, comes across as a drab interlude that pulls against the remainder of the brochure, all of which focuses on Cather's pioneering achievements as a writer. In addition, this interlude leads immediately into the *Alexander's Bridge* section, which describes Alexander's realization that his "success" has landed him in just the sort of life he had hoped to avoid, and which explicitly mentions Cather's decision not to focus this novel on "the newspaper and magazine world," that very world she was then fleeing in order to write this novel.

The topic resurfaces at the end of the *Song of the Lark* section, which notes that Cather "has gained her knowledge of the ways of the operatic world through journalistic work," and the brochure's final section places Cather firmly in New York, the place where she had come to work for *McClure's*, and where she had indeed come to know the inner workings of the publishing world, including its reliance on advertising. And advertising expertise is what she brings to this brochure, her most extended exercise in preparing promotional copy about herself. As such, the brochure is one more Cather tribute to S. S. McClure, whose advertising bent she had stressed in her recent autobiography of the publisher. But it is also evidence of the continuing impact of the extended period she had spent, on her first *McClure's* assignment, with another consummate master of the craft, Mary Baker Eddy. For one cannot doubt that as Cather wrote and reviewed copy for a brochure whose purpose was to sell more books and bring in larger royalty checks, she had in mind Eddy's constant focus on advertising, the role that sales of her books had played in her astonishing success, and the envy-inspiring royalties her books had reaped. And just as Eddy's focus on "the Truth" never stopped her from crafting convenient untruths about herself, so in this brochure, in which Cather lays so much emphasis on artistic truthfulness, she does not hesitate to stretch the truth repeatedly in the interest of selling herself and her books.

Implicit in both the existence of this brochure and the character of its salesmanship is the double life Cather was leading in 1915: on the one hand, a novelist intent on scaling the heights, on producing works that met her own high standards for artistic honesty and integrity; on the other, a working professional spending increasing amounts of time on just the sort of promotional work she had thought to flee when she left *McClure's*. Perhaps most interesting is what the brochure suggests about the uneasy but clearly successful complementarity of these two sides of Cather's life at this juncture—the sort of pragmatic synergy she had many years before admired in Sarah Bernhardt. It is a complementarity implicit in the balance between, on the one hand, the tribute paid throughout to Jewett's influence on Cather's writing and, on the other, the central role Cather plays in creating a brochure whose character and purpose embody what she had learned from McClure and Eddy. This complementarity finds expression also in the heroine of the novel this brochure is advertising, who ends up living two very different lives, both of which are essential to her success. The concurrent production of *The Song of the Lark* and of this brochure suggests the similar nature of the double life Cather herself was living.[6] She clearly sees the novel as embodying all she is striving for as an artist, and she portrays it as such in the brochure; like Thea, she is not entirely comfortable with the promotional side of her life, hence the anonymity of her role in creating the brochure, but, again like Thea, she sees this side as essential to what she wants to achieve and takes it on with energy, determination, and a willingness to accept the compromises that will make the brochure effective. Three years before, as she faced the need to leave *McClure's* and devote herself to writing, she had described Bartley Alexander as "not a man who can live two lives." In *The Song of the Lark* she creates a heroine who does just that, and in 1915 Cather herself deftly pulls off a similar balancing act when she both completes her novel and shapes this substantial promotional brochure. In contrast to the absolute divide she had once proposed, she and Thea, though "vexed by human hobbies [and] human follies," nonetheless manage to inhabit "the clear firmament of creation where the world is not."

And Diverge Again: 1915–1920

We have seen that even as Cather began work on *My Ántonia*, a work that so nobly fulfils the spacious and heroic promises of the two novels that preceded it, she herself was living a very different life in New York

City, a gulf reflected in the novel's divided focus between Ántonia and Jim Burden—an obvious change from *The Song of the Lark*, where the different lives Thea is living are at least united in a single person. We saw also that these were years in which Cather felt pressed for funds, was frustrated by her perception that Houghton Mifflin was doing less than it might to advertise and sell her books, and was herself frequently involved—as in her work on the 1915 *Song of the Lark* brochure—in trying to complement and improve their efforts.

It was nagging concerns of this sort, combined with the disappointing sales of *My Ántonia*, that in 1920 and 1922 led Cather to publish her next books with Knopf. These same concerns find expression also in the stories Cather wrote in the second half of the teens, virtually all of which contain, and in most cases focus on, women deeply concerned with money. Stella in "The Bookkeeper's Wife" and the wife and daughters of the dying Paul Wanning in "Her Boss" are so obsessed with having the wherewithal to live well that they are impervious to the plights of the men who have been supporting them. Both Ardessa and Becky in "Ardessa" are concerned with getting ahead in the firm where they work, although they go about doing so in very different ways; even Annie, the young secretary who shows such compassion for Mr. Wanning in his last months, finds herself fired for her generosity and cheated of the modest bequest she had hoped for. Cressida Garnet, Kitty Ayrshire, and Eden Bower are successful singers, but it is the pursuit of money and success that dominates their lives, not the artistic ideals of a Thea Kronborg.

As suggested earlier, the structure of *Youth and the Bright Medusa* underscores the pragmatic cast of these singers' lives by posing their stories opposite four from *The Troll Garden* which contain intimations of the loftier worlds that art and artists can inhabit. The unusually copious jacket copy on this book, the first Cather published with Knopf, reflects the pressures—many of them also pragmatic—she was facing in these years. The jacket sounds familiar themes—Cather's penchant for exploring new areas, her ability to probe human character—but the specific topics it mentions differ sharply from those in the promotional materials for the novels of the teens. The jacket mentions no story that "embod[ies] a new idea and a new country," no "story of aspiration and conflict, of the magnificent courage of young ambition"; no character "who dares and achieves," or who represents "the flame and driving force of unconquerable youth." Youth is present, as it was on the jackets of those novels, but here it is pitted against the enigmatic Medusa. The jacket describes only one story in detail, "Coming, Aphrodite!," calling it a "story of a young painter, drawn by accident under the overwhelming obsession of a woman's beauty," a description that scarcely suggests youth's triumph. The jacket comments on the "savage and purely pagan theme" of "Coming, Aphrodite!," its similarity to "a fragment of Greek art," and notes that "The Diamond Mine" is "a whole novel resolved into its elements and foreshortened with an ironic simplicity." But it contains nothing about the artistry of Eden Bower or Cressida Garnet, nothing about their careers as singers, a lack especially apparent in contrast with what both the brochure and the jacket for *The Song of the Lark* say about Thea. In fact, though the *Youth* jacket identifies "the many-colored Medusa of art" as its theme, it says little about art—as if Cather, like Don Hedger and the singers in the first four stories, has been "drawn under the overwhelming obsession" of more immediate concerns.

At the start of her jacket comments on "Coming, Aphrodite!" Cather notes the story's backdrop of "New York asphalt streets and studio skylights," and it is true that all four of the collection's new stories focus on eastern cities, and on New York in particular. (Though much of the action in "The Diamond Mine" and "A Gold Slipper" takes place elsewhere, both end with their heroines headed for New York.) Even this fact, however, cannot fully explain the degree to which the jacket downplays Cather's background on the prairies, the topic that looms so large in her other autobiographical descriptions and to which the *Song of the Lark* brochure just five years earlier had traced so much of her artistic growth—and which is in fact relevant to three of the four *Troll Garden* stories included in *Youth*. In deference to these earlier stories, the jacket does devote considerable attention to *The Troll Garden*, but the biographical material on its inner flap is truly astonishing in what it includes and what it omits about Cather's earlier career. *My Ántonia* receives but passing comment ("her last published work prior to the present one"), and there is no mention of *O Pioneers!* or *The Song of the Lark*: so much for Cather's three great novels of the past decade! Instead, the blurb focuses on McClure's acceptance of her *Troll Garden* stories and on the years Cather had spent "devot[ing] herself to editorial work in New York and abroad." A reference to a London trip "on magazine business" provides a segue to the intriguing mention of "Alexandra's Bridge," and enclosed between these allusions to work at *McClure's* is the comment that "[i]t was in Italy, curiously enough, where she wrote her first story about the prairie country of the West, where she spent her childhood, and which has since become so much her field." It is the only mention of her Nebraska background on the entire jacket.

We saw that the contents and form of the 1915 brochure mirror Cather's feelings at the time: a long first section filled with the energy and inspiration of her prairie childhood, four sections that vigorously capture the creative surge that led to three novels in the past four years and that was soon to produce *My Ántonia*, and tucked between these two poles a small section, pedestrian in tone, about the intervening twenty-one years, including the jobs in Pittsburgh and New York which had impeded her writing, and from which she had recently escaped. The *Youth* jacket reverses these thematic foci. In 1920 Cather is deeply involved in New York's competitive publishing world, and the jacket's biographical blurb gives full play to the experience she has had of that world through her work at *McClure's*. Her childhood on the prairies now feels distant, and one recalls that in the novel she is writing at this time, *One of Ours*, her hero flees the prairies to pursue his dream. Even the three great novels of recent years are now things of the past, with two of them not even named and the third mentioned summarily. It is in comments on her *Troll Garden* stories that the jacket marks the "ardor and restless energy of imagination which give her work the stamp of genius," in these "earlier tales" that these qualities "flame out amazingly," while more recent work is characterized by its "finish and execution." The jacket's focus places Cather squarely in the New York world she had sought to escape in 1911; the works now on her mind are those that reflect current concerns (the new stories in *Youth*) and those that grew out of her Pittsburgh years and her early years in New York (*The Troll Garden* and *Alexander's Bridge*). Her heroic novels of the teens have become a world apart from that which she now inhabits, and the one mention of the West alludes to an early story, "The Enchanted Bluff," which identifies a youthful dream but then watches that dream become ever more distant as the boys' lives move on; and even that story is not named.

The Ultimate Divide: Through 1926

The metaphor of a retreating mirage is apt for Cather's mindset in the 1920s, and for the books she writes up through *My Mortal Enemy*. In 1915 Cather had portrayed Thea Kronborg as balancing soaring artistry with attention to the practical demands of an artist's life, a synergy that both recalls what Cather had admired in Sarah Bernhardt and also resembles her own life as she simultaneously wrote great novels like *The Song of the Lark* and worked at publicizing and selling them. As she moves toward 1920, however, the mundane side of her life increasingly intrudes upon the higher quest she has always associated with great art—and with her own art—a trend implicit in the pragmatic cast of the artists who inhabit her 1916–19 stories. And it is these artists who set the tone in *Youth and the Bright Medusa*—Cressida Garnet, Kitty Ayrshire, Eden Bower—scarcely the artistic heroines one would expect from the author who had written that "[a]n artist . . . should be among men but not one of them, in the world but not of the world."

When in 1918 Cather begins work on "Claude," her original title for what would become *One of Ours*, it is as if she is pushing back in the opposite direction, for this is a novel whose hero consciously seeks to flee the crass concerns that dominate the lives of those around him and to commit his life to "something splendid." It is tempting also to see Cather's placement of "Paul's Case" within *Youth* as reflecting the same mindset. Coming immediately after Cather's four stories about artists who, for all their courageous tenacity, are surely "vexed by human hobbies [and] human follies," Paul stands immediately apart as someone who, like Claude

Wheeler, is resolutely (if misguidedly) seeking something that will "lift himself up into the clear firmament of creation where the world is not." This search for "something splendid" carries over to the next three novels Cather writes as well. Marian Forrester, even amid her visible decline, seeks always to rise above her circumstances and surroundings, even at her lowest ebb refusing to surrender to drabness, "to grow old gracefully" (*LL* 125). Godfrey St. Peter and Tom Outland express similar urges, though at different stages of the quest, with Tom's youthful discovery of his lofty city juxtaposed with the aging professor's reluctant farewell to the high aspirations that had once animated his life. Myra abandons society's standards when she chooses romance over an inheritance, struggles always—like Marian—to live in ways that rise above mere survival, and even in death contrives to escape the shoddiness of her daily life and to end her life with "something splendid" before her eyes.

Our metaphor of "the enchanted bluff" as a vision that haunted Cather's mind even amid the mundane toils of the late teens is not entirely fanciful. Cather was working on a first draft of "Tom Outland's Story" as early as 1916, and not until she published *The Professor's House* nine years later did it find a home. After that, the "enchanted bluff" remains very much in mind as she writes her next three novels, becoming Myra's headland in *My Mortal Enemy*, recurring in both the Enchanted Mesa and the great rock of Ácoma in *Death Comes for the Archbishop*, and transmuting into the Rock of Quebec in *Shadows on the Rock*. Though the image of the bluff regularly carries intimations of transcendent accomplishment, even from its appearance in 1908 it is associated also with unattainability and death: the boys who talk about it in the story do just that—talk. We feel sure they will never reach it, and even as they imagine the peaceful lives that its inhabitants enjoyed on its summit, they recall also the dreadful death these inhabitants suffered. When Tom Outland finally scales the Blue Mesa, he finds a city as dead and mummified as Mother Eve, a city whose inhabitants, he realizes, somehow died with it, probably violently. And Myra, of course, seeks her "enchanted bluff" as a sequestered place where she can die alone.

The contrasting associations of the bluff accord with the "mortal" rift that is basic to Cather's thinking throughout the twenties, and that in different ways shapes all the novels of that decade. On the one hand, humans have the capacity to imagine better, more orderly worlds than they inhabit, to build their lives around such visions, and to create art inspired by them; on the other, such "enchanted bluffs" are but visions: we can never fully attain them, and our inability to do so is inextricably bound up with our mortality. Cather's life in the late teens and twenties brings home both sides of this rift. Even as in the late teens she tries "to lift [her]self up into the clear firmament of creation where the world is not," an effort implicit in the drafting of "Tom Outland's Story" and the inception of "Claude," she begins to confront realities yet more troubling than the erosive frustrations of the daily round: she is becoming older, she is beset by illness and discomfort, she wearies of the daily "bother and fatigue" in part because her strength and energy are not what they once were. Like Professor St. Peter, whom she so resembles, she begins to realize that much of life is behind her, that death is pressing closer, and that her time for dreaming dreams and following the gleam—Jewett's words—is fading. The degree to which marketing concerns help shape her 1924–25 collection of Jewett's stories poignantly suggests the increasingly cynical mindset of these years: "dreaming the dream" is no longer natural or easy.

As we have seen, the first four novels of the twenties reflect these concerns in a variety of ways. Their lead characters all still reach for something extraordinary, even heroic, in their lives, but the reminders of their mortality are more insistent than they were in the novels of the teens. To be sure, death sounds its knell in the novels of the teens—one thinks of Emil and Marie, of Ray Kennedy, of Mr. Shimerda—but the central characters, Alexandra, Thea, and Ántonia, remain very much alive as their novels end. In contrast, Claude, Marian, Tom, and Myra all die, and St. Peter finds himself preoccupied with death at the end of *The Professor's House*—indeed, almost dies. Claude Wheeler and Tom Outland die while still young, before they suffer the erosion life would otherwise bring, but the diminishments that come with age are central to Cather's portrayals of Marian Forrester, Godfrey St. Peter, and Myra Henshawe.

Poignantly complementing this decline is the gradual shift in the gender of Cather's protagonists. In the teens Cather had, we might say, crossed "Alexandra's bridge" from Bartley Alexander to the three conquering women—"Alexandras"—of *O Pioneers!*, *The Song of the Lark*, and *My Ántonia*, each with her share of mortal failings, but each cast in the mold of "heroic womanhood." Even in the late teens, as she herself feels worn down by the pressures of daily life, Cather still builds her stories around women who, like herself, find ways of dealing with life, of making their way—Cressida Garnet, Kitty Ayrshire, Eden Bower, even Ardessa Devine and Becky Tietelbaum and Annie Wooley. As she begins once again to lift her gaze beyond this daily round, once again to seek "the enchanted bluff" and to confront its dual implications, however, she turns back to male protagonists—Tom Outland, Claude Wheeler—the same thing she had done when she fastened on Bartley Alexander for the hero of her first novel. She places women at center stage in the two short novels of the twenties, investing both Marian and Myra with the courage and resilience she had written into her artists and office workers of the late teens, but also tracing in both a process of inexorable decline. "Heroic womanhood" still applies, but their heroism lacks the epic cast of Alexandra's, Thea's and Ántonia's. And for the character who in these novels most closely approximates her own experience and feelings, she again chooses a man—Godfrey St. Peter.

Once again, the promotional materials associated with these books— the jacket blurbs, the 1926 biographical sketch, and the 1926 "interview"— reflect these developments in illuminating ways. The four jackets all suggest larger public and moral themes and concerns, a return to the mode of the teens, and a sharp contrast to that of the *Youth and the Bright Medusa* jacket. Thus the *One of Ours* jacket concludes with the "ever deepening sense of national drama, of national character," that lies behind the book's personal drama; the *Lost Lady* jacket locates "this romance of the old West" against its historic context—"the railroad aristocracy that grew up when the great trans-continental lines were being built across the plains" and "all the idiosyncrasies of that lavish, generous, careless era." The jacket on *The Professor's House* singles out Cather's "portraiture of

America's many social groups," and that for *My Mortal Enemy* places its "entire life of a woman" against "the nineteenth century surroundings that produced her greatness of character."[7] There is simply not language of this sort on the *Youth* jacket. To some extent the difference reflects that these jacket blurbs are for novels, the *Youth* blurb for a book of stories. That said, major themes and issues, especially those relating to the artist's place in society, run through all the stories in *Youth*, but they find little reflection in the jacket copy. Similarly, the *Youth* jacket speaks of Cather's "cutting into the very tissues of human experience and emotion," of each story as "a separate new discovery about character and life," but it contains nothing about the psychological explorations found throughout the collection—the way the stories lead us into the hearts of Don Hedger, of Paul, of Aunt Georgiana, for instance. In contrast, the jackets for the novels of the twenties emphasize the innerness of Cather's focus. Claude is a "young Hamlet of the prairies," the novel an "intimate story of a young man's life," its climax the "releas[ing of] the baffled energy of the boy's nature." Internal character and its contradictions are at the heart of the jacket descriptions for *A Lost Lady* and *My Mortal Enemy* as well: "Through the whole story one figure stands out with irresistible fascination—the figure of Marian Forrester, full of feminine mystery and charm, inscrutable in her weakness and her reckless courage." "My Mortal Enemy is . . . an astounding and profound study of a woman's heart." This focus on the inner lives of the characters carries over to the way these jackets describe Cather and her writing. Cather's portrayal of Claude reflects "all the passion of her daring, impatient mind"; Marian's story is a "moving drama," with every page characterized by "a melancholy beauty, a thrilling pathos"; *My Mortal Enemy* is "a work of tragic passion." Implicit in several of these jackets are riddles, enigmas: Claude is Hamlet, his energy baffled; Marian is "inscrutable"; and the *My Mortal Enemy* jacket ends with the riddle of who *is* the "mortal enemy"—all reminiscent in their different ways of youth confronting Medusa in 1920 on the first of Cather's Knopf dust jackets.

To compare such phrases with what we met on the jackets from the teens is to confront the radical shift in tone that has occurred from the earlier novels to the later: love stories, yes, but none that "is the very story of Youth" or that exemplifies "the magnificent courage of young ambition"; and though Claude even more than Ántonia is a product of the western plains, he certainly does not have "the freshness and vitality of the new soil from which [he] springs," or "the vigor of the great prairies." The first three of these jackets do—like the jackets of the teens—celebrate achievement and triumph, but it is Cather's, not her characters': *One of Ours* is "a novel to rank with the finest of this or any age"; Marian Forrester "is one of Miss Cather's greatest triumphs"; *The Professor's House* "represents her highest achievement in the art of fiction." Instead of youth, vigor, freshness, and vitality, motifs sounded so often in the teens, the increasingly dominant leitmotif is the fact of our mortality, and this theme provides the context for understanding what appears—and does not appear—on the jackets of these books. The comparison of Claude to Hamlet, especially in light of Cather's published comments on Shakespeare's hero, suggests not only his capacity for delusion but also his early death. The "melancholy beauty" and "pathos" of *A Lost Lady* are explicitly posed against the "easy brilliance of the writing" and the "vivacity" with which Cather limns "that lavish, generous, careless era," Marian's "mystery and charm" against "her weakness and her reckless courage," balances which capture the chiaroscuro of the novel, its dark palette of colors. As for *The Professor's House* and *My Mortal Enemy*, the perfunctory blurb of the one, the lack of self-promotion in the blurb of the other, are the proper, even necessary, response to the two novels' focus on how mortality both shadows our daily round and undermines our highest dreams. Godfrey's weariness with the mortal struggle has its complement in Cather's apparent failure to put much effort into the jacket, and Myra's confrontation of her "mortal enemy" is a topic that scarcely invites its author to trumpet her mortal wares on its dust jacket.

Discussion of the blurbs for these two books leads naturally to Cather's two anonymous 1926 "puff pieces," both written shortly before the appearance of *My Mortal Enemy*, and each in its way signaling Cather's gradual retreat from such self-promotion. The 1926 biographical sketch repeats some of the familiar untruths—Cather's age when the family moved to

Nebraska, and when she graduated from the university—and it mentions (with justification) that two stories in *The Troll Garden*, "The Sculptor's Funeral" and "Paul's Case," have attracted particular attention, but it is unencumbered by the laudatory adjectives and phrases that characterize the 1903 and 1915 statements. It also offers balanced assessment in place of the skewed perspectives of the earlier pieces. The 1903 note paid a great deal of attention to the reading Cather had done at home and at the university, while the 1915 statement completely ignored this side of Cather's background; the 1926 sketch grants due notice to the topic, but it does so in the context of other critical influences on her development. While both of the earlier statements stress Cather's Nebraska background far more than the nine-plus years she had spent in Virginia, the 1926 sketch treats this earlier period as an important countersubject to Cather's subsequent years on the plains. And while the 1915 statement deals with the years in Pittsburgh and at *McClure's* in a manner that feels lackluster after the energy of the opening section, the 1926 sketch identifies these years as providing "all that work and experimenting that every writer and painter must do at some time or other to find and perfect his medium."

A word that I used of this 1926 sketch in the last paragraph is important: unencumbered. Four years earlier in "The Novel Démeublé" Cather had argued that the novel had become "over-furnished" and had advocated "throw[ing] all the furniture out of the window; and along with it, all the meaningless reiterations concerning physical sensations, . . . leav[ing] the scene bare for the play of emotions" (*WCOW* 35, 42–43). Jackets from this period reflect the same inclinations: the jacket for *One of Ours* praises the novel's "epic simplicity," that for *The Professor's House* its "great economy of words and an equally great simplicity of manner." And *My Mortal Enemy*, the novel about to appear at the time Cather was writing the 1926 sketch, is, as one critic has written, "the most unfurnished of her novels, a remarkable example of the novel *démeublé*."[8] Against this background it is both significant and appropriate that not only is the 1926 sketch itself "unencumbered" in style but also that in it Cather highlights the unencumbered, raw nature of the plains. The third and fourth paragraphs stress the traditional elegance of the world from which Cather had moved—an "old conservative society" in the Valley of Virginia, a life that was "ordered and settled," "rich and kindly"—and point out that this background made Cather the more aware of the very different world she found in Nebraska: "An imaginative child, taken out of this definitely arranged background . . . naturally found something to think about." Later in the sketch, when she is talking about the nostalgia she felt when she was in France, she again emphasizes the "unfurnished" nature of "the flat country . . . . A great many people find it dull and monotonous; they like a church steeple, an old mill, a waterfall, country all touched up and furnished, like a German Christmas card."

Not only does the unencumbered character of this land—that it is not "all touched up and furnished"—appeal to Cather and accord with her esthetic tastes at this time, but she portrays its barrenness as the proper setting for the elemental struggles she witnessed: "Struggle appeals to a child more than comfort and picturesqueness, because it is dramatic. No child with a spark of generosity could have kept from throwing herself heart and soul into the fight these people were making to master the language, to master the soil, to hold their land and to get ahead in the world. . . . Lightning and hail and prairie fires and drouths and blizzards were always threatening to extinguish this family or that."

In her 1915 statement Cather had suggested a variety of ways in which the plains and the people on them had affected her—the challenge of trying to understand their language, the intellectual excitement of spending time with them, the trove of stories she picked up from them, the early experience of getting inside another person's skin. In 1926, in keeping with her emphasis on stripping away nonessentials, she stresses one basic fact: the transition from the refinements—the furnishings, if you will—of life in Virginia to the raw simplicity of the plains brought her face to face with the basic human condition. On the one side she saw aspiration—to master the language and the land, to get ahead in the world; on the other, the forces pitted against such human dreams, including the ultimate threat of extinction. It is the very tension that is focal to the novels Cather has just written, and that culminates in Myra Henshawe's confrontation with "her mortal enemy." Given this thematic link to *My Mortal Enemy*, it is probably no accident that in this 1926 sketch, written soon after she had finished the novel, Cather stresses an emotion similar to what Myra feels on her headland overlooking the sea: "[W]hen I strike the open plains, something happens. I'm home. I breathe differently. That love of great spaces, of rolling open country like the sea,—it's the grand passion of my life."

Among the topics of which Cather seemingly disencumbers herself in the 1926 sketch is that of Sarah Orne Jewett's impact on her writing. It is an omission that contrasts sharply with the centrality of this topic in the statement she wrote in 1915 for the brochure promoting *The Song of the Lark*—and that is especially surprising given that Cather had just recently, in 1924–25, immersed herself in Jewett in compiling her collection of Jewett stories and writing the preface for this collection. A closer look at this 1926 biographical sketch, however, reveals Jewett's pervasive impact, especially in the sketch's close reminders of passages from Cather's recent preface to Jewett's stories. One feels Jewett's presence in the stripped-down eloquence and control of this, Cather's last such statement, in its avoidance of needless puffery (compare the preface's comparison of Jewett's writing to a "modern yacht, where there is no ornamentation at all" [*Best Stories* xviii]). One feels Jewett's influence also in the way this brief sketch evokes so powerfully the land and people that shaped Cather's voice, sensibilities, and soul, and to which she constantly returns for inspiration—indeed, one readily recalls her recent description of Jewett: "She early learned to love her country for what it was. What is quite as important, she saw it as it was. She happened to have the right nature, the right temperament, to see it so—and to understand by intuition the deeper meaning of all she saw" (xvi). Jewett-like too is Cather's moving portrait of herself traveling in France and finding herself longing for the people and prairies of her home: compare Cather's comments on Jewett's fondness for "The Hiltons' Holiday": "[T]hat story simply *is the look*—shy, kind, a little wistful—that shines out at one from good country faces on remote farms ..." (xiv). Jewett may not be mentioned in Cather's 1926 sketch, but she is constantly there, "the inexplicable presence of the thing not named, of the overtone divined by the ear but not heard by it." The familiar phrases from "The Novel Démeublé" feel the more apt in that they so recall what Cather had recently written in her Jewett preface about the great story's capacity to "leave in the mind of the sensitive reader an intangible residuum of pleasure; a cadence, a quality of voice that is exclusively the writer's own, individual, unique" (xi). The very indirection of Cather's 1926 sketch makes it one of her most moving tributes to the woman who had, at the end of her life, taught Cather so much—and who had again, during Cather's 1924–25 immersion in her stories, spoken to her so powerfully yet again. Indeed, her very title for this 1926 piece again suggests Jewett: "Biographical *Sketch*," the word she uses in her preface to describe Jewett's own semiautobiographical masterpiece, "The 'Pointed Fir' *sketches*" (x; italics mine).

In her preface Cather had praised Jewett's ability to find the "voice that is exactly suited to the song" (xi), and Cather shows the same pitch-perfect skill in her 1926 interview. If the 1926 biographical sketch gives a portrait of the author that is relatively unencumbered by promotional flourishes, this "Interview" written a few months later is totally unfurnished, and—in the portion she composed—contains no promotion at all. This "Interview Démeublé" too recalls the familiar words just quoted from "The Novel Démeublé." About all we are told is that we are at Grand Central station, that it's a hot July day, and that Cather's train is about to leave. But because of so much that "is felt upon the page without being specifically named there," we take from this brief piece a vivid sense not only of the setting, with the train about to leave, but also of Cather's personality, the tone of the conversation, and the imagined actions that accompany it.

We also take from it a strong sense of direction, and that direction is toward departure. The direction is signaled in Cather's first words, "Yes, I'm going out of town," and line after line sustains it: "Now I'm going up into New England"; "I'm going away to work and don't want to be bothered"; "I need a rest from resting"; "My train is called"; "He's calling 'all aboard'"; "Goodbye." This momentum foreshadows what Cather will later say about writers: "In this country a writer has to hide and lie and almost steal in order to get time to work in,—and peace of mind to work with." If one is going to write, one must do what Cather is doing here—get away from addressing the public, from getting hooked on the public's approbation, from becoming puffed up with the importance of the activity itself. Once again we hear Jewett reminding Cather that she must find her "own quiet centre."

Behind the light touch of Cather's remarks ("Try it out yourself; go lecture to a Sunday School . . ."), there is a serious and self-referential subtext, and with it typical Cather cross-currents. In the Cather heading off on her train and the Cather who knows so much about the lure and danger of addressing the public we have those two sides we have met so often—on the one hand, the artist seeking "the clear firmament of creation where the world is not," on the other, the artist "vexed by human hobbies or human follies." Just as Cather upon arriving in Nebraska suddenly saw human life stripped to its essentials—aspiration poised against mortality—so in this bare-bones interview she lays out the dilemma that she herself has faced for so long, and that is exemplified by the conflicting demands of this very summer. She desperately wants and needs to find the quiet and seclusion to work on *Death Comes for the Archbishop*, but here she is in New York, composing promotional copy—first the sketch for the Knopf brochure, and now this interview to advertise *My Mortal Enemy*: yet once again we recall her envy of Eddy's book sales and royalties.

Such promotional work, like lecturing, is something she has now been doing for years, and doing with style and success; the very fact that license to engage freely in such activities was one of Knopf's attractions suggests how much one side of her enjoyed them. The speech she gives at the end of the interview suggests the same thing. For if the interview as a whole moves toward departure, toward escape from the world's intrusions, line after line of this concluding speech moves in the opposite direction—toward the world and its enticing temptations: "[L]ecturing is very dangerous for writers. If we lecture, we get a little more owlish and self-satisfied all the time. We hate it at first, if we are decently modest, but in the end we fall in love with the sound of our own voice. There is something insidious about it, destructive to one's finer feelings. All human beings, apparently, like to speak in public.

. . . Really, I've seen people's reality quite destroyed by the habit . . . . It's especially destructive to writers, ever so much worse than alcohol, takes their edge off . . . . Try it out yourself . . . [Y]ou'll see how puffed up and important you begin to feel. You'll want to do it right over again." If for "lecturing" and "speaking to the public" we read "playing to the public" or "promoting one's wares," the whole speech fits Cather's promotional activities—like this very interview—perfectly, activities she sees as addictive and dangerous, but whose attraction she knows too well, and still feels within herself.

At the end, in a passage she revised to make it more forceful, Cather reminds herself to resist the temptation to "do it right over again": "*But don't!*" That she apparently had little to do with the *Professor's House* blurb suggests that she was already pulling away from these activities, as does the lack of hard-sell language in the 1926 sketch and the *My Mortal Enemy* jacket. Perhaps most telling, her next book, *Death Comes for the Archbishop*, will carry no promotional blurb whatsoever, only reviews of other books.[9] Finally, there is the fact that this interview was never used for promotional purposes—that on the two occasions when it does appear, it is simply as an interview, without the addendum pushing *My Mortal Enemy*. Was it perhaps Willa Cather herself who decided not to use it as a puff piece? That we will probably never know. What we do know, though, is that the form in which the interview *was* published in the Nebraska papers lays bare, unfurnished, the essential struggle between a writer's need to escape the world and the strong temptation to pander to that world; that in this interview Cather portrays herself as caught on the divide between these pulls, and as knowing both of them well; and that at its end it is the momentum of departure that wins out: "Goodbye." It is no accident that her next novel feels like she has at last truly found her "own quiet centre."

Part VII
"In the End Is My Beginning"

Cather's writing of anonymous promotional sketches peaks in the 1926 sketch and interview, and after that she produces no independent pieces of this sort. Her involvement in the writing of jacket copy falls off around the same time, but in the decade that follows it gradually resumes, reaching a climax in *Sapphira and the Slave Girl*, on the blurb for which she expends special care. That *Death Comes for the Archbishop* has no jacket blurb is itself revealing, and the novel touches in intriguing ways on a number of issues we have been considering.

CHAPTER SEVENTEEN

Death Comes for the Archbishop

It is ironic that in the same Boston years when Mary Baker Eddy, who preached health and the power of goodness, was inadvertently focusing Cather's attention on the reality of evil and the certainty that we are flawed and mortal, Sarah Orne Jewett, who was mortally ill, was urging Cather "to dream your dreams and go on to new and more shining ideals." *My Mortal Enemy*, in which issues raised by Eddy figure so prominently, and in which Myra Henshawe so recalls Eddy herself, is in many ways Cather's aptly titled tribute to the grim but profound lessons she learned from Eddy, including those about herself. Despite "Death" as the first word of its title, Cather's next novel is her glowing tribute to the woman who had shown her that life and art can rise above violence and death, our mortal enemies.[1] Its extraordinary evocation of a part of the country that had haunted Cather's mind for years further acknowledges Jewett's continuing influence, and its luminous beauty matches what Cather had found and described as she worked on Jewett's stories in 1924–25—"the kind of beauty we feel when a beautiful song is sung by a beautiful voice that is exactly suited to the song" (*Best Stories* xi).

Death Comes for the Archbishop, coming as it does after *My Mortal Enemy*, breathes an aura of resolution and release reminiscent of what Myra seeks on her Pacific headland at dawn: "[I]t's as if all our sins were pardoned; as if the sky leaned over the earth and kissed it and gave it absolution." Contributing to the sense of serenity Cather evokes is the unaccented style she developed for the novel, with its roots in Puvis de Chavannes and the Golden Legend:

I had all my life wanted to do something in the style of legend, which is absolutely the reverse of dramatic treatment. Since I first saw the Puvis de Chavannes frescoes of the life of Saint Geneviève in my student days, I have wished that I could try something a little like that in prose; something without accent, with none of the artificial elements of composition. In the Golden Legend the martyrdoms of the saints are no more dwelt upon than are the trivial incidents of their lives; it is as though all human experiences, measured against one supreme spiritual experience, were of about the same importance. The essence of such writing is not to hold the note, not to use an incident for all there is in it—but to touch and pass on. (*WCOW* 9)[2]

Also contributing to this sense that human lives, and everything that happens in them, are all *sub specie aeternitatis* is the Catholic faith that suffuses the book, a natural next step from the role Catholicism had played in Cather's two preceding novels.[3] Though at several points in *The Professor's House* Augusta's strong but simple faith evokes the professor's irony, her faith underpins the succor she brings St. Peter in the final scenes of the novel.[4] When he wakes from his near-death experience, she is reading the "little much-worn religious book that she always carried in her handbag," and though her Catholic faith does not specifically come into play in their final conversation, her down-to-earth, faith-inspired rootedness helps him face his mortality. Indeed, his thoughts on Augusta in this scene foreshadow the "unaccented" style Cather will adopt for *Death Comes for the Archbishop*: "She hadn't any of the sentimentality that comes from a fear of dying. She talked about death as she spoke of a hard winter or a rainy March, or any of the sadnesses of nature" (*PH* 277, 281). The next stage is the far more explicit role that Myra's faith plays in her last days, as she spends increasing amounts of time with Father Fay, receives the sacrament as death approaches, and dies with her ebony crucifix clutched in her hands.[5]

Also carrying over from these two earlier works is the association of such faith with towering rocks, an association made explicit early in *Death*. When the bishop first sees the Enchanted Mesa and Ácoma, he meditates on the role such places have played in the lives of the natives: "The rock, when one came to think of it, was the utmost expression of human need; even mere feeling yearned for it; it was the highest comparison of loyalty in love and friendship. Christ Himself had used that comparison for the disciple to whom He gave the keys of His Church" (98). Though without the Catholic overtones, the Blue Mesa carries similar associations for Tom Outland, as does her rocky headland for Myra Henshawe—awe, exaltation, the sense of something holy and untainted.[6] As we have seen, Cather's use of this powerful image predates even the "Enchanted Bluff"—and will carry over directly to the Rock of Quebec in her next novel, *Shadows on the Rock*.[7]

In all of these appearances the towering rock suggests something strong and unshakeable that outlives its human inhabitants, an embodiment of the eternal in a world of change. By the same token, however, the very fact that it rises above transience is a reminder of human mortality, and we have seen that in Cather's fiction the motif is constantly associated with death. Both the Enchanted Bluff of Cather's early story and Tom Outland's Blue Mesa are places where humans seek refuge only to meet sudden and violent death, and it is as a place to die that Myra seeks out her headland. The association continues in *Death*. When Ácoma and the Enchanted Mesa first come into sight, Jacinto tells Latour that the people who had many centuries ago lived on the Mesa had perished there of hunger when a storm destroyed the stairway that was their only access to food, and the grim story of Fray Baltazar being hurled to his death from Ácoma follows soon after and provides the climax to this section of the novel. Even the building of the great cathedral in Santa Fe, constructed from the trove of golden rock that Latour has found, provides the backdrop to the archbishop's death, just as the Rock of Quebec will provide the setting for the death of the count in *Shadows on the Rock*.[8]

For me at least, *Death* projects its aura of resolution above all because Latour and Vaillant are able to translate into human terms, and into human life, the lasting strength of a faith whose symbol is the unyielding and ultimately inhuman image of the rock. Though very different from each other, both priests have extraordinary ability to respond to people, including those very unlike themselves. Both can bend when necessary, can make compromises, and some of their greatest achievements flow from a flexibility that is anything but rocklike. They both understand that to render their faith meaningful to the natives they must build bridges between Christianity and these peoples' native faiths. Both are candid in recognizing their own flaws and frailties. And the novel's most moving episodes are those in which they connect with other mortals: one thinks of Latour's supple handling of Doña Isabella's vanity about her age, or of how he reaches out to Sada in the "December Night" episode; of the very human skills by which Vaillant wangles the two donkeys from Manuel Lujon, and the way in which these two animals come to suggest both Vaillant's earthiness and also the partnership of these two priests. Underscoring their humanity is the very title Cather has chosen for her novel, which reminds us that for all the rocklike permanence of their faith, these two priests are mortal, and indeed death comes to both of them before the novel ends. While in style and theme *Death* sounds the triviality of human experiences when "measured against one supreme spiritual experience," the most powerful after-images it leaves are of mortals making better the lives of other mortals, and of mortals using well their allotted years, a theme implicit in what Latour says as he prepares for his last return to Santa Fe: "I shall die of having lived" (270).[9]

To see the book in this way is to understand its close relationship to the tension between our immortal dreams and our mortal nature that runs through Cather's previous novels of the 1920s. But where these books emphasize the degree to which mortality pulls against and even undercuts human aspiration, in *Death* Cather casts Latour and Vaillant as mortal, flawed humans whose accomplishments feel immortal in kind. As Vaillant says to Latour upon his return from France, "To fulfil the dreams of one's youth; that is the best that can happen to a man. No worldly success can take the place of that" (263–64).

The ancient bell that awakens Latour in an early scene plays many roles in *Death Comes for the Archbishop*. Its ringing of the angelus, nine strokes divided into three groups of three, mirrors the structure of the novel. Its purity of tone embodies the crystalline clarity that suffuses the entire novel, and the ancient and diverse metals that are melted into its substance and that account for its unique timbre parallel the rich mixture of old and new that the bishops create in their work in the New World. But the description of this bell contains as well a cautionary note: "Full, clear, with something bland and suave, each note floated through the air like a globe of silver" (43). For implicit in, even necessary to, the novel's glorious clarity is "something bland and suave": it attains its aura of resolution and serenity at the price of skirting significant aspects of human experience, including ones that are focal in the four darker novels that precede it.[10] Scholars in recent years have pointed out the book's apparent acquiescence in American expansionism and white superiority, its occasional insensitivity toward Native Americans, and they have noted that such issues are the more troubling in light of the unspoken, underlying assumptions they suggest; there seems something "bland and suave" in the way the novel avoids probing into such matters.[11]

Other issues go yet deeper. Cather herself commented at one point that *Death Comes for the Archbishop* is "a story with no woman in it but the Virgin Mary," and that such a story "has very definite limitations."[12] Her comments exaggerate, for the novel contains a number of unforgettable female characters, among them Sada, Doña Isabella, and Magdalena, the woman rescued from the brutal Buck Scales. That said, it is true that the book contains no women who approach the complexity of a Marian Forrester or a Myra Henshawe—or of a Willa Cather.

Female sexuality, so powerful a motivating force in Marian and Myra and Eden Bower, and so integral to Thea Kronborg's artistic blossoming, figures only in passing in the women of this novel. Book 4, "Snake Root," comes closest to approaching the theme, but the way Latour responds to its intimations of female sexuality is characteristic of the novel as a whole. The cave where Latour and his native guide Jacinto find refuge during the blizzard is a landscape as patently female as is Panther Canyon in *The Song of the Lark*.[13] Latour and Jacinto enter by an "orifice" with a "mouth-like opening" that suggests "two great stone lips, slightly parted and thrust outward" (128–29). Inside is a lofty cavern, at the back of which is a hole "about as large as a very big watermelon, of an irregular oval shape" (130), which Jacinto immediately tries to seal off. The bishop welcomes the life-saving shelter provided by the cave, but from the first he is "struck by a reluctance, an extreme distaste for the place. . . . [H]e detected at once a fetid odour, not very strong but highly disagreeable" (129). His initial distaste remains long after the episode: "[T]he cave, which had probably saved his life, he remembered with horror. No tales of wonder, he told himself, would ever tempt him into a cavern hereafter" (135). That for the rest of his life he avoids such places mirrors the way the book itself deals with sex and especially female sexuality.[14] Cather had repeatedly explored this theme in previous novels, usually focusing on the destructive power of sexual passion—one thinks of Bartley and Hilda, Emil and Marie, Claude and Enid, Marian and Frank Ellinger, Myra and Oswald. Cather wrote approvingly about a review that found in *My Mortal Enemy* "the steady rhythm of the fundamental hatred of the sexes one for the other and their irresistible attraction one for the other," a theme underscored by Myra's comment on two lovers whose affair she is abetting: "[V]ery likely hell will come of it!" (*MME* 41).[15] In *My Mortal Enemy* Cather explores this hell with devastating candor and directness; in *Death Comes for the Archbishop* she avoids it—just as Latour for the rest of his life steers clear of caves.

The title of book 4, "Snake Root," suggests another focus of the episode—evil itself. Lurking throughout this section are tales about the natives of the Santa Fe area, tales intimating that they are "peculiarly addicted to snake worship, that they kept rattlesnakes concealed in their houses, and somewhere in the mountain guarded an enormous serpent which they brought to the pueblo for certain feasts" (124). The truth of these tales is never confirmed, but Latour's conversation with Zeb Orchard toward the end of book 4 suggests that there may be something to them. It is again in the cavern episode that these tales come closest to the bishop himself. Latour has noticed an "extraordinary vibration in [the] cavern . . . like a hive of bees, like a heavy roll of distant drums." When he asks Jacinto about it, the guide scrapes open another aperture deep in the cavern, this one in the floor, and directs the bishop to place his ear on the opening. When he does so, he hears "the sound of a great underground river, flowing through a resounding cavern. The water was far, far below, perhaps as deep as the foot of the mountain, a flood moving in utter blackness under ribs of antediluvian rock. It was not a rushing noise, but the sound of a great flood moving with majesty and power. 'It is terrible,' he said at last, as he rose" (131–32). Later in the night Latour wakes and sees Jacinto with his ear pressed to this other aperture, "listening with supersensual ear, it seemed, and he looked to be supported against the rock by the intensity of his solicitude" (134). The run of the narrative implies that this cavern, whose location Jacinto warns the bishop never to mention, may be the place the natives associate with the sacred snake mentioned elsewhere in "Snake Root."

As we have seen repeatedly, the association of evil with snakes is ubiquitous in Cather's work, and *Death Comes for the Archbishop* is no exception. Well before the climactic episode of "Snake Root," Latour and Vaillant confront Buck Scales, a vicious murderer "with a snake-like neck, terminating in a small, bony head. Under his close-clipped hair this repellent head showed a number of thick ridges, as if the skull joinings were overgrown by layers of superfluous bone. With its small, rudimentary ears, this head had a positively malignant look" (67). Warned by Buck's wife, the bishops escape and help bring Scales to justice and then take his wife, Magdalena, the unwilling witness of his former crimes, into service at their school. The motifs of the tale resonate with Eden and with Christianity: the snake-headed, aptly named Scales, the embodiment of evil; a woman saved from this vile life, and named Magdalena. But whereas Latour and Vaillant deal handily with this snakelike menace in book 2, in "Snake Roots," which follows soon after, Latour shies away from confronting the snake that is so intimately associated both with the cave and with the native women of the area.

Latour's reaction to the cave's great underground river is comparable, and similarly revealing: "It is terrible." Once again his instinct is to turn away: in what follows, he avoids the river, does not seek to understand or know more about it. Contrast this with Alexandra in *O Pioneers!*: "Her personal life, her own realization of herself, was almost a subconscious existence; like an underground river that came to the surface only here and there, at intervals months apart, and then sank again to flow on under her own fields. Nevertheless, the underground stream was there . . ." (*OP* 203). It is an intensely female image, one that suggests a complexity central to what Alexandra is and achieves; in "Snake Roots" this underground river, so important to Jacinto, and again with complex overtones, is something the bishop finds frightening, and from which he distances himself.[16]

Also missing in *Death Comes for the Archbishop* is any character who embodies the aggressive human ambition Cather builds into so many of her fictional characters, an ambition that reaches high but that by its nature often has division and divisiveness as its corollaries. To make this point is not to overlook the daunting goals Latour and Vaillant set for themselves, or their remarkable attainments. We get moving glimpses of the private lives that lie behind their public accomplishments, including the unforgettable passage where the dying Latour recalls his efforts many years earlier "to forge a new Will in that devout and exhausted priest" (303) who would later become the comrade of his labors.[17] But the book's very absence of accent and drama entails skirting both the fever pitch of human ambition so central to many Cather characters and also the divisions within and between humans that such ambition often spawns.[18] Near the end of *My Mortal Enemy* Myra comments to Father Fay, "Religion is different from everything else; *because in religion seeking is finding*" (*MME* 111). She is referring to the life of faith, but her words are apt for the way Cather presents the achievements of Latour and Vaillant in *Death*. In keeping with Cather's intention "not to hold the note, not to use an incident for all there is in it—but to touch and pass on," there is in the book from its first chapter to its last a sense of inexorable forward progress in which the bishops' extraordinary achievements feel foreordained, the fruit of careful thought and great labor, but untouched by the driving ambition that so dominates many human lives, and that has so often been Cather's focus in previous books: this is a novel in which "seeking is finding," and such is not the way of the world.[19]

That the dust jacket of *Death* contains no blurb plugging this sublime novel is appropriate to its manifest avoidance of aggressive ambition and self-advertisement. As we have seen, it is also in keeping with where Willa Cather found herself in 1926 and 1927, the years when she was writing this novel: weary of the constant push for more sales and revenues, of her own long involvement in advertising efforts, and increasingly aware of how addictive such activities can become, how "destructive to one's finer feelings." It is a time when such matters increasingly seem mere mortal vanities, passing and unimportant in the larger scheme of things; a time when Cather's attention is increasingly focused on what is lasting, on what rises above "mortal mind" and our mortal lives; and a time, consequently, when the divide within Willa Cather between creating immortal art and taking the world by storm feels distant, with worldly ambition temporarily subdued.

If the absence of a jacket blurb on *Death* both echoes its skirting of the uglier sides of human ambition and signals its assured attention to more important matters, the centrality of the rock in its landscape also points in two directions. On the one hand, the rock, whether it is the rock of Ácoma or the rock of St. Peter's Church, is an image of the faith that undergirds the book and its characters, something that reaches high, is unfailingly strong, and outlives its human inhabitants; as Latour says of the natives who lived on Ácoma, they "share[d] the universal human yearning for something permanent, enduring, without shadow of change,—they had their idea in substance. They actually lived upon their Rock; were born upon it and died upon it" (99). His very words, though, recall a similar statement, but one with a very different resonance: "We come and go, but the land is always here. And the people who love it and understand it are the people who own it—for a little while" (*OP* 308). Alexandra's comment to Carl near the end of *O Pioneers!* strikes the same poles as does Latour's comment on Ácoma, but there is a great difference, and one that again reflects the world of *Death Comes for the Archbishop*. The rock is secure, stable, unchanging, something to which one can hold fast from birth to death, to which one can flee to avoid danger, something that outlives mere mortals.[20] But how different it is from Alexandra's land, which fosters growth and change, which people love and understand and own for a while—and which provides the Garden in which Emil and Marie confront the sexual passion and the temptations that are so much part of human life, and that are largely marginalized in *Death*.[21] And just as the bishop finds the underground river within the rock something "terrible," something to avoid, while Alexandra's very life is like an underground stream that feeds the land, so the land—like the rock—outlives us but has its own human qualities, including our place in the ongoing life that it nurtures: "Fortunate country, that is one day to receive hearts like Alexandra's into its bosom, to give them out again in the yellow wheat, in the rustling corn, in the shining eyes of youth!"

CHAPTER EIGHTEEN

Fiction of the 1930s

In her 1926 "Interview" Cather commented on the addictive dangers of courting the public, and in the years following she tries to skirt these dangers. *Death Comes for the Archbishop* has no blurb promoting the novel itself, though the jacket does contain review excerpts for the six books Cather had published with Knopf between 1920 and 1926. By the time *Shadows on the Rock* appears in 1931, the earlier pattern begins to reassert itself, with the jacket featuring a short blurb about the novel on the front cover and a slightly longer one on the back. *Obscure Destinies* the following year contains a more detailed jacket description, as does *Sapphira and the Slave Girl* in 1940. As for *Lucy Gayheart* in 1935, we know that Cather herself became directly involved with production details (including the typeface to be used), but its jacket blurb is brief and generic.[1] As mentioned earlier, the two works in which Cather herself appears as a character—as Vickie in "Old Mrs. Harris" and as her five-year-old self in the epilogue to *Sapphira*—have jacket blurbs that probe into the books' characters and the emotional issues at stake. In contrast, Cather herself plays no such roles in *Shadows on the Rock* and *Lucy Gayheart*, and their jacket blurbs focus on the books' ambience and say little about the characters. In addition, consuming personal ambition, largely absent in *Death* and *Shadows*, and muted at best in Lucy Gayheart's musical life until just before she dies, reappears as an important theme in both *Obscure Destinies* and *Sapphira*; as it does, the blurbs on these books, one index of Cather's investment in them—and ambition for them—show a corresponding resurgence.

Shadows on the Rock

Shadows on the Rock builds on a number of Cather's personal interests, among them French cooking, the history of Catholicism in the New World, and knowledge of Canada gained from summers spent on Grand Manan and trips taken to Quebec itself.[2] And the loving portrait of the apothecary Auclair draws on childhood memories of her father, who had died not long before she began work on this novel.[3] Like *Death*, however, *Shadows* for the most part skirts the intense emotional issues that had loomed so large in Cather's earlier fiction. She herself spoke of the book as organized around "[a]n orderly little French household" and claimed that the book "had no fire at all and almost no energy."[4] Her judgment is far too negative: the novel's varied cast of characters creates a fascinating and moving web of human relationships, and I agree with Stout's characterization of the book as often "luminous and significant."[5] As in *Death*, however, several themes central to earlier novels are again peripheral at best—the compulsions, good and bad, that attend fierce ambition; the complex double life of the artist; the loves and hates innate to sexual passion; the gulf between our soaring dreams and the fact of our mortality. Hermione Lee, who finds much to praise in *Shadows*, nonetheless describes it as "a children's book for adults," pointing out that its heroine Cécile is "innocent and presexual" and that the realities of life in late seventeenth-century Quebec are "softened and muted."[6] That Jeanne Le Ber, the one woman in the novel associated with female sexuality and passion, ends up cloistering herself behind the altar of her church fits this mode, as does the fact that Cécile is deftly assimilated to the Virgin Mary and miraculously leapfrogs from being a twelve-year-old in the book proper to being the mother of four in the epilogue (compare the full sequence of a woman's life that Cather gives us in *My Ántonia*).[7]

Although the novel projects something of the affirmation felt in *Death*, it does so far less unambiguously.[8] Replacing the brilliant sun-bathed colors of *Death* are the muted, often fog-covered hues of *Shadows*, an apt complement to its more shaded textures of life.[9] Not only had Cather's father died in 1928, but later that same year her mother suffered a debilitating stroke and continued to decline during the years when Cather was working on this novel. It is accordingly not surprising that reminders of our mortal frailty run throughout—sickness, hunger, aging, cruelty, death itself, with the death of Count Frontenac at the end of the novel proper cast in darker colors than is that of Latour at the end of *Death*.[10] Replacing Latour and Vaillant's synergy of opposites in *Death* are the new bishop's petty efforts to undermine the old in *Shadows*, and replacing the heroic quests of Latour and Vaillant is the quite different heroism of "an orderly little French household that went on trying to live decently, just as ants begin to rebuild when you kick their house down . . ." (*WCOW* 16). The image of the rock becomes even more prominent, though as the title suggests, the Rock of Quebec, in contrast to the sun-bathed mesas that dot the landscape of *Death*, is often darkened by shadow. In addition, as human striving in *Shadows* diminishes in scope from the heroic journeys of *Death*, the rock looms even larger: "To me," Cather wrote, "the rock of Quebec is not only a stronghold on which many strange figures have for a little time cast a shadow in the sun; it is the curious endurance of a kind of culture, narrow but definite. There another age persists" (*WCOW* 15).[11]

It is revealing that the jacket for *Shadows* says nothing about the novel's characters and their concerns but instead focuses on the novel's atmosphere, and the rock: "[Cather] recaptures the very tone and feeling of the seventeenth century in this old French city, built on a rock on the great St. Lawrence." Even the short blurb on the front of the book, with its comment that *Shadows* "is of the same superb vintage" as *Death* (fig. 13), focuses on ambience rather than substance, albeit in a manner in keeping with the French setting of the novel and its frequent emphasis on culinary matters (to say nothing of the importance both Cather and the Knopfs attached to fine French wines!). It is also significant that a slightly later issue of the first edition introduces a jacket that abandons any cover blurb in favor of an image of the rock so imposing that at first one scarcely notices the buildings of the Upper Town that peek over its top, or the smaller buildings—the Lower Town—that huddle at its base (fig. 14). It is an image that suggests the "obscure destinies" of the two towns' inhabitants, and the limited place humans occupy in this harsh world.[12] Although an inner flap and the rear of this new jacket quote from Wilbur Cross's comments on the novel, the rock itself, which spills over onto the jacket's spine, makes the major statement about the novel. As critics have commented, the diminishment in stature of the novel's human agents mirrors Cather's own sense of diminishment in the difficult years when she was writing it. Cather's jacket blurbs are in many ways an embodiment of her ambition, her drive to preeminence: that even the short blurb on the original jacket soon yields to the domination of the rock on the new one poignantly captures her sense of being overwhelmed, pitted against unfeeling adversaries, during these years.[13] A similar picture emerges from her description of Thea Kronborg in the new preface to *The Song of the Lark* that she writes in 1932, the year after she published *Shadows*: "As the gallery of her musical impersonations grows in number and beauty, as that perplexing thing called 'style' (which is a singer's very self) becomes more direct and simple and noble, the Thea Kronborg who is behind the imperishable daughters of music becomes somewhat dry and preoccupied. Her human life is made up of exacting engagements and dull business detail, of shifts to evade an idle, gaping world which is determined that no artist shall ever do his best."[14]

One reason that *Shadows* yet manages to breathe such serenity is that it lacks any character, and especially any woman, who is possessed by the powerful ambitions, and torn by the acute divisions, of a Kronborg or a Cather. How far we have come from the heroine of *A Lost Lady*, who as she ages and dies yet remains relentlessly hungry for life, in search of new possibilities, and rebellious in the face of death and decline![15] A natural line leads from Godfrey St. Peter's reluctant acceptance of a life without delight to Myra Henshawe's willing participation in her own death to the Cécile and Jeanne Le Ber of *Shadows*, the former deeply appealing for the grace with which she embraces a woman's traditional roles, the latter memorable for the absoluteness of her withdrawal. In the books of Cather's final decade—*Obscure Destinies, Lucy Gayheart, Not Under Forty, Sapphira*—she will move back toward women of Marian Forrester's and Thea Kronborg's rich complexity, women who in their different ways reveal the passionate drives, and the wrenching divisions, that are largely suppressed in Cécile and Jeanne Le Ber. Complementing this progression in her late books, and inherent within it, will be the resurgence of Cather's own energies and ambitions as well as her final confrontations with the attendant rifts in her own life.

Obscure Destinies

That the jacket for *Obscure Destinies* tells us so much both about the stories themselves and also, indirectly, about the author suggests the degree to which Cather was emotionally caught up in the book's three stories. Just as these stories return, as the jacket notes, to the western backdrop of her earlier fiction, so also they plunge again into the human issues that Cather had largely skirted in *Death* and *Shadows*. "Neighbour Rosicky" not only confronts mortality more directly, and on a more personal level, than do these novels, but it also probes the complex generational, ethnic, and emotional dynamics of mature family relationships. In "Old Mrs. Harris" such dynamics play an even more central role, and with a focus on three women who contrast sharply with the preadolescent Cécile of *Shadows*: the adolescent, ambitious Vickie; her mother, Victoria, caught in the full range of adult female life—nursing one baby, finding herself pregnant with another, dealing with two lively young sons and a rebellious daughter, trying to keep herself young for her husband; and "old" Mrs. Harris, who not only understands in retrospect what her daughter and granddaughter are going through but also faces her own painful issues.[16] "Two Friends" may be shorter, but at its heart are again central human concerns—the importance, and fragility, of friendship; the complex codes by which humans communicate, and fail to communicate; the swiftness with which that which is beautiful and good, and seems so strong, can reveal its mortality.[17] A phrase from the description of "Old Mrs. Harris" in fact applies to all three stories, "the old riddle of human relationships," and we recall the riddles implicit in jacket blurbs from *Youth* through *My Mortal Enemy*—youth facing Medusa, Claude as Hamlet, the inscrutable Marian, the enigma as to the identity of the "mortal enemy."

If we can take Cather's draft for the *Sapphira* jacket as a model, we may expect to hear her voice most clearly in the three paragraphs of the *Obscure Destinies* jacket that deal with the stories themselves, and indeed those paragraphs contain comments that seem to reflect the author's own insights. We have noted the connections she makes between *My Ántonia* and "Neighbour Rosicky," *A Lost Lady* and "Two Friends," with the former further signaled by the jacket's implicit link between "Ántonia" and "Anton." These links to the past match both the jacket's comment about Cather's "return . . . to the Western scene of her earlier novels" and also its emphasis on retrospective elements in the stories themselves: Rosicky's years on his prairie farm are seen against the backdrop of his Bohemian origins and his experiences in London and New York, while "Two Friends" sweeps us back to those earlier days "when business was still a personal adventure."

This emphasis on returning to the past sets the stage for the final description of the blurb, that of "Old Mrs. Harris," a story in which Cather simultaneously returns to "the old riddle of human relationships" and to her own childhood. Just as Cather gives this story, the longest and most personal in the collection, the central position in the book, so also she lends it special emphasis in the jacket blurb.[18] Not only does she vary the order in which she discusses the three stories so that this one comes last, but she also describes it in ways that underscore its uniqueness. It has its own place in her oeuvre: "Miss Cather has never written anything . . . like this before." Its manner is distinctive: "Tragic human meanings underlie its apparently careless and light-hearted mood." Its theme is universal: "[T]he story is the old riddle of human relationships, the struggle of three women who live under one roof each to live her own life and follow her own destiny." That Victoria and Vickie are modeled on Cather's mother and herself carries special poignancy here: not only had their relationship long been stormy, but Cather wrote these stories at the time when her mother was dying.[19] In speaking of the story's "tragic meanings" and its "riddle of human relationships," Cather is turning the retrospective cast of the whole jacket blurb very much on herself and her family. In particular, one suspects a highly personal reference when she speaks of the three women under one roof each trying to live her own life and find her own destiny: it is precisely what Cather spent her childhood doing, and the ambitious, headstrong, alternately caring and selfish Vickie is Cather's unsparingly candid portrait of herself as a child, someone not easy to live with, or always thoughtful of others, but what she had to be if, like Thea Kronborg, she were to fulfill her ambitions and her potential.[20]

It is not only in Vickie, of course, that *Obscure Destinies* gives us humans with strong personal ambitions. Anton Rosicky's oldest son, Rudolph, for all his care for his father, talks about leaving the farm for a job where he "can always make good wages . . . and be sure of my money." Noting that his father has not kept up with his neighbors during his years on the prairie, Rudolph thinks that "[t]here must be something wrong about his . . . way of doing things" (*OD* 45, 50). As for Vickie, her ambition is clearly something she has inherited from her mother, whose ambition is apparent in how she reacts to her pregnancy: "She was still young, and she was still handsome; why must she be for ever shut up in a little cluttered house with children and fresh babies and an old woman and a stupid bound girl and a husband who wasn't very successful?" (178). Indeed, the final paragraph of the story lumps Victoria and Vickie together in its comments on how they have treated Mrs. Harris—and on the driving ambition they share: "They will regret that they heeded her so little; but they, too, will look into the eager, unseeing eyes of young people and feel themselves alone. They will say to themselves: 'I was heartless, because I was young and strong and wanted things so much. But now I know'" (190).[21]

R. E. Dillon and J. H. Trueman, the title characters of "Two Friends," differ in many respects, but they too are both ambitious: they have aimed high in life and are proud of what they have achieved. The young narrator describes Dillon as "according to our standards, a rich man," and Trueman as "what we called a big cattleman"; of the two together the narrator says, "In my childhood they represented to me success and power" (194–95). The narrator ascribes similar qualities to him- or herself, [22] speaking of early youth as that time "when the mind is so eager for the new and untried" (193), and he or she is clearly drawn into Dillon's and Trueman's aspirations just as they themselves, in recalling plays they have seen, are drawn into those imaginary worlds: "But they saw the play over again as they talked of it, and perhaps whatever is seen by the narrator as he speaks is sensed by the listener . . . . This transference of experience went further: in some way the lives of those two men came across to me as they talked, the strong, bracing reality of successful, large-minded men who had made their way in the world when business was still a personal adventure" (218).[23]

Although the three stories of *Obscure Destinies* were written in the same general period as *Shadows on the Rock*, Cather—like her narrator in "Two Friends"—seems drawn into the "personal adventure" in a way that does not happen in that novel, caught up in the lives and aspirations of her characters just as the narrator and her "Two Friends" are transfixed by the transit of Venus near the center of the story (one recalls Alexandra, whose lofty ambitions seem so perfectly reflected in her rapt attention to the stars, "their ordered march" [*OP* 70]). Cather's jacket blurbs are both indices of her degree of involvement in a particular book and outlets for her ambitions on its behalf, ambitions that also (like Mary Baker Eddy's) often reached to the stars. That *Obscure Destinies* once again sports a jacket blurb so substantial and substantive, especially coming as it does after what we find (and do not find) on the jackets of *Death* and *Shadows*, is the corollary to the sense of personal adventure, of new possibilities, that Cather felt in writing these stories during these dark years. As in the past, the blurb is an avatar of her ambition, a revealing sign of how passionately—once again—she wanted to lure readers into her fictional world.

Two final points. First, as Cather returns to the theme of ambition, division again begins to loom large. We have seen that Rosicky's son feels his father has lacked ambition, and that this feeling opens a slight gulf between the generations. The gulfs are wider in "Old Mrs. Harris," where the ambitions of both Victoria and Vickie create divides around them. And in "Two Friends," the aspirations of both Dillon and Trueman are such that it takes only a petty issue to catalyze the ultimate split. Second, Cather's choice to discuss "Old Mrs. Harris" last on the jacket blurb not only highlights the story's importance within the collection but also dramatically underscores the change of gender from the male figures she has described in the first two stories—Anton Rosicky, Dillon and Trueman—to the three women evoked at the end. "Old Mrs. Harris," placed at the heart of this new collection, represents the first time she has given central roles to strong and mature female characters since *My Mortal Enemy*. In its three courageous and distinctive women, the story both returns to the "heroic women" of earlier novels and foreshadows the central role women will play in the three books yet to come, *Lucy Gayheart*, *Not Under Forty*, and *Sapphira and the Slave Girl*.[24]

Lucy Gayheart

Although in *Lucy Gayheart* Cather focuses on some of the issues that are absent from *Death* and *Shadows*—the life of the artist, the interweaving of love and hate, our high hopes as against our mortality—she herself expressed weariness with the novel's central figure, and Lucy Gayheart falls short of the heights and the depths of both artistic ambition and human passion.[25] To see this, one need merely juxtapose similar moments from Lucy's life and Thea's.[26] Here is Thea as she heads back to Chicago to resume her studies: "She realized that there were a great many trains dashing east and west on the face of the continent that night, and that they all carried young people who meant to have things. But the difference was that *she was going to get them*. That was all. Let people try to stop her! She glowered at the rows of feckless bodies that lay sprawled in the chairs. Let them try it once!" (*SOL* 218). And here is Lucy, also en route to Chicago to study music: "At last she was alone, lying still in the dark, and could give herself up to the vibration of the train,—a rhythm that had to do with escape, change, chance, with life hurrying forward. That sense of release and surrender went all over her body; she seemed to lie in it as in a warm bath" (*LG* 23–24).[27] Here again is Thea, now in Chicago: "Thea glared round her at the crowds, the ugly, sprawling streets, the long lines of lights, and she was not crying now. . . . All these things and people were no longer remote and negligible; they had to be met, they were lined up against her, they were there to take something from her. Very well; they should never have it. They might trample her to death, but they should never have it. As long as she lived that ecstasy was going to be hers" (*SOL* 201). And Lucy: "She went slowly across the town, getting a kind of comfort out of the crowded streets and the people who rushed by and bumped into her, hurrying away from the rain. . . . [T]onight all these people seemed like companions, and she felt a kind of humble affection for them" (*LG* 62–63).

Thea's fierce, angry ambition is simply absent in Lucy: her piano teacher comments that she is someone who does not get nervous "because she [is] not ambitious—that it was her greatest fault" (*LG* 34). Although the performance of "The Bohemian Girl" near the end of the book makes Lucy want to return to "a world that strove after excellence" and, for what is really the first time, inspires "something that was like a purpose forming" (181–82), her life ends before she is able to act on this new sense of resolve (compare the transformations that occur in Eddy's life after she meets Quimby, in Thea's when she changes from piano to voice).[28] The 1915 brochure describes the impact on Thea of the cliff-dweller ruins, where "for the first time in her life, she grew all at once into a powerful and willful young creature, got her courage, and began to find herself." Partly because of her early death, Lucy never reaches this point, never fully "gets her courage."

The final words of the book, describing the footprints Lucy leaves imprinted in the cement of the sidewalk, are apt: "running away." Despite her love of life, her winning exuberance, and her swift stride, Lucy's essential impulse is toward escape.[29] She goes to Chicago less to become a great musician than to flee Haverford, and her human relationships reflect a similar inclination: with both Harry Gordon and Clement Sebastian her instinct is repeatedly to flee. She flees Chicago after Clement's death, and she is in flight from Pauline, and from Harry, when she takes her final and fatal skate on the river.[30]

In light of all this, the novel's somewhat perfunctory jacket blurb—a sharp contrast to the specificity and emotional depth of the *Obscure Destinies* blurb three years earlier—is not surprising: "Willa Cather's new novel needs no introduction: I will comment only as to place and time. It is Romantic . . . Western . . . Modern . . . a story of the passionate enthusiasms of youth, which triumph even when they seem to fail." Its final phrase is significant, though, especially given Cather's own comment that book 3 was the best part of the novel, and the one that made sense out of book 1.[31] Joseph Urgo argues cogently that what matters in the novel is not Lucy herself but the powerful, even mythic images she leaves in people's minds, images to which her inclination toward flight is essential: "Lucy Gayheart is the personification of motion, of the quality of human movement so vital to Cather's understanding of social and cultural existence. . . . By all standards Lucy Gayheart is a limited young woman . . . . Nonetheless, the need of the living for images of irrepressible light-heartedness, for gaiety and grace, is not qualified by fact or by the limitations of empirical reality."[32] The jacket blurb makes a similar point when it speaks of "the passionate enthusiasms of youth, which triumph even when they seem to fail."

CHAPTER NINETEEN

Cather, Jewett, and *Not Under Forty*

From *Death Comes for the Archbishop* to *Lucy Gayheart*

Sarah Orne Jewett plays a central role in *Not Under Forty*, the book of essays Cather published in 1936, and this book in turn feeds directly into her final novel, *Sapphira and the Slave Girl*, which she began writing in 1937. Even prior to that, Cather's work in 1924–25 on *The Best Stories of Sarah Orne Jewett* had exerted a strong influence on the fiction she wrote in the late twenties and the first half of the thirties.

Although Cather does not specifically name Jewett in the public letter she wrote in 1927 about the recently published *Death Comes for the Archbishop*, her language reveals how much Jewett was on her mind. Cather begins that letter by evoking the strong impressions left by her first trip to the Southwest "some fifteen years ago," emphasizes the frequency with which she returned there in the years that followed, speaks of other specific influences on the novel—the statue of Archbishop Lamy in Santa Fé, Howlett's *Life of the Right Reverend Joseph P. Machebeuf*, the Puvis de Chavannes' St. Geneviève murals that Cather had seen in Paris in her student days—then concludes, "I did not sit down to write the book until the feeling of it had so teased me that I could not get on with other things" (*WCOW* 10). It is hard to imagine a clearer allusion to the advice from Jewett with which two years before Cather had begun her preface to *Best Stories*: "The thing that teases the mind over and over for years, and at last gets itself put down rightly on paper—whether little or great, it belongs to Literature" (iv).[1] Further sealing the connection is Cather's comment a bit later in the same letter that "[w]riting this book

. . . was like a happy vacation from life, a return to childhood, to early memories" (*WCOW* 11), lines that strongly recall Cather's emphasis in that same preface on the ways in which Jewett's childhood memories had fed into her fiction—how in "driving about the country with her doctor father" Jewett "learned to love her country for what it was" and "saw it as it was"; how "[f]rom childhood she must have treasured up those pithy bits of local speech, of native idiom, which enrich and enliven her pages" (*Best Stories* xvi).

In addition, the very style and character of *Death* at point after point recall what Cather had written about Jewett in that same preface. How better to describe *Death*'s evocations of the Southwest than through Cather's words on the "'Pointed Fir' sketches": "[They] are living things caught in the open, with light and freedom and air-spaces about them. They melt into the land and the life of the land until they are not stories at all, but life itself" (*Best Stories* x)? How better to portray the easy structural mastery of *Death*, its calm, understated beauty, than by Cather's description of Jewett's writing: "[I]t has an organic, living simplicity and directness. . . . [It] is the beauty for which the Greek writers strove" (xviii)? Other passages from Cather's Jewett preface are equally apt. There is the Louise Imogen Guiney excerpt that Cather chose as epigraph, "But give to thine own story / Simplicity, with glory." There is her comment on the capacity of Jewett's *Country of the Pointed Firs* to "confront time and change so serenely. [It] seems to me fairly to shine with the reflection of its long, joyous future" (xviii–xix). Finally, as mentioned earlier, in *Death* more than in any other Cather novel one feels that Cather has, as Jewett had urged, found her "own quiet centre of life" and is "writ[ing] from that to the world" (SOJ *Letters* 249).

Several of the same ties to Jewett carry over to Cather's next novel, *Shadows on the Rock*. Although her interest in Canada in general and Quebec in particular was relatively recent, her mind had long been teased by France, French culture, and French cuisine, all of which figure prominently in *Shadows*. If the mood is darker, the sense of resolution more muted, the mastery with which Cather evokes the landscape, the way the episodes of her novel "melt into the land and the life of the land until they are not stories at all, but life itself," remains constant. In her 1925 preface Cather had praised Jewett's ability to find the timeless and the significant in the modest turns of everyday life: "Miss Jewett wrote of the people who grew out of the soil and the life of the country near her heart, not about exceptional individuals at war with their environment. . . . She happened to have the right nature . . . to understand by intuition the deeper meaning of all she saw" (*Best Stories* xv–xvi). Cather's description of Jewett is close to what she would in 1931 write about herself and *Shadows*: "An orderly little French household that went on trying to live decently . . . interests me more than Indian raids or the wild life in the forests" (*WCOW* 16).

Jewett's counsel to "find your own centre of life" is also apt. In an eloquent article about Jewett's influence on *Shadows*, Ann Romines focuses on a passage in the same letter that carries this advice a step further: "To work in silence and with all one's heart, that is the writer's lot; he is the only artist who must be a solitary, and yet needs the widest outlook upon the world."[2] Noting that Jewett was still very much on Cather's mind in 1928 when she began writing *Shadows*, Romines proposes that in this novel for the first time Cather explores what it means to "be a solitary." She does so both through Cécile, an only child who when her mother falls ill is removed from the convent school and thereafter spends most of her days "alone in her father's house, performing the domestic tasks her mother taught her," and through Jeanne Le Ber, the beautiful heiress who at seventeen takes vows of chastity and later retreats to an isolated chapel from which she will never emerge.[3] Romines finds counterparts to these Cather characters both in the narrator of Jewett's *Country*, a solitary female who comes to a remote Maine village to spend a summer writing, and in "poor Joanna," a young woman who when jilted by her fiancé flees for the remainder of her life to a shack on a small, barren island. In *Shadows*, writes Romines, Cather, "bearing the wide experience of her rich, intense life in the world . . . returned to the traditional parish of women to probe the meanings it might yield to a woman artist. . . . No figure among her American literary predecessors could have offered more support and impetus for such work than the advice and example of Sarah Orne Jewett."[4]

Romines's comment on Cather's return "to the traditional parish of women" points to a further aspect of Jewett's influence. We have seen that from her focus on the two bishops in *Death*, with women cast in largely subsidiary roles, Cather begins in her subsequent fiction again to give prominent roles to female characters. Cécile and Jeanne Le Ber are the most memorable figures in *Shadows*. The central story in *Obscure Destinies*, "Old Mrs. Harris," revolves around three women who exemplify quintessential female roles, and both Mary and Polly are memorably evoked in that book's opening story, "Neighbour Rosicky." The heroine of *Lucy Gayheart* may lack the heroic temperament of Thea Kronborg, but the fullness of her portrait, especially in the novel's final section, clearly shows Cather moving back toward the richly imagined women of her earlier novels—Alexandra and Marie, Ántonia, and Thea in the teens, Marian Forrester and Myra Henshawe in the twenties. One cannot doubt that Cather's return to Jewett in 1924–25 contributed to this progression, which will climax in the memorable female cast of *Sapphira*. For remarkable women dominate the Jewett stories Cather selects in *Best Stories*: in *Country* Mrs. Todd, Mrs. Blackett, "poor Joanna," the unnamed narrator, and a host of others—including Mrs. Hight and Esther in the later stories Cather chose to retain in *Country*. Memorable female figures populate the remaining *Best Stories* as well: the almost adolescent "Sylvy" in "A White Heron"; the title character and her two friends, Peggy Bond and Aunt Lavina Dow, in "The Flight of Betsey Lane"; the Dobin sisters and their mother in the "The Dulham Ladies; and so on through the whole book. It is for good reason that in her preface to *Best Stories* Cather quotes Jewett as saying, "laughingly," that "her head was full of dear old houses and dear old women, and that when an old house and an old woman came together in her brain with a click, she knew that a story was under way" (xvi). We shall see that in *Not Under Forty* Cather places Jewett herself in the company of other "old women," and Jewett's comment on "an old house and an old woman [coming] together with a click" to create a story aptly describes what happens when Cather writes *Sapphira*.

Before we consider *Not Under Forty* and *Sapphira*, however, it's worth mentioning two other ways in which Jewett's influence makes itself felt in

Obscure Destinies and *Lucy Gayheart*. Most obviously, both of these have their origins in people and stories that have long haunted Cather's mind, and that finally push their way to the surface many years later. "Neighbour Rosicky" returns to the Shimerdas, "Two Friends" to two Red Cloud leaders whose stories Cather had enjoyed hearing as a child—even to the particular place where she had sat and listened, and "Old Mrs. Harris" takes us back to the Cather household in the years—the late 1880s— when Cather was preparing to head for the university, with the teasing of Cather's mind, and the dynamics of the story, obviously colored by current thoughts of her mother, then incapacitated in California. *Lucy Gayheart* has its origins in Cather's recollections of two women she had known many years before: a "vivacious young schoolteacher Cather had met and instantly liked when she was visiting Red Cloud in the summer of 1896," and whose name was Gayhardt; and Sadie Becker, a young musician whom Cather remembered "skat[ing] on the old rink in a red jersey."[5]

Second, *Obscure Destinies*, Cather's title for the book that follows *Shadows*, perfectly captures what she had in her 1925 preface described as Jewett's persistent focus: "the people who grew out of the soil and the life of the country near her heart." In the attention paid to the profound themes implicit in the "obscure destinies" of a handful of people from Cather's small-town Nebraska past, the three stories of this wonderful collection represent a natural next step from Cather's focus in *Shadows* on "an orderly little French household that went on trying to live decently." The opening of *Lucy Gayheart* emphasizes the small-town provenance of its heroine and her story, and the fact that her "obscure destiny" survives time's passing: "In Haverford on the Platte the townspeople still talk of Lucy Gayheart. They do not talk of her a great deal, to be sure; life goes on and we live in the present. But when they do mention her name it is with a gentle glow in the face or the voice, a confidential glance which says: 'Yes, you, too, remember?'" It is language that recalls what Cather had written ten years earlier in her preface to *Best Stories*: Jewett's characters may be obscure, but her stories about them have lasting resonance.[6]

From *Not Under Forty* to *Sapphira and the Slave Girl*

Jewett's presence, strongly felt in the works that stretch from *Death* through *Lucy Gayheart*, comes fully to the fore in the book Cather publishes in 1936, *Not Under Forty*. Its brief jacket blurb begins with what might be a subtitle for the book, an impression furthered by the italics in which it is set: *Studies of Literary Personalities and Certain Aspects of Literature*.[7] The brief description that follows, no doubt vetted by Cather herself, underscores the book's personal nature, its roots in the author's own predilections: "Its revealing chapters concern some of the authors she admires and what she admires in them, so that the result is a considerable expression of her convictions about the art of writing generally." Given the mention of "authors she admires" and "her convictions about the art of writing," the surprise would be if Jewett did not figure prominently. In fact, Jewett's impact extends throughout, a fact signaled by the word Cather uses in her prefatory note to describe the essays of *Not Under Forty*: "sketches." As we have seen, it is the very word she had used of Jewett's stories in her 1925 preface. She repeats this passage when she expands the 1925 preface into "Miss Jewett" in *Not Under Forty*, and she underscores the point in one of the new sections: "[Miss Jewett] spoke of 'the Pointed Fir papers' or 'the Pointed Fir sketches'; I never heard her call them stories" (*NUF* 89).

"Miss Jewett" begins at the same place as did Cather's 1925 preface, with Jewett's advice about "[t]he thing that teases the mind over and over for years, and at last gets itself put down rightly on paper." But this familiar passage here takes on new meaning, for it proves relevant to the essays that surround it in *Not Under Forty*. Although the first sketch goes back to a "chance meeting" with Madame Grout just six years before, in 1930, its opening words, "It happened at Aix-les-Bains," seem to evoke a more distant past, an impression subtly enhanced by other touches in the same paragraph: the reference to Queen Victoria and her visits "to that old watering-place"; the mention that the hotel "was built for the travellers of forty years ago"; Cather's comment that "long ago [she] used to hear old Pittsburghers and Philadelphians talk of it." The impression is apt, for as the essay unfolds, it draws us further and further into the past—to Flaubert and his various works, all of which have long teased Cather's mind, especially *L'Éducation sentimentale*, "a story of youth" (19); to other authors that are part of her own past and of her own "sentimental education"—Balzac, Turgenev, James, Sand, among others; and, at the very end, to the childhood relationship between Madame Grout and her uncle. The whole essay has the feeling of taking the reader, the narrator, and Madame Grout herself back to all manner of things that have teased the mind over the years. Only at the end are we abruptly jolted back to the present by the quotation of the notice, in French, of Madame Grout's death.

"148 Charles Street," the second of the five longer sketches, follows a similar path. Again the opening words draw us immediately into the past: "Late in the winter of 1908 Mrs. Louis Brandeis conducted me along a noisy street in Boston and rang at a door hitherto unknown to me. Sometimes entering a new door can make a great change in one's life." Not only does this door lead us "up a steep, thickly carpeted stairway" into "'the long drawing room,' where Mrs. Fields and Miss Jewett sat at tea," but even before that we have been taken back to the earlier time when Annie Adams, a girl of nineteen but now an elderly widow, married James T. Fields, the famous publisher (*NUF* 53). No sooner have we met Annie Fields and Sarah Orne Jewett than we enter another door to a yet more distant past, M. A. De Wolfe Howe's book of extracts from Mrs. Fields's diaries, published in 1922 with the evocative title *Memories of a Hostess*. Even here there is a further inset, for Cather reminds us that what follows is her largely unrevised review of Howe's book, written when that book first appeared. And once inside this central section of the sketch, we meet the people who have haunted Mrs. Fields's memory across so many years—Dickens, Thackeray, and Matthew Arnold; Winslow Homer and Sargent; "Longfellow, Emerson, Whittier, Hawthorne, Lowell, Sumner, Norton, Oliver Wendell Holmes—the list sounds like something in a school-book; but in Mrs. Fields' house one came to believe that they had been very living people—to feel that they had not been long absent from the rooms so full of their thoughts, of their letters, their talk . . ." (*NUF* 56–57). The remainder of the sketch moves easily between this more distant past and Cather's memories of the times she herself spent with Mrs. Fields in 1908–9, with the two periods sometimes merging: "It was at tea-time, I used to think, that the great shades were most likely to appear; sometimes they seemed to come up the deeply carpeted stairs, along with living friends . . . ." Cather sketches the fire in the long room, the view of the sunset "flaming, or softly brooding, upon the Charles River and the Cambridge shore beyond," then adds, "It was indeed the peace of the past, where the tawdry and cheap have been eliminated and the enduring things have taken their proper, happy places" (*NUF* 62–63). As in "A Chance Meeting," so too at the close of this sketch we are jolted back to the present: "Today, in 1936, a garage stands on the site of 148 Charles Street. Only in memory exists the long, green-carpeted, softly lighted drawing-room, and the dining-table where Learning and Talent met . . ." (73). More recently, "In England and America the 'masters' of the last century diminished in stature and pertinence, became remote and shadowy," Cather notes, but she ends with the theme that has infused the whole sketch, the memories of the past: "It was thus Mrs. Fields died, in that house of memories, with the material keepsakes of the past about her" (74–75).

I have dealt at some length with these first two long sketches to suggest how deeply they respond to Jewett's comment about "the thing that has teased the mind." The same theme carries over strongly to the three that follow. A principal focus in the final sketch—and the one that dominates its closing pages—is on how at the very end of her life Katherine Mansfield finally returned to the memories of her New Zealand childhood as the basis for three of her greatest stories—stories "[s]he could not have written . . . when she first came to London" (*NUF* 144; compare the return to Madame Grout's childhood at the end of the first sketch). Once again, as in "148 Charles Street," Cather adds to her original essay an opening section that enhances our sense of probing with her into past memories. This new opening sets her subsequent picture of Mansfield against the backdrop of shipboard conversations with a man whose name she can no longer recall but whom she dubs "Mr. J." (as in Jewett, perhaps?). In turn, he recounts memories that have haunted him across the years—of his chance meetings, also on shipboard, with Katherine Mansfield as a child, and of catching a glimpse of her years later in London. The theme surfaces as well in the essay on Thomas Mann's *Joseph and His Brothers* when Cather discusses the "two ways in which a story-teller can approach a theme set in the distant past" (97); noteworthy too, and typical of the way Cather links the essays of *Not Under Forty*, is the mention in the next sentence of Flaubert's *Salammbô*, a work that figures prominently in the first sketch.

"Miss Jewett," the centerpiece of the five longer sketches, itself revolves around this same theme. Not only does the portion of the essay reprised from Cather's 1925 preface use Jewett's familiar words as the entrée to showing how Jewett's own stories grew out of her childhood memories and experiences, but Cather expands this 1925 core to include her own recollections of the "short period when I knew her, 1908 and 1909" (*NUF* 85), the very period with which "148 Charles Street" also begins. In contrast to this immersion in the past in most of the essay, Cather's final section, in a manner familiar from the closing portions of "A Chance Meeting" and "148 Charles Street," again jolts us back to the present. Cather had ended her 1925 preface by imagining the "sense of rich discovery" with which a "young student of American literature in far distant years to come will take up this book and say, 'A Masterpiece!' as proudly as if he himself had made it" (*Best Stories* xix). The closing pages of her new version instead remind us of the different "young students" of 1936: "It is easy to understand why some of the young students who have turned back from the present to glance at Miss Jewett find very little on her pages. Imagine a young man, or woman, born in New York city, educated at a New York university, violently inoculated with Freud, hurried into journalism, knowing no more about New England country people (or country folk anywhere) than he has caught from motor trips or observed from summer hotels: what is there for him in *The Country of the Pointed Firs?*" (*NUF* 92–93).

In putting together *Not Under Forty*, Cather included also her famous 1922 essay, "The Novel Démeublé." Although in character and length this essay differs from the five other sketches, Cather weaves it too into the tight fabric of her book. We have seen that this 1922 essay found echoes in both the themes and the language of Cather's 1925 Jewett preface, and in 1936 she creates similar ties between it and the other sketches of *Not Under Forty*. Her description in the first sketch of *L'Éducation sentimentale* could well come out of "The Novel Démeublé," though with a darker shading: "One is 'left with it,' in the same way that one is left with a weak heart after certain illnesses. A shadow has come into one's consciousness that will not go out again" (20). The same is yet more apparent in what Cather writes about Mansfield in the last essay: "She communicates vastly more than she actually writes. One goes back and runs through the pages to find the text which made one know certain things about Linda or Burnell or Beryl, and the text is not there . . . . It is this overtone, which is too fine for the printing press and comes through without it, that makes one know that this writer had something of the gift which is one of the rarest things in writing, and quite the most precious" (137–38). And Cather's comment on the refuge Mrs. Fields's home offered from "the tawdry and cheap" echoes her comparison of the modern novel to "a cheap soap or a cheap perfume, or cheap furniture" in "The Novel Démeublé," the sketch she has placed immediately before "148 Charles Street."

By now it will be clear that Cather has in preparing *Not Under Forty* frequently expanded and revised the essays, all of which had been published earlier, so as to create structural and thematic bridges among them. The way Cather weaves intimations of Sarah Orne Jewett into the other essays is central to this process and extends well beyond what we have seen so far—and in ways that prove prophetic of directions she will explore as she writes *Sapphira* in the years immediately ahead. Most obviously, Jewett's influence is felt in the overall cast of characters of *Not Under Forty*, with women playing lead roles in four of the five longer sketches—a natural extension of the way Cather's work on Jewett in the midtwenties had helped lead both to her use of female narrators in "Uncle Valentine" and *My Mortal Enemy* and to a return to women as her central characters in the novels of the 1930s. In addition, these women of *Not Under Forty* have much in common—further evidence of the care with which

Cather has shaped her collection into a cohesive whole. To begin with, all of them, though in very different ways, live up to what Cather writes about Jewett: "'The distinguished outward stamp'—it was that one felt immediately upon meeting Miss Jewett: a lady, in the old high sense. It was in her face and figure, in her carriage, her smile, her voice, her way of greeting one" (84–85). The whole description clearly fits both Madame Grout and Mrs. Fields. As for Katherine Mansfield, she is scarcely "a lady, in the old high sense," but the young girl Mr. J. meets surely has her "distinguished outward stamp," as he recalls so clearly: "She struck him as intensely alert, with a deep curiosity altogether different from the flighty, excited curiosity usual in children. She turned things over in her head and asked him questions which surprised him. She was sometimes with her grandmother and the other children, but oftener alone, going about the boat, looking the world over with quiet satisfaction" (131).

The women of these sketches are also, albeit again in different ways, all strong-minded and artistically ambitious. They know what they think and what they want, and they do not hesitate to speak their minds. Part of the strength that distinguishes all of them is their courage in the face of adversity and disability. Once again Cather's description of Jewett, this time in her last years, sets the pattern: "After the carriage accident she was not strong enough to go out into the world a great deal; before that occurred her friendships occupied perhaps the first place in her life." Nonetheless, "[e]ven after her long illness she was at home to a few visitors almost every afternoon; friends from England and France were always coming and going" (85–86). Cather is both impressed and slightly put off by the way Madame Grout, despite her age and her physical limitations, drives herself, going out to paint each day despite the hot sun and determinedly attending every symphony and opera performance. Of Mrs. Fields Cather writes, "Although [she] was past seventy when I was first conducted into the long drawing-room, she did not seem old to me. Frail, diminished in force, yes; but, emphatically, *not* old. 'The personal beauty of her younger years, long retained, and even at the end of such a stretch of life not quite lost,' to quote Henry James, may have had something to do with the impression she gave; but I think it was even more because, as he also said of her, 'all her implications were gay'" (57). As for Katherine Mansfield, the final portion of Cather's sketch repeatedly reminds us of her "long struggle with illness, made more cruel by lack of money and by the physical hardships that war conditions brought about in England and France" (138). She quotes from Mansfield's account of the tragic last years but stresses that "[t]he *Journal*, painful though it is to read, is not the story of utter defeat. She had not, as she said, the physical strength to write what she now knew were, to her, the most important things in life. But she had found them, she possessed them, her mind fed on them" (144–45).[8]

It is noteworthy that the passages quoted about Jewett in the two previous paragraphs again come from portions of "Miss Jewett" that Cather has added for this 1936 publication. The 1925 preface concentrates on Jewett's writing and says very little about Jewett herself. Aside from a passing comment that her attitude toward the people of her stories is "a little arch in its expression," there is no hint of Jewett's "distinguished outward stamp," of how she struck one immediately as "a lady, in the old high sense." And there is no mention of her carriage accident, her subsequent illness, or the decline in "working energy" during her last years. It is clear that in shaping *Not Under Forty* Cather wished to create close ties among the women of her collection, and that in expanding her Jewett preface she did so in such a way as to assure that Jewett was part of this larger pattern.

Just as noteworthy is the fact that the traits we have found in these four women also fit one other woman who plays a major role in *Not Under Forty*: Willa Cather herself. She too, in 1936, was a woman of "distinguished outward stamp," "a lady, in the old high sense. It was in her face and figure, in her carriage, her smile, her voice, her way of greeting one" (84–85).[9] She too was strong-minded and artistically ambitious, knew what she thought and what she wanted, and did not hesitate to speak her mind. Indeed, a notable feature of these sketches is that, like Jewett in so much of her fiction, Cather herself is the narrator, and in a voice that is decidedly her own. Like the other women in these sketches, Cather too persevered courageously in the face of hurdles posed by age and disability. We recall the chronic maladies from which she suffered for so many years, the persistent focus on age and mortality in her novels of the twenties—it is no accident that death hangs over all the women of *Not Under Forty*, with the deaths of Madame Grout and Katherine Mansfield bracketing the collection. In the years preceding the publication of *Not Under Forty* Cather had to stop writing for several months in 1934 because of hand injuries and faced further medical problems in 1935. Nonetheless, she saw *Lucy Gayheart* to publication in 1935, revised her essays for *Not Under Forty* in 1936, and began work on *Sapphira* in 1937. What she writes about Mansfield near the end of *Not Under Forty* aptly describes herself in the late 1930s: "No one was ever less afraid of the nettle; she was defrauded unfairly of the physical vigour which seems the natural accompaniment of a high and daring spirit" (140). Finally, that Cather shares so much with these women befits her role in these sketches: she is not just narrator but also, again in the manner of Jewett, a fellow actor. She participates in the events of "A Chance Meeting" from start to finish. She is involved throughout "148 Charles Street" as well, not least in the new sections that she added in 1936. Similarly, it is in the portions of "Miss Jewett" that are new to *Not Under Forty* that Cather herself takes the stage, and it is the new opening section of "Katherine Mansfield" that gives her occasion, through her conversation with Mr. J., to become directly part of the action in that sketch.[10] The close affinities between Cather and the women whose stories she tells—and reshapes—in these sketches exemplify yet again her capacity to inhabit, and to breathe herself into, a variety of roles.

Underpinning the courage of all the women of *Not Under Forty* is a certain feistiness. This quality is most apparent in Madame Grout, and one suspects that Cather placed this sketch at the start of the collection to fix this character trait in our minds. While Cather's Madame Grout scarcely lives up to Ellen Moers's description of her as "the worst bitch in nineteenth-century French literature," she nonetheless comes across, in Sharon O'Brien's words, as "opinionated, selfish, domineering, and even a bit cruel."[11] Although Cather's respect, even awe, are apparent throughout "A Chance Meeting," there is also a side of her that resents

Madame Grout's intrusive and imperious manner. We sense both Cather's respect and her resistance when Madame Grout tries to prevent her from departing a concert early: "'Oh, no,' said she, 'that is not necessary. You can have your tea here at the Maison des Fleurs quite well, and still have time to go back for the last group.' I thanked her and went across the garden, but I did not mean to see the concert through. Seeing things through was evidently a habit with this old lady . . ." (11).

Though to a lesser degree, the feistiness of Madame Grout that is so firmly established in this opening sketch carries over to the other women of the collection. Mrs. Fields, for all her gentility and warmth, has a frostier, imperious side as well. Cather captures this combination of opposites in her description of Mrs. Fields's laugh (compare the laughs of Marion Forrester and Myra Henshawe): "I had seldom heard so young, so merry, so musical a laugh; a laugh with countless shades of relish and appreciation and kindness in it. And, on occasion, a short laugh from that same fragile source could positively do police duty! It could put an end to a conversation that had taken an unfortunate turn, absolutely dismiss and silence impertinence or presumption" (57–58).[12] As a child, Katherine Mansfield reveals a certain impertinence in her conversations with Mr. J. ("I thought they would astonish you," she says of the yellow ducks that decorate her dress [NUF 131]); and when Mr. J. sees her later as a rising literary light in London, he comments, "She scorned conventions, and had got herself talked about. . . . She looked . . . almost demure,—except for something challenging in her eyes, perhaps" (132–33). Cather's later description of Mansfield as the author of *Bliss* goes still further: "[S]he throws down her glove, utters her little challenge in the high language which she knew better than did most of her readers . . . . A fine attitude, youthful and fiery: out of all the difficulties of life and art we will snatch *something*" (139–40). Given the ties Cather creates among the women of her book, it is no surprise that—again in material added when she revised her essays for *Not Under Forty*—Cather finds something of this same sharpness as well in Sarah Orne Jewett. She describes Jewett's reaction (including *her* two-sided laugh!) to a story about a mule written by a young man who, his publisher averred, could write authentically about his subject because he himself "was a mule-driver and had never been anything else. When I asked Miss Jewett if she had seen it, she gave no affirmative but a soft laugh, rather characteristic of her, something between amusement and forbearance, and exclaimed: 'Poor lad! But his mule could have done better! A mule, by God's grace, is a mule, with the mettle of his kind. Besides, the mule would be grammatical'" (*NUF* 88–89).

If the other qualities associated with these women seem also to suggest Cather, their feistiness seals the connection. Not only did Cather throughout her career win the reputation of being prickly, but that quality is rarely more apparent in her writing than it is in *Not Under Forty*.[13] Her brief prefatory note throws down *her* glove when it announces that this book "will have little interest for people under forty years of age" and that "[i]t is for the backward, and by one of their number, that these sketches were written." The new portion of Cather's Jewett essay, with its description of the young men and women of the current day, "educated at a New York university" and "inoculated with Freud," further inflamed readers and critics, especially in conjunction with her comment in the following paragraph that "[t]his hypothetical young man is perhaps of foreign descent: German, Jewish, Scandinavian" (93). Not only does her manner align her with Madame Grout, whom we—and she—will soon meet in the opening sketch, but her insertion of such language into the Jewett essay has the effect of lending some of her own feistiness to Jewett herself.[14] As if to underscore the connection, she echoes the prefatory note's comment that her own essays have nothing to offer the young reader in her similarly curt dismissal of the possibility that the same sort of reader might find anything of interest in Jewett: "what is there for him in *The Country of the Pointed Firs*?"

The qualities we have associated with these five women—"the stamp of distinction"; strength of mind and heart and will; courage, even defiance, in the face of diminishment or disability; a certain feistiness underpinning them all—lead inevitably to yet another woman, Cather's next great heroine, Sapphira Colbert.[15] For just as the strong and distinctive women of *Not Under Forty* grow naturally out of the increasing interest in women that Cather displays in the fiction that begins with *Shadows*, so this same trajectory will find its natural completion in her final novel and its heroine.

Worth noting are two other ways in which *Not Under Forty* prepares for *Sapphira*, and again we look to the additions Cather made in revising her 1925 Jewett preface into the "Miss Jewett" of 1936. For one thing, Cather now includes a famous Jewett apothegm that was missing in 1925: "You must know the world before you can know the village" (88).[16] Not only does Cather here give these words a unique provenance, attaching them to Jewett's laughter over the story of the mule driver (who apparently knew only his village, and not even that very grammatically!); she also recalls this advice at a time when it is uniquely applicable to herself. For just as Mansfield was only ready near the end of her life to write stories about her early childhood, as Cather reminds us, so only now, after a lifetime of coming to know the world, is Cather ready to write about hers in *Sapphira*.

Second, in the new sections of "Miss Jewett" Cather expands on a theme that she had introduced in her 1925 preface. Commenting on Jewett's extraordinary sensitivity to the Maine natives who were her primary subject, Cather had written, "If [a writer] achieves anything noble, anything enduring, it must be by giving himself absolutely to his material. And this gift of sympathy is his great gift; is the fine thing in him that alone can make his work fine" (*Best Stories* xii).[17] In Cather's 1936 sketch, she significantly extends this theme of sympathy. She now attaches it not only to the author but also to the reader, and she does so in such a way as to create a complex interpenetration between the two, with the reader aware of, and sensitive to, the very elements that distinguish the writer's craft: "To enjoy [Miss Jewett] the reader must have a sympathetic relation with the subject-matter and a sensitive ear; especially must he have a sense of 'pitch' in writing. He must recognize when the quality of feeling comes inevitably out of the theme itself; when the language, the stresses, the very structure of the sentences are imposed upon the writer by the special mood of the piece" (*NUF* 92). A couple of pages later Cather returns to the same theme: "When we find ourselves on shipboard, among hundreds of strangers, we very soon recognize those who are sympathetic to us. We find our own books in the same way. We like a writer much as we like individuals; for what he is, simply, underneath his accomplishments" (94). And it is with this same author-reader sympathy that Cather ends her essay: "During the twenty-odd clamorous years since her death 'masterpieces' have been bumping down upon us like trunks pouring down the baggage chutes from an overcrowded ocean steamer. But if you can get out from under them and go to a quiet spot and take up a volume of Miss Jewett, you will find the voice still there, with a quality which any ear trained in literature must recognize" (95). It is precisely the sort of meeting of minds of which Cather despairs both in her prefatory note and in her snide comments on the gulf between Jewett and the young modern reader. That she chooses to end "Miss Jewett" on this more harmonious note is both moving and significant. So is the fact that the shipboard imagery of these two passages foreshadows the opening section of the Mansfield sketch, again a 1936 addition: for what we find in those opening pages are passengers who encounter sympathetic strangers—Cather's chance meeting with Mr. J., and the crusty Mr. J.'s chance shipboard meetings with the young Katherine Mansfield.

Just as Cather's 1936 Jewett essay speaks of knowing the world before writing about one's village at the very time when Cather herself is preparing to do just that, so the same essay's focus on sympathy sounds a theme that will be central to Cather's final novel. Not only will sympathy be a touchstone for the novel itself, but in the blurb Cather writes for that novel she describes herself as "a sympathetic artist." What's more, in *Sapphira*, as in *Not Under Forty*, Cather will—like Jewett in her fiction— both be the sympathetic narrator throughout and also, in the epilogue, a sympathetic participant in the action.

One final point, which leads directly into our discussion of *Sapphira*. The qualities shared by the women of *Not Under Forty*, and which also suggest both Cather herself and Sapphira Colbert, seem tailor-made as well for another woman who has loomed large in Cather's life, and whose presence will be marked in her last novel: aristocratic bearing that bespeaks one's station, determination and willpower, courage in the face of both age and physical disability, feistiness. Are not all of these descriptive of Mary Baker Eddy? And indeed we shall find that in *Sapphira*, as in so many of her great earlier works, Cather draws on both Jewett and Eddy in constructing her novel and imagining her heroine, in the process crafting sympathetic resonances between the discordant alter egos she had met in her Boston years. Further, in retrospect we can see that in shaping *Not Under Forty* itself Cather has taken care to suggest Eddy's presence: not only does she end with a Katherine Mansfield who shares Eddy's delight in throwing down the gauntlet, not only does she begin with a prefatory note imbued with her own feisty challenge to both readers and critics, but to lead off her collection she chooses her portrait of Madame Grout, bypassing Annie Fields and Sarah Orne Jewett in the process. In doing so, Cather gives pride of place to a woman who throughout her life had demonstrated not only her literary skills but also an Eddy-like genius in promoting herself and her uncle through the writing and marketing of books—and who, like Eddy in *her* old age, continued to delight in issuing and confronting tough challenges. I expect too that Cather began her collection with "A Chance Meeting" because of the particular fascination Madame Grout exerted over her. One part of this fascination lay in Grout's brilliant literary heritage, her astonishing range of associations. Every bit as important, though, was that in 1930 Cather had seen in Grout so close—and so uncomfortable—an image of herself and her own indomitable ambition. It is precisely the sort of recognition she had experienced many years before in her chance encounter with Mary Baker Eddy, and it is this keen and feisty independence that sounds in the prefatory note and in the sketch of Flaubert's niece with which she begins her collection—and that is echoed in the sketch of Katherine Mansfield with which she ends it.

CHAPTER TWENTY

Sapphira and the Slave Girl

"My end is my beginning," wrote Cather about *Sapphira and the Slave Girl*, acknowledging the novel's return to her childhood home and childhood memories.[1] The same words fit this book as well, for Cather's last novel takes us back to our starting point—her creation of promotional material, including dust-jacket copy. In the case of *Sapphira*, we know that Cather composed the central portion of the jacket blurb, and its sharp differences from the copy that had been proposed to her are revealing as to her conception of the novel.

For ease of comparison, here are the two versions:

Original draft of central section:

The period is the middle of the nineteenth century. Sapphira, a rather willful, haughty, and attractive child of the Tidewater aristocracy had "broken away from her rightful station" to marry Henry Colbert a sober, hard-working miller. Together they had moved to the uplands, to live among poor people who had no liking for Sapphira's fashionable Anglican creed and even less for her cavalier attitude toward slavery.

On the whole the Colberts, who rank with Miss Cather's finest character creations, lived well together—until the slave girl, Nancy, came between them. How the conflict that then arose is resolved and how the resolution influenced Sapphira and Henry, form the heart of the novel.

Cather's revised copy (used on the published jacket):

The chief theme of the novel is the subtle persecution of a beautiful mulatto girl by her jealous mistress. The unconventional opening chapter at the breakfast table strikes the keynote of the whole story, in which strong feelings and bitter wrongs are hidden under the warm atmosphere of good manners and domestic comfort. The period is 1856, just before the outbreak of the Civil War. The setting is the beautiful Virginia countryside, and the narrative is peopled with unusual characters: the mountain people, grim disapproving "Republicans," and Sapphira's African slaves, who are, and doubtless were meant to be, the most interesting figures in the book. These colored folk are presented in an unusual way. They are attractive to the writer as individuals, and are presented by a sympathetic artist who is neither reformer nor sentimentalist.

The original draft highlights the marriage of Sapphira and Henry, with Nancy as the barrier that comes between them; Cather's revision makes no mention of Henry but stresses the relationship between mistress and slave, the same relationship that her title also stresses. The proposed draft gives thumbnail descriptions of Sapphira and Henry and ranks them among "Miss Cather's finest character creations"; Cather's revision tersely evokes Sapphira and Nancy ("beautiful mulatto girl," "jealous mistress") but identifies Sapphira's African slaves as "the most interesting figures in the book." The draft concentrates on plot—a marriage disturbed by the threat of a third party, the resulting conflict and resolution; Cather's revision ignores plot but stresses how the opening chapter introduces "the keynote of the whole story," the gulf between surface appearances ("the warm atmosphere of good manners and domestic comfort") and emotional realities ("strong feelings and bitter wrongs").[2] The draft stresses differences of class and location—Sapphira's aristocratic heritage as against Henry's more humble background and calling, Sapphira's religious and social beliefs as against those of the uplands poor among whom she ends up living; the revision notes different groups represented in the novel—"the mountain people, grim disapproving 'Republicans,' Sapphira's African slaves"—but focuses not on the tensions among them but on their inherent human interest: "the narrative is peopled with unusual characters"; its "colored folk are presented in an unusual way. They are attractive to the writer as individuals . . . ." The draft sets the novel "in the middle of the nineteenth century"; Cather's revision dates it specifically to "1856, just before the outbreak of the Civil War," introducing by mention of the war the theme of internal conflict that is central to the novel on so many levels.[3] The draft's reference to Sapphira's "cavalier attitude toward slavery" subtly evokes the social and moral issues involved in this institution, while the revision limits its comments to the fact of Sapphira's slaves, and to their intrinsic human interest. The draft ends with plot resolution, Cather's revision with herself as "a sympathetic artist who is neither reformer nor sentimentalist."[4]

This final comment, which we know is Cather's own, provides a valuable entrée to the novel. We have seen that Cather's revised blurb focuses not on plot but on the inherent interest of her characters. "A sympathetic artist who is neither reformer nor sentimentalist" points in the same direction. Cather's purpose is neither to suggest how humans should be, to reform them, nor to sentimentalize human existence by making it correspond to what we'd like it to be. Cather will confront our mortal lives as they are, replete with our failings and contradictions, much as Sapphira herself will in the end confront the ultimate mortal condition, her death, face to face. This artist's role is to *suffer with* her characters—the root meaning of *sympathetic*—rather than to judge them.

Accordingly, the book at every level also poses questions and puzzles rather than offering answers and solutions. Henry Colbert searches his Bible for unambiguous answers about slavery but finds statements that pull against each other. When Michael Blake "drop[s] from the clouds . . . to deliver Rachel from her loneliness" (138), it seems a fairytale ending to her mother's doubts that Rachel will ever find a husband—and, to Rachel, a dream come true. The sentimental prince-saves-princess fairytale fractures, however, when both Michael and their beloved son Robert die of yellow fever, and when the widowed Rachel then loses one of her two surviving daughters to diphtheria. The novel is populated with figures who themselves are ambivalent: Till, so strong and so good, but so invested in maintaining her status in the household and in serving her mistress properly that her own daughter cannot seek her help when she is threatened by rape; Henry Colbert, a man of conscience and generosity, but one who lacks the courage to stand up to his wife and who, as in his Bible study, has such trouble knowing what is right that he ends up leaving action to others; Rachel, who saves Nancy by her clever intervention, but who as a nurse is so deficient in medical knowledge, and so willing to act out of ignorance, that she helps bring about her daughter's death; Martin Colbert, the rake who accedes to Sapphira's plan to ruin Nancy, but who ends up a Civil War hero.[5]

Critics have commented that Cather's deliberately nonjudgmental portrayal of 1856 southern society at times approaches equivocation, and that ways in which the text speaks of class distinctions in general, and of slaves and slavery in particular, betray the author's seemingly unquestioned prejudices and presuppositions.[6] Though such comments deserve to be taken seriously, they need also to be considered within the context of Cather's interests in writing the novel, and once again her revised jacket copy proves helpful. In changing the focus of the *Sapphira* blurb from plot to character and by commenting that "the keynote of the whole story" is the way in which "strong feelings and bitter wrongs are hidden under the warm atmosphere of good manners and domestic comfort," Cather underscores the novel's innerness, its pervasive and nonjudgmental probing of human complexity. She has chosen to accept the realities of pre–Civil War slave-owning society, depicted with all their ugliness, as backdrop for exploring the moral complexities of the human soul and human interaction, a purpose for which, as Merrill Skaggs has suggested, the twists and turns of the double-S road so prominent in the novel's setting are an apt metaphor.[7] Surely Henry Colbert speaks for this nonreforming, nonsentimental author when, following the tragic death of his beloved granddaughter, he says, "There are different ways of being good to folks" (268).

Sapphira herself is the novel's supreme example both of human complexity and of the variety of ways in which one can be good, or bad, to folks. Skaggs describes her as "capable of infamous villainy, but also of extraordinary generosity—an audacious mix."[8] Most readers will seize first on the negative side of this mix, on Sapphira's arrogance, willfulness, selfishness, vengefulness; her capacity both for subterfuge (e.g., her use of Martin to undermine Nancy, and to get back at her husband) and for open cruelty (she is beating Nancy when we meet her in an early scene). But along with these huge flaws she also has great and even appealing strengths, a number of which, as with the typical tragic hero or heroine, are flip sides of her weaknesses.[9] That she is headstrong and arrogant has as its complement her willingness to act, something that differentiates her from her husband, who is both more thoughtful, more ready to see the complexities of a possible course of action, and also less decisive. If she is smart in devising schemes to get at her enemies, she is also smart in running a house, and even a farm. She believes in keeping slaves in their place and does so by a mix of harshness, manipulation, and imperious distance, but she can also be kind and generous to them, as in the episode of Jezebel's death; and for the most part, her slaves admire her and serve her well.[10] When Rachel helps Nancy escape, Sapphira quickly figures out what has happened and severs ties with her daughter, but when she learns of her granddaughters' illness, she promptly secures proper medical attention, and after one of them dies, she invites Rachel and her surviving daughter back, and does so in such a way as to assure that Rachel will indeed return.[11]

Sapphira's strengths become yet more apparent when we set her beside Lucy Gayheart. Lucy is young and lovely and moves with grace and alacrity, while Sapphira is aging, physically deformed, and dependent on others either to push her wheelchair or to help her walk. But despite her youth and mobility, Lucy is characteristically in flight, while Sapphira seems always on the advance, whether literally or metaphorically; Lucy lacks self-reliance and conviction while Sapphira is invariably sure of herself; Lucy, despite her name (Lucy—*lux*, light—Gay-heart), frequently weeps, while Sapphira, whose name suggests darkness and may be cognate with saturnine, weeps not once in the novel, smiles frequently (albeit often maliciously), and—like Marian Forrester and Myra Henshawe—has a distinctive laugh (which, like Myra's, can be either malevolent or jovial).[12] Lucy ends up defined more by her death than by her life, while Sapphira, who faces death so bravely, remains in our minds as someone defiantly alive.

Sapphira's courage in facing challenge and misfortune—her life in the back-creek area, Nancy's flight, the deaths in Rachel's family, her wasting disease and impending death—recalls Cather's description of how the rebels dealt with what they found when they returned from defeat in the Civil War. They came back to find that their fields had been neglected, that their livestock—including their horses—were gone, that "[e]ven the cocks and hens had been snapped up by the foragers." They themselves were "tired, discouraged, but not humiliated or embittered by failure." They could accept defeat with such dignity because they had for years lived a life in which "[a]lmost every season brought defeat of some kind to the farming people. Their cornfields, planted by hand and cultivated with the hoe, were beaten down by hail, or the wheat was burned up by drouth, or cholera broke out among the pigs" (276). In short, they were people whose experience had taught them what it means to be human, and who were prepared to make the best of it, the same spirit that Sapphira brings to her life. One of the loveliest touches in the novel is that when Henry Colbert imagines what awaits Nancy after her flight, his description reads into Nancy qualities he has come to know in Sapphira, Nancy's tormentor: "She was to go out from the dark lethargy of the cared-for and irresponsible; to make her own way in this world where nobody is altogether free, and the best that can happen to you is to walk your own way and be responsible to God only" (228). And not inappropriately, when Nancy returns to Virginia twenty-five years later, she displays the same self-possession, the same ability to respond to life's vagaries, that had once distinguished Sapphira. She even has Sapphira's stylishness of dress and bearing.

If woven into the texture of this novel are surprising similarities between the novel's contrasting title characters, Sapphira is also similar to other, more distant Cather heroines. Like Alexandra, she is single-minded in pursuing what she wants, prefers making decisions to mulling over problems, has a fine head for business, is an excellent manager of her house and farm, is more impressive than her husband, and does not hesitate to go after her enemies. Like Ántonia, she is at her best when faced with the toughest challenges, has a soft spot for the spunky mischief-maker (compare her delight in Martin with Ántonia's fondness for the impish Leo), has an irrepressible love of life, is better than her husband at running a farm, and towers above everyone else in the novel. She is most similar to Thea—indeed, phrases from the 1938 jacket description of Thea fit Sapphira perfectly: "a powerful and willful . . . creature"; "sublimely egotistic." Like Thea, Sapphira readily defines others as her enemies, is fiercely determined to come out on top, and doesn't hesitate to do what she must to succeed. Both women display strengths and weaknesses that are larger than life, and that are often the reverse images of each other.

Larger than life, strengths and weaknesses that are complementary, an unflagging determination to prevail: such are quintessential traits of the great heroes and heroines. And though Sapphira's unappealing side has frequently deterred both readers and critics from applying the word to her, in stature, power, and range of influence she clearly belongs with Cather's other "heroic women." It is a designation that in this novel reaches beyond Sapphira, however. We have already noted similarities between Sapphira and Nancy, the other woman singled out in Cather's title, and given both the courage Nancy finally musters for her trip north and the strength and confidence she exudes upon her return, she has by the end earned the same designation.[13] "Heroic womanhood" suggests two others as well within the novel's cast: Till and Rachel. Till brings almost superhuman strength and loyalty to everything she does, so much so that she can seem—as perhaps she does to her own daughter—cold and unfeeling. But her courage extends from far in the past through the epilogue twenty-five years later; and when the confusion and noise of the nut-picking episode provide her the cover she has been seeking, she quickly reveals in her snatched conversation with Rachel her understanding of what has happened to Nancy, her gratitude that she has escaped, and her desperate eagerness for word of her. As for Rachel, she strikes many of those around her as unbending and disapproving, but her deep compassion—the Latinate equivalent of sympathy—comes through not just in the way she handles the terrified Nancy but also in her relationships with her father, with Mrs. Bywater, and with Mrs. Ringer. She too is remarkable in her courage, whether in fashioning a life after the death of her husband and son, in taking matters swiftly in hand each time Nancy appeals to her, or in confronting the illness that threatens her two remaining children. To a degree unusual even in Willa Cather, *Sapphira* is a novel that abounds in "heroic womanhood."[14]

That phrase, in turn, takes us back to the two women whose influence on Cather in her 1906–8 Boston years so contributed to her shift from the hero of *Alexander's Bridge* to the great heroines of the teens. Not surprisingly, the influence of both Sarah Orne Jewett and Mary Baker Eddy is strongly felt in *Sapphira and the Slave Girl*, Cather's final exploration of heroic womanhood. Perhaps even more than in the novels of the teens and *A Lost Lady*, Cather in *Sapphira* is following Jewett's advice to write about that which has long haunted the mind.[15] We know from correspondence with Blanche Knopf that as early as 1931 Cather was actively considering writing a story based on her Virginia childhood.[16] Moreover, five years before that, in her 1926 biographical sketch, she had given fuller place to her Virginia background than she had in her earlier such statements and had sounded some of the very motifs that reappear in *Sapphira*, among them the old traditions, the accompanying patterns of behavior, and the rigid distinctions that define southern life. And once embarked on *Sapphira*, Cather found that much she had thought forgotten came flooding back, as she wrote to Dorothy Canfield Fisher.[17] Jewett had promised that one day Cather would write about her own country, and here she returns to an "own country" that predates even her Nebraska years. That only now does she do so recalls, as we have seen, the familiar piece of Jewett's advice that Cather had included in *Not Under Forty*: having spent a lifetime coming to know the world, Cather is now at last fully ready to write about her childhood parish.

Mary Baker Eddy is also very much part of *Sapphira*, and especially of its title character. Willful, arrogant, thoughtless, egotistical, vengeful, manipulative—the words fit both women.[18] Both can turn swiftly from affection to hate, as Sapphira does with Nancy; both can be fiercely jealous and distrustful; both assume and demand full obedience from those around them and readily use people for their own at times demonic purposes; both are stronger than their husbands and order their husbands about.[19] Sapphira as we see her in the novel is ill and needs to be helped around by others; Eddy was frequently ill and often had to be carried by others. Not least, Sapphira's flaws are such as to make her almost repugnant, a response Cather certainly encourages at many points in her biography of Eddy. At the same time, though, Sapphira has also the strengths Cather wrote about in Eddy: an indomitable will to succeed, keen business acumen, and resilience in the face of adversity.

Once again, *Not Under Forty* has prepared the way, for the women we meet in its sketches prefigure much of what we find in Sapphira—"the stamp of distinction," strength of will and character, courage in the face of adversity, little tolerance for fools (think of Jewett and the mule driver!). That Cather chose "A Chance Meeting" as the lead story of *Not Under Forty* seems prophetic, for of the women in that collection, it is Madame Grout who most closely resembles Sapphira. As we have seen, she is also the one most similar to Eddy, and of the women sketched in *Not Under Forty*, the only one who elicits from Cather the mixture of admiration and resistance that also colors her portrait of Eddy. Cather's 1930 encounter with Madame Grout clearly left a strong impression, for not only does it inspire her 1933 essay, but Cather is still thinking about Madame Grout three years later when she both places "A Chance Meeting" at the beginning of *Not Under Forty* and also writes "The Old Beauty," a story clearly modeled on the same chance meeting. Indeed, it is tempting to surmise that one reason Madame Grout so fired Cather's imagination was that she reminded her of *both* Jewett and Eddy. Madame Grout was an aging woman, long past her prime as a writer, when Cather met her, and this serendipitous meeting with a literary figure she had long admired from a distance may well have recalled similar features of her first meetings with Jewett in Boston; that her distinguished literary genealogy had its roots in Flaubert, an author both Jewett and Cather deeply admired, can only have strengthened the connection.[20] At the same time, Madame Grout's domineering manner inspired a mix of repugnance and respect similar to that which Eddy had evoked in Cather, and the fact that Madame Grout had been highly successful at publishing and promoting her uncle's works recalled Eddy's brilliance in similar activities.[21] What is without question is that Cather's complex response to Madame Grout feeds directly into her portrait of Sapphira, just as her 1936 collection of sketches feeds into her 1940 novel.

There is yet another telling link between Sapphira and Eddy. Sue Rosowski points out that in a January 1938 letter to Sinclair Lewis Cather comments at length on this country's inclination to ignore the mounting evil in the world: "Americans tend to refuse to believe evil exists, she summarized. . . . This is the idea Cather put at the heart of *Sapphira and the Slave Girl*."[22] The American attitude that so troubled Cather in these prewar years recalls the issue that also engaged her attention with Eddy—the problem of evil, and the folly of glossing it over. In this final novel she returns once again to her exploration of this theme, and with a strikingly Eddy-like woman as her protagonist.

The other Cather heroine in whom Eddy-like flaws are carried to the extreme is Myra Henshawe, and not surprisingly she, like Eddy, at times comes across both to us and to those around her as repellent. And it is she whom, among Cather heroines, Sapphira resembles most closely.[23] Not only do they share most of the character traits we have noted—jealousy, arrogance, cruelty, and hatred among them—but both have married down; both at the ends of their lives find themselves ill and dependent on others; and both lash out at those around them, including their husbands. In an earlier chapter, we read *My Mortal Enemy* as Cather's most probing and despairing confrontation of those "mortal enemies" that Eddy had downplayed—the body's subjection to sexual passion, to aging, to disease, to death, to mortality itself. And we saw that Cather's next two novels attain their aura of resolution in part by skirting these issues, especially as they relate to women and to relationships between the sexes. In *Sapphira* Cather again confronts these issues head on, pitting her heroine, as she had Myra, against "this original injustice" of our mortality. Sapphira—aging, ill, crippled, soon to die, still tormented by sexual jealousy—stares it all in the face, and without the religious supports on which Myra comes to rely at the end of her life. If part of Cather's design in this novel is to make Sapphira repugnant to the reader, another part is clearly to make her admirable, even heroic, in the way she faces up to her mortality and all its cruel accompaniments.

That in this last novel we feel once again the presence of Mary Baker Eddy is further testimony to the profound and troubling impact Eddy had on Cather during those early years in Boston. Like any traumatic experience, especially one of as long duration as this one, the Eddy confrontation keeps coming back to Cather, keeps taking on new forms, inspiring new directions in her writing. In the teens Cather responds to Eddy's false optimism about evil by crafting novels in which again and again evil reveals itself as the dire reality it is; at the same time, however, in these same novels she also creates heroines—Alexandra, Thea, Ántonia—who achieve the same mythic stature that Eddy had attained in the minds of her followers. In the stories and novels of the late teens and the twenties, Cather continues to create heroines who embody Eddy's toughness and resilience and determination, but her focus shifts ever more toward what Eddy had dubbed "mortal mind," the fact of our mortality and the limitations it places on our immortal dreams. Cather's obsession with this theme reaches its peak in Myra Henshawe and her confrontation with "our mortal enemy." In the late thirties, the pervasive reality of evil in the world, and the fact that so many people seemed blithely unaware of it, again calls Eddy to her mind. In *Sapphira*, a novel with an Eddy-like heroine at its center, Cather attempts, as she put it, to evoke "an elusive sense of evil, which she called 'the Terrible,' lurking within everyday domestic life."[24] In *Death Comes for the Archbishop*, "Terrible" is the word Latour uses of the underground river he listens to but then avoids; in contrast, in *Sapphira* Cather dares to confront "the Terrible" head on.

I suggested earlier that the most traumatic aspect of the Eddy project was that it obliged Cather to confront the many ways in which she herself resembled Eddy. This aspect of the trauma too keeps recurring: Thea and Myra are the most Eddy-like heroines of the teens and the twenties, respectively, and both resemble Cather very closely; Madame Grout, who looms large in *Not Under Forty*, seems to fall into the same category. The pattern repeats in the late thirties as Cather creates Sapphira, who shares so many traits with Eddy—and with Cather herself. Cather too was ambitious, could be heartless, didn't hesitate to use people; she too had aristocratic leanings, placed great emphasis on dressing well and eating well; she too liked people with spirit and disliked whiners; she too could turn in anger on her friends, had a great capacity for hate, and had no hesitation in resorting to subterfuge when it availed her (as, for instance, in her many anonymous self-promotional pieces, and their freedom with the truth). Not least, Cather as she wrote this novel was, like Sapphira, facing old age, constant physical pain, and debilitating injuries to her hand (compare Sapphira's deformed extremities).

Cather resembles Sapphira also, however, in another and far more appealing respect—their common ability to understand others, to get inside another person's skin. For despite her hardness, Sapphira shows keen intuition into other people. One thinks first of the slaves, so different among themselves and from Sapphira, whose souls she yet understands so well—Tanzy Dave, Jezebel, Till (compare the jacket comment on the author's special interest in these same figures). But Sapphira also understands the members of her family, including those she torments. She sees into Henry and can respond to him with warm sympathy, as in the scene when he comes home from seeing his granddaughter die.[25] She may banish Rachel from her house, but when she learns of the sickness that has struck Rachel's children, she immediately feels deeply for her daughter—indeed reads herself enough into Rachel's mind to understand how to counteract what she knows will be Rachel's reluctance to move home. The irony of her jealousy toward Nancy is that she suspects her husband less of sexual dalliance with the slave girl than of developing the close and sympathetic relationship with a slave on which she prides herself (and, of course, she suspects this because she can read her husband so well).

"Sympathy"—suffering with someone else—depends on the capacity to feel as another person does, to get inside another person's skin, a capacity that Sapphira has, and that Cather claims in her 1915 statement first to have learned from her contact with the women she met on the prairie. It is a skill that any great novelist must possess, and Cather singles it out in the *Sapphira* jacket description of herself as "a sympathetic artist." And what Cather does in this novel is indeed to *sym-pathize*: to suffer with.[26] Not only does she herself serve as omniscient narrator, but she clearly suffers with all her characters, and especially with Sapphira and Nancy, for she frequently inserts little hints of her own involvement—words and phrases that remind us that she is always there, part of the action.[27] The ultimate source of Cather's sympathy is her knowledge of her own soul and the divides within it, her capacity for playing many roles and living such diverse lives. Once again we are taken back to that crucial period in Boston when Cather encountered such divergent alter egos in Jewett and Eddy, the one the image of her highest artistic aspirations, the other a less welcome reflection of her own mortal mix of good and bad, strength and weakness, a mix that will so shape some of her most fascinating characters. And if Sapphira's character owes much to Eddy, the sympathy that everywhere colors Cather's portrait of her and the other characters in the novel is very much in debt to Jewett. We have seen it as a quality Cather emphasizes in her 1936 expansion of her Jewett sketch, as well as a quality Jewett herself emphasized in her own characters. In turn, Willa Cather's capacity to suffer with others is one reason she can bring to life such a range of unforgettable characters, can so "produce what voice is needed" for each of them. Here again her debt to Jewett is apparent, for inherent in Jewett's capacity for sympathy was her ability, as Cather reminds us, to find the "voice that is exactly suited to the song."

Two of Cather's internal personae come on stage in the epilogue to *Sapphira*, where she both inserts her five-year-old self into the tale and also identifies herself as the narrator—indeed, at the end even appends a brief authorial note to which she signs her name. The novel's cast of heroic women accordingly includes herself, and it ends up a story of victory, albeit bittersweet.[28] It is alone and often smiling that Sapphira confronts her mortality—"Though the bell was beside her, she had not rung it," reports Till of her mistress's death (294). When Nancy, in her last appearance in the novel, asks Mrs. Blake about her would-be rapist,

Martin Colbert, it is also with a smile. And when Willa Cather ends this book, which features a heroine so much like herself, and one confronting mortal ills such as she herself was facing at the time, she too concludes with a smile: "For some reason I found the name of Mr. Pertleball especially delightful, though I never saw the man who bore it, and to this day I don't know how to spell it" (295).

Her implicit triumph goes beyond this characteristically ironic conclusion, for her signature at the end reminds us that the five-year-old who witnessed Nancy's return is now the woman who has written this novel. "My end is my beginning," Cather's comment on *Sapphira*, proves true in yet another way, for the book ends both with the youngster who will become the storyteller and with the story to which Cather herself always reverted, the return of Nancy Till. But the whole epilogue is filled with stories—the stories Nancy and Till and Rachel tell each other of the years they have been apart, the stories Nancy hears of what happened to the Colberts after she left, the stories Rachel Blake and her mother share over tea. It is also characteristic of Cather that if Nancy fled in 1856, as we here are told, her return twenty-five years later must be placed in 1881, whereas in fact we know that her actual return occurred in 1879: it is yet one more story, one told to make Willa Cather five years old in 1881, thus preserving the "story" she has told for so many years—that she was born in 1876, not 1873.[29]

The stories this five-year-old hears in the days shared with Nancy and Till and Rachel become part of her repertoire, though it is not until the end of her writing career that she goes back to them.[30] When she does, it is to make them the final chapter in her saga of heroic women, a tale that begins with the great heroines of the midteens, continues through the gutsy singers of the late teens, the "lost" but undaunted Marian and the mortal but defiant Myra of the twenties, and then rises from the brave trio of "Old Mrs. Harris" to the heroic women of her last novel. Unmistakably present among the "heroic women" of *Sapphira*—like the literary ghosts that appear for tea at 148 Charles Street—are Sarah Orne Jewett and Mary Baker Eddy, and this last novel fittingly ends with one more woman of the same ilk, Willa Cather, who, true to form, appears on stage in two roles—both as the child she once was and as the author she has now become.

The *Sapphira* jacket is a reminder of how fortunate we are to have in Cather's jacket blurbs a body of promotional copy that she herself either wrote or vetted and that provides insights not only into how she saw her books and herself and but also how she went about promoting both. As we have seen, valuable information often lurks not only in the individual jackets but also in the relationships between and among different jackets. One example of such relationships that we have not discussed earlier involves the jacket blurbs on *My Mortal Enemy* and *Obscure Destinies*—and, like so much else in Cather's writing, leads ultimately to *Sapphira*. The blurb for *My Mortal Enemy* describes this novel as "a work of tragic passion"; five years later the blurb on *Obscure Destinies* uses similar language to describe "Old Mrs. Harris" as rich in "tragic human meanings." The two jackets tell us that the novel deals with "the growing intensity of relations between the characters," the story with "the old riddle of human relationships." *My Mortal Enemy* is billed as "a . . . study of a woman's heart" that "sketches unforgettably the entire life of a woman," while "Old Mrs. Harris" charts "the struggle of three women who live under one roof each to live her own life and follow her own destiny." Tragedy, the tangle of human relationships, women: these are the topics that had been focal to the novels of the teens, that had been implicit, though with a less heroic ambience, in *Youth and the Bright Medusa* and *A Lost Lady*, that had surged to the surface in *My Mortal Enemy*, and that had been largely absent in *Death Comes for the Archbishop* and at best implicit in *Shadows on the Rock*. The relationships between what these blurbs say about *My Mortal Enemy* and "Old Mrs. Harris" not only hint at intriguing lines of connection between these two works (which are, in fact, of comparable length) but also suggest the way in which both works belong to Cather's ongoing exploration of "heroic womanhood," a quest that subsequently leads through *Lucy Gayheart* and the strong women of *Not Under Forty* to *Sapphira*.[31] And a further link, this time between the *Obscure Destinies* and *Sapphira* jackets, suggests that this last relationship is scarcely accidental: the *Obscure Destinies* jacket describes "Old Mrs. Harris" as a story in which "tragic human meanings underlie its apparently careless and light-hearted mood," language that closely foreshadows what Cather in the blurb for *Sapphira* will identify as "the keynote of the whole story"—the way "strong feelings and bitter wrongs are hidden under the warm atmosphere of good manners and domestic comfort." The thematic and even verbal ties among these three jackets thus provide valuable hints of the close relationships, even the natural sequence, among three of Cather's most probing and emotionally wrenching pieces of fiction—hints especially valuable since they seem to come from Cather herself.

Though decidedly "fictional" in their own ways, Cather's dust-jacket blurbs and her four longer autobiographical pieces differ in purpose and character from her other fiction and even from her essays: they are written to advertise and promote, and in shaping them, Willa Cather is deliberately and consciously assuming a different role from that of artist. That she kept this side of her writing anonymous suggests at least some discomfort about this bifurcation of roles—a discomfort reminiscent of that which led her throughout her life to distance herself from one of her largest writing projects, the Eddy biography. In this connection, it is of particular interest that in her blurb for *Sapphira*, her final exercise in the genre, she reduces the distance between these roles. In writing this blurb, she speaks less as promoter than as author, in fact volunteering information that only the author could give. She stresses the novel's central theme—the tension between surface appearances and underlying emotional realities; identifies the way she has used the first scene to set up this thematic contrast; speaks of the characters she has created and her efforts to differentiate them one from another, even reveals her special interest in one group—the "colored folk"; and finally expresses her vision of herself as "a sympathetic artist who is neither reformer nor sentimentalist." In turn, her role within the book itself mirrors this description, for her authorial comments throughout remind us that she is part of the action, and at the end she brings herself on stage both as the child who heard many of these stories when she was young and, in the concluding italicized paragraph, as the mature artist who has shaped them into this novel.

The word Cather uses of herself in this jacket blurb, sympathetic, proves apt for the way in which, by the end of the novel, characters move toward each other, and toward suffering with each other. Following the death of Rachel's younger daughter there is the moving scene in which Henry and Sapphira, at odds through so much of the novel, sit together and, in every sense of the word, sympathize. The result of their conversation is to renew Sapphira's feelings for her daughter, and we learn in the epilogue that Rachel did indeed move back and that mother and daughter found pleasure and comfort in each other. The epilogue also brings Till and Nancy together, and its scenes are largely given over to people talking with each other, sharing stories and memories and sorrows—again, sympathizing. Willa Cather herself, a woman so divided for so much of her life—within herself, from others—participates in this concluding movement toward reunion. Not only does the five-year-old Willa Cather whom we meet at the start of the epilogue come together with the sixty-seven-year-old artist who signs her name at the end, but the stories that we see the youngster listening to become the stories the mature author tells us. That in her blurb for this book Cather merges the two roles so often separated in her life—author and advertiser—is one more variation on this pattern of unifying persons long divided. Given all this, it is supremely appropriate that she speaks in that blurb of her capacity for sympathy, a capacity central both to her work as a novelist and to the personal reunions that take place in this last novel's final section, including those of her own diverse selves. For her capacity to see her own different and often warring sides, to understand her own penchant for playing diverse roles, and to recognize how characteristic such complexity is of human nature, is at the heart of her ability as a novelist to create characters so torn, so fascinating, and so profoundly human, with Sapphira herself among the supreme examples. And in the end, may not sympathy, our capacity to "suffer together," be the one response we humans can make to "the seeming original injustice," our fatal mix of good and evil, of immortal aspiration and mortal failing?

Notes

Introduction

The epigraph is taken from "Willa Cather: The Secret Web," Murphy 1974, 1.

1. See esp. Lindemann, e.g., 140: "[Q]ueerness did indeed have a hold on Cather, and the radical sense of alienation and otherness she experienced . . . would inflect her relationships to the discourses of normativity and nationality throughout her long, productive career. In the nation built in Cather's fiction, the 'queer' may . . . be a utopian agent of challenge and change—may be curative, salvific . . . ."

Part I: Cather on Cather

1. Skaggs 1990, 10.
2. Lewis 173 refers to a "Line-a-day" that Cather began keeping around 1933, but it apparently contained little more than brief comments; one assumes it was destroyed.
3. Leonard Woolf, *Growing: An Autobiography of the Years 1904–1911* (New York: Harcourt Brace, 1961), 9.

Chapter 1. Three Autobiographies and an (Auto)interview

This chapter draws on Porter 2002 and 2003.

1. Crane 5 notes that "a copy of *April Twilights* with a tipped-in 'Literary Note'" had sold at a 1930 auction, but that neither she nor Frederick B. Adams Jr. had ever seen the note.
2. Though she does not name her source, Edith Lewis clearly drew on this passage for her description of Cather's childhood in *Willa Cather Living* 13–14: "Willa Cather spent a great deal of her time on horseback, riding about through the thinly-settled countryside, visiting the Bohemians and Danes and Norwegians who were their nearest neighbours, tasting the wild plum wine the old women made, eating watermelons with the little herd girls, who wore men's hats, and coolly

killed rattlesnakes with clods of earth. Although she did not go to school, she read many of the English classics aloud to her two grandmothers in the evenings, and she learned to read Latin at this time. In a box of books brought from Virginia she found an old copy of Ben Jonson's plays, and a set of Shakespeare, and a Byron. *The Pilgrim's Progress* she read through eight times one of those winters."

3. On the spelling, see Bintrim 52–53.

4. For Lewis's borrowings from the 1926 sketch, see note 27 below.

5. Cf. Stouck 39: "The feeling which pervades the whole collection . . . is that of youthful insecurity and self-doubt—the hesitation of a university graduate going out into the world."

6. From a 1915 article in the *Lincoln Daily Star*: Bohlke 1986, 12.

7. A 1903 *Poet-Lore* article (see note 9 below) follows the "Literary Note" in dating Cather's birth to 1876: Bohlke 1986, 3. For the usual view, see Brown 17 n. 1; Lee 81; Woodress 1987, 516; O'Brien 293–94.

8. On Cather's actual date of birth, see Brown 17; Woodress 1987, 516; Stout 2000, 6. Though Lewis 13 rightly places the 1883 move to Nebraska in Cather's ninth year, she nowhere mentions Cather's birthdate. Lewis protected her friend's adjustment of her age to the end, for it must be she who chose the birthdate of 1876 for Cather's Jaffrey gravestone.

9. "Glimpses of Present-Day Poets: Willa Sibert Cather," reprinted in Bohlke 1986, 3–4.

10. The postcard, done in the same colors as the brochure's cover, has on its front side a smaller reproduction of the Bréton painting along with yet one more blurb for the book.

11. Cather received no middle name at birth. At some point prior to 1900 she added "Sibert," a version of her grandmother Boak's maiden name, and a name common among other earlier family members as well. See, e.g., O'Brien 106–7; Woodress 1987, 18–19.

12. On these motifs—getting inside another's skin, being eaten by a tiger—see Woodress 1987, 38–40. On their relevance to *The Song of the Lark*, see Harbison, esp. 145–46.

13. Cather's emphasis here on these minority groups, like her mention at the end of the *O Pioneers!* section of those "settlers who are becoming more and more a power in the political and economic life of the country," is typical of the way she consistently locates her fiction against the backdrop of national traits and trends. On the topic, see Urgo passim.

14. Greenslet letters of July 21 and 26, 1915, to Cather (Houghton Library, Harvard University).

15. The second paragraph of section 5 is directly from the jacket and is Cather's; the heart of the next paragraph is also hers, though it was not used for the jacket: see her letter of June 30, 1915, to Greenslet. On September 2, 1915, he sent Cather a mock-up of the brochure for her review; her letter of September 13 expresses her gratitude for his work on it (Houghton Library).

16. "Willa Cather Talks of Work," in Bohlke 1986, 7–11. Cather had already taken a first step toward self-quotation in the 1903 note: "and *The Pilgrim's Progress*, which latter she said she read through eight times in one winter"; cf. later, "where she says she found . . ."

17. But she keeps her actual age for the move West—nine; cf. "ten" in the 1903 "Literary Note."

18. See Woodress 1987, 42; Stout 2000, 13.

19. Stout 2000, 49–50, describes the "discouragement and uneasy delay" of this period and cites Cather's comparison of it to being "exiled to Siberia." Slote grants the frustrations but also notes the many activities in which Cather was engaged at the time: *KA* 22–29.

20. On Cather's teaching career, see Woodress 1987, 150ff.; Stout 2000, 54.

21. On the episode, see Woodress 1987, 261–62, and Cather's letter of July 24 [?], 1915 (= Stout 2002, #315), to Ferris Greenslet, where she stresses the financial motives for the trip.

22. Cf., for instance, Cather's accounts of her meetings with Stephen Crane and Edward Burne-Jones (see p. 67); Woodress 1990, 111–12, on Cather's account of her first meeting with Alfred A. Knopf; Stout 2000, 300: "[O]ne must have the facts in mind in order to appreciate the fiction. One also needs to have the fiction in mind in order to appreciate the nonfiction."

23. *WCOW* 92. On the rapidity with which Cather realized that *Alexander's Bridge* did not represent her best work, see Woodress 1987, 222, and Cather's preface to the 1922 edition.

24. The sketch apparently dates from the second half of 1926. On May 28 Cather wrote Blanche Knopf about a publicity booklet that would include Porterfield's "An English Opinion." She indicates she would like to review the proofs, including any biographical information, but does not mention writing anything for the booklet herself (Stout 2002, #834).

25. The version printed here is that of the 1926 pamphlet (cf. notes 29–31 below); for its minor variations from Cather's corrected typescript, see below, note 39.

26. Cather recalls riding the prairie as a child in all three of her statements. In later years she used the same metaphor to describe writing *O Pioneers!*: see *WCOW* 92–93.

27. Lewis 14 uses this passage, without attribution, in her account of Cather's childhood: "She gave herself with passion to the country and to the people, the struggling foreigners who inhabited it; became at heart their champion, made their struggle her own—their fight to master the soil, to hold the land in the face of drouths and blizzards, hailstorms and prairie fires. Many of the friendships she formed in these years lasted throughout her life."

28. Lewis 14 uses these sentences too: see above, note 2.

29. Cather changes "about" to "around" in the 1933 and 1941 versions of this sketch.

30. Cather changes this to "manuscripts" in the 1933 and 1941 versions.

31. This list is updated in the later versions—through *OD* in 1933, and through *SSG* in 1941.

32. Compare, e.g., the modifiers that dot the 1903 statement—"delightful volume of poems," "remarkably discriminating dramatic criticism," "clever dramatic and literary criticism"—or the 1915 statement's concluding reference to Cather's "position in the front rank of American writers," her place "in the little group of American novelists that count."

33. Cf. Sergeant 194–95 on Cather in the midtwenties: "The increase in her literary reputation helped . . . to give her a basic confidence in her own direction. Successful, handsome and blooming, even accessible at last, she allowed the world to have its charms for her."

34. The whole sketch abounds in artful contrasts—riding around the country by day, reading in the evenings; winters in Pittsburgh, summers in the West; Europe vs. home.

35. The self-citation in 1926 is invented for the occasion, whereas those in the 1915 statement are drawn from an actual earlier interview.

36. Although *Willa Cather in Europe* was not published until 1956, it consists of only slightly edited versions of Cather's 1902 essays for the *Nebraska State Journal*.

37. In Lewis 57 the fiction continues: "I remember her telling me of her first visit to Chartres, and of how the wheat-fields of the Beauce filled her with an almost unbearable homesickness for Nebraska; from the train window she saw a little girl riding on a cultivator with her father, and the sight filled her eyes with tears."

38. Cather used materials from this same essay to suggest the sense of familiarity Claude Wheeler feels in his first days in France. See *OO* 339ff.; *WCE* 115–16.

39. The published version of the sketch differs only slightly from Cather's revised typescript. It corrects "lightening" to "lightning" and changes "offerred" and "travelled" to the usual American spellings. At one point it changes a common

Cather punctuation, the comma plus a dash (,—), to a simple dash but leaves it intact at another. The typescript is written with a purple typewriter ribbon; most of Cather's handwritten corrections are in black ink, though three minor adjustments, all apparently at the last stage, are in pencil.

40. Cf. St. Peter's comment on Tom Outland's journal: "If words had cost money, Tom couldn't have used them more sparingly" (*PH* 262). Cather's comfort level with the 1926 sketch is implicit when she sends a copy of the pamphlet to a 1929 correspondent who has requested biographical information in connection with an article he is writing: Stout 2002, #988.

41. "Prefatory Note" to *Not Under Forty*.

42. Bohlke 1986, 89–91. Bohlke notes that the origin of the interview is uncertain but surmises that it probably appeared first in a New York newspaper.

43. The interview also appeared on September 16 in the *Webster County Argus*, with credit to the *NSJ*. My thanks for this information to Dr. Kari Ronning, who also provided copies of these articles, neither of which gives any hints as to how the interview found its way to the *NSJ*. Indications that the typing is Cather's include her distinctive purple typewriter ribbon and her frequent use of "z" (usually alternating with "x" or the hyphen) to type over letters and words she wishes to delete.

44. The text published here is that of Cather's typescript; it differs in only minor details from that published in Bohlke 1986, 90–91.

45. Cather's 1926 New Mexico trip in fact lasted closer to six weeks than three months. She stopped in Red Cloud on the return trip, then left for New York on July 21 (as reported in the July 22 *Webster County Argus*). Her immediate destination in New England (artfully camouflaged in the interview) was the MacDowell Colony in Peterboro, N.H.: see Woodress 1987, 393–96.

46. Cf. her delight in the variety of life on the Divide in the "Biographical Sketch," or the comment in the 1915 sketch that "[o]ne thing is certain—she will not repeat herself."

47. One assumes this note must have been added by a Knopf editor working with Cather on promotion of *My Mortal Enemy*, but no one has yet identified the handwriting.

48. On the publication history of *DCA*, see Crane 128–29. A composition date of summer 1926 for the interview squares also with its early September appearance in the *Nebraska State Journal*.

49. Cather's manner in this interview approximates the description given by Burton Rascoe in 1924: "Her conversation is staccato; she chops her spoken sentences out incisively, in short, neat links." "She is free from the usual inhibitions to comfortable and easy discourse; she uses good, colloquial and pungent words"

(Bohlke 1986, 66, 63). Cf. the comment of Allene Sumner in a 1925 interview: "Her sentences are crisp and almost terse" (Bohlke 1986, 87).

50. Bohlke 1986, 87.

51. Lewis 136. *The Professor's House*, written in the years preceding this interview, reflects Cather's frustration with the intrusions on her life in this period: see Brown 237–39. Cf. St. Peter's response when Louie Marsellus speaks of attending his lecture in Chicago: "Come if you wish. Lectures seem to me a rather grim treat, Louie" (*PH* 77).

52. See Woodress 1987, 319–22; Stout 2002, #552, #555, #560, #562 #574, #580, #608, #612, etc.

53. Stout 2002, #673, #709, #721, #727, including an invitation to return to Bread Loaf in 1924.

54. Woodress 1987, 361, 378–79; Stout 2002, #779, #782, #799–802, #805.

55. On the self-referential quality of her interview comments, see Bohlke 1986, 140.

56. Stout 2002, #861, #864.

57. The only real exception is a speech she gave at Princeton University in 1933, with simultaneous broadcast over NBC: see Woodress 1987, 450–51; Bohlke 1986, 168–70.

58. Cf. what Cather wrote in 1896 on orator Robert G. Ingersoll: "His magnificent talents as an orator have really been greatly against him, for they have made him popular and that is the greatest calamity that can befall a man of bold and original thought" (*KA* 211).

Chapter 2. Dust-Jacket Copy

This chapter draws on and expands Porter 2005.

1. See, respectively, Stout 2002, #383, #394, #398, #401–2, #407–8, #411–13, #420–21, #423–24.

2. For Cather's correspondence regarding *The Song of the Lark*, see Stout 2002, #312, #324, #328 (cf. #330, #348), #329, #344–45; also Woodress 1987, 274–75. On the move to Houghton Mifflin, see Cather's letter of January 12, 1921, to Greenslet, indicating that this move to Knopf is based solely on issues involving promotion of her books (Houghton Library, Harvard). Cather had used Knopf in 1920 for the publication of *Youth and the Bright Medusa*, but this 1921 letter, in which she indicates that Knopf will also publish "Claude," sealed the decision. On the change, see Woodress 1987, 307–11, 316–18, and 1990, 111–12; *LL* (CSE) 177–85; Lewis 108–16.

3. Stout 2002, #311 (*SOL*), #454 (*MA*).

4. Brown 213–14; Woodress 1990, 112: "Knopf . . . allowed her to pick her own typeface and to write advertising and jacket copy if she wished."

5. Note its different typewriter font and its use of spaces before and after the double hyphens.

6. Typeface matches that in the two typescripts discussed in chapter 1, as does the use of "z" to cross out words (see chapter 1, n. 43).

7. The only changes are one correction of punctuation and one transposition of words.

8. Knopf 211. Cather herself mentions Lewis's assistance in such work: Stout 2002, #455, #475.

9. Location of blurbs is indicated only when jackets have more than one original blurb. For information on other copy on jackets (e.g., excerpts from reviews), see Crane.

10. *LL* (CSE) 327.

11. Bréton's picture is eliminated in later editions: see Stout 2002, #1087; Harbison's edition, 421 n. 6, 433; and Woodress 1987, 259.

12. See Cather letters of May 24, 1915, to Miss Van Tuyll and undated (but near the same time) to Greenslet, and his responses of May 25 and June 7, in the latter of which he thanks her for the "jacket text" and indicates that he "like[s] it very much" (Houghton Library).

13. Contrast Greenslet's prosaic description of Alexandra in his house memo: "The chief character, a girl who grows into a woman, takes hold of an enlarging farm, becomes herself one of the successful 'pioneers' of the region,—a most attractive person" (Houghton Library).

14. See Cather to Houghton Mifflin and Greenslet, October 30 and November 1, 1915 (Houghton Library), on the heavy-handedness of their advertising suggestions; on Greenslet's keen admiration for *My Ántonia*, see, among others, his letters to Cather of February 18 and September 23, 1918.

15. Bohlke 1986, 77.

16. Preface to the 1932 edition, used again for the 1938 reissue of the novel.

17. The jacket also contains a plug from Booth Tarkington. Here too one suspects Cather's hand, for though his words purport to be about "McClure's story," in fact they focus on the writing, and do so in language Cather would have approved: "Nothing I have ever read was more touching than the early passages; nor more perfectly and beautifully written. What is told is very wonderful, and the *way* it is told just plain noble. It can stand, right now as a *model* of 'literary workmanship'— only it doesn't seem to be 'workmanship,' it just seems to be truth. It's as simple as a country church—or a Greek statue."

18. The original *April Twilights* (1903), Cather's first book, was issued without a dust jacket. The signed and limited 1923 first edition also had no dust jacket; the jacket copy reprinted here is that of the second 1923 edition. Cather mentions the book in her 1926 sketch but gets the title wrong: *April Twilights and Later Verse*.

19. In his historical essay for the Cather Scholarly Edition of *One of Ours*, 623–24, 657, Richard Harris clearly shows that Cather herself provided copy for the blurb of this novel. Sinclair Lewis alluded to its phrase "Hamlet of the Prairies" in the ironic title he gave his negative review of the novel in the *Literary Review*: "Hamlet of the Plains"; see Trout 106.

20. On Cather's distaste for the original *AT*, see Stout 2002, #152, #232; Woodress 1987, 165.

21. The 1923 edition contains new poems about which Cather felt real satisfaction (cf. Stout 2002, #415), and she brought energy and enthusiasm to the tasks associated with its reissue: she is eager to finish the proofs (Stout 2002, #650, #665), is pleased with the book's handsome appearance (#668), and makes a special effort to be on hand when it comes out (#682).

22. See Crane 98.

23. The original blurb for *The Professor's House* was short-lived: in a first-edition copy I own, this blurb has already been replaced by a comment on the novel by Grant Overton. This same jacket also substitutes a rich purple for the blue in the cover illustration, a change interesting in view of the novel's explicit mention of the Blue Mesa's purple cast (*PH* 186).

24. On Cather's frustration with Houghton Mifflin concerning reviews, see her letter of May 19, 1919, to Greenslet (Houghton Library). On the whole transition from Houghton Mifflin to Knopf, and the complex reasons behind it, see Lindemann 87–88.

25. The theme of youth sounds also on the 1903 *April Twilights* mail-in order form, which compares the collection's tone to "a beautiful April evening, when the old world is young again" (fig. 2).

26. Lee 318.

27. See Woodress 1987, 301; Stout 2002, #650, #1529, #1633, #1671.

28. See, e.g., Skaggs 1990, 2–3; Porter 2002, 59.

29. On Cather's disinclination to be a reformer, see Lee 65. Cf. also her comments on Tolstoy the novelist as against Tolstoy the reformer (*KA* 378).

30. Regarding the Wharton model, cf. Stout #369 and #577, for example. Ferris Greenslet, who in his house memo on *Alexander's Bridge* stressed the Wharton connection, subsequently rejected it: see Greenslet 118. Regarding Cather's rejection of the traditional mode of novel writing, cf. her comments in Bohlke 1986, 77; also Woodress 1987, 290; Skaggs 1990, 3.

31. Stout 2000, 71, calculates that before the January 1903 publication of "A Death in the Desert," the earliest of the *Troll Garden* stories, Cather had already *published* twenty-seven stories.

32. *WCOW* 91–92; Cather's 1922 preface to the novel does not mention the London tie.

33. Woodress 1987 discusses both the Italy trip and "The Enchanted Bluff" (198–99, 205), but neither he nor others I have read trace the origin of this story to that time in Italy.

34. Lewis 70 and Brown 149 date the writing of the story to 1909; both Brown (ibid.) and O'Brien 370 see it as following Jewett's advice to write about the country of her childhood.

35. On the transition from Alexander to Alexandra, see Stout 2000, 112–13.

36. During this same period, jacket covers with illustrations (*LL, PH, DCA*) and bold designs (*MME*) replace covers dominated by promotional copy (*YBM, OO*). This increased emphasis on graphic elements does not, however, fully explain the gradual diminution of copy over this period: *OD* and *SSG* have brilliant designs that fill their covers—but their inner flaps also contain substantial blurbs about the books.

Part II: Entering the Kingdom of Art

1. On attacks in the 1930s on Cather's reputation, see Acocella 24–25, who points out also that many criticized Cather even in the 1920s (18–24); also Woodress 1987, 333–34, 433, 469.

2. Adding to the complexity is the fact that Cather had frequently attacked self-advertisement in general: see esp. Stout 2000, 51.

3. Cf. Stout 2000, 75, on Cather's early days as a newspaper writer: "Conflicting impulses are evident, too, in the contrast between Cather the aesthete and Cather the practical mover and shaker, the young woman wanting to get ahead in what was still a man's world."

Chapter 3. The Quest to Excel

1. On Cather's emphasis on the link between acting and power, see Stout 2000, 59–68.

2. Lewis 21–22 suggests that Cather had a model of the type in the Mr. Ducker with whom she studied Latin and Greek in Red Cloud for so many years.

3. The following year, 1896, Cather criticizes the high fees paid operatic prima donnas, noting that "America has become the gold field for foreign artists" and

seeing in this pattern an index of American values—and a threat to the artists: see *W&P* 315; also *KA* 195.

4. See also *W&P* 91ff., but note Stout 2000, 77, on the context of Cather's remarks about Wilde.

5. O'Brien 447. Stout 2000, 62–63, notes that though Cather admired artists who were less self-assertive, she favored those of "strong individuality" or "eccentricity," and she herself came more to resemble this latter type.

6. *KA* 33; Sergeant 163.

7. O'Brien 121; with these epithets, cf. the character of Vickie in "Old Mrs. Harris."

8. Edel 1959b, 5.

9. See Woodress 1987, 70–103.

10. Woodress 1987, 114ff. Lewis xv notes that as a child Cather "had known how hard and humiliating poverty can be" and that "[h]er first years in Pittsburgh were years of constant worry about money."

11. Woodress 1987, 150–55, including information on her rapid rise in compensation (155).

12. For Cather on *The Home Monthly*, see Woodress 1987, 115. For the Crane reference, see *W&P* 776.

13. O'Brien 227. One hears Cather's own sentiments in the comment made by the singer heroine of a story she wrote for the *Home Monthly* in 1896: "You must give the people what they want" ("The Count of the Crow's Nest," *CSF* 464).

14. O'Brien 227.

15. See Lee 46–49.

16. See O'Brien 178–80.

17. *KA* 20; Slote's reference is to the article Crane was writing for the Bacheller-Johnson news syndicate on a major drought in Nebraska.

18. For the details, see *W&P* 912.

19. *KA* 409 (1895). The other two passages quoted in this sentence are from 1896 (*KA* 417) and 1895 (*W&P* 262), respectively.

20. See O'Brien 229–30.

21. In contrast, the heroine of "A Singer's Romance," written three years later, has taken a different path, becoming "industrious," "thoroughly competent," invaluable to her managers, and a source of support to her gambler husband, but someone who has abandoned art's highest quest. The type will become familiar in several Cather stories from 1916 to 1919.

22. O'Brien 282–85; Lee 21, 49–50; Murphy 2000, 21.

23. Cf. Lee 77: "But she makes a case for [Paul], too, so that we are absorbed

into his dream-world, and follow with pleasure his release into the world of music and theatre, his escape to New York. . . ."

24. Cather's use of pseudonyms, especially in this early period, undoubtedly reflects also the sense of alienation and otherness that attended her lesbianism. For a brilliant analysis of the ways in which Cather's early letters to Louise Pound reveal these tensions in her language, including the words she uses to identify herself, see Lindemann 17–31.

Chapter 4. Cather Caught in the Eddy

This chapter draws on Porter 2000 and 2007.

1. *AB* 1922, vii. For Jewett's impact on Cather, see, among many, O'Brien, esp. 334–78.

2. *SOJ Letters* 246.

3. See Stout 2000, 98. On the episode, see also Woodress 1987, 192–98; O'Brien 291–92.

4. See Bohlke 1982, 291–93; Woodress 1987, 194; Stouck's edition of *MBE* xvii; Stout 2000, 330 n. 6.

5. See, e.g., Rosowski 1986, 33; O'Brien 291–94.

6. For divergences between the *McClure's* essays and the book, see Crane 218–22.

7. Crane 220.

8. Cather adds that "lucid, clean-cut expression was almost impossible to Mrs. Glover." For still other comments on Eddy's writing, see *MBE* 330, 447.

9. See also *MBE* 179–207, 227ff. The final *McClure's* segment is especially scathing on this theme: "Sin, sickness, and death, she says, are beliefs which originated in mortal mind. And how and when did mortal mind originate? Mortal mind does not exist, she answers, therefore it had no origin. This reasoning satisfies her; she believes it perfectly adequate" (*McC* 184). On Cather's attention to this aspect of Eddy's work, and the way it is reflected in her writing, see Hudson's comments, xix ff. On the Christian underpinnings of much of Cather's criticism of Eddy, see Murphy in *DCA* (CSE) 330–31.

10. Cf. *MBE* 480: "The result of Mrs. Eddy's planning and training and pruning is that she has built up the largest and most powerful organisation ever founded by any woman in America. Probably no other woman so handicapped—so limited in intellect, so uncertain in conduct, so tortured by hatred and hampered by petty animosities—has ever risen from a state of helplessness and dependence to a position of such power and authority."

11. Stouck xvii–xviii. In her 1922 letter to Edwin Anderson, Cather speaks of the project as a sort of discipline, an exercise; the portraits she gives of people like James Henry Wiggin, Eddy's editor (327ff.), and Calvin Frye, her business manager and all-around amanuensis (293ff.), show her burgeoning ability in evoking character.

12. Though Cather told Edwin Anderson that she did not write the book's first chapter, she did edit the whole book for publication and knew that first chapter well.

13. Bennett 1.

14. For representative examples of how Eddy mythologized her life, see *MBE* 18–20, 346–48, 415, 417–19.

15. For Cather's description of Eddy's room, see *MBE* 154. For her study at the McClung home, see Woodress 1987, 140. Cather used it as a model for the study where St. Peter writes *his* books in *The Professor's House*: ibid. 369.

16. For other passages on Eddy's charismatic impact, see 65, 123, 158, 314, 444.

17. Indeed, Cather adds a pointed footnote to the very pages where she cites Eddy's comments about "church rites" and Christianity: "Since 1875 Mrs. Eddy's ideas of church buildings and church organisations have been considerably broadened. Her organised churches are now more than six hundred in number, and her congregations worship in costly temples, and have a very complete ecclesiastical system; and the founder of the church and the head of the entire church system is Mrs. Eddy herself" (*MBE* 198 n. 8).

18. James Henry Wiggin, Eddy's editor, describes her as "[a]n awfully (I use the word advisedly) smart woman, acute, shrewd" (*MBE* 337) and adds a page later, "No, Swedenborg, and all other such writers, are sealed books to her. She cannot understand such utterances, and never could, but dollars and cents she understands thoroughly" (338).

19. *MBE* 140, 146, 416–17, 419–20, 451, 399–400, 405, 410.

20. Eddy emphasized that "health and self-satisfaction and material prosperity [were] high among the moral virtues—indeed, they were the evidences of right living…" (*MBE* 375). Eddy advertised *Science and Health* as a book that "affords opportunity to acquire a profession by which you can accumulate a fortune" (209).

21. *MBE* 168, 417, 315.

22. Cather recorded her royalties in minute detail in a small ledger, recently added to the Cather collection at the University of Nebraska.

23. *MBE* 164, 191, 212. For other passages where Eddy uses "Truth" with reference to Christian Science, see *MBE* 200, 203, 248, 268, 345, 350–51, the last noting that Eddy saw the proper interpretation of this "Truth" as falling to her alone.

Like so much else in Christian Science, Eddy took over this usage of "Truth" from Quimby.

24. *MBE* 71–104, 161ff.

25. For two such instances, see *MBE* 222ff. (Richard Kennedy), 247ff. (Daniel Spofford).

26. Eddy's hypochondria is, of course, one more link to Cather, who even early in her life was constantly subject to illness: see, e.g., O'Brien 90, 290; Stout 2000, 124, 280, 301.

27. Crane 217. Cf. *MBE* 410: "[F]rom the time the Boston church was reorganised, Mrs. Eddy's power over it was absolute. She was the church. She wrote its bylaws, appointed its officers, selected its membership, and virtually owned the church property."

28. This verse was taken from Longfellow's "Santa Filomena," a tribute to Florence Nightingale (cf. Stouck *ad loc.*).

29. Stout 2000, 59, comments that in the Eddy project Cather "examined the sources and meaning of a woman's power"; noting Cather's willingness to take on S. S. McClure's autobiography, she comments also that in the Eddy biography "she had presented another character of 'masterful will and great force of personality' as an unlikely leader 'groping for a vocation'" (127; the inner quotations are from *MBE* 57, 62).

30. See Lee 29.

31. *CSF* 29. On the passage and its heroic connotations, see Stouck 22; Romines 1992, 136.

Chapter 5. Two Alter Egos

1. O'Brien 335, drawing on a 1921 article in the *Omaha World-Herald* (Bohlke 1986, 33–39). On Jewett's influence, see the excellent comments of Stout 2000, 98–101.

2. *NUF* 76.

3. Introduction to the 1922 edition of *Alexander's Bridge*, vii.

4. O'Brien 335. The distancing began while Cather was still in Boston. A 1908 letter to Annie Fields "reveals Cather's attitudes toward Mary Baker Eddy in a specific, and caustic, way; throughout, she is both wry and ironic as well as more than a bit condescending in her characterization of Eddy and the followers of Christian Science" (Thacker 290).

5. Skaggs 1990, 182.

6. For a detailed account of this episode and its background, see Madigan 119–23, 127.

7. On the reaction this story evoked among family and friends in Nebraska, see Romines 1992, 133; on these and other instances of Cather's habit of using people, see Stout, 2000, 36–38.

8. Skaggs 1990, 183.

9. O'Brien 293, paraphrasing Cather's December 19, 1908, letter to Jewett.

10. O'Brien 344.

11. O'Brien 294–95. McClure actively discouraged Cather's efforts as a writer of fiction: see Woodress 1987, 203–4.

12. See esp. *MBE* 305–6; also 274–75. The story of Richard Kennedy, which begins on *MBE* 134 and weaves through the next 100 pages, exemplifies the pattern. Cather sent the finished version of "The Willing Muse" to *Century* on June 5, 1907 (Stout 2002, #128).

13. *CSF* 108. For Eddy's impact on the story, see Hudson's edition of *MBE* xxix–xxx.

14. Hudson's edition of *MBE* xx–xxiv.

15. For the date, see Cather's letter of December 18, 1904, to Canfield (Stout 2002, #100).

16. *SOJ Letters* 246–47. On Jewett and the story, see O'Brien 367–70.

17. For a sensitive reading of the story, see Rosowski 1986, 31. Lewis 70, who dates its composition to 1909, captures the breakthrough that this story represented for Cather.

18. The motif had, however, appeared in the "Dedicatory" to her 1903 *April Twilights*, as Stouck 18 notes: "Let it [the moon] work again its old enchantment. / Let it, for an April night, transform us / From our grosser selves to happy shadows / Of the three who lay and planned at moonrise, / On an island in a western river, / of the conquest of the world together. / Let us pour our amber wine and drink it / To the memory of our vanished kingdom . . ."

19. O'Brien 370–71.

20. Just when Jewett told Cather that "one day she would write about [her] own country" is not clear—this advice is not explicitly contained in her letter of December 1908 to Cather. But Cather's acquaintance with Jewett had begun just prior to the 1908 European trip, and Jewett's close mentoring of Cather belongs more to the period after Cather's return.

21. Cf. the suggestion of O'Brien 328–32 that "The Namesake," a story published in March 1907, already suggests how ready Cather was for what she would find in Jewett.

22. See *SOJ Letters* 246–47.

23. *SOJ Letters* 247–48.

24. Cf. Stouck 215: Nelly's death (cf. her baptism) is "a kind of death by water."

25. On "Behind the Singer Tower," see O'Brien 383ff.

26. Sergeant 62 recounts a spring 1911 meeting in which she and Cather discussed the "temptations" of continuing to work for McClure's: "Well, the lure of big money rewards in the crude sense—for cheap work—magazine success—writing to pattern . . . ."

27. *WCOW* 41, in "The Novel Démeublé."

28. See Cather's letter of December 19, 1908 (= Stout 2002, #145) and O'Brien's paraphrase on p. 86. For Alexander's perception of his life, see esp. *AB* 16, 46–51.

29. The phrase "like his youth calling to him" is from the 1915 brochure—cf. related language at *AB* 52, 70, 99, 107, 109; in contrast, his marriage "was everything but energy; the energy of youth" (144).

30. One thinks of the description of Cather as editor in the opening chapter of Sergeant. On similarities between Bartley Alexander and Cather, see Rosowski 1986, 39; Stout 2000, 103–4.

31. Woodress 1987, 204.

32. See Stout 2000, 103–4.

33. Lee 84 calls the novel "Cather's first extensive treatment of her deep and lifelong obsession with doubling." Rosowski 1986, 35, comments on how the two women of the novel mirror the two lives Alexander is leading. Urgo 2000 brilliantly reads the novel as commentary on leaders of the time who both destroyed themselves and betrayed their societies by the double lives they led.

34. "Moor" may well also carry overtones of death, as in the French "mort."

35. Cf. Lewis 79.

36. *SOJ Letters* 246.

37. Romines 1992, 139.

38. For Alexander's vision of what awaits him if he abandons Winifred, see *AB* 142–43.

39. Rosowski 1986, 36, reads the novel to be about the bridging of the worlds of reality and the imagination—"the voyage perilous"—another bridging Alexander fails to accomplish.

40. Cf. Lewis 78: "But when [the novel] at last moves into its true theme, the mortal division in a man's nature, it gathers an intensity and power which come from some deeper level of feeling . . . . It is as if [Cather's] true voice . . . had broken through . . . ."

41. Cf. Lee 86, who sees the illicit love of Alexander as leading to death, that of Clara in "The Bohemian Girl" as leading to life.

Part III. At Home on the Divide

1. Cather's sounding of Wagner's "bridge motif" at the climactic moment of *The Song of the Lark* both recalls the theme of bridging in Cather's first novel and also reminds us of the tensions by which Thea is torn in this one: "The cold, stately measures of the Walhalla music rang out, far away; the rainbow bridge throbbed out into the air, under it the wailing of the Rhine daughters and the singing of the Rhine. But Thea was sunk in twilight . . ." (*SOL* 199). On the passage, see Giannone 92.

Chapter 6. *O Pioneers!* and *My Autobiography*

Portions of this chapter again draw on Porter 2000 and 2007.

1. Cf. Eddy's "resourcefulness and energy in the prosecution of her plans" (*MBE* 460).

2. Cf. *OP* 175: "those clear, deliberate eyes, that saw so far in some directions and were so blind in others."

3. Cf. O'Brien 436.

4. Cf. *MBE* 245: "From 1877 to 1879 Mrs. Eddy was in the law-courts so frequently that the Boston newspapers began to feature her litigations and to refer to them and to her with disrespectful jocularity."

5. There are even striking similarities between the house Alexandra builds and Eddy's home outside Concord, N.H.: see Porter 2000, 40.

6. On the sharply contrasting qualities in Alexandra's character, see Lee 104–6, 109–10.

7. Cf. the colorful costume Marie wears as a fortune teller (*OP* 216): "a red skirt . . . , a white bodice and kirtle, a yellow silk turban wound low over her brown curls, and long coral pendants in her ears"; also Carl's vivid recollection of her eyes (*OP* 135–36, 305).

8. The language recalls Cather's repeated comment on Lyra Garber: "Wasn't she a flash of brightness in a grey background, that lady?" (Bennett 75).

9. *SOJ Letters* 249.

10. Eddy showed "a curious aversion" to her natural son from the beginning and abandoned him early in his life (*MBE* 26ff.), and she avoided any sort of rapprochement later in her life (*MBE* 453ff.). As for her adopted son, Foster Eddy, the tale of how Mrs. Eddy dispatches flowers and a group of Christian Scientists to cheer him on his way as he sails for Philadelphia is one of the great set pieces of Cather's biography: "[A]s the adopted son stood by the deck-rail with his bouquet in his hands, and watched the water widen between him and Boston, he realised

the import of this cordiality, and knew that, through the crowd on the shore, his mother had waved him a blithe and long adieu" (*MBE* 422).

11. See *MBE* 291ff., including Cather's editorial comment: "Explained as the work of animal magnetism, Mr. Eddy's death, which might otherwise have been a blow to his wife professionally, was made to confirm one of her favourite doctrines."

12. On the open-ended character of the conclusion, see Blanche H. Gelfant's introduction to the Penguin Books edition of *O Pioneers!*, xxvii.

13. Stars figure prominently both in *O Pioneers!* (including in its prefatory poem) and in the Eddy biography. Eddy associated herself with the apocalypse of "a woman clothed with the sun, and the moon under her feet, and upon her head a crown of twelve stars," a vision reproduced in a window of the Mother Church. In addition, Eddy's personal room in this church, the "Mother Room," was so created that when she occupied it "through the open skylight shines the star of Bethlehem, enveloping her in its rays" (*MBE* 344, 408).

14. *SOJ Letters* 247.

15. Cf. Eddy's query, which Cather cites in her final *McClure's* article: "Is marriage nearer right than celibacy?" (*MCC* 187).

16. One wonders if Cather is echoing the description of Helen in Yeats's "No Second Troy," which had appeared in 1910: "Why, what could she have done, being what she is? Was there another Troy for her to burn?" On Cather and Yeats, see Woodress 1987, 217.

17. Cf. Stouck 31: "The two stories woven together in *O Pioneers!* stretch back to Genesis. Alexandra's is the story of creation. . . . Emil and Marie's is the story of lovers cast from the earth's garden through sin." Cf. also Rosowski 1986, 54. Reinforcing the echoes of the Garden are the connections to Gounod's *Faust* that are set up when Emil whistles the "Jewel Song" as he cuts the grass: see Giannone 78–79.

18. On the origins of *O Pioneers!* in two separate novellas, see Woodress 1987, 231ff.

19. When Amédée goes off to work despite severe stomach pains, Angélique's assumption that all will be well recalls Emil's fallacious optimism as he heads to his final meeting with Marie: "Only good things could happen to a rich, energetic, handsome young man like Amédée, with a new baby in the cradle and a new header in the field" (*OP* 242).

20. On the many similarities between Cather and Alexandra, see Stout 2000, 111–12.

21. See p. 75.

22. On other links between these two novels, see Lindemann 49–50.

23. For the background of *My Autobiography* and the way it was written, see Woodress 1987, 249–50. On Cather's willing acknowledgment of her role in writing it, see Thacker's introduction, v.

24. On the similarities between them, and Cather's identification with aspects of McClure's story, see Stout 2000, 126–27.

25. A comment in Ferris Greenslet's house memo on *Alexander's Bridge* reminds us of yet one more tie between McClure and Cather—his efforts on her behalf as publisher of her work in *McClure's*: "[The novel] is to be serialized in McClure's [*sic*] in three long installments ending with their April number. Mr. McClure, I am told, is writing the advertising in person. This will unquestionably give it an excellent start..." (Houghton Library, Harvard).

26. Cf. Acocella 2. In her 1932 introduction to *The Song of the Lark*, Cather mentions that she had at one point thought of calling the novel "Artist's Youth."

Chapter 7. *The Song of the Lark*

1. Stout 2000, 120–21, 127, suggests several other models for Thea, including the heroine (an actress) of Mary Austin's *A Woman of Genius*.

2. Woodress 1987, 255, paraphrasing a letter of late April 1913.

3. Cather uses the word "awakening" twice in her introduction to the 1932 edition of *The Song of the Lark*. On Thea's similarity to Cather, cf. Rosowski 1986, 62: "Thea Kronborg is Willa Cather in essentials, though Olive Fremstad was her external prototype"; Stout 2000, 120: "In *The Song of the Lark* Thea Kronborg may be a composite of singer Olive Fremstad and Mary Austin's actress figure in *A Woman of Genius*, but she is also, unmistakably, Willa Cather ...." Stout 2000, 129, 132–35, explores a number of the similarities; see also Lewis 39, 92–93; Giannone 85; Lee 122–24.

4. Woodress 1987, 266.

5. Cf. Rosowski 1986, 62.

6. Woodress 1987, 266ff.

7. Stout 2000, 142, makes this same connection. On the episode itself, see Romines 1992, 146.

8. On the female landscape of Panther Canyon, see Moers 258. Rosowski 1986, 70–72, points out that the feminine connotations extend far beyond the description of Panther Canyon.

9. *SOJ Letters* 249.

10. Cf. *SOL* 101, where Thea is twice compared to a wildcat!

11. Cf. Cather on Bernhardt: "[H]eaven preserve me from any very intimate relations with her" (*W&P* 49).

12. As Stouck 191 points out, Thea's willingness to fight her way to the top is implicit in her choice to decorate her first Chicago room with a photograph of the Naples bust of Caesar (*SOL* 170) and in the special delight she takes in the Art Institute's "great equestrian statue of an evil, cruel-looking general with an unpronounceable name" (*SOL* 196).

13. On Thea's capacity to hate, see Skaggs 1995, 26.

14. Rosowski 1986, 69, speaks of Thea's "talent, ambition, hard-headedness, egocentricity, and a certain ruthlessness"; cf. Urgo 138: "Thea is, if we place ourselves at a distance, away from the narrator's obvious affection for her, a ruthless woman."

15. Cf. Lee on the way Cather associates Thea with "domineering male heroes" (126) and with heroic elements in Wagnerian opera (129–32).

16. As Thea's musings continue, she thinks about the "second self" that people have: "How deep they lay, these second persons, and how little one knew about them, except to guard them fiercely" (217). Lee 23–24 comments on the degree to which the image "of a talented girl, ruthlessly committed to her own ambitions, shutting out the family from her own room," is drawn from Cather's own life; she also compares Cather's 1936 essay on Katherine Mansfield, in which every individual in an everyday "happy family" "is clinging passionately to his individual soul, is in terror of losing it in the general family flavour."

17. Cf. Stouck 191: "But as Thea's sense of heroic purpose grows stronger, the gap for her widens between the claims of ordinary life and the desire to be an artist. Throughout Part II we are reminded of the necessary and often sordid details of everyday existence, which harass and impede the striving artist."

18. Cf. Skaggs 1990, 28: "*Lark* is the story of a young woman with nothing who achieves success and personal fulfillment as an artist, at the cost of almost everything deriving from personal feeling."

19. Both incidents reflect actual experiences Cather had with Fremstad; see Woodress 1987, 253; Stout, 2002, #257.

20. 1932 preface, which Cather used also for the 1938 edition. See Stouck 183–84 on the light this preface casts on Cather's "double vision of art" and its roots in her own life. Sergeant 137 also comments poignantly on the close ties between Cather and Thea.

21. Cf. Giannone 97 on a passage where Cather quotes Balzac: "Single names for Cather, after Balzac, are noble epithets, 'names that tell all and make the passer dream.'"

22. The conditions under which Cather ghosted McClure's autobiography also prevented her from telling his full story: we hear nothing of the staff exodus at *McClure's* just before Cather's arrival, an exodus motivated by the restlessness, the

endless search for new directions, that were so much part of McClure; nor do we hear of the financial and managerial problems that beset McClure in Cather's own years at *McClure's*—and that even as she wrote the book were bringing about McClure's financial ruin. In contrast, Cather tells all of Eddy's story—and enough of Thea's that we see not only her triumph but also the diminished and separate personal existence that is its corollary.

23. O'Brien 447.

Chapter 8. *My Ántonia*

1. On the Edenic character of the first of these, see Rosowski 1986, 77.

2. On the significance of the snake in the last of these, see Rosowski 1986, 80.

3. Cf. the comment on Wick Cutter when we first meet him—"a man of evil name" (57). The Eddy connection is underscored by Mrs. Cutter, whom Stewart Hudson calls Cather's "most explicit transmogrification of Mrs. Eddy" (introduction to *MBE* xxv). Cather herself underscores the connection by having Jim Burden comment, "I have found Mrs. Cutters all over the world; sometimes founding new religions . . ." (*MA* 243).

4. Cf. her comment about herself: "The trouble with me was, Jim, I never could believe harm of anybody I loved" (388).

5. Cf. Cather on A. E. Housman: "That is what it means to write poetry; to be able to say the oldest thing in the world as though it had never been said before" (*W&P* 708).

6. *NUF* 77–78. Cather's comment that Jewett's sketches feel like they were "caught in the open, with light and freedom and air-spaces about them" is important to what she sought to achieve in *My Ántonia*. In a 1918 letter she asks that the illustrations for the novel be set "a little lower on the page to give an effect of spaciousness overhead" (Stout 2002, #408).

7. The lamp is an important motif elsewhere in the novel: see Lee 137.

8. On Cather and Plato's Allegory of the Cave, see Acocella 82–83. Romines 1992, 142, comments on the cave's similarity to "the stifling dugout in which the Shimerdas spent their first year in America"—but now "redeemed" from the past by Ántonia's will and energy.

9. Although she does not specifically mention Plato, Rose's excellent "Modernism: The Case of Willa Cather" is all about Cather's ability to move from the particular to the universal.

10. As Stout 2000, 156–62, notes, the novel's implicit ethnic and racial attitudes,

and the resulting divisions, also pull against the aura of unity: the book's virtual ignoring of German settlers, its treatment of both Native Americans and African Americans, and its hierarchical attitudes toward even those immigrants whom Cather does honor, all "disrupt *Ántonia*'s celebration of inclusiveness" (156).

11. Stout 2000, 145–50.

12. Lena's independence is stressed from the start: in her first appearance she deprecates marriage and says she doesn't want to "have to ask lief of anybody" (184). The novel's first description of Frances calls her "as good a judge of credits as any banker in the county" (171), a phrase that immediately recalls Alexandra and her keen business sense.

13. See 363 and 388, and cf. Ántonia's comment about Mary's children having "a grand chance" (393). On these alternatives that Cather works into the final sections of the novel, cf. Stout 2000, 150: "The stories of Tiny, Lena, and Frances, all stories of career development and geographic mobility, comprise a distinct contrast to the story of Ántonia. . . . Clearly, Ántonia is a powerful emotional center of nostalgic import. At the same time, she herself points toward other possibilities for women."

14. On ways that Cather reads her New York life into Jim, see Murphy 2000, 32.

15. On this dual ownership of "My" Ántonia, and on the differences between Cather's 1918 and 1926 introductions, see Lindemann 62–64.

16. On the central divide between Jim and Ántonia, a divide of understanding as well as of place and profession, see Romines 1992, 143, 148–49.

17. On this passage, see Lee 137; also Woodress 1987, 298.

18. Cf. Acocella 3.

19. On this passage and its relation to pastoral, see Stouck 50–58; also Lee 137–38.

Chapter 9. "Hard and Dry"

The phrase is from a letter of March 1916: see Woodress 1987, 277, 539. Cf. Sergeant's comment on *Youth and the Bright Medusa* (cited in chapter 10, n. 3).

1. E.g., Stout 2002, #328–32, #335–37, #339, #344–46, #348, #370, #377; also Woodress 1987, 274–75; Lindemann 87–88.

2. Stout 2002, #356, 399–400. A similar crisis relating to typesetting changes in *My Ántonia* erupted in 1919: see Stout 2002, #461; Woodress 1987, 306–8.

3. See Woodress 1987, 279, 282–83, 286.

4. Cf. Stout 2000, 130: "All but one of the eight stories she published between 'The Bohemian Girl' and *Youth and the Bright Medusa* (1920) are related in one way or another to women's work and careers. The one exception, 'Consequences,' . . . concerns the *lack* of a career."

5. By the time of a March 7, 1916, letter to W. H. Boynton "her next novel was planned pretty well": Woodress 1987, 277. Greenslet's house memo notes receipt of the complete novel on November 21, 1917 (Houghton Library, Harvard).

6. Woodress 1987, 279, 282.

7. In creating Cressida, Cather draws on what she had written earlier about Nordica: see *W&P* 382–83, 620, 642–46. In "Three American Singers" Cather praised Farrar but noted that she "never aspired to climb the frozen heights reached by her teacher, the great Lilli Lehmann" (Woodress 1987, 256). On Cather and Farrar, see also Giannone 83–85.

8. Cather had already in 1898 created an artist of the same ilk in the heroine of "A Singer's Romance," where Selma Schumann is described as an "industrious and . . . indefatigable student" who "could sing a large repertoire at the shortest notice" (*CSF* 336). Again, Cather's model was Nordica—indeed, her language is at points lifted verbatim from what she had written about Nordica in an 1896 review (*W&P* 382).

9. Cf. *W&P* 402: *Tannhäuser* is "one of the most intense and direct of all operas."

10. Cf. Lee 161: all four of the new stories are "about American opera singers struggling against their 'natural enemies' in a philistine, envious, interfering world. It's a mark of Cather's mood that these are not, like Thea's, stories of triumphant escapes, but of compromises and spoilings."

11. *UV* 124; cf. 132: "It was his wife's restlessness and her practical turn of mind that had made him a money-getter."

12. Cf. Mrs. Cutter in *MA*, who is clearly modeled on Eddy (see chapter 8, n. 3).

13. Note esp. *UV* 133–34: "Annie had no shining merits of character, but she had the gift of thinking well of everything, and wishing well. When she was there Wanning felt as if there were someone who cared whether this was a good or a bad day with him."

14. On the many connections, see Thacker's introduction to *My Autobiography*, xii–xiii.

15. Stout 2000, 130, comments that "The Bookkeeper's Wife," "Her Boss," and "Ardessa" all reveal "that Cather well understood the power structures in such work environments."

16. See Thacker xii–xiii.

17. *Youth* was out by October 2, 1920: Crane 81.

18. H. L. Mencken described it as a "novelette": *UV* xvii.

19. Stout 2000, 130. Lee 162 also takes Hedger's art too seriously for my taste, though she does admit that our sympathies are torn between him and Eden Bower (163).

20. Cather explicitly alludes to the myth of Diana and Actaeon: even before Don begins spying on Eden, he meets her in the hall after she has had her bath and is reminded of the myth (*UV* 149); there is an indirect allusion later when his dog tugs at him as he watches Eden through the knothole. Cather had used the same myth to suggest Alexander's realization of the danger Hilda poses: *AB* 130. As Stouck 199–200 points out, Eden also evokes Delilah, another beautiful and dangerous woman. There are intimations as well of Danae, who is portrayed at times (e.g., by Rembrandt) as receiving Jupiter in the form of brilliant light, at others (e.g., by Titian) with intimations of her prostituting herself. Both images fit Cather's portrait of Eden Bower.

21. Cf. the opening of Rossetti's "Eden Bower": "It was Lilith the wife of Adam: / (Sing Eden Bower!) / Not a drop of her blood was human, / but she was made like a soft sweet woman" (*Collected Poetry and Prose* [New Haven: Yale University Press, 2003] 43).

22. Cf. the description of Thea Kronborg in Cather's 1938 jacket blurb: "[E]very influence, natural and human, she turns into account to help her in her career."

23. In an unpublished autobiography, Achsah Barlow Brewster, a friend of Cather and Edith Lewis for many years, describes the first time (c. 1903) she met Cather, who was "rustling out to a dinner party in a shimmering rose charmeuse satin and an opera cloak. We hung over the banister to watch her sweep down the hall majestically—that dingy hall of 60 South Washington Square that she describes in 'Coming, Aphrodite'" ("The Child," 318; the manuscript is in the Brewster Archive at Drew University).

24. Cf. sections 5 and 6 from the 1915 brochure: "[O]ne book in no way prepares [the reader] for what is coming next"; "One thing is certain—she will not repeat herself."

Chapter 10. *Youth and the Bright Medusa*

1. On the differences, see Woodress 1987, 315–16; *UV* xvii ff.

2. On the counterpoint between the new and old stories of *Youth*, see Giannone 100.

3. Cf. Sergeant's comment on the new collection: "The noticeable change in Willa's first Knopf book, *Youth and the Bright Medusa . . .* was one of tone. *My Ántonia* had been notably warm and glowing. The new book was dry, almost sardonic at times" (161).

4. Lee 164.

5. An artist does play a central role in her 1925 story, "Uncle Valentine," on which see chapter 14, n.13.

6. Lee 163 speaks of the "Medusa-like dangerousness of desire" and notes that this theme "will be a very strong subject in the post-war novels."

7. See her 1932 introduction, where she identifies the focus on Thea's success as a flaw.

8. Cf. Stout 2002, #470, dated July 28, 1919: "Only reason she does short stories is for the income."

9. Flo Field, quoted by Woodress 1987, 312.

10. Not until *One of Ours* did a Cather book achieve real financial success: see Lee 167; Stout 2000, 184–85.

Chapter 11. *One of Ours*

1. Cather began work on *One of Ours* in the fall of 1918 and did not complete it until late in 1921: see Woodress 1987, 303–5, 318–19; Lee 164–65.

2. See Stout 2000, 169–81, on the ways in which Cather reveals her assessment of Claude's choice. Stout notes that Cather regarded the choice her cousin—the model for Claude—had made to escape Nebraska by going to fight in France as "leading to nonsense" (169).

3. Cf. Skaggs 1990, 40: "The central fact about *One of Ours* that one must see in order to read it intelligently at all is that the book is bathed and saturated in irony."

4. See Skaggs 1990, 41, on Cather's use of Lindsay's "bombastic, jingoistic, crudely chest-thumping and repetitious poem"; also Stout 2000, 179. Urgo 143–67 demonstrates how fully the novel reflects this country's "persistent, national narrative of imperial ascendancy" (145).

5. On this "rhythm of disillusionment," cf. Rosowski 1986, 103–5, who subsequently speaks of "affirmation, then denial" as "the pattern of the novel" (108). Trout reads the novel as "an effort to render simultaneously the attractions and repulsions of war. True to the paradoxes at the heart of its subject, this difficult novel asks its audience to confront and even identify with the desires (not ignoble in themselves) that find fulfillment in the ultimately anything but noble activity of killing" (190).

6. The cherry-tree episode early in the book follows the same pattern: see Skaggs 1990, 31–32.

7. Skaggs 1990, 33, notes how these clouds recall the clouds of dust pictured in the earlier picture of the Nebraska fields.

8. That book 2, "Enid," echoes Tennyson's "Idylls" of Enid and Geraint enhances the sense of disillusionment: see Rosowski 1986, 99–100.

9. On this episode, see Trout 117–18, 120; Skaggs 1990, 31.

10. Stout 2000, 176–77, lists a series of instances where Claude's dreams prove delusory.

11. See Stouck 82–83 on this change in the way Nebraska is portrayed.

12. Reynolds 118–19. Cf. Lee 179, who points out that Claude's mother used to read to him from *Paradise Lost*: "The loss of Eden, we are meant to feel, is taking place now."

13. See, e.g., the description of the unused machines at the Wheeler farm, the junk in their basement (18–20), and Claude's thoughts on the obsession with machines (43). On materialism as the enemy that Claude is fleeing, see Lee 176–77.

14. On the numerous similarities between Claude Wheeler and Willa Cather, see Richard Harris in *00* (CSE) 638–39.

15. See Stout 2000, 180, on Cather's doubt that the war effort could in any way be a "triumph."

16. On his mother's astute understanding both of Claude and of the tragedy of his quest and its outcome, see Stout 2000, 174, 178.

17. Cf. 28: "A violent temper and physical restlessness were the most conspicuous things about Claude when he was a little boy." Cf. his reaction in the cherry-tree episode (27–28), and the jacket's mention of his "stormy youth" and "the baffled energy of the boy's nature."

18. See Harris in *00* (CSE) 623–24, 657.

Part V: "The Seeming Original Injustice"

1. Cf. Romines 1996, 101: "Cather's post-1922 fiction is one of our invaluable cultural resources for confronting the coming of age."

2. Giannone 105–6 finds the same theme in the four more recent stories of *Youth*.

Chapter 12. *A Lost Lady*

1. Cf. Stouck 59: "Marian Forrester's disintegration is not just an individual story but a chronicle of a society's decline."

2. Stout 2000, 190.

3. Rosowski 1986, 117–18, 124–25, 127–28, comments on the same persistent rhythm.

4. See Skaggs 1990, 52, on the erotic connotations attached to Marian's removal of her rings.

5. Cf. 152: "[W]ithout him, she was like a ship without ballast . . . ."

6. Cf. the description of Thea as "uncommon in a common, common world" (*SOL* 212).

7. Cf. Skaggs 1990, 48: "a phrasing oddly suggestive of a brothel"; also Stout 2000, 195.

8. Cf. Claude Wheeler's fear that Gladys will eventually marry Bayliss: "He had believed in her fine feelings; believed implicitly. Now he knew she had none so fine that she couldn't pocket them when there was enough to be gained by it" (*OO* 113).

9. See Stout 2000, 222–24, who also notes, however, that the very frequency with which Cather's fiction raises such questions suggests her own uncomfortable awareness of them.

10. On roses in the novel, see Rosowski 1986, 123–24; also Stout 2000, 207.

11. The freshness of morning is a motif throughout the novel: cf., for instance, the boys' expedition on "a summer morning long ago" (14) with Niel's comment that "men like Ivy Peters . . . would drink up the mirage, dispel the morning freshness" (106)—just as Ivy does when his intrusion sullies the Eden of that first morning outing.

12. Lee 185. Note even Niel's fall from the tree!

13. On the echoes of Robin Hood and Maid Marian, see Skaggs 1990, 50; Lee 202–4. On Niel's name, including the wordplay on "kneel," see Skaggs 1990, 50–51.

14. On the values at play in Captain Forrester's choice, see Skaggs 1990, 58–59.

15. As Niel says, "She was one of the people who ought always to have money" (83).

16. Cf. Thea Kronborg's comment that being rich is "the only thing that counts. . . . To do any of the things one wants to do, one has to have lots and lots of money" (*SOL* 242).

17. Urgo 75–76 contrasts Marian's capacity to move with the Captain's stability—and immobility.

18. "'A Lost Lady' was a beautiful ghost in my mind for twenty years before it came together as a possible subject for presentation" (from a 1925 article on Willa Cather in the *Nebraska State Journal*: see Rosowski 1986, 114–15, 260 nn. 3, 4).

19. Cf. Lee 207: "Her will to survive gives her more affinity with the earlier women-heroes, Alexandra, Ántonia and Thea, than might appear: they are all, as A. S. Byatt puts it, products of 'a great novelist's capacity to show human beings almost as forms of energy.'"

Chapter 13. *The Best Stories of Sarah Orne Jewett*

1. *A Lost Lady* was published in September 1923; Cather's first letter to Greenslet about the Jewett project is dated February 17, 1924 (Stout 2002, #718).

2. On the shift of publishers and its complex overtones, see Lindemann 86–91.

3. Lindemann 94.

4. While Cather in her letter of February 17, 1924, indicates her intention to begin with Jewett's original volumes, she also indicates that "of course" the three later Dunnet Landing stories will be included with the Pointed Fir sketches. For a good summary, see Marco A. Portales, "History of a Text: Jewett's *The Country of the Pointed Firs*," *New England Quarterly* 55 (1984): 586–92.

5. Romines 1999, 155. Cather's inclusion of "William's Wedding" not only confuses the chronology of the volume but also introduces "the heterosexual love plot that Jewett's text had assiduously avoided" (Lindemann 96).

6. Lindemann 94–95 suggests that Cather shapes both the collection and the preface to promote qualities she associates with her own books: "In selling Jewett, she sells herself" (95).

7. On the crosscurrents in Cather's Jewett collection, see Romines 1999; Lindemann 90–100. Cf. the tangled echoes of Jewett and Eddy in *Alexander's Bridge*: pp. 93–97.

8. Jewett was clearly on Cather's mind when she visited Bowdoin College in May 1925. In her talk she paid tribute to both Jewett and Bowdoin, which had conferred an honorary degree on Jewett even though she was not a graduate: Bohlke 1986, 154–55, 157, 161, 165.

9. Romines 1999, 164, comments that until Cather "introduced her first specifically female narrative voice . . . in *My Mortal Enemy*," she had ignored Jewett's advice "with stunning success." She had experimented with a female narrator in "The Joy of Nelly Deane" (1911), but she does not repeat the experiment until "Uncle Valentine."

Chapter 14. *The Professor's House*

1. The letter, dated February 21, 1923, is in the Brewster Archive of the Drew University Library.

2. Stout 2002, #673, #709, #727, #758.

3. Stout 2002, #686, #690, #693, #714.

4. Impatience with demands: e.g., Stout 2002, #606, #611, #652, #668, #710, #713, #750, #751. Various medical problems: tonsillectomy (#600), appendicitis (#615, #618, #623, #637), neuritis of her arm (#698, #701, etc.), back problems and a cold (#706), ringworm (#708), a stiff neck (#719, #722).

5. Stout 2002, #719, #755.

6. Stout 2002, #736.

7. Lewis 136. Rosowski 1986, 132, finds these concerns echoed in *The Professor's House*: "St. Peter's extreme fatigue suggests the toil of these demands and the question of the book: Where is the true or authentic self in it all?"

8. Stout 2002, #743.

9. Cf. Romines 1999, 159; also Lindemann 107–11.

10. On the similarities between Cather and St. Peter, see Lee 228–29. Leon Edel 1959a, 114–21, suggests a web of connections revolving around the comfort Cather felt in the study she had on the top floor of Isabelle McClung's Pittsburgh home (it too a sewing room with its dressmaker's dummies) and the discomfort she experienced when, not long before beginning *The Professor's House*, she tried to work in the new study Isabelle had created for her at Ville d'Avray.

11. Cf. Romines 1999, 160. On the "grotesque ironies" of this mansion, see Trout 174–77.

12. Tom's discovery that to win support in Washington entails taking one's potential patron out for an expensive lunch plays a cynical variation on the same theme (229).

13. Note the centrality of the same theme in Cather's closely contemporary story, "Uncle Valentine." It sounds most poignantly in the scene at the end where Charlotte and Valentine associate their nighttime view of Pittsburgh with Wagner: "As possession of the ring made from the Rhinegold causes the conflict and downfall in Wagner's Ring Cycle, so does money destroy the happiness of the characters in this story" (Woodress 1987, 361).

14. Cf. Moseley 202: "Suspended between the tall round tower and the deep canyon, Tom inhabits spatially an 'ideal' plane of vision that is almost Platonic . . . ."

15. Cf. the similar language used of the lake that St. Peter so loves (30).

16. See Lee 251. On St. Peter's callousness, esp. toward his wife and daughters, see Stout 2000, 208–10.

17. For a similar analogue to the novel's structure, see Lee 233: "[Cather's] title page quotation from Louie Marsellus, 'a turquoise set in dull silver', refers to Tom's blue stone from the mesa—simple, glowing, ancient . . . ; it also describes the shape of the novel."

18. On how the novel's broken structure mirrors its themes, see Skaggs 1990, 79; Stout 2000, 213–15.

19. See Schwind 84. The evidence is subtle but clear: see esp. the conversation between Kitty and Scott on 109–10.

20. On Tom's story, cf. Stout 2000, 211: "In contrast to the story of Godfrey's aging and disheartenment and weariness, it is a story of youth and excitement and discovery. It is a story, too, of aspiration and hope . . . ."

21. On the "sacramental" character of Tom's quest, see Lee 242–44.

22. On the associations of Mother Eve with Eden and the Fall, see Skaggs 1990, 71.

23. Cf. Rosowski 1986, 133: "[A] troubling undercurrent of human values betrayed runs through the story." Steven Trout shows that the shadow of World War I, "the thing not named," permeates the novel, undercutting human ambition, the search for meaning, even the possibility of rational narrative itself (147–91).

24. The phrase "mortal, subject to the chances," is from Archibald MacLeish's poem, "Calypso's Island," *Collected Poems, 1917–1953* (Boston: Houghton Mifflin, 1952), 146. As for Godfrey and the devil, Skaggs 1990, 75, points also to the smell of smoke that he leaves behind him (*PH* 17); cf. Rosowski 1986, 215, who finds in St. Peter intimations of "the Faustian Gothic Hero."

25. Sergeant 139–40.

26. On the relationship of these themes to Cather's artistic goals, see Lee 244ff.

27. On the similarities in language, see Romines 1999, 156.

28. On St. Peter's willful "separatism," see Lee 238.

29. On this association, cf. Moseley 202–3. Romines 1999, 156–57, makes telling comments on the differences between the *living* women storytellers of the Jewett stories Cather was anthologizing at this time and the ossified, flawless order that preoccupies the male writers she creates in *Professor's House*, Tom Outland and Godfrey St. Peter.

30. Lindemann 110–11, whose whole treatment of the relationship between *The Professor's House* and Cather's Jewett collection is brilliant (albeit, as she herself comments, to some degree a "more or less arbitrary construct of the interpreter" [101]). See also Romines 1999.

31. On the scene between Augusta and St. Peter, see Skaggs 1990, 81–83. Rosowski 1986, 133–43 gives an evocative interpretation of the resolution St. Peter attains, but to say that in the novel "Cather had cast off outside connections and affirmed a unity that lay beneath them" (144) seems to me too positive a reading. Cf. Skaggs 1990, 91: "Writing *The Professor's House* was not cathartic. To judge by her next year's activities, Cather's distress had intensified."

32. T. S. Eliot, *The Complete Poems and Plays, 1909–1950* (New York: Harcourt Brace, 1952), 363. Celia, it should be noted, turns down this reconciliation to the "human condition" and holds to her saintly vision, which soon leads to her violent death.

Chapter 15. *My Mortal Enemy*

1. On the structure of the novels, see Stouck 65, 117. The brief jacket blurb on the English first edition comments that *My Mortal Enemy* is "small and fine" and compares it to *A Lost Lady*.

2. Woodress 1987, 340.

3. Woodress 1987, 380.

4. Johanningsmeier 237–72. On other possible models, see Skaggs 1990, 85–89.

5. On fairytale elements in Myra's story, see Skaggs 1990, 98, 199 n. 19.

6. Nellie's language recalls "The Novel Démeublé," with its emphasis on that which is felt without being seen. On the rich resonances of the *Norma* scene, see Giannone 179–83.

7. On their many similarities, see Lee 193–94. The jacket blurb on the English first edition comments that after her marriage Myra "never relapsed into a placid week-day contentment" but "kept bright with much use of her faculties of love and hate."

8. Cf. *LL* 100, where Niel speaks of Marian in terms of "a blade" and of "tempered steel."

9. Cf. Lee 210.

10. Romines 1999, 164.

11. Myra's amethyst necklace nicely suggests these crosscurrents in *My Mortal Enemy*. Late in the novel, Myra gives it to Nellie, just as Jewett had late in her life given Cather a similar necklace. The way Myra taunts Nellie for staring at the necklace at their first meeting, however, embodies her domineering, Eddy-like side. Cf. Romines 1999, 164.

12. See Stouck's introduction to *MBE* xix–xx. Lee 214 describes Myra's combination of "generosity, extravagance, love of luxury, talent for friendship, jealousy, superstitions, greed, passion, cruelty, and appetite for control." She could well be describing Mary Baker Eddy as Cather portrays her.

13. On Myra and mirrors in this scene, see Skaggs 1990, 99.

14. Cf. Rosowski 1986, 152, speaking of both Myra and her uncle: "[D]espite the yearnings of their immortal souls, human beings are doomed to failure by their mortality."

15. On these and other early signs of the tensions in the marriage, see Stout 2000, 217–18.

16. On the undermining of Nellie's illusions about Myra, see Rosowski 1986, 146–48.

17. On the self-referential nature of her words, see Stouck 120–21.

18. Nellie's reaction to Myra's outburst in part I is significant: "Everything about me seemed evil" (64). Cf. the similar elements in a comment Kitty makes about her sister Rosamond: "When she comes toward me, I feel hate coming toward me, like a snake's hate" (*PH* 85).

19. Cf. Skaggs 1990, 104–5: "The real facts of her life—including her love of Oswald, her sponsorship of that adoring younger self, Nellie, and her aging body that reminds her of her entrapment in the flesh—are Myra's (as they are also Nellie's and Oswald's) mortal enemy."

20. On Myra's heroism, see Lee 216–18.

21. On the strong Catholic overtones and the Dante-esque echoes of the progression that begins in *The Professor's House* and leads through *My Mortal Enemy* and *Death Comes for the Archbishop* to *Shadows on the Rock*, see Murphy 1990. Gervaud 78 traces Cather's interest in this motif back to her fascination with the Rocher des Doms in Avignon, on which see also Sergeant 96.

22. On similarities between Cather and Myra Henshawe, see Stouck 117; Stout 2000, 216.

23. Cf. Skaggs 1990, 91: "*My Mortal Enemy* stands in my mind as Willa Cather's most brilliant—in the sense of technically astonishing—tour de force."

Part VI: Recapitulation

1. Tobias Wolff, *Old School* (New York: Vintage Books, 2004) 156.

Chapter 16. Cather Talks with Cather

1. *SOJ Letters* 247–50.

2. *SOJ Letters* 247–48.

3. Both Jewett ("the 'Troll-Garden'") and the jacket ("A Troll Garden") get the title of *The Troll Garden* wrong.

4. *SOJ Letters* 248.

5. We noted in chapter 1 that Ferris Greenslet apparently worked on the three sections of the 1915 brochure that describe Cather's earlier work, and one can find connections between those sections and the house memos Greenslet had written

on the three novels in question. In the case of all three, however, there is also much new material, and much that strongly suggests Cather's own involvement. This is especially true of the passages about *Alexander's Bridge* considered in this paragraph, which are unlike anything found in Greenslet's house memo on the novel—and very reminiscent of language Cather uses elsewhere.

6. The brochure "was distributed before publication of the novel," which appeared on October 2 (Crane 313, 48). Cather was correcting proofs of the novel from spring into late summer; she wrote her portion of the brochure in late July (Greenslet memos, cited by Crane 314). In early September Greenslet sent Cather both a first copy of the novel, fresh off the presses, and a final mockup of the brochure for her review (letter from Greenslet to Cather, September 2, 1915, Houghton Library, Harvard).

7. These jackets thus emphasize a feature of both Cather's early novels and these novels of the 1920s—their reference to larger historical and national issues: see Urgo passim.

8. Woodress 1987, 379.

9. In the end, Cather can't resist helping promote even DCA. Soon after its September 2 appearance, she proposes advertising copy, and in November she identifies a review she thinks apt for promotional use: see Stout 2002, #901, #902, #913.

Chapter 17. *Death Comes for the Archbishop*

1. Cf. Lindemann 118: "[T]he serenity of *Archbishop* rests in part on a recuperation of Jewettian optimism . . . ."

2. On Puvis and *Death*, see Keeler and Giorcelli. Cather knew Puvis before the 1902 trip and often encountered his work in later years: see Woodress 1987, 199; Stout 2000, 138–39.

3. On the topic, see esp. Murphy in *DCA* (CSE) 326–42. Skaggs 1990, 66, notes the theme's continuity from *The Professor's House* through *Shadows*.

4. See, e.g., their first conversation, *PH* 19–25.

5. On the role of religion at the end of Myra's life, see Rosowski 1986, 151.

6. St. Peter's name links him to the Rock, as does his interest in Tom's Blue Mesa. Cf. Skaggs 1990, 76–77: "The Professor must ask as the novel proceeds whether any rock exists on which one might eventually imagine erecting some systematic and sustaining faith." See also Gervaud 77.

7. On the persistence of this motif, see Rosowski 1986, 183–84; also Murphy, *DCA* (CSE) 331.

8. Typical of the progression from *My Mortal Enemy* to *Death* is that amethysts,

so associated with Myra's bitterness, reappear in Latour's beloved ring: see Skaggs 1990, 19.

9. Cf. Skaggs 1990, 113: "[Myra Henshawe] seeks and finds the confidence in human potential which gathers to a greatness in *Death Comes for the Archbishop*."

10. Rosowski 1986, 162–63, comments on the "attitude of acceptance" that runs through *Death* and notes that Latour and Vaillant "characteristically turn away from worldly matters." Lee 260 notes that *Death* "stays above the complicated tensions of *The Professor's House* and *My Mortal Enemy*. . . . Something ferocious and unreconciled, that goes right back to the dark primitive troll-self of the hero of her first novel, is placed at arm's length . . . ."

11. Stout 2000, 239ff.

12. Woodress 1987, 396. See Lee 285–86 on the way in which the Virgin Mary gives sublimated expression to the sexuality that otherwise is largely suppressed in the novel.

13. On the episode, see Stout 2000, 241–43; Rosowski 1986, 173–74, 217–18; Lindemann 131–32.

14. Cf. Romines 1996, 108: "In *Archbishop*, the undying powers of a goddess have gone underground, in the great and terrifying river of 'Stone Lips.'" Lee 285 notes that "*Death Comes for the Archbishop* is a deliberately chaste book," with "[s]ensuality . . . safely placed on the periphery."

15. Woodress 1987, 385. There are hints of the same anxieties about sexual passion in the description of Mother Eve's downfall in *The Professor's House*: see Romines 1999, 158.

16. Noting that "guadalupe" may be Mexican for "snake," Lee 286 suggests that the Lady of Guadalupe may represent a conflation of an Indian snake goddess with the Virgin Mary.

17. On the passage, see Swift 64–65; Urgo 179.

18. Cf. Rosowski 1986, 161–62, on the opening scene, where Latour's mission is decided entirely by others: "The effect is to contradict any notion of the heroic individual determining his own and the world's fate . . . ." Romines 1996, 101ff., points out that the serene dignity with which Cather invests the archbishop's death comes at the cost of avoiding the more complex issues of female aging and dying that had been so much on her mind—and that she will finally confront in "Old Mrs. Harris" and *Sapphira*.

19. Among others who have sensed an element of retreat and withdrawal in *Death*, see esp. Edel's *Willa Cather: The Paradox of Success* and Granville Hicks's 1937 essay "The Case against Willa Cather."

20. Cf. *DCA* 244: "But the Cathedral is not for us, Father Joseph. We build for the future. . . ."

21. Cf. Brown 111 on the volcanic rock of Italy evoked in Cather's poem "Recognition" (*AT* 1923, 64): "that sense of time immutable, the cave-dwellers and the Rock."

Chapter 18. Fiction of the 1930s

1. Woodress 1987, 464; Stout 2002, #1229 and #1230, dated July 25 and 26, 1934.

2. Cf. Woodress 1987, 426. On Cather and French culture in general, see Gervaud.

3. See Woodress 1987, 426–27.

4. *WCOW* 16; Woodress 1987, 425.

5. Stout 2000, 254.

6. Lee 300–301.

7. See Rosowski 1986, 184–87; also Lee 304. On Jeanne le Ber, see Lee 305; Skaggs 1990, 140–41. Romines 1992, 152–63, wisely resists interpreting either the novel or its heroine too simplistically.

8. Cf. Murphy 1976, 37: "The Catholicism [the novel] depicts is one of tradition, authority, ritual, miracles—an orderly, arranged, safe world . . . ." Note also, though, the theme of change and mobility—as in the shadows moving across the rock: Urgo 98–99.

9. On the contrasting colors, see Lee 293.

10. Cf. Lee 306–8.

11. Cather herself in a May 1, 1931, letter to Dorothy Canfield Fisher spoke of the book itself as a rock of refuge in these difficult years: see Murphy-Stouck's "Historical Essay" in *SOR* (CSE) 357; also Skaggs 1990, 128–29, 139.

12. *Shadows* was published on August 1, 1931; the new jacket appeared in September with the fifth printing (Crane 155–56). The new jacket also mirrors the novel's political world, "a hierarchy well symbolized in the verticality of its setting . . ." (Stout 2000, 255).

13. Leon Edel 1959a, 121, notes the "deep feeling of insecurity" present in all of Cather's later works and her "choice of the Rock as the symbol of endurance."

14. The jacket copy for a 1938 English edition similarly compares an earlier time—1915—with the present. It begins, "This is Miss Cather's favourite among her works. In these pages Miss Willa Cather has rewritten one of her earlier stories; to the freshness of spring she has added the wealth of summer; what began as a novel of charm has ripened into a masterpiece." Its conclusion returns to the "ripening" metaphor and ends with the theme Cather emphasizes in her 1932

preface—the way an artist's professional life supplants all else: "[The novel] tells of her hopes, her little ambitions that ripened and grew, her gradual successes; of the men who helped her and loved her; of the ever-increasing absorption of her soul in her art. Willa Cather."

15. Cf. Moers 238–39, who vigorously protests the notion that this novel is a "[p]rairie pastoral! *A Lost Lady* is an Electra story, raw and barbarous. Marian Forrester is a queen and a whore as well."

16. The emotional complexities between Vickie and her grandmother that are explored here appear also in one of Cather's early poems, "Granmither, Think Not I Forget," as Stouck 40–41 points out. Cather retained this as her lead poem in the revised 1923 *April Twilights* and also published it separately in a circular advertising this reissue: see Crane 98.

17. See Rosowski 1986, 199–204, and Lee 310–15 on the issues at stake in "Two Friends."

18. Romines 1992 calls this story the "buried heart" of the collection (164) and comments that it is "as deeply, rigorously autobiographical as anything [Cather] ever wrote" (173).

19. For the longstanding difficulties of this relationship, see Stout 2000, 131–32, who also reads the story as Cather's "forgiving reassessment of her dying mother" (256). Romines 1996, 109–10, argues that in this story Cather finally confronts the issues of female aging and dying that she had largely skirted in *Death*, *Shadows*, and even *My Mortal Enemy*.

20. Cf. Woodress 1987, 444, on how the story reflects Cather's own earlier self-absorption.

21. Mrs. Harris has her own strong sense of family pride: "She wouldn't for the world have had Victoria go about every morning in a short gingham dress, with bare arms, and a dust-cap on her head to hide the curling-kids, as these brisk housekeepers did" (134).

22. The narrator's gender is unclear: Lee 311 reads the child as "not sexed, but seemingly boyish"; Rosowski 1986, 200–201, and Romines 1992, 164, relate the child closely to Cather herself and hence suggest that the narrator is female.

23. It seems clear that Cather read into both men qualities she admired in S. S. McClure.

24. Cf. Romines 1992, 173: the "subject is women and how they repeat each other's destinies."

25. Lee 334–35 suggests that it was Cather's growing friendship with the Menuhin children that inspired her to return to the life of the artist in *Lucy Gayheart*. Skaggs 1990, 156, speaks of Lucy's "lack of high seriousness, her lack of ambition."

26. On the comparison of Lucy with Thea, see Skaggs 1990, 151; 1995, passim. Lee 339 finds Lucy more like the "pointlessly aesthetic Paul" than "the ferociously ambitious Thea."

27. On "escape" as a focus in *Lucy Gayheart* and many Cather novels, see Woodress 1987, 452.

28. See Stout 2000, 264, 269–70.

29. Cf. Lee 338: "The language of Lucy's aspiration is always fragile and escapist."

30. On Lucy's pervasive inclination toward flight, cf. Skaggs 1990, 154.

31. See Stout 2000, 271, 347 n. 29.

32. Urgo 118, 125. Stout 2000, 265–74, also finds ways in which Lucy, for all her weaknesses, leaves behind much that is lasting and significant.

Chapter 19. Cather, Jewett, and *Not Under Forty*

1. On the background experiences that Cather returned to in writing *Death*, see Murphy, *DCA* (CSE) 325ff.

2. *SOJ Letters* 250.

3. Romines 1990, 149.

4. Romines 1990, 156.

5. Woodress 1987, 449. On the background of the novel, see also Lee 336–37.

6. Both Sergeant 58 and Romines 1992, 173, note Jewett's particular fondness for Flaubert's "Écrire la vie ordinaire comme on écrit l'histoire."

7. Cf. the new title Cather gives the collection when it appears in 1938 in the autograph edition: *Literary Encounters*.

8. Interestingly, older women facing disabilities are central to two of the sections Cather inserted into *Country*—the immobilized Mrs. Hight in "A Dunnet Shepherdess" and the somewhat dotty Mrs. Martin in "The Queen's Twin." Romines 1996, 111, comments that *My Mortal Enemy* "initiated an important project of [Cather's] later years, a complex and nuanced exploration of the experience of aging women" that included "Old Mrs. Harris" and *Sapphira*. The women of *Not Under Forty* clearly belong to the same project.

9. On this side of Cather, cf. Woodress 1990, 113: "She never lived ostentatiously, but one of the several dichotomies of her life was her ability to love and write glowingly about the immigrants in Nebraska and at the same time to live elegantly the life of a New York sophisticate with aristocratic tastes and little interest in the masses."

10. Cather even appears briefly in the Thomas Mann essay: see *NUF* 100.

11. Slote and Faulkner 82. In the same passage Moers also calls Madame Grout "a very tough cookie" and muses thoughtfully about how much Cather really knew about her, and why, if she really understood her, she chose to write about her. For the second quote, see O'Brien 322, who comments also on the affinities between Madame Grout and Mrs. Fields (324).

12. On both this passage and Mrs. Fields in general, see O'Brien 315–22, esp. 321.

13. On the feisty spirit Cather brings to *Not Under Forty*, see Lindemann 134–35.

14. Cf. Lee 350: "Cather puts a good deal of herself . . . into Madame Grout: this is the kind of difficult old lady she is becoming, or would like to become."

15. Cf. Lee 349 on "the now-familiar trope" of Cather's late writings, "the lost lady who brings back the past. The last lost ladies are old ladies: Madame Caroline Franklin-Grout [of] 'A Chance Meeting'; the 'old beauty' of the slightly later story; Sarah Orne Jewett and Annie Fields . . . ; and the formidable Sapphira."

16. Cf. Jewett's strikingly similar language in "The Queen's Twin," one of the stories that Cather added to *Country*: "[T]he sea captains and the captains' wives of Maine knew something of the wide world, and never mistook their native parishes for the whole instead of a part thereof . . ." (*Best Stories,* vol. 1, 243).

17. The theme is underscored later in the preface by Cather's famous comment that the writer "must be able to think and feel in that speech—it is a gift from heart to heart" (xvii). Jewett herself frequently sounds the same theme—e.g., in the description of Mrs. Blackett in *Country*: "Sympathy is of the mind as well as the heart, and Mrs. Blackett's world and mine were one from the moment we met" (*Best Stories,* vol. 1, 73).

Chapter 20. *Sapphira and the Slave Girl*

1. Skaggs 1990, 166.

2. Cf. Rosowski 1986, 234: the novel creates "a world of unsettling contradictions, where a graceful façade of civilization covers actions of dark cruelty . . . ."

3. Cather also twice calls attention to this date on the first page of the novel: Urgo 84–85.

4. On Cather's aversion to dogmatism, see Skaggs 1990, 174, 207 n. 12; Stout 2000, 76; and esp. Cather's own 1931 essay, "Escapism" (*WCOW* 18–29).

5. On Till's complexities, see Romines 1992, 179–81; on her relationship with Nancy, see Morrison 21–23. On Henry, see Stout 2000, 286–88, who calls his response "at best passive" but also provides the historical context for his reluctance

to become directly involved in facilitating Nancy's escape. On Rachel, see Skaggs 1990, 180, and cf. Cather's comments on her own grandmother, Rachel Boak, on whom she modeled Rachel Blake: Skaggs 1990, 165. On Martin Colbert, see Skaggs 1990, 179. Though Morrison's reading of the novel is very different from mine, she too recognizes the courage and honesty of the undertaking: "In her last novel [Cather] works out and toward the meaning of female betrayal as it faces the void of racism. She may not have arrived safely, like Nancy, but to her credit she did undertake the dangerous journey" (28).

6. See, e.g., Stout 2000, 284–85; Lee 365. For a powerful reading of the sexual and racial issues in the novel, see Morrison 18–28.

7. Skaggs 1990, 179. See also Urgo 87–88.

8. Skaggs 1990, 176.

9. Skaggs 1990, 177.

10. Cf. Skaggs 1990, 175: "To her servants she appears more generous and merciful than the juster Rachel or Henry."

11. See Rosowski 1986, 240–41, on the overwhelming power Sapphira exerts in the novel.

12. On the name Lucy Gayheart, see Skaggs 1990, 153–54; Stout 2000, 264.

13. On the heroic qualities of Nancy, see Romines 1992, 186–87.

14. Romines 1992, 174–89, captures the heroism of the novel's women, including that of Jezebel and of the young Mary, who contrives to save her own life.

15. Cf. Wolff 222: "Willa Cather paraphrased [Jewett's advice] many times herself, and in her last novel she breathed personal meaning into it by reviving those ancient memories from her own life that had 'teased the mind over and over for years'. . . ."

16. See Woodress 1987, 481; Stout 2000, 280.

17. Woodress 1987, 484; the letter to Fisher is Stout 2002, #1497, dated October 14, 1940.

18. See Stout 2000, 282, on Sapphira's "manipulative, powerful" side and its echoes of Cather's Eddy.

19. Cf. 50: "You're the master here, and I'm the miller. And that's how I like it to be."

20. Cf. O'Brien 338–39.

21. The obituary notice with which "A Chance Meeting" ends pays tribute to Madame Grout's work in publishing her uncle's works.

22. Rosowski 1986, 244. Cf. Lee 357.

23. See Lee 369.

24. Cf. Stout 2000, 276–77. Cf. Lee 357.

25. See Rosowski 1986, 242–43, on the mutual compassion/sympathy of this scene.

26. Rosowski 1986, 199, comments in similar terms on the "sympathy" Cather brings to the characters of "Old Mrs. Harris"—and the sympathy her approach evokes in the reader.

27. See Skaggs 180–81; Urgo 85, 91. On the epilogue, see Stout 2000, 282–83, 294–96.

28. Cf. Hoover 251: "*Sapphira and the Slave Girl* represents women with power over their lives: Sapphira to run her household and to maintain a position in the community, Rachel to defy her mother's principles, Nancy to escape from Sapphira's tyranny, Till to spin stories, the 'I' to piece the stories into a larger design, and Willa Cather to create a text that marks them all."

29. Stout 2000, 133, shows Cather playing similar tricks with Thea's age in *The Song of the Lark*.

30. On the stories told in the epilogue, and the way these stories continue in Willa Cather's own storytelling, see Romines 1992, 185–88.

31. "Old Mrs. Harris" is in fact longer than *My Mortal Enemy*: in the Library of America edition of Cather's *Stories, Poems, and Other Writings*, "Old Mrs. Harris" runs 53 pages, *My Mortal Enemy* 49.

Works Cited

Acocella, Joan. *Willa Cather and the Politics of Criticism*. Lincoln: University of Nebraska Press, 2000.

Bennett, Mildred R. *The World of Willa Cather*. Lincoln: University of Nebraska Press, 1961.

Bintrim, Timothy. "A Note about Spelling Cather's *Pittsburg*." *WCPMN&R* 46 (Winter/Spring 2003): 52–53.

Bohlke, L. Brent. "Willa Cather and *The Life of Mary Baker G. Eddy*." *American Literature* 54 (1982): 288–94.

———. *Willa Cather in Person*. Lincoln: University of Nebraska Press, 1986.

Brown, E. K. *Willa Cather: A Critical Biography*. New York: Alfred A. Knopf, 1953.

Cather, Willa. *Alexander's Bridge*. Boston: Houghton Mifflin, 1922.

———. *April Twilights*. Boston: Gorham Press, 1903.

———. *April Twilights and Other Poems*. New York: Alfred A. Knopf, 1923.

———. *Collected Short Fiction, 1892–1912*. Lincoln: University of Nebraska Press, 1965.

———. *Death Comes for the Archbishop*. New York: Alfred A. Knopf, 1927.

———. *Death Comes for the Archbishop*, Willa Cather Scholarly Edition. Lincoln: University of Nebraska Press, 1999.

———. *A Lost Lady*. New York: Alfred A. Knopf, 1923.

———. *A Lost Lady*, Willa Cather Scholarly Edition. Lincoln: University of Nebraska Press, 1997.

———. *My Ántonia*. Boston: Houghton Mifflin, 1918.

———. *My Mortal Enemy*. New York: Alfred A. Knopf, 1926.

———. *Not Under Forty*. New York: Alfred A. Knopf, 1936.

———. *Obscure Destinies*. New York: Alfred A. Knopf, 1932.

———. *O Pioneers!* Boston: Houghton Mifflin, 1913.

———. *O Pioneers!* Ed. Blanch A. Gelfant. New York: Penguin Books, 1994.

———. *One of Ours*. New York: Alfred A. Knopf, 1922.

———. *One of Ours*, Willa Cather Scholarly Edition. Lincoln: University of Nebraska Press, 2006.

————. *The Professor's House*. New York: Alfred A. Knopf, 1925.

————. *Sapphira and the Slave Girl*. New York: Alfred A. Knopf, 1940.

————. *Shadows on the Rock*. New York: Alfred A. Knopf, 1931.

————. *Shadows on the Rock*, Willa Cather Scholarly Edition. Lincoln: University of Nebraska Press, 2005.

————. *The Song of the Lark*. Boston: Houghton Mifflin, 1915.

————. *The Song of the Lark*. Ed. Sherrill Harbison. New York: Penguin Books, 1999.

————. *Uncle Valentine and Other Stories*. Lincoln: University of Nebraska Press, 1973.

————. *Willa Cather in Europe*. New York: Alfred A. Knopf, 1956.

————. *Willa Cather on Writing*. New York: Alfred A. Knopf, 1949.

————. *Youth and the Bright Medusa*. New York: Alfred A. Knopf, 1920.

Crane, Joan. *Willa Cather: A Bibliography*. Lincoln: University of Nebraska Press, 1982.

Curtin, William M. *The World and the Parish: Willa Cather's Articles and Reviews, 1893–1902*. Lincoln: University of Nebraska Press, 1970.

Edel, Leon. *Literary Biography*. Garden City: Doubleday, 1959a.

————. *Willa Cather: The Paradox of Success*. Washington DC: Library of Congress, 1959b.

Gervaud, Michel. "Willa Cather and France: Elective Affinities." *The Art of Willa Cather*. Ed. Bernice Slote and Virginia Faulkner. Lincoln: University of Nebraska Press, 1974. 65–83.

Giannone, Richard. *Music in Willa Cather's Fiction*. Lincoln: University of Nebraska Press, 1968.

Giorcelli, Christina. "Willa Cather and Pierre Puvis de Chavannes: Extending the Comparison." *Literature and Belief* 23.2 (2003): 70–88.

Greenslet, Ferris. *Under the Bridge: An Autobiography*. New York: Houghton Mifflin, 1943.

Harbison, Sherrill. "Cather, Fremstad, and Wagner." *Willa Cather's New York: New Essays on Cather in the City*. Ed. Merrill Maguire Skaggs. Madison: Fairleigh Dickinson University Press, 2000. 144–58.

Hicks, Granville. "The Case Against Willa Cather." 1937. Reprinted in *Willa Cather and Her Critics*. Ed. James Schroeter. Ithaca: Cornell University Press, 1967. 139–47.

Hoover, Sharon. "Reflections of Authority and Community in *Sapphira and the Slave Girl*." *Cather Studies* 3 (1996): 238–55.

Jewett, Sarah Orne. *Letters of Sarah Orne Jewett*. Ed. Annie Fields. Boston: Houghton Mifflin, 1911.

———. *The Best Stories of Sarah Orne Jewett.* Edited and with a preface by Willa Cather. 2 vols. Boston: Houghton Mifflin, 1925.

Johanningsmeier, Charles. "Unmasking Willa Cather's 'Mortal Enemy.'" *Cather Studies* 5 (2003): 237–72.

Keeler, Clinton. "Narrative Without Accent: Willa Cather and Puvis de Chavannes." *American Quarterly* 17 (1965): 117–26.

Knopf, Alfred A. "Miss Cather." *The Art of Willa Cather.* Ed. Bernice Slote and Virginia Faulkner. Lincoln: University of Nebraska Press, 1974. 205–24.

Lee, Hermione. *Willa Cather: Double Lives.* New York: Pantheon Books, 1989.

Lewis, Edith. *Willa Cather Living.* New York: Alfred A. Knopf, 1953.

Lindemann, Marilee. *Willa Cather: Queering America.* New York: Columbia University Press, 1999.

Madigan, Mark J. "Willa Cather and Dorothy Canfield Fisher: Rift, Reconciliation, and *One of Ours.*" *Cather Studies* 1 (1990): 115–29.

McClure, S. S. *My Autobiography.* New York: Frederick A. Stokes, 1914. Reprint, Willa Cather, *The Autobiography of S. S. McClure.* Introd. by Robert Thacker. Lincoln: University of Nebraska Press, 1997.

Milmine, Georgine. *The Life of Mary Baker G. Eddy and the History of Christian Science.* New York: Doubleday Page & Co., 1909. Reprint, ed. Stewart Hudson. Grand Rapids: Baker Book House, 1971. Reprint, ed. David Stouck. Lincoln: University of Nebraska Press, 1993.

———. "Mary Baker G. Eddy: The Story of Her Life and the History of Christian Science, XIV: Mrs. Eddy's Book and Doctrine." *McClure's Magazine,* June 1908: 179–89.

Moers, Ellen. *Literary Women.* Garden City: Doubleday & Co., 1976.

Morrison, Toni. *Playing in the Dark: Whiteness and the Literary Imagination.* Cambridge: Harvard University Press, 1992.

Moseley, Ann. "Spatial Structures and Forms in *The Professor's House. Cather Studies* 3 (1996): 197–211.

Murphy, John J. "The Art of *Shadows on the Rock.*" *Prairie Schooner* 50 (1976): 37–51.

———. "Cather's New World Divine Comedy: The Dante Connection." *Cather Studies* 1 (1990): 21–35.

———, ed. *Five Essays on Willa Cather: The Merrimack Symposium.* North Andover: Merrimack College, 1974.

———. "From Cornfield to the Big Apple Orchard: New York as School for Cather and Her Critics." *Willa Cather's New York: New Essays on Cather in the City.* Ed. Merrill Maguire Skaggs. Madison: Fairleigh Dickinson University Press, 2000. 21–42.

O'Brien, Sharon. *Willa Cather: The Emerging Voice*. Oxford: Oxford University Press, 1987.

Porter, David H. "'She had only to touch an idea to make it live': Willa Cather and Mary Baker Eddy." *WCPMN&R* 44 (Fall 2000): 38–44.

———. "Cather on Cather: Two Early Self-Sketches." *WCPMN&R* 45 (Winter/Spring 2002): 55–60.

———. "Cather on Cather II: Two Recent Acquisitions at Drew University." *WCPMN&R* 46 (Winter/Spring 2003): 49–58.

———. "Cather on Cather III: Dust-Jacket Copy on Willa Cather's Books." *WCPMN&R* 48 (Winter/Spring 2005): 51–60.

———. "From Violence to Art: Willa Cather Caught in the Eddy." *Violence, the Arts, and Willa Cather*. Ed. Joseph R. Urgo and Merrill Maguire Skaggs. Madison: Fairleigh Dickinson University Press, 2007. 295–309.

Reynolds, Guy. *Willa Cather in Context: Progress, Race, Empire*. New York: St. Martin's Press, 1996.

Romines, Ann. "The Hermit's Parish: Jeanne Le Ber and Cather's Legacy from Jewett." *Cather Studies* 1 (1990): 147–58.

———. "Her Mortal Enemy's Daughter: Cather and the Writing of Age." *Cather Studies* 3 (1996) 100–114.

———. *The Home Plot: Women, Writing and Domestic Ritual*. Amherst: University of Massachusetts Press, 1992.

———. "The Professor and the *Pointed Firs*: Cather, Jewett, and Problems of Editing." *Jewett and Her Contemporaries: Reshaping the Canon*. Ed. Karen L. Kilcup and Thomas S. Edwards. Gainesville: University Press of Florida, 1999. 153–66.

Rose, Phyllis. "Modernism: The Case of Willa Cather." *Modernism Reconsidered*. Ed. Robert Kiely and John Hildebidle. Cambridge: Harvard University Press, 1983. 123–45.

Rosowski, Susan J. *The Voyage Perilous: Willa Cather's Romanticism*. Lincoln: University of Nebraska Press, 1986.

———. "Willa Cather's Subverted Endings and Gendered Time." *Cather Studies* 1 (1990): 68–88.

Schwind, Jean. "This Is a Frame-Up: Mother Eve in *The Professor's House*." *Cather Studies* 2 (1993): 72–91.

Sergeant, Elizabeth Shepley. *Willa Cather: A Memoir*. Lincoln: University of Nebraska Press, 1963.

Skaggs, Merrill Maguire. *After the World Broke in Two: The Later Novels of Willa Cather*. Charlottesville: University Press of Virginia, 1990.

———. "Key Modulations in Cather's Novels about Music." *WCPMN&R* 39 (Summer and Fall 1995): 25–30.

———. "Young Willa Cather and the Road to Cos Cob." *Willa Cather's New York: New Essays on Cather in the City.* Ed. Merrill Maguire Skaggs. Madison: Fairleigh Dickinson University Press, 2000. 43–59.

Slote, Bernice. *The Kingdom of Art: Willa Cather's First Principles and Critical Statements, 1893–1896.* Lincoln: University of Nebraska Press, 1966.

Slote, Bernice, and Virginia Faulkner, eds. *The Art of Willa Cather.* Lincoln: University of Nebraska Press, 1974.

Stouck, David. *Willa Cather's Imagination.* Lincoln: University of Nebraska Press, 1975.

Stout, Janis P., *Willa Cather: The Writer and Her World.* Charlottesville: University Press of Virginia, 2000.

———, ed. *A Calendar of the Letters of Willa Cather.* Lincoln: University of Nebraska Press, 2002.

Swift, John N. "Cather's Archbishop and the 'Backward Path.'" *Cather Studies* 1 (1990): 55–67.

Thacker, Robert. "Four 'New' Cather Letters to Annie Fields at the Huntington Library." *Cather Studies* 3 (1996): 285–91.

Trout, Steven. *Memorial Fictions: Willa Cather and the First World War.* Lincoln: University of Nebraska Press, 2002.

Urgo, Joseph R. *Willa Cather and the Myth of American Migration.* Urbana: University of Illinois Press, 1995.

———. "Willa Cather's Political Apprenticeship at *McClure's* Magazine." *Willa Cather's New York: New Essays on Cather in the City.* Ed. Merrill Maguire Skaggs. Madison: Fairleigh Dickinson University Press, 2000. 60–74.

Woodress, James. *Willa Cather: A Literary Life.* Lincoln: University of Nebraska Press, 1987.

———. "Writing Cather's Biography." *Cather Studies* 1 (1990): 103–14.

Wolff, Cynthia Griffin. "Time and Memory in *Sapphira and the Slave Girl*: Sex, Abuse, and Art." *Cather Studies* 3 (1996): 212–37.

Index

role of artist, 241–42; in *DCA*, 241, 256; in *MME*, 224–25, 254; in *PH*, 203–4, 205, 206, 208. *See also* rocks, image of

Boak, Virginia Sibert (mother). *See* Cather, Virginia Sibert Boak (mother)

"The Bohemian Girl," 83, 92, 96, 230

book jackets. *See* jacket copy

"The Bookkeeper's Wife," 146, 150, 152, 237

Brandeis, Mrs. Louis, 281

Bréton, Jules, 7, 37, 317n11, fig. 4

bridges motif, 94–95, 96, 100–101

Burne-Jones, Edward, 67, 79

business instincts: in Alexandra Bergson, 104; in Ántonia, 139; in Eddy, 104, 301; in Sapphira, 299, 301

Canfield, Dorothy and "The Profile," 85, 89

Cather, Charles Fectigue (father), 7, 265

Cather, Virginia Sibert Boak (mother), 7, 119, 265–66, 269–70

Cather, Willa: and aging, 286; ambition, 58, 264, 271, 286, 304; and Ántonia, 140, 141; as applause-seeker, 57; aristocratic leanings, 304; birthdate, 6, 14, 20, 76, 306, 312nn7–8, 313n17; capacity for hate, xxv, 304; as character in her fiction, 54, 264, 268, 270, 287, 305; childhood, 21–24, 75–76; in "Coming, Eden Bower!", 157–58; competitiveness, 84–85, 92; complexities of, xxv, 59; desired qualities in her work, 211–12; desire for public recognition, 58; difficulty to live with, xxv; distortions of facts, 12–16, 27, 30, 67,

79, 235, 245–46; diverse lives of, 305; divisions in, xx, 30, 112, 116, 142, 158; double lives of, xx, 86, 127–28, 235–36; dressing well, 304; Eddy assessment, 72–74; facing passage of time, 195; feistiness of, 289; heartlessness, 304; as heroic woman, 305–7; on her own writing, 102–3; illnesses, 182–83, 202–3, 286, 304; importance of jacket copy to, 33; and Jewett stories, 196–201; as journalist, 66, 67, 234–35; lesbianism, xx, xxv, 320n21; loss of idealism, 177; McClure as model for, 116, 328n25; middle name of, 7, 312n11; money and financial concerns of artists in, 58; and mortality, 182, 242; New York side, 140–42, 143–44; as one who never repeats herself, 26, 50, 158, 233, 269, 315n45, 333n24; outspokenness, 65, 286; presentation of self, 52–55; role-playing by, xx, 129–30, 305; search for something splendid, 168; sense of diminishment in the difficult years, 267; shaping of her myth, 67; similarities to characters of *PH*, 203, 211–12, 338n10; similarities to characters of *YBM*, 165–66; similarities to Eden Bower, 158; similarities to Godfrey St. Peter, 212–13, 226, 241, 242; similarities to Jim Burden, 140–41; similarities to Marie Shabata, 111–12; similarities to Myra Henshawe, 226; similarities to Sapphira, xxv, 304; similarities to Thea, 141–42, 270, 329n16; similarities to women of *NUF*, 286–87; study room of, 76, 338n10; and success of *OO*, 202;

Cather, Willa (*cont.*)
   sympathy, 304–5; as teacher, 8, 14, 66; temper in, xxv, 304; at university, 65–66; using people for her own ends, 85–86, 304; as Western writer, 24, 193. *See also* Eddy, Mary Baker; Jewett, Sarah Orne; promotional activities
Catholicism: in *DCA* and *PH*, 255; in *MME*, 225
cave, Plato's, 138, 330n8
cave as female symbol: in *DCA*, 258–59, 343n14
Cécile (*SOR*), 265, 267, 277. *See also* *Shadows on the Rock*
"A Chance Meeting" (*NUF*), 280–81, 287–88, 301
character studies in jacket copy, 244, 264
charismatic powers: of Marie Shabata and Eddy, 106, 109
childhood: of Cather in promotional materials, 21–24; as Garden of Eden, 31; leaving behind by Thea and McClure, 124–25, 128; similarity of Cather's childhood to Eddy's, 75–76
Christian Science, 72–74
Clara Vavrika ("The Bohemian Girl"), 96, 230
"Claude," 240, 242. *See also* *One of Ours*
Claude Wheeler (*OO*), 169–75; in jacket copy, 245; male protagonist, 243; and mortality, 242; and *PH*, 203, 209; rejection of material wealth, 197. *See also* *One of Ours*
Cleveland Press interview, 28–29
Columbus, Christopher, 90
"Coming, Eden Bower!" (*YBM* as "Coming, Aphrodite!"), 153–59, 164, 238

compassion: absence of in Eddy, 73; absence of in "The Bookkeeper's Wife," 152; in Rachel, 299–300
compromisers: in early writing, 63–64; in *YBM* and *OO*, 176
conquerors: and Alexander the Great, 94; Bernhardt as, 63–64; Cather's desire to, 96; Cather's praise of artists, 60–61; Eddy as, 82; in Pittsburgh years, 66
Coronado, 90
courage: of Cather in leaving McClure's, 232; in *NUF*, 287–88, 289; in Rachel, 300; in Sapphira, 298; and stories of 1916–17, 150
Crane, Stephen, 63, 66, 67, 79
Crawford, Marion F., 62, 67, 79
Cressida Garnet ("The Diamond Mine"): abandoned dreams of, 175; Eddy-like qualities, 150; life force of, 161–62; and Marian Forrester, 190; model for, 146, 147, 332n7; and place of the artist, 162–63; survivor, 150; and women obsessed with money, 237. *See also* "The Diamond Mine" (in *YBM*)

death as theme: and bluffs/rocks, 256; in Christian Science belief, 73, 223; in *MME*, 226; in novels of the twenties, 182; in *OO*, 178–79; in *PH*, 214–15; in *Troll Garden* stories, 161
Death Comes for the Archbishop, 254–63; absence of promotion in jacket copy for, 47, 49, 251, 261–62, 307; headlands in, 241, 256; and Jewett, 275–76; Mary the Virgin in, 258, 343n16; and *PH*, 215; sexuality in, 343n14; snakes motif in, 343n16; and *SOR*, 265, 266; and *SSG*, 303

"A Death in the Desert" (in *Troll Garden*, YBM), 83, 162. *See also* Katharine Gaylord ("A Death in the Desert")

design, feeling for, 207–8, 211–12

"Development of an American Novelist." *See* 1915 sketch (*SOL* brochure)

"The Diamond Mine" (in YBM), 146, 148, 238

disillusionment. *See* idealism, loss of/ disillusionment

"Divide, the," xix

division and dividedness: in Cather, xx, 30, 112, 116, 142, 158; in Myra Henshawe, 219; in *OD*, 271–72; in *OO*, 168, 177–78; in *OP*, 110–11, 112; in *SOL*, 128–30. *See also* double lives

Don Hedger ("Coming, Eden Bower!"), 154–55, 158

double lives: in *AB*, 94–96; of Cather, xx, 86, 127–28, 235–36; in "Coming, Eden Bower!", 158; of Eddy, 78, 79–80, 86, 125–26; in *MA*, 133; in *OO*, 177–78; in "Paul's Case," 68; in *PH*, 210; in *SOL* 1932 preface, 126–27; in Thea, 117, 125–26, 236. *See also* division and dividedness; tension between artistry and promotion

dream your dreams (Jewett advice): in *OO*, 175; in *SOL*, 120

duality: conqueror *vs.* artist, 63–64; of heroes and heroines, 100–101

Duse, Eleanor, 63–64

dust jackets. *See* jacket copy

Eddy, Asa, 107, 326n11

Eddy, Foster, 326n10

Eddy, Mary Baker: in 1915 brochure, 103, 129, 235; ambition, 71, 81, 104–5, 124; and *Best Stories of Sarah Orne Jewett*, 199; birth date, 76; Cather distancing herself from, 308; and "Coming, Eden Bower!", 159; effect on young men, 88; illnesses, 79–80, 109, 151; impact on Cather, 71, 72–74, 92–93, 250, 303; inconsistencies in, 79; lack of compassion in, 108; and *LG*, 273; and *LL*/Marian Forrester, 189, 224; and *MA*, 135–36, 136–37; and *MME*/Myra Henshawe, 220, 223, 224, 254; and novels of the teens, 99–100; and *NUF*, 291–92; and *OO*, 178–79; public image and private reality in, 72; similarities to Cather, xxi, xxv, 72, 74–80, 84–87, 229; and *SOL*/Thea, 120–21, 123, 124, 125–26; and *SSG*/Sapphira, 300–301, 301–2; and stories of 1916–17, 150; temper in, 120–21, 179, 223; and "The Bookkeeper's Wife," 152; using people for her own ends, 85–86, 107; and YBM, 166

Eden, garden of: childhood as, 31; in "Coming, Eden Bower!", 157, 165; in *DCA*, 260, 262–63; in Eddy, 78; in *LL*, 188–89, 191; in *MA*, 131–32; in *MME*, 220, 224; in *OO*, 176, 335n12; in *OP*, 110–12; and *PH*, 208–9, 211

Eden Bower ("Coming, Eden Bower!"/"Coming, Aphrodite!"), 155–57, 333n20; abandoned dreams of, 175; dominance of life, 161; and Marian Forrester, 190; obsession with money, 237; and place of the artist, 162–63; sexuality of, 258; and Thea, 164; as woman who acts, 161

"Eleanor's House," 88

Emil (*OP*), 109–12; and *DCA*, 259, 262–63; and *LL*, 188, 189

"The Enchanted Bluff": and *AB*, 95; and *DCA*, 256; and Jewett, 90, 229; and *MME*, 225; and *YBM*, 53, 240

energy: character of in university years, 65; in *OP* jacket copy, 233; and protagonists of 1916–19 stories, 161

equivocation in *SSG*, 296

"Escapism" (essay), 182

Europe, trip to: in 1926 sketch, 247; in blurb to *YBM*, 53, 239; and nostalgia for plains, 22, 248, 314n37; and writing about your own country, 91

evil: Cather on Eddy's theory of, 73, 109–12; in *DCA*, 259–60; development of Cather's attitudes, 182, 230, 303; in *LL*, 189–90; in *MA*, 131–32; in *MME*, 220, 341n18; in *OO*, 178–79; in *OP*, 109–12; in *SSG*, 301, 303

fact and fiction in Cather's writings: in 1915 brochure, 12–16, 235; in 1926 biographical sketch, 27, 245–46; in reporting, 67; as split in Cather, 30

fairytale aura: in Marian Forrester and Myra Henshawe, 216–17; in *SSG*, 295

Fall from Eden: in *LL*, 188–89, 191; in *PH*, 208, 211. *See also* Eden, garden of

Farrar, Geraldine, 146, 332n7

father of Cather. *See* Cather, Charles Fectigue

Fechin, Nicolai, portrait of Cather, xx

feistiness in *NUF*, 287–88

Fields, Annie, 95, 196, 281–82, 285–86, 288

financial concerns of artists. *See* money and financial concerns of artists

Flaubert, Gustave, 283

"Flavia and Her Artists," 85

France and nostalgia for Nebraska, 22, 314n37

Frances Harling (*MA*), 139, 331n12. *See also* My *Ántonia*

Fremstad, Olive, 64, 118, 124, 129, 146–47

Garber, Lyra, 196, 216, 326n8

Garden, Mary, 146

The Garden of the Heart, 4, fig. 1

Glasgow, Ellen, 1

Godfrey St. Peter (*PH*): double life of, 210; dreams of, 205–7; as male protagonist, 243; and *MME*, 224; mortal limitations, 214–15; and the rock, 342n6; similarities to Cather, 203, 226, 241; and *SOR*, 267. *See also The Professor's House*

"A Gold Slipper" (in *YBM*), 146, 148, 149

Greenslet, Ferris, 12–13, 313n15; 1915 brochure, 341n5; and *AB* dust jacket, 99; edited Jewett stories for, 196; house memos, 34, 38–40, 317nn12–14. *See also* Houghton Mifflin

Grout, Madame Caroline: ambition in, 285; Eddy-like qualities of, 292, 303–4; feistiness, 287–88, 347n11, 347n14; and Sapphira, Jewett, and Eddy, 301–2; and teasing the mind, 280–81

Guilbert, Yvette, 61

Hambourg, Isabelle McClung, 1, 14, 66; and study room used by Cather, 76, 338n10

Hamlet (character of Shakespeare), 180, 184

Jewett, Sarah Orne (*cont.*)
  AB jacket copy, 38; and *DCA*, 254, 275–76; and *LL*, 193; and *MME*, 219–20, 226; and *NUF*, 280–92, 284; and *OP*, 102–3, 106–7; and *PH*, 212, 213–14; in *SOL* brochure, 10, 15; and *SOR*, 276–77; and *SSG*, 300, 305; and *YBM*, 166; and Thea, 124; women characters of, 278. See also *Best Stories of Sarah Orne Jewett*; "The Hiltons' Holiday," "Miss Jewett" (*NUF*)
Jim Burden (*MA*), xxii, 140–41. See also *My Ántonia*
"Joseph and His Brothers" (*NUF*), 283
Joseph Vaillant (*DCA*), 256–57
journalism of Cather, 66, 67, 234–35
"The Joy of Nelly Deane," 92, 230, 337n9
Julia Wanning ("Her Boss"), 150–52

Katharine Gaylord ("A Death in the Desert"), 83, 160–61, 162, 165
"Katherine Mansfield" (*NUF*), 282–83, 284
Keats, John, 61, 211
Kenneth Gray ("The Willing Muse"), 87–88
kingdom of art, 60–64, 130, 166. See also art and the artist
Kipling, Rudyard, 116
Kitty Ayrshire ("Scandal," "A Gold Slipper"): abandoned dreams of, 175; dominance of life, 161; Eddy-like qualities, 150; life force of, 162; and Marian Forrester, 190; model for, 146–47; obsession with money, 237; and place of the artist, 162–63; selling instinct, 148–49; survivor, 150
Knopf, Alfred A., and Knopf publish-ing house: and desire for better promotion, 237, 250; and jacket copy, 34, 44; move from Houghton Mifflin, 33, 316n2, 317n4; return to Houghton Mifflin from, 197; use of reviews on jackets, 49

"lady with a lamp" (Longfellow quote): Ántonia as, 137; Eddy as, 82
laughter: in Marian Forrester, 219, 288; in Myra Henshawe, 219; of Sapphira, 298; of women in *NUF*, 288–89
Leader (Pittsburgh), 14, 66
lecturing, dangers to writer, 26–27, 29–31, 250–51. *See also* addictive dangers of courting the public; success, perils of
Lena Lingard (*MA*), 139, 331n12. See also *My Ántonia*
lesbianism, of Cather, xx, 320n21
Lewis, Edith, 1, 5–6, 34, 311n2, 317n8
Lindsay, Vachel, 171, 334n4
"Literary Note" (1903), 4–6, 57, 232, fig. 3; text, 4–5
Longfellow, Henry Wadsworth, 82, 137, 214
A Lost Lady, 184–95; dawn motif, 225; gulf between aspirations and mortal failings in, 220–21; jacket copy, 44–45, 54, 190, 193, 243, 244, 245, 307; jacket copy text, 43; and Jewett, 336n18; and *MME*, 224; and *PH*, 208, 215; and *SOR*, 267, 345n15; as story of loss, 184, 192; and "Two Friends," 269; women protagonists in, 216
lost past, nostalgia for: in "148 Charles Street," 281–82; in Alexandra, 112; in Cather, 30; in *MA*, 24, 141; in *PH*, 205–6. *See also* past, possession of
Lucy Gayheart, 272–74; jacket copy, 49,

mortality: in jacket copy, 245; in later
novels, 181–83; in *MME*, 226; in
novels of the twenties, 220, 222,
242; in *SSG*, 302–3. *See also* tension
between immortal aspirations and
mortal limitations
Mother Eve (*PH*), 205, 206, 208,
213–14
mother of Cather. *See* Cather, Virginia
Sibert Boak
mundane side of life: in *MME*, xxii–
xxiii; in *PH*, xxii–xxiv, 209, 328n7;
in writing of early twenties, xxii–
xxiii, 240; in writing of teens, 168;
in *YBM*, 166, 237–38
My Ántonia, 131–42; and Cather
as Western writer, 24; contrast
with New York Stories, xxii, 146;
division between characters, 101,
236–37; Eddy-like overtones in,
135; jacket copy, 33, 39–40, 52,
140–41, 231; jacket copy text,
37–39, fig. 10; and "Neighbour
Rosicky," 269, 279; passage of time
in, 141, 193, 194; and *SOR*, 265; in
YBM jacket copy, 238–39. *See also*
Ántonia Shimerda (*MA*); Frances
Harling (*MA*); Jim Burden (*MA*);
Lena Lingard (*MA*); Wick Cutter
(*MA*)
My Autobiography. See McClure, S. S.
My Autobiography
"My First Novels (There Were Two)"
(essay), 102–3
My Mortal Enemy, 216–26; and 1926
sketch, 247–48; bluffs motif in,
224–25, 254; and *DCA*, 259, 261;
evil in, 220–24, 341n18; jacket
copy, 45, 46, 54, 244–46, 307,
340n1; jacket copy text, 44–47; and
Jewett, 200, 201, 284; and *PH*, 215;

quest for life above the mundane,
xxii–xxiii, 340n14; religion in, 225,
261; woman's voice in, 201. *See also*
Myra Henshawe (*MME*)
Myra Henshawe (*MME*): and *DCA*, 255,
256, 258, 259; Eddy-like qualities,
220, 223, 224, 254, 302, 303–4; and
enchanted bluff, 241; fairy tale aura
of, 216–17, 221; jealousy in, 218;
laughter of, 288; and mortality,
242, 303; and Sapphira, 297–98,
302; and *SOR*, 267. See also *My
Mortal Enemy*

"The Namesake," 324n21
Nancy (*SSG*), 298, 299–300
"Nanette: An Aside," 67–68
Napoleon, 85, 90
nature: Eddy's and Alexandra's differ-
ing attitudes on, 108–9
Nebraska: in 1926 sketch, 21–22, 246,
314n37, fig. 5; influence on char-
acter of Cather, 65; and obscure
destinies, 279; in *OO*, 168, 176; in
YBM jacket copy, 239. *See also* West,
decline of
"Neighbour Rosicky" (*OD*), 50, 268,
269. See also *Obscure Destinies*
Nelly Deane ("The Joy of Nelly
Deane"), 92, 230
New Mexico trip in 1926 "interview,"
26, 315n45
New York scene in Cather's writing,
xxi, xxii, 140–44, 150, 153, 234–35,
238, 239–40
Niel Herbert (*LL*), 184, 189–90, 197,
225
Nordica, Lillian, 146, 332nn7–8
Not Under Forty, 280–92; aging in,
346n8; jacket copy, 49, 280, 307;
jacket copy text, 48–50; and *SSG*,

301–2. *See also* "148 Charles Street," "A Chance Meeting," "Katherine Mansfield," "Miss Jewett," "The Novel Démeublé" (*NUF*)

"The Novel Démeublé" (*NUF*), 196–98, 246, 249, 283–84. See also *Not Under Forty*; "unfurnished style"

Obscure Destinies, 268–72; ambition in, 264; jacket copy, 49–50, 54, 264, 268, 308; jacket copy text, 47–48; and Jewett, 278, 279. *See also* "Neighbour Rosicky" (*OD*); "Old Mrs. Harris" (*OD*); "Two Friends" (*OD)*

Olaf Ericson ("The Bohemian Girl"), 96

"The Old Beauty," 301

"Old Mrs. Harris" (*OD*), 268; Cather as character in, 264; and influence of Jewett, 278; in jacket copy, 50; jacket copy and *SSG*, 307, 308; sympathetic artist and, 349n26. See also *Obscure Destinies*

One of Ours, 168–80; and Cather's changing mindset as artist, 240; gulf between aspirations and mortal failings in, 220; jacket copy, 44, 45, 46, 54, 179, 243, 245, 246, 318n19; jacket copy text, 42, fig. 12; and Jewett, 198; and *PH*, 204, 205; Pulitzer prize for, 198, 202. *See also* Claude Wheeler (*OO*)

"On the Gulls' Road," 70, 89–90, 99, 200, 229

O Pioneers!, 102–12; Cather finds own voice in, xix, 100; and *DCA*, 262; division between characters, 101; influence of Eddy on, 103–6, 109–10; influence of Jewett on, 84, 106–7; jacket copy, 38, 39, 52, 58, 100, 231, 233; jacket copy text, 35–36; and *LL*, 188; similarities of Alexandra and Marie to Cather, xxii, 111–12; in *SOL* brochure, 9–11, 162

original injustice, 182–83, 220, 222. *See also* mortality

past, possession of: in *LL* and *MA*, 192–93. *See also* lost past, nostalgia for

"Paul's Case" (in *Troll Garden*, *YBM*), 68; and Claude Wheeler, 169, 171; death in, 161, 162; and ideal of the artist, 163–64; placement within *YBM*, 240; in promotional pieces, 246; and role-playing, 80

Paul Wanning ("Her Boss"), 150–51

pilgrim: artist as, 62; Cather as, 228; and Eddy, 76–77

Pittsburgh Leader, 8, 14

Pittsburgh years, xxi, 66, 246, 320n10

Plato's cave, 138, 330n8

Poe, Edgar Allan, 62, 63

Poet-Lore (journal), 6

Pound, Louise, 66–67

prima donna/diva: Eddy as, 124; Thea as, 124

"The Professor's Commencement," 68

The Professor's House, 202–15; Catholicism in, 255; gulf between aspirations and mortal failings in, 221; and "Her Boss," 151; intrusions on life in, 316n51; jacket copy, 45–46, 54, 243–44, 245, 246, 318n23; jacket copy text, 43–44; and Jewett stories, 200; and *MME*, 226; mortality in, 210, 214–15, 242; quest for life above the mundane, xxii–xxiv, 328n7; snakes motif in, 209, 341n18; study room in, 206,

Sapphira Colbert (*SSG*): and Cather, xxv; complexity of, 296–97; Eddy-like qualities of, 300–301, 304; Marian Forrester and, 297–98; and Myra Henshawe, 302; and *NUF*, 289. See also *Sapphira and the Slave Girl*

savvy about land: of Alexandra Bergson and Eddy, 107–8

"Scandal" (in *YBM*), 146, 148, 149

"The Sculptor's Funeral" (in *Troll Garden*, *YBM*), 160, 246

self-promotion: by Cather, 77–78, 166; in "Coming, Eden Bower!", 122, 158; by Eddy, 77–78; need for, 129–30; in *OP* jacket copy, 100; in *SOR*, 58; and *SSG*, 307; and stories of 1916–17, 150, 165; in *YBM*, 197. *See also* promotional activities

self-quotation, 14, 22, 313n16

Selma Schumann ("A Singer's Romance"), 147

setting sun, image of: in *MA*, 131, 142

sewing forms in study room: of Cather, 338n10; in *PH*, 206

sexuality: of Cather, xxv, 320n21; in Cather's novels, 259; in *DCA*, 258–59, 343n14; in *LL*, 190; in Marian Forrester, 191; in Marie Shabata, 109; in *MME*, 223; in *SOR*, 265; in Thea and Eden Bower, 156–57

Shadows on the Rock, 265–68; headlands, 241, 344n11; jacket copy, 2, 49, 54, 58, 264, 266–67, 307; jacket copy text, 47, fig. 13–14; and Jewett, 276–77; and *LL*, 345n15

simplicity in art: in 1926 sketch, 246; and Jewett, 276–77; in *OP* jacket copy, 233; in *PH* and Cather, 211–12

singers as embodiments of Cather, 68, 147–49

"A Singer's Romance," 147, 320n21

snakes, motif of: in *DCA*, 259–60, 343n16; in *LL*, 188, 191; in *MA*, 132–33; in *MME*, 223–24; in *OP*, 110; in *PH*, 209, 211, 341n18

SOL brochure, fig. 4. *See also* 1915 sketch (*SOL* brochure)

solitariness of writer and Jewett, 229, 277

The Song of the Lark, 118–30; in 1915 brochure, 7, 11–12, 235, 236; 1932 preface to, 126–27, 267, 334n7; and "Coming, Eden Bower!", 157; contrast to stories of 1916–17, 147–48; double life in, 117, 125–26, 236; gulf with *YBM*, 164; influences of Jewett and Eddy, 119–25, 136; jacket copy, 3, 38, 39, 231, 238, 344n14; jacket copy text, 37; promotion of, 33, 145; sources of Thea's success in, 181; transcendent values in, 181. *See also* Madison Bowers (*SOL*); Thea Kronborg (*SOL*)

southern life and *SSG*, 300

stamp of distinction: in *NUF*, 289; in Sapphira, 301

Stevenson, Robert Louis, 116

stylishness of dress: in Cather, 304; in Sapphira and Nancy, 298

success, material: in Alexandra, 104–5, 112; in Eddy, 80–83, 104–5; for McClure, 114, 116; and self-promotion, 58

success, perils of: in Bartley Alexander and Alexandra Bergson, 113; for Cather, 85, 95; in Eddy, 85; in *PH*, 203, 204; in "A Singer's Romance," 320n21. *See also* lecturing, dangers to writer success, struggle for: in 1926 sketch, 247; in *MA* jacket copy, 40; in Pittsburgh years, 66

survivors: Eddy and Ántonia as, 136–37; Marian Forrester as, 193; in 1916–19 stories about singers, 149–50

sympathetic artist: Cather as in *SSG*, 309; in Cather's biography of Eddy, 74; and Jewett, 290–91, 305; in "Old Mrs. Harris," 349n26; in *SSG*, 304–5; in *SSG* jacket copy, 52, 295, 308–9

Tarbell, Ida, 153

Tarkington, Booth, 317n17

teasing the mind for years (Jewett advice): and *DCA*, 275–76; in *LL*, 193, 336n18; in *MA*, 136; in "Miss Jewett," 280–81; and *NUF*, 282; in *OD* and *LG*, 279; and *SSG*, 300, 348n15

temper: in Cather, xxv, 304; of Claude Wheeler, 179; of Eddy, 120–21, 179, 223; of Thea, 120–21

tension between artistry and promotion: in 1915 brochure, 16, 234; in 1926 interview, 250; artist *vs.* entrepreneur, 86; in Cather's early writing, 60–69, 230; in *SOL*, 128–30, 178; and *YBM*, 166. *See also* double lives; duality

tension between immortal aspirations and mortal limitations: in 1926 sketch, 247; avoidance of in *DCA*, 258; in *DCA*, 256, 257; and Eddy, 303; in Myra Henshawe, 223; in novels of the twenties, xxiii–xxiv; in preface to Jewett stories, 200; in *LG*, 272; in *MME*, 220–21, 224, 340n14; in *PH*, 208, 211–12,

212–13, 214–15; in *SOR*, 266; in *SSG*, 295; in *YBM*, 170–71. *See also* mortality

tension between surface appearances and emotional realities: In "Old Mrs. Harris," 308; in *SSG*, 294, 308

Thea Kronborg (*SOL*): in 1932 preface, 267; and Ántonia, 133–34; contrast with heroines in stories of teens, 146, 149–50, 161; dualities of, 100, 101, 178, 236, 240; Eddy-like qualities of, 120–21, 124, 125–27, 303–4; and Eden Bower, 156, 164; and Harvey Merrick, 163; influence of McClure on, 117; in jacket copy, 233, 234, 238; Jewett-like qualities in, 119–20, 124; and Lucy Gayheart, 272–73; and Godfrey St. Peter, 215; and quest for life, 182; and Sapphira, 299; sexuality of, 156–57, 258; similarities to Cather, xxii, 166, 267, 270; success, 181; tensions within, 101; transcending the ordinary, 193; tricks with Thea's age, 349n29; uncommonness of, 221. *See also* *The Song of the Lark*

Till (*SSG*), 296, 299, 305–6

"Tommy the Unsentimental," 67

Tom Outland (*PH*), 203–4; and Cather's changing mindset as artist, 241; and *DCA*, 256; dreams of, 205; male protagonist, 243; and mortality, 242. *See also* *The Professor's House*

transcendent values: in *LL*, 193; in *MME*, 226; in *PH*, 203–4, 208; in *SOL* and *OO*, 181; in *YBM*, 166

Troll Garden: absence of jacket copy, 35; Jewett's comments on, 230–31; in promotional pieces, 246; in *SOL*

Youth (cont.)
244, 307; jacket copy text, 40–42,
fig. 11; and *LL*, 190, 191; mundane
side of life in, 237–38; and *OO*,
170–71; self-promotion in, 197;
tension of opposing pulls in artist's
life, xxii, 237–38. See also *Troll
Garden*; *specific stories*
youthfulness: in jacket copy of early
books, 53, 54, 231–32; in Marie,
112; in McClure, 114; in *LG*, 274;
in *YBM*, xxii